The Siberian Curse

S THE
iberian
Curse

How Communist Planners
Left Russia Out in the Cold

Fiona Hill

Clifford G. Gaddy

BROOKINGS INSTITUTION PRESS
Washington, D.C.

Copyright © 2003

THE BROOKINGS INSTITUTION
1775 Massachusetts Avenue, N.W., Washington, D.C. 20036
www.brookings.edu

Library of Congress Cataloging-in-Publication data

Hill, Fiona.
   The Siberian curse : how communist planners left Russia out in the
cold / Fiona Hill and Clifford Gaddy.
      p.   cm.
Includes bibliographical references and index.
   ISBN 08157-3644-4 (cloth : alk. paper)
   ISBN 08157-3645-2 (pbk. : alk. paper)
   1. Siberia (Russia)—Economic conditions. 2. Russia (Federation)—
Economic conditions. 3. Economic geography. 4. Forced migration—
Russia (Federation)—Siberia—History—20th century. 5. Land
settlement—Russia (Federation)—Siberia—History—20th century.
6. Industrial location—Russia (Federation)—Siberia. I. Gaddy, Clifford
G. II. Title.
   HC340.12.Z7S53343 2003
   330.957—dc22   2003016801

9 8 7 6 5 4 3 2 1
The paper used in this publication meets minimum requirements of the
American National Standard for Information Sciences—Permanence of Paper for
Printed Library Materials: ANSI Z39.48-1992.

Typeset in Minion

Composition by Circle Graphics
Columbia, Maryland

Printed by R. R. Donnelley
Harrisonburg, Virginia

Dedicated to the memory of
Frederick H. Hodder

Contents

Foreword

This book takes something everyone knows about Russia—it is very big and a lot of it is very cold—and makes of that commonplace the basis of path-breaking analysis that should be of considerable utility to the people who govern Russia today.

Rumination on Russian "reform" has become something of a cottage industry in the United States over the last decade. Few books on the subject get much below the surface to look at the hidden forces—the deep structural dynamics—of what is under way in that vast, complex, and immensely important country. This book by Fiona Hill and Clifford Gaddy, senior fellows at Brookings, does just that. It explains why Russia has had so much difficulty breaking free of its Soviet past. Bringing together pioneering research in politics and economics, *The Siberian Curse* poses a provocative question: Can Russia actually achieve the goals it has set for itself, given the persistence of economic habits and structures it inherited from the U.S.S.R.? Fiona and Cliff suggest that even the most comprehensive and targeted reforms may be doomed unless there is an active and conscious effort to face up to—and correct—the mistakes of the Soviet past.

The Siberian Curse uses the tools of economic statistics and economic geography, as well as historical analysis looking back over several centuries, to argue that what traditionally has been perceived as one of Russia's major strengths—its enormous size—is in fact its greatest weakness. Russia's size gave successive Soviet governments the excuse to blunder on an unprecedented and monumental scale. For almost seventy years, communist planners forced people and economic activity out into the vast, resource-rich territory of Siberia—through the GULAG prison labor system and later costly incentive schemes—to colonize, urbanize, and industrialize this last great, but inhospitably cold, frontier. This massive relocation of population and industry into Siberia's icy wastes burdened Russia with enormous problems associated with the costs of transportation over great distances and of keeping warm, or just staying alive, in conditions of great cold.

Fiona and Cliff explain why and how the dislocation of population and the accompanying misallocation of resources have impeded the development of a market economy and fully functioning democracy in Russia. People, cities, and factories languish in places communist planners (and the GULAG) put them, not where market forces and free choice would have attracted them. They also help us understand why this fundamental problem was not rectified, or even recognized, by a series of post-Soviet Russian governments in the 1990s, and why it is likely to persist given the difficulties of effecting a mass migration back out of Siberia toward warmer western regions of Russia.

The only way for Russia to rid itself of the economic burdens of maintaining huge populations in some of the coldest inhabited places on the planet is to turn to the West—not just in theory but in practice. And the West means Europe: Russian leaders must fully embrace the idea of a "European Russia"—a Russia in which population and economic activity are concentrated west of the Ural Mountains, close to Europe and its markets. That means Moscow has to support and facilitate the desires of the population to move away from Siberia and encourage people to move from Siberia's largest cities, not just from its most remote towns and villages.

The challenges facing the Russian leadership in this regard are daunting. There is no historical precedent for the shrinkage of cities on the scale that will be required in Russia. As a result, changing Russia's economic geography will be a costly and wrenching process, even if it will eventually put Russia on a sustainable path of development.

Fiona and Cliff emphasize that Russian leaders are not faced with a black-and-white choice: develop Siberia or reject it and cast it off. Russia can and should exploit the resources of Siberia. But it has to do so by reducing the dependency on huge fixed pools of labor. Siberia's resources can contribute to Russia's future prosperity, and the regional economy can one day be viable, but not if the Russian government persists in trying to maintain the cities and industries that communist planners left for it out in the cold.

In keeping with our growing emphasis on multidisciplinary research and cross-program collaboration within Brookings, and collaboration with outside partners, *The Siberian Curse* is inspired by, and draws on research from, a number of centers and scholars not previously presented to a broader audience, as well as original research by Fiona and Cliff. Scholars at the Brookings Institution's Center on Social and Economic Dynamics, employing the pioneering agent-based computer modeling techniques that are the hallmark of the center's research activities, a Russian-American team of economists at Pennsylvania State University, researchers at Moscow's New Economic School, and World Bank experts, among others, were all actively involved in the research project that produced this book.

The Brookings Institution gratefully acknowledges the financial support provided for this project and this book by Carnegie Corporation of New York. Research related to the study on the sustainability of the Russian economy was also conducted under projects supported by the John D. and Catherine T. MacArthur Foundation, and the Alcoa Corporation.

STROBE TALBOTT
President

Washington, D.C.
September 2003

Acknowledgments

This book could not have been written without the assistance and support of numerous colleagues in the United States, Russia, and elsewhere. Their generosity in sharing ideas, sources, and time to brainstorm with us is greatly appreciated.

The intellectual roots of this book reach deep and have received nourishment from many people. Fiona Hill began serious work on the issue of Russia's obsession with territorial size during her time at Harvard University. Richard Pipes, her Ph.D. thesis adviser at Harvard, was a great inspiration in thinking about this topic. Work with other Harvard scholars, including Akira Iriye, Ernest May, Roman Szporluk, and the late Adam Ulam, also helped guide some of the discussions of major trends in Russian imperial and Soviet history.

Barry Ickes, a longtime collaborator of Clifford Gaddy, was a cooriginator of one of the important precursors to this book, a project entitled the Cost of the Cold. He and his colleagues at Pennsylvania State University and the New Economic School in Moscow were instrumental in shaping the conceptual aspects of this work, including "temperature per capita" (TPC). The empirical analysis done by Tatiana Mikhailova, a Ph.D. student under Barry at Pennsylvania State, was critical for the arguments we present in the book.

Preliminary findings from the Cost of the Cold project were first presented publicly in 2000 at a workshop at Columbia University entitled Geographies of Russia's Transition: Questions of Space, Place, and Time, sponsored by the Association of American Geographers. Three of the participants in that conference, individuals with different fields of expertise on Russia, made contributions at that early stage and remained supporters of the project in its current form. Economist Richard Ericson endorsed the key concept embodied in TPC, stressing not only its potential value as a means of estimating the hidden cost of cold, but also its ability to serve as an "economic rationality index." Historian and urban specialist Blair Ruble urged us to study the example of Canada and pointed us to research conducted in that country on issues of the cold and its effects on productivity. Demographer Timothy Heleniak suggested several fruitful empirical uses of the TPC concept.

As the project evolved, Tim's contributions became even more valuable. He allowed us to draw on his unique knowledge of the theory and practice of migration, demography, and labor markets in Russia and the rest of the former Soviet Union. He offered detailed responses to many questions, shared data with us, and provided assistance in tracking down information, sources, and supporting materials. We are grateful to Tim and his World Bank colleagues, such as Andrei Markov in the Moscow Office, who clarified numerous issues related to the development and status of the World Bank's Northern Restructuring Project.

All of these ideas of size, cold, and distance have benefited from our conversations with a long list of scholars of Russian affairs. Charles William Maynes and S. Frederick Starr—two senior scholars and practitioners with many decades between them of living and working in, and thinking about, Russia—were early interlocutors on the topic of book, taking part in numerous brainstorming sessions and pointing us toward ideas and sources. Bill and Fred later provided thoughtful comments and critical feedback on the first draft of the book, suggested numerous areas for improvement and elaboration, and were unflagging enthusiasts of the project.

As we began thinking about the nature of the book we wanted to write, we also depended on the reactions to our ideas from a number of knowledgeable colleagues with extensive personal experience reporting on Russia. Journalists Peter Baker, Robert Cottrell, Susan Glasser, Edward Lucas, Maura Reynolds, Paul Starobin, and Marcus Warren offered their observations on the big themes of the book. Michael Thumann contributed his conclusions and materials from extended trips through remote areas of Siberia.

Boris Brevnov, the former head of Russia's electric power monopoly, Unified Energy Systems (UES), was kind enough to come to Washington, D.C., expressly for an early discussion of the book concept. His insights and information about his attempts to reform the Russian utility system were critical in solidifying our ideas about the political importance of this project.

Several scholars shared their work on specific issues. Michael Alexseev offered his perspective on Chinese migration in the Russian Far East and sent us copies of materials. Anne Applebaum provided us with an advance copy of her new book, *GULAG: A History*, at a critical stage in editing our final manuscript. Bruce Blair, Mark Kramer, William Odom, and John Steinbruner all shared information on the Soviet security buildup in Siberia and the Russian Far East after World War II and thoughts on its ideological underpinnings. Michael Bradshaw provided his insights on Russia's economic geography, Siberia, and the Russian Far East, and on Soviet planning, pointing us toward key sources. He also offered valuable comments on an early draft of the book. Murray Feshbach gave us his information on Russia's demographic situation, including an early copy of his book, *Russia's Health and Demographic Crises*. Nancy Ries sent us her unpublished paper on informal social safety nets and the role of personal networks in Russia. Anara Tabyshalieva spent time discussing the implications of Central Asian migration to Siberia. Kiril Fisenko from the *Eastview* database service and David Johnson of *Johnson's Russia List* helped to track down specific articles in Russian and English.

We were also fortunate to have colleagues and friends (including many of those above) willing to devote time and intellectual energy to our project, from discussing initial concepts to reviewing the first draft of the book. These included Richard Burger, Ronald Childress, Jonathan Elkind, Alla Eskina, Florence Fee, Amy Gordon, Thomas Graham, Graeme Herd, David Kramer, Anatol Lieven, Jenny Lo, Bruce Parrott, Jenny Savill, and Jonas Store. Pavel Baev, Alexander Bakastov, Georgi Derlugian, Sergei Grigoriev, Aliona Kostritsyna, and Nikolai Zlobin offered valuable Russian perspectives as well as critiques of general ideas. Adel Yusupov also helped us work through many conceptual and linguistic issues and make contacts in Moscow for verifying sources. Harley Balzer, Bjorn Brunstad, Timothy Colton, John Litwack, Pekka Sutela, and Vladimir Treml read and commented on the first draft. Kenneth Keen showed great patience in listening to "tales from the book" on an almost daily basis and read the entire first draft at one sitting to see if it held together as a manuscript.

We presented our thesis in various stages of development and levels of detail to a range of audiences in the United States and abroad. Participants at workshops and seminars held by the American Enterprise Institute, the Brookings Institution, the Canadian Foreign Ministry, the Defense Department's Office of Strategic Assessment, the Defense Intelligence Agency, the European Central Bank, the Foreign Service Institute of the U.S. State Department, the International Monetary Fund, the National Security Council, and the World Bank offered valuable feedback at various stages of the research.

The initial and ongoing research project could also not have been undertaken without the generous and sustained support of Carnegie Corporation of New York and the continued commitment of Vartan Gregorian, David Speedie, Deana Arsenian, and their colleagues to our work. This book is, in fact, the culmination of more than twelve years of individual and joint research funded by Carnegie Corporation.

We owe, in addition, a special note of thanks to our colleagues at the Brookings Institution, many of whom were present at the birth of the first ideas and who helped us to see the project and the book through to their conclusions. Richard Haass was the initial advocate of our collaboration, encouraging us to join forces on an economic, historical, and political inquiry into the roots of Russia's structural problems. James Steinberg and Carol Graham have been enthusiastic supporters of the project, spurring us along in the writing process, offering insightful observations and suggestions on early versions of the text, and helping us push through numerous obstacles in getting the manuscript completed.

Robert Axtell first drew the authors' attention to spatial aspects of economic activity. Work by Ross Hammond and Timothy Gulden, Rob's colleagues at the Brookings's Center on Social and Economic Dynamics (CSED), contributed to our understanding of the skewed and artificial nature of Russian city size distribution. In addition, Tim offered his ideas on how best to organize and present critical data, and he produced all of our maps for us.

Jeremy Shapiro engaged in many brainstorming exercises, helped to generate ideas for cross-country comparisons from other contexts, and offered detailed comments on the first draft of book. Helmut Sonnenfeldt also provided perspicacious comments on the first draft and great enthusiasm for the project. Richard Bush, Bridget Butkevich, Timothy Crawford, Bates

Gill, Aaron Lobel, Suzanne Maloney, Meghan O'Sullivan, and Alex Sokolowski offered helpful tips and pointers along the way. Michael Aller and Karla Bilafer provided company and moral support for late writing sessions. Eric Eisinger and Sarah Chilton in the Brookings library helped us to track down and obtain "hard-to-get" and obscure materials.

The book could certainly not have been completed without the help and hard work of our talented and dedicated research assistants and interns at Brookings, who threw themselves wholeheartedly into the venture. Marjory Winn Schleicher assisted in the book project from inception to completion. She was a genuine collaborator in a joint endeavor. We are especially grateful to Marjory for a heroic effort to compile, systematize, and analyze vast amounts of meteorological data from across the Russian Federation, as well as to conduct comparative research on Alaska and Canada and numerous other related subjects. Catherine Yusupov researched Russian federalism, migration, and the *propiska* system limitations, among other issues. She carried out invaluable, painstaking work on Russian source material, resolved transliteration issues, and played a critical role in all the final stages of the manuscript preparation. Regine Spector participated in the early brainstorming sessions, pulling together background sources and helping us to flesh out the general ideas and concepts in the first two years of the project. Regine's contribution was crucial to the initial research. Janine Toth spent a summer investigating Russian energy utility systems. The information she compiled shaped our understanding of the challenges facing Russian municipalities and households east of the Urals and the dilemmas of city shrinkage. Irina Sivachenko scoured an enormous collection of Russian language materials and articles on Siberia. She also offered a Russian perspective and thoughtful critique of the first draft of the book.

Debbie Styles gave us excellent editorial support in the end stages. We greatly benefited from her suggestions and keen eye in improving the final manuscript. Susan Woollen did wonderful work on cover conceptions and design, and Brenda Szittya enthusiastically offered support in thinking of ways to present the book's conclusions to different audiences.

Finally, we want to acknowledge the immense contribution of our late colleague, collaborator, and friend Frederick H. Hodder. The project that led to this book truly began when he came to Brookings in June 2000. Working as an unpaid intern and given little more than the germ of an idea about trying to quantify the magnitude of a country's "cold," he was left alone to put the idea into empirical reality. By the end of the summer, this gifted young Cambridge mathematician had accumulated the data to implement the first empirical realization of "temperature per capita," applying it to

Russia, Canada, Sweden, and the United States. Thanks to his elaboration of the basic ideas and his pioneering empirical work, the project on the Cost of the Cold was launched. Fred stayed on for another year as a research assistant, and during his time here, he benefited us and all our colleagues through his intellect, his enthusiasm, his humor, and his generosity of spirit. We owe a lot to Fred; we miss him; and we dedicate this book to his memory.

FIONA HILL AND CLIFFORD GADDY

Note on Transliteration

There are a number of different systems for transliterating Russian Cyrillic into the Latin alphabet. Throughout the text, we have used the United States Board on Geographic Names's standard for transliteration of Cyrillic into Latin. Exceptions were made in cases of names commonly rendered differently in English (for example, Yeltsin, Oryol, Kasyanov). When citing English language materials, we have preserved the transliteration from the original source. Russian words that have entered into standard English usage in literature on this region are not italicized in the text and are treated as English words (for instance, tsar, Duma, oblasts, polpreds).

OZYMANDIAS

I MET a Traveler from an antique land,
Who said, "Two vast and trunkless legs of stone
Stand in the desert. Near them, on the sand,
Half sunk, a shattered visage lies, whose frown,
And wrinkled lip, and sneer of cold command,
Tell that its sculptor well those passions read
Which yet survive, stamped on these lifeless things,
The hand that mocked them and the heart that fed;
And on the pedestal these words appear:
'My name is OZYMANDIAS, King of Kings:
Look on my works, ye Mighty, and despair!'
Nothing beside remains. Round the decay
Of that Colossal Wreck, boundless and bare,
The lone and level sands stretch far away."

PERCY BYSSHE SHELLEY (1792–1822)

An ode to Soviet folly in Siberia's snowy wastes

Russia, Showing Places Mentioned in Text

1

The Great Errors

A s observers have looked at reform in Russia over the decade since the collapse of the USSR, they have assumed that if the old system that produced the wrong results in the past is now changed, the new system will produce the right results in the future. Unfortunately, to be able to put a new system in place, countries in transition must not only dismantle the old system and replace it with a new one; they must also rectify the consequences of operating under the old system for a long period of time. In the case of Russia, the time frame was especially long. For more than seventy years after the Russian Revolution, the Soviet centrally planned economic system produced a certain set of outcomes, which became part of Russian history, society, and political culture.

One of these outcomes was a peculiar and unique economic geography that continues to define Russia and puts it completely out of step with the requirements of a market economy irrespective of system change. Today, despite the abolition of central planning, Russia still has a nonmarket distribution of labor and capital across its territory. People and factories languish in places communist planners put them—not where market forces would have attracted them. Russia cannot build a competitive market economy and a normal democratic society on this basis.

Another specific outcome of the Soviet system is the development of Siberia. In this instance, the freedom of the market was deliberately defied and perversely turned on its head by the use of the GULAG prison-camp system in order to conquer and industrialize Siberia's vast territory. Beginning in the 1930s, slave labor built factories and cities and operated industries in some of the harshest and most forbidding places on the planet, where the state could not otherwise have persuaded its citizens to go en masse on a permanent basis. In the 1960s and 1970s, leaders in Moscow decided to launch giant industrial projects in Siberia. Planners sought to create permanent pools of labor to exploit the region's rich natural resources, to produce a more even spread of industry and population across the Russian Federation, and to conquer, tame, and settle Siberia's vast and distant wilderness areas. This time, new workers were lured to Siberia with higher wages and other amenities— rather than coerced there and enslaved—at great (but hidden) cost to the state. Today's Siberia is the economic legacy and the embodiment of the GULAG and of communist planning.

Thanks to the industrialization and mass settlement of Siberia, at the beginning of the twenty-first century and a new era in Russia's economic and political development, Russia's population is scattered across a vast land mass in cities and towns with few physical connections between them. Inadequate road, rail, air, and other communication links hobble efforts to promote interregional trade and to develop markets. One-third of the population has the added burden of living and working in particularly inhospitable climatic conditions. About one-tenth live and work in almost impossibly cold and large cities in Siberia, places where average January temperatures range from −15 to −45 degrees Celsius (+5 to −49 degrees Fahrenheit).* Given their locations, these cities (as they did in the Soviet period) depend heavily on central government subsidies for fuel and food; they also rely on preferential transportation tariffs. Costs of living are as much as four times as high as elsewhere in the Russian Federation, while costs of industrial production are sometimes higher still. The cities and their inhabitants are cut off from domestic and international markets. Russia is, as a result of its old centrally planned system, more burdened with

---

* In the remainder of this book, we will cite temperatures only according to the Celsius (centigrade) scale. A Celsius to Fahrenheit temperature conversion chart is in appendix A.

problems and costs associated with its territorial size and the cold than any other large state or country in northern latitudes, like the United States, Canada, or the Scandinavian countries.

From the perspective of today's market-economy imperative, looking back over Russia's history reveals that *misallocation* was the dominant characteristic of the Soviet period. Resources (including human resources) were misused from the point of view of economic efficiency. The system produced the wrong things. Its factories produced them in the wrong way. It educated its people with the wrong skills. Worst of all, communist planners put factories, machines, and people in the wrong places. For a country with so much territory, especially territory in remote and cold places, location matters a great deal. Not only did Russia suffer from the irrationality of central planning for more than seventy years, but Russia's vast territorial expanse offered latitude for a system of misallocation to make mistakes on a huge and unprecedented scale. Had the Bolshevik Revolution taken place instead in a country as small and contained as, say, Japan, the damage could not have been as great. While central planning would still have distorted the economy, it would not, and could not, have distorted it as much in terms of locational decisions. In Russia, Siberia gave the Bolsheviks great room for error. Towns and cities grew to huge size in places they would never have developed under the influence of free-market forces.

Of course, the Bolsheviks inherited Siberia and the rest of Russia's vast territories from the tsars. It was the tsars who, over the course of five centuries, made Russia the world's largest country—a state defined by its physical geography, with a national identity rooted in the idea of territorial expansion and size ("gathering the Russian lands"). It was also the tsars who first pushed people out into Siberia and planted the seeds of cities on the farthest frontiers of the state to establish and affirm Russian sovereignty. But it was the Bolsheviks—the Soviets and their central planners—not the tsars, who shaped modern Russia's economic geography. Where the tsars had placed forts, villages, and towns in Siberia, the Soviets built cities of over a million. Where the tsars exiled thousands of prisoners to Siberia, the Bolsheviks and Soviets deployed millions of labor camp inmates to build factories, mines, and railways, as well as cities. The tsars bequeathed to the Bolsheviks a huge swathe of the world's coldest territory. The Bolsheviks chose to defy the forces of both nature and the market in developing it. Soviet planning subsequently gave modern Russia a supremely distorted economic geography with a huge portion of the bequest (cities, factories, and people) lost in the distance and cold of Siberia. It was a costly gift that can neither be easily maintained nor adapted to the market.

This book uses economic statistics, economic geography, and history to describe the extent to which people in Russia live and work in the wrong (distant and cold) places and to examine the implications of this for the modern Russian economy. Reviewing the history of Russian territorial expansion and the conquest and development of Siberia, the book outlines when and how this misallocation of resources happened. It explains why market mechanisms alone were not able to rectify economic distortions in the 1990s and why these distortions are likely to persist in the immediate future—given desires at all levels of the Russian government to redevelop and repopulate Siberia, and the fact that Russia's size and ideas of battling the elements continue to define the modern state. Finally, the book considers ways in which the Russian government might be able to address some of the distortions by rethinking the relationship between Russia, its economy, and its territory, especially Siberia.

This last point is especially important. Because the spatial misallocation was on such a massive scale, and went on for so long, it has actually become part of Russia's profile. Russia continues to be defined by its size. In spite of all its upheavals, including the loss of territories associated with the Soviet Union and the Russian Empire, Russia remains the world's biggest country. The discrepancy between its sheer size and its economic potential continues to draw the attention of even the most renowned economists and radical reformers in Russia as well as international observers. Consider, for example, this formulation attributed by Russian journalists to Andrey Illarionov, President Putin's economic adviser, in a December 2002 presentation on Russia's persistent economic difficulties and the prospects for growth:

> Today the way Russia looks on the map of the world is as follows: it occupies 11.5 percent of the world's territory, it has 2.32 percent of the global population total, and its share of world gross domestic product (GDP) is 1.79 percent in terms of purchasing power parity and 1.1 percent at market exchange rates. The unavoidable conclusion here is a cruel one. Human history has no precedent of a gap this wide between "territorial power" and economic "insignificance" holding for any extended length of time.[1]

We argue in this book that trying to tie GDP to territory is precisely the *wrong* way to think about Russia and its economic development. Instead, we should first remember that economies are "big" not because of their territorial expanse or quantity of raw materials, or even because of the amounts of physical output. Economic size is a matter of the *quality* of the output as measured by *value created*. Today's "big" economies are big because of the number of transactions that take place within them. Since the time of Adam Smith, we have known that the rate of value creation depends on the degree of special-ization of the economy and the intensity and complexity of exchange within it. In this context, Russia is a large economy, but only as measured in the num-bers of plants, machines, and the physical quantity of other inputs. The cen-tral issue to be resolved in the Russian economy is, therefore, how to put those inputs to their highest-value uses. To accomplish this, Russia needs *not* to try to bring its population, purchasing power, GDP, or any other economic index into line with its territorial size, but to concentrate people and resources within that territory.

In essence, to become competitive economically and to achieve sustainable growth, Russia needs to "*shrink*." It must contract not its territory (its physical geography), but its economic geography. "Being big" is a serious impedi-ment to development unless distances can be reduced and connections between population centers and markets can increase. Shrinking distance and increasing connections has been the consistent trend in other large countries over the course of their histories. Responding to market forces, the United States, Australia, and Canada, for example, have concentrated and connected their populations within their own vast territories much more than Russia. For the purposes of both economic productivity and good governance, this gives them a distinct advantage over Russia.

Russia's greatest dilemma today is that it must connect an economy that is both physically vast in size and terribly misdeveloped. This is a costly endeavor, and it is also likely to be inefficient once accomplished if connec-tions are pursued within the framework of Russia's current economic geog-raphy. Reconnecting the Russian economy is not simply a question of refurbishing and upgrading the existing systems of road, rail, and air trans-portation, or of constructing new infrastructure and creating new means of communications. This will simply improve the connections between exist-ing towns, cities, and enterprises—especially those in Siberia—which should never even have been located where they are in the first place. New infra-structure will, at high cost, have made places more livable where, from an eco-nomic point of view, few should live. As a result, the Russian government and the population will have forgone alternatives that are better.

In the final analysis, if Russia is to "shrink"—contract its economic geog-raphy, concentrate its population, and ultimately connect its economy—then *mobility* is the key to the future. Modern economies are characterized by mobility of factors of production. Today the world is becoming more mobile as people seek new and better opportunities for themselves and their families. This means that people in Russia need to move to warmer, more productive places, closer to markets and away from the cold, distant cities placed by the GULAG and communist planners in Siberia. Unfortunately, the dominant trend in Russia's imperial and Soviet history has been to constrain as well as direct the movement of population. Today, although the legal right to move is enshrined in the new Russian constitution, Russians are still not really free to relocate to places where they would like to live and work. Residence restrictions in cities like Moscow, resource constraints, poorly developed job and housing markets, and the absence of social safety nets all work against personal mobility, while the Russian government also attempts to direct investment to target locations of its choosing. Ensuring mobility, not just changing the system, will be the major challenge for Russia in the coming decades.

2

Size Matters

Throughout history, Russia's size has been its most significant attribute. Its physical geography has defeated aggressors, endowed it with substantial natural resources, and made it a major factor in the geopolitical calculations of Europe, Asia, and the Pacific Rim. But in today's world size is less an asset than a liability. It makes normal economic and political interaction extremely difficult. The primary issue is not just Russia's physical expanse, but *where* people are located within that space.

Size as Salvation . . .

Russia has long been a country of daunting proportions. For at least four centuries, Russia—the Russian Empire, the USSR, the Russian Federation—has been the largest state in the world. Already in the sixteenth century, Russian rulers reveled in the fact that awe-struck Europeans considered Russia's territory to be larger than the surface of the full moon.[1] No matter what else happened with Russia, its size was the constant that gave it stature in the world.

It was seen as the source of wealth, power, and even invincibility. Russian historians claim that Russia's huge territory saved not just Russia itself, but all of western civilization from devastation by serving as a buffer against the impact of Tatar-Mongol expansion.[2] Even the celebrated Russian poet Alexander Pushkin wrote that "[Russia's] vast plains absorbed the force of the Mongols and halted their advance at the very edge of Europe. . . . [T]he emergent enlightenment was rescued by a ravaged and expiring Russia."[3]

By the late nineteenth and early twentieth centuries, when the race to divide the globe up into colonies had firmly established a state's size—or, at least, the size of its colonial possessions—as a primary indicator of its influence in international affairs, Russia could scarcely be ignored. With a territory that covered a sixth of the world's surface in one single sweep from the Baltic Sea to the Pacific Ocean, Russia far outstretched both of the only two other contiguous land empires in Europe—Austria-Hungary and the Ottoman Empire. In the course of time, European observers said, Russia— along with the other great continental power, the United States—would eventually dominate global affairs.[4]

The idea that size is power was particularly promoted by British observers, who were used to admiring the attributes and enormous proportions of their own empire, on which the sun famously "never set." One British historian wrote in 1914: "The Russian Empire is an organism unique in the world's history. It embraces an area greater than Alexander's conquests, than the solid dominion built up by Rome, than the realms overrun by Chinghiz or Timur; it is surpassed only by Greater Britain [the British Empire]."[5] The eminent British geographer Halford Mackinder went so far as to describe Russia and the Euro-Asian landmass that it occupied as "the geographical pivot of history." All other areas of Europe and Asia to the east, south, and west of Russia and its great steppe lands were, Mackinder argued, merely marginal to it.[6]

Even today, after the collapse of the USSR, western observers remain in awe of Russia's size and resources. They marvel at a country that sprawls across eleven time zones with a potential market of nearly 150 million consumers. They typically cite a long list of its natural resource holdings: 40 percent of world natural gas reserves, 25 percent of the world's coal, diamonds, gold and nickel, 30 percent of its aluminum and timber, 6 percent of global oil, and so on, and so on.[7]

It goes without saying that such words are music to the ears of Russia's nationalist politicians and ideologues. For them, size in the most abstract sense of pure and empty "space" (*prostranstvo*) has near-mystical power and appeal. But even respected mainstream politicians fall prey to the temptation of invoking Russia's physical size to justify its international influence. One top political figure—Alexander Livshits, a former finance minister and adviser to President Boris Yeltsin—expressed a typical sentiment when he remarked in July 2001, after a high-level international meeting in Italy, that Russia could never accept the status of a junior partner to the United States. "The country is too large to be a younger brother."[8]

. . . and as Stumbling Block

But being "big" has always come at a cost. At the same time that observers in past centuries looked at the advantages of Russia's size, they—or at least some of them—saw its size as a burden. The most obvious was the difficulty of defending the territory. To contend with its huge sprawl across Eurasia, Russia in the nineteenth century was forced to maintain the largest standing army in Europe. The bulk of this force of more than one million men was stationed either on its borders or in potentially rebellious provinces like Poland. Maintaining the army consumed as much as three-quarters of state revenues in times of war, even though Russia spent less per soldier than other European countries such as Germany (Prussia) and France. It was the huge numbers that accounted for Russia's military budget, not the provision of weaponry and equipment or investment in technological advance.[9] Nor was there money available to provide the infrastructure on the necessary vast scale. Russia lacked a strategic railroad network for the transportation of men, weapons, and supplies thousands of kilometers from home to the frontiers of the empire. In military crises, even in war, troops often had to move on foot.

Time and again, conquering distance proved to be as much of a challenge as overcoming the military foe. The difficulties of mobilization and transportation contributed to Russia's defeat in the Crimean War in 1854–56. The European powers massed against Russia had imposed a naval blockade in the Black Sea that cut off all Russian sea approaches to the Crimean Peninsula. Russia's already overtaxed and disorganized land supply and communication lines eventually broke down into complete disarray.

In 1875, during Russia's military expeditions into Central Asia, the war ministry in St. Petersburg informed the Russian commander, General Kaufmann, that although he could have additional troops to support an offensive in Kokand, he should not count on seeing them for almost a year. The new units would "have to walk from Europe to Asia."[10] A quarter of a century later, during the 1904–05 Russo-Japanese War, the Russian Baltic fleet needed nine months to sail the 30,000 kilometers from its home port to the Far East—only to be blasted from the water by the Japanese navy at the Battle of Tsushima Strait.[11]

By this time (1904–05), there was a way to move by land from Europe to Asia, as the construction of the Trans-Siberian Railway was almost complete. But that route extended for more than 9,000 kilometers, was only single track, and had a vital section missing around Lake Baykal. Although it no longer took months to travel by land from one side of Russia to the other, it was still several weeks before reinforcements and supplies could be dispatched to support battles with the Japanese in northern Manchuria. Likewise, in World War I, although Russia's railway network had been expanded in its western regions, it was still insufficient to meet the demands of war across a huge and shifting western front that extended from the Baltic to the Black Seas.[12]

Some analysts, both in Russia and abroad, identified the roots of Russia's problems. Writing shortly before the Russo-Japanese War, one observer noted that Russia had become "the greatest power on earth, territorially considered, exceeding even the size of the United States." But, he quickly added, Russia's very weakness as a Great Power lay in that size because the country's defense required such vast outlays in manpower and capital. Russia, he concluded, was not in fact a Great Power, but a country teetering on the edge of domestic disaster. "Russia [was] invulnerable only in one narrow, definite sense—in the sense of her unwieldiness."[13]

Long after World War I, when the Russian Empire had become the USSR and had armed itself with intercontinental ballistic missiles and nuclear weapons, its Soviet rulers still relied heavily on sheer manpower. The Soviet Union continued to maintain the world's largest conventional military force. Since the collapse of the USSR, even with the loss of considerable territory, Russia today still has more neighbors and more international land borders than any other state (with the exception of China), and it has attempted to keep more than one million men under arms to defend them.*

Territory and Economics

It is when we turn from nineteenth-century notions of geopolitics to the ideas of global society prevalent in the late twentieth and early twenty-first centuries that we see size in its correct market economic perspective. If "size

---

* China borders fifteen countries, Russia fourteen. Russia too would have fifteen if Japan were included as a neighbor on the ground that the two countries claim possession of the same territory—the Kurile Islands.

of territory equals power" is an old nineteenth-century idea, then the formula now is "size of the economy equals power." Today, there seems to be little correlation between territorial size and economic size. If there is one, it is negative—as in Russia's case.

Historically, when wealth came from the land by virtue of extensive agriculture and harvesting of raw materials, size could be seen to have economic advantage for a country. As technology developed, size—raw land area—offered fewer and fewer advantages and more disadvantages. To the extent that there is an enduring belief that territorial size conveys strength, it is perhaps because of the fact that a large territory offers a greater chance of having an abundance of natural wealth. As economists Dwight Perkins and Moshe Syrquin have noted: "Geographic size is important because minerals and other natural resources are more apt to be present in larger quantities and greater variety in a large territory than in a small one. It is possible to have a huge expanse of territory and few petroleum reserves, but the odds are against it."[14]

Today, economists see distance and space overwhelmingly as obstacles. The reason why is simple. All economies beyond the most primitive ones are based on exchange (trade). The easier it is to engage in exchange and the more trade there is, the greater the degree of specialization is possible and, therefore, the more productive the citizens can be. Complex exchange is virtually synonymous with a high level of economic development.

The history of economic development is to a large extent the story of overcoming the obstacles posed by distance between trading partners. One of the great institutional innovations in economic history—wholesaling—came about as a way of facilitating long-distance trade.[15] Similarly, technological progress has been and continues to be driven by the need to reduce the time and cost of transporting goods, people, and now, increasingly, information, across space. Consequently, distance per se is not the point. What is relevant is the ease or difficulty of traversing the physical distance. Consider two sets of towns, each pair one hundred miles apart. In one case, the towns are on opposite sides of a high mountain range. In the other, the towns lie on the banks of a large navigable river. Clearly, the "economic distance" in the latter case is much shorter. Geography matters. But technology matters, too. Canals, railroads, and so on shrink physical distance. Such infrastructure projects are investments in raising productivity by lowering the costs of distance.

The appropriate economic map of a country would not represent a physical space of miles or kilometers but a space where distance is measured in terms of the cost of traversing it. But how could that be done? It is something that defies accounting. Distance—even "technologically modified" distance—affects different types of economic activity in different ways.

Moving bulk quantities of raw materials puts demands on transportation that differ from those involved in moving finished goods or people. Moving information is different still. Information is a good that was once subject to many of the same constraints of distance as moving people, because information had not only to be gathered by people, but also transmitted by them. Moving information meant moving the people that carried it. The telegraph, the telephone, and today's Internet changed that, dramatically reducing the cost of moving information across space.

The importance of technological progress in shrinking distance can be seen clearly in the economic history of the United States, especially in the way that the country has grown to become a true single national economy rather than an agglomeration of regional economies.

Becoming Connected

When the United States settled the continent, it was as an economy based overwhelmingly on land as the source of wealth. An initial phase of "harvesting natural resources" was followed by farming as the dominant activity. In 1860, 59 percent of the American labor force was in agriculture.[16] There were not many true cities. Most urban settlements were towns and cities serving agriculture. Nationally, the United States was a set of regional economies. Because transportation costs were high, factors of production were immobile. Even the infant industries used local resources. As a result, regions were not highly specialized.

In the period from 1860 to 1914, as the United States built its industry, the development of railroads lowered transportation costs—that is, they "shrank economic distance," making it cheaper to transport final goods, especially relative to inputs such as energy. Large-scale production processes, combined with relatively immobile energy sources, allowed regions to begin to specialize. At the same time, regional specialization made sense only because the national economy was more integrated. Final goods produced in one region could be sold to consumers in another. Thus while regions increasingly began to play specialized roles, they were doing so in the context of a country that was becoming more connected at the national level.

This process of regional specialization reached a peak in the interwar period of the twentieth century. After World War II and to the present, a remarkable change has occurred, thanks again to technological developments related significantly to transportation. As factors of production became even more mobile and as new technologies were developed that offered a greater range of choice of inputs for production, more and more industries freed themselves of the constraints of specific location. People could do and make the same or equivalent things in different regions. Regions again "despecialized." This time, however, lack of specialization did not reflect a process of primitivization, or regional self-sufficiency, as had been the case in the earlier, pre-1860 period. Rather, it was the opposite: the economy was moving to an even higher level of integration and complexity.

The "Death of Distance"?

The process of national integration in the United States continues today, thanks in large part to shrunken distance and thus greater mobility of all factors of production. From steel production to computers and biotechnology— America's industries seem increasingly less tied to specific regions of the country. It is tempting to suggest that in today's "postindustrial" world, geography has lost its importance. Even in the most modern information economy, however, space still claims its due because goods still need to be physically transported. Although the means of transportation of goods can be organized more efficiently, they remain the same: rail, road, water, air. Moreover, in one important sense, geography may be growing in importance. A pioneering line of research suggests that in the present phase of business development in the United States, location continues to matter a great deal. This is no longer because capital needs to be close to sources of raw materials, to immobile energy sources such as coal or water power, or to markets. Rather, it is because capital needs to be where labor is, or, more correctly, where labor *would like* to be. The most valuable workers—the highly productive individuals who belong to what has been called the "creative class"— increasingly choose their region of residence based on locational amenities. That is, they move to where they think they will be comfortable, in terms of both the natural climate and the social environment, confident that capital will come to where they are.[17] While the "creative class" thesis may as yet apply to only a small portion of businesses in high-tech sectors of the most advanced economies, it identifies a trend that may shape the future for countries that aspire to be competitive in these most advanced technology areas.

Choosing Location

The evolution of the U.S. economy shows the importance of technological and infrastructure development in overcoming the obstacles of size and distance to integrate the nation. But this is not just a story of trying to reduce distance between preexisting settlements. Where the settlements are in the

Table 2-1. *Territory and Population, Selected Countries*

Country	Land area (000 km²)	Population (millions)	Population density (people per km²)
Russia	17,068	145	9
European Russia[a]	*3,948*	*106*	*27*
Asiatic Russia[b]	*13,120*	*39*	*3*
China	9,322	1,273	137
Canada	9,217	32	3
United States	9,163	278	30
U.S. without Alaska	*7,682*	*277*	*36*
Brazil	8,453	175	21
Australia	7,615	19	3
Ukraine	603	49	81
Sweden	411	9	22
Germany	350	83	237
Norway	308	5	15
Finland	305	5	17
United Kingdom	241	60	247

Sources: Land area and mid-2001 population for all countries except Russia, *Statistical Abstract of the United States: 2002* (U.S. Census Bureau, 2001), tables 18, 1308. Russian land area from *Rossiyskiy statisticheskiy yezhegodnik, 2001* (Goskomstat Rossii, 2001), pp. 41–43. Russian population figures are preliminary 2002 census results as reported in *Interfax Statistical Report*, no. 18 (2003).

a. European Russia: the territory of the Central, Northwestern, Southern, and Volga federal districts.

b. Asiatic Russia: the territory of the Ural, Siberian, and Far Eastern federal districts.

first place is subject to technological constraints and, most generally, to dictates of economic rationality. In a market economy, populations are not arbitrarily distributed across space, leaving it to technology and infrastructure to then connect those settlements. Rather, as businesses and people chose where to locate originally, they evaluated the costs and benefits of trading in input and output markets. As a result, spatially large economies typically evolve in a certain pattern. This can be seen by reflecting on patterns of population distribution in the world's largest countries. Table 2-1 gives an overview of the territories, populations, and densities of some major countries.

Canada and Australia both have huge territories, small populations, and, therefore, low overall population densities (even lower than Russia). In contrast to Russia, however, their populations are actually rather compactly settled. Approximately 85 percent of Canada's population is concentrated within three hundred kilometers of the U.S. border. In Australia, the population is concentrated on the eastern and southeastern coasts, and there is virtually no settlement in the interior of the country. The population of the United States is also primarily clustered in the east and west of the continent, with much lower population densities in the interior. Clearly, this phenomenon of clustering and concentration of population reduces the challenge of large size and facilitates the construction of critical infrastructure. The United States, Canada, and Australia have all managed to reduce distance in spite of their large territories and relatively low overall population densities, but Russia has not. Russia has not followed the trend of concentration of population because of a persistent belief that all its territory must be *populated* to be possessed and governed.* Instead, Russia has spread its population out across its territory.

Density Is Good . . . Most of the Time

Density of population is commonly singled out as a prerequisite for economic development and technological advancement. One prominent recent example of this is Jared Diamond's thesis in his 1999 book *Guns, Germs, and Steel*. Diamond describes why "modern civilization" arose on the Eurasian continent, while peoples indigenous to the Americas, central and southern Africa, and the Asian-Pacific islands (including Australia) failed to make similar technological, agricultural, and political-organizational advances. He argues, in part, that complex societies ruled by advanced political administrations could only be achieved, historically, where population densities were high and where there were few ecological and geographic barriers to impede movement of people and the relatively quick transmission of information.[18]

From the economist's point of view, there are several straightforward reasons why one would expect regions with more concentrated populations to be more productive. The first is that if the various stages of production occur close to one another, transportation costs will be lower. Second, when many firms are located close to one another, they all benefit from increased technological spillovers from one to another. Third, denser activity facilitates greater specialization: firms will have access to a greater variety of intermediate inputs.[19] (These factors are referred to as the positive externalities of agglomeration.)

There are, however, countervailing forces. Concentration can become too great if congestion lowers productivity and comfort in an area. The disadvantages of density (so-called disamenities of agglomeration) that stem

---

* This refers to the concept of *terra nullius*, which will be discussed in greater detail in chapter 4.

mainly from congestion are especially important to households, both as workers and as consumers. In equilibrium, the positive and negative effects balance, giving an optimal density.

A major problem in determining the actual effect of density on economic development is how to measure it correctly. Clearly, comparing average national population densities does not seem to be right. Another look at table 2-1 shows the problem. Germany and the United Kingdom, large and productive economies, have population densities that are one hundred times as great as those of Canada and Australia, two other advanced economies. Average national density therefore appears to be a very poor predictor of economic success.

It turns out that the same is true of density even at lower levels, such as the average densities for individual U.S. states. One attempt to go beyond the crude measures and look at the idea of structure and economic performance with a more refined notion of density was made by economists Antonio Ciccone and Robert Hall. In their work, they used a measure of internal densities—local density within states—and compared that with the states' productivity. They concluded that differences in density of economic activity by this measure account for more than half of the variation in average labor productivity across U.S. states.[20] To illustrate the point more concretely, they estimated that an average worker in one of the least dense counties in the United States produces less than half the output of a worker in New York City, even if the two have the same levels of education and are engaged in exactly the same sort of activity.[21]

In sum, the results of this and other research indicate that in a normal market economy like that of the United States, the favorable effect of density tends to outweigh the negative effect of congestion. As a result, the mere fact of being located in a dense region makes economic activity more productive. What is important is to realize that concentration of population in specific regions is another way of shrinking space—and a more powerful way than building railroads and highways to connect distant settlements.*

At the same time, it is important to realize that the fact that density is better in a *market* economy may have little relevance to Russia. After all, density

---

* A further point is that technology allows concentrated areas to better deal with the negative effects of density and thus draw benefits from the positive aspects. Individuals in most of the world—from Los Angeles to Moscow—appear to have great faith that technology will be able to solve congestion problems. They move to big cities because of the advantages of density. Meanwhile, their very presence there further increases the positive and negative sides, both for themselves and for others. But people usually assume that the negative sides will somehow be "fixed" as municipal policymakers order the construction of new highways, bridges, parking garages, and so on.

is not just a matter of lumping many people together in one spot. The positive forces of density are related to how well the market functions. Russia, an imperfect market economy, might possibly exhibit the same nominal degree of density at various levels, regional or local, even using a refined notion like Ciccone and Hall's, and yet reap none of the benefits that the U.S. economy does. Intuitively, one can understand this by realizing that having a lot of people congests. If those are not the "right" people (that is, people with the proper education and skills and matched to the productive industries), the mere fact that there are a lot of them in a close space will produce no gains to offset the negative effects of congestion. This suggests that something more than density is needed to capture the essence of countries' internal spatial-economic structure. The questions are: (1) what is concentrated; (2) where is it concentrated; (3) how is it connected? The key is *cities*—how large they are, how many there are, and where they are located, in relation to one another, in relation to the rest of the world, and, as we will see in the next chapter, in relation to the range of climatic conditions that Russia offers.

City Size

Russia has two true metropolitan areas—Moscow and St. Petersburg, both relatively old and established world-class cities. Already in 1800, these two Russian cities had populations of more than 100,000, making them the fifth and eighth largest cities in Europe, respectively.[22]* Even today, they are in the same class as the largest U.S. cities. By one reasonable definition, Moscow is as big as or bigger than the very largest U.S. metropolitan areas of New York, Los Angeles, and Chicago, while St. Petersburg would fit comfortably in a comparison with the next tier of U.S. cities (Philadelphia, Washington, or Detroit).† The difference in the size structure of the cities in the two coun-

---

* The top ten European cities in 1800 were: London, Paris, Constantinople (Istanbul), Naples, Moscow, Lisbon, Vienna, St. Petersburg, Amsterdam, and Adrianople (modern Edirne in Turkey).
† These comparisons hold if one defines the U.S. cities according to the notion of so-called primary metropolitan statistical areas. The U.S. Census Bureau distinguishes three levels of metropolitan areas: metropolitan statistical areas (MSAs), primary metropolitan statistical areas (PMSAs), and consolidated metropolitan statistical areas (CMSAs). An MSA consists of either (1) a central city with a population of at least 50,000 and the surrounding communities with which it has a high level of social and economic integration or (2) an area with no central city containing at least 100,000 people. Areas with more than a million people are often designated as CMSAs, and they are made up in turn of PMSAs. To see the difference between CMSAs and PMSAs, consider the "New York-Northern New Jersey-Long Island, NY-NJ-CT-PA CMSA," with a population of 21.2 million in 2000, and the "New York, NY PMSA," with a population of 9.3 million. For an explanation of these concepts, see the Census Bureau website: www.census.gov/population/www/estimates/aboutmetro.html.

Table 2-2. *Largest Russian and U.S. Cities*

Russian cities	Population (thousands)	Rank	U.S. cities (metro areas[a])	Population (thousands)
Moscow	10,102	1	New York	21,200
Saint Petersburg	4,669	2	Los Angeles	16,374
Novosibirsk	1,426	3	Chicago	9,158
Nizhniy Novgorod	1,311	4	Washington–Baltimore	7,608
Yekaterinburg	1,293	5	San Francisco	7,039
Samara	1,158	6	Philadelphia	6,188
Omsk	1,134	7	Boston	5,819
Kazan'	1,105	8	Detroit	5,456
Chelyabinsk	1,078	9	Dallas–Fort Worth	5,222
Rostov-na-Donu	1,070	10	Houston	4,670
Ufa	1,042	11	Atlanta	4,112
Volgograd	1,013	12	Miami	3,876
Perm'	1,000	13	Seattle	3,555
Krasnoyarsk	912	14	Phoenix	3,251
Saratov	874	15	Minneapolis–St. Paul	2,969

Source: For U.S. cities, 2000 census figures from *Statistical Abstract of the United States: 2002* (U.S. Census Bureau, 2001). For Russian cities, 2002 preliminary census results as reported in *Interfax Statistical Report,* no. 18 (2003).

a. The U.S. cities listed are CMSAs (consolidated metropolitan statistical areas), with the exception of Atlanta, Phoenix, and Minneapolis–St. Paul, which are MSAs (metropolitan statistical areas).

tries begins after that. While the United States has a nearly continuous range of cities of increasingly smaller size, Russia does not. Table 2-2 lists the largest cities in each country. Russia's two largest cities would fit in among the top ten American cities, but Russia's third largest city would not appear until number thirty-five on the American list.

Russia's lack of urban areas between about 1.5 and 4.0 million people is one of the most striking formal differences between the U.S. and Russian urban structures. Put another way, nearly 80 million Americans (about one in three) live in a large urban environment (the cities of 1.5–4 million people like Orlando, Phoenix, Atlanta, Pittsburgh, and St. Louis) that is altogether unknown to Russians. Relative to its total size, Russia has roughly the same number of cities smaller than half a million as the United States, but the United States has many more large cities—including more than three times as many cities with over a million people. As table 2-3 shows, more than half of

Table 2-3. *Percentage of Total U.S. and Russian Population*
in Medium and Large Cities

Country	Proportion of total population living in cities of various size ranges			
	100,000–250,000	250,000–500,000	500,000–1,000,000	Over 1,000,000
Russia	9.4	10.7	10.0	15.5
United States	8.0	10.0	9.6	51.9

Source: Authors' calculations based on latest census results: Russia, 2002, as reported in *Interfax Statistical Report*, no. 18 (2003); United States, 2000, from U.S. Census Bureau.

the U.S. population lives in urban agglomerations of more than one million people, while fewer than 16 percent of Russians do. Again, this reflects the large gap between Moscow and St. Petersburg, on the one hand, and the rest of urban Russia on the other. Another way to see this pattern is to look at the relationship between cities' populations and their size rankings.

Breaking the Law

One of the most interesting regularities in economic development is a phenomenon called "Zipf's law" for cities.[23] Zipf's law says that across all countries and across time, cities generally seem to obey a curious mathematical law with respect to their relative sizes: a country's largest city is approximately twice as large as the second-largest city, three times as big as the third city, four times as large as the fourth, and so on. Zipf's law is most easily visualized when the cities' populations and ranks are plotted on logarithmic scales. Then the Zipf result is that the cities fall along a straight line with a slope of -1. Figure 2-1 shows that U.S. cities do indeed closely follow Zipf's law.[24]

In view of our observations about table 2-2, it is perhaps not surprising to find that the Russian city size distribution is a very poor fit along the Zipf line (figure 2-2). The sharp drop in size from St. Petersburg (the second dot) to Novosibirsk (the third dot) shows up clearly on the graph. But it is also not surprising to learn of Russia's deviance from the law for the simple reason that if indeed Zipf's law were the result of the play of natural (market) economic forces over time, it would be strange if Russia did obey it.[25]

Russia is not the only case of a country that has failed to follow the regular pattern. But the Russian cities deviate from Zipf's law in a way not seen for any other country. In most other notable cases of deviation, the first city

Figure 2-1. *U.S. City Size Distribution, 2000*

Population of city in thousands

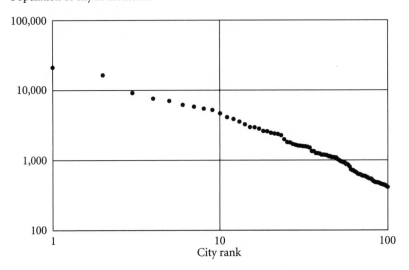

Source: *Statistical Abstract of the United States: 2002* (U.S. Census Bureau, 2001).

Figure 2-2. *Russian City Size Distribution, 2002*

Population of city in thousands

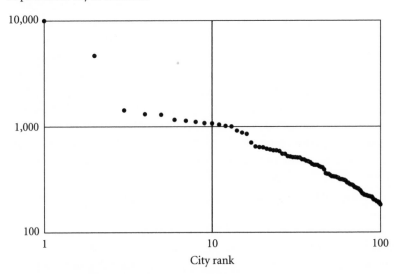

Source: *Interfax Statistical Report*, no. 18 (2003).

is too large. This is often referred to as the "super-city" case, or the "Paris syndrome," since France is the paradigmatic case: Paris is much larger than it "should be." The basic picture in Russia, in contrast, is that a group of cities, ranking from number three through about number fifteen, are all too small to make the line fit. And they are not off by just a small amount. According to Zipf's law, one would expect that Russia's third largest city should have a population of around 5 million. That city should be followed by cities of, roughly, 4 million, 3 million, 2.5 million, 2.3 million, and 2 million. But those are all missing. What is the reason? An answer suggests itself when we look at exactly which cities follow St. Petersburg as number three and lower: Novosibirsk, Nizhniy Novgorod, Yekaterinburg, Samara, Omsk. These are all defense industry cities, whose size was tightly regulated by Soviet economic and defense planners. We will return to this question of the defense industrial cities in a later chapter. For now, let us present some recent work by colleagues at the Brookings Institution that may shed a somewhat different light on the peculiarities of the Russian city-size distribution.

Too Many Cities?

Brookings researchers Timothy Gulden and Ross Hammond have designed a model that shows that a Zipf distribution is the natural result of very simple forces. They show that, given the "proper" number of cities relative to total population, unconstrained movement of people among the cities according to fairly simple rules of attraction will produce a Zipf distribution. What is interesting to see is what upsets the Zipf result. It turns out that if the number of people and cities in an urban system are badly mismatched, systematic deviations occur, even with the free movement of people. If there are not enough cities (for a given number of people), the largest city will end up with far too many people. This resembles the "super-city," or the Paris case described above. If, on the other hand, the number of cities is too large, the result will be a distribution that bears an uncanny resemblance to Russia—it produces a group of second-tier cities that are close to one another in size and that are also smaller than expected.[26]

Does Russia, then, have "too many" cities? This would be consistent with the idea that Soviet economic planners, in their attempt to nominally fill the space from the Urals to the Pacific, spread the population out too thinly. On the one hand, they prevented some large cities from growing. On the other, they created and maintained a range of cities that under more normal market conditions would not have evolved to that size.

However, it is important to stress that this does not imply that just unleashing market forces will grow Russia's current second-tier cities to fit the Zipf distribution. Why not? Because market forces not only determine the relative size of cities; they also affect their location. And in the case of Russia, those second-tier cities are mislocated.

Where Cities Grow

Economists and economic geographers have long studied the functioning and roles of cities and their internal dynamics. What they have not done well is explain how and why large cities end up where they do in space. Recent research tends to reject the idea that "nature" or geography predetermines the sites of great cities (even though, of course, many cities historically began as small settlements that were sited because of an advantageous geographical feature like a river crossing or a valley). There was, however, a time when such theories were in vogue. In the United States, right before the mid-nineteenth century, for instance, some of the biggest enthusiasts of the theory that geography—natural location—is destiny were real estate speculators. They wanted to use "science" to justify their marketing claims that the patch of territory they were selling would likely become the "next great metropolis."

There is no consensus theory today, but there are several alternatives. The good news is that the leading contending theories may be complementary rather than rivals. To simplify somewhat, the various hypotheses stress the importance of local trade, long-distance (international) trade, and financial mediation.* The latest thinking combines the three by saying that whatever forces may have initially placed towns and even cities on the map in particular locations, successive waves of economic factors later determined which of those cities would grow to become large urban centers. In other words, as countries develop into the phase of open, industrialized economies, powerful market forces shape the initial "inherited" constellation. The seeds, as it were, of future cities may have been scattered rather randomly—at least in relation to the later forces that prevail in determining their ultimate destinies—and only a few of the seeds develop into viable, healthy plants.

The urban structure of a large country typically evolves as the country passes through successive phases of economic development: from harvesting

---

* These theories are, respectively: the central place theory, the mercantile theory, and the metropolitan dominance theory.

of natural resources, to farming, and then to industrial and postindustrial phases. The uniquely Russian problem is that as the country moved from the land-intensive agricultural phase to the urban-dominated industrial phase, economic allocation was guided by distinctly nonmarket rules. Thus for Russia (to continue the metaphor of seeds of cities) it was not the case that market economic forces acted differentially on the seeds planted randomly, selecting the locations that made sense commercially to become the large centers. Rather, the Russian, and especially the Soviet, state artificially nurtured some seeds (town sites) to become large plants (cities), far larger than they "naturally" would have become. But, up until the early twentieth century, despite the state-directed development of cities in the Russian Empire, Russia's urban structure may not have been significantly more "unnatural" than that of the United States, say. Plenty of U.S. cities began in serendipitous ways. Some began as frontier military forts. More than a few were the result of the commercial marketing schemes (even scams) of real estate speculators. But in the end, market economic forces prevailed, choosing some to prosper and leaving others to stagnate and even fade away. It is not clear whether there is a distinct size cut-off for a city's viability, a point beyond which a city will be able to continue to live and develop despite strong shifts in the economic climate. But empirically, it is interesting to note that while there have been many, many cases of small towns in the United States and Europe that have grown, reached a peak of population, and then shrunk, this does not seem to happen to cities of over several hundred thousand in population. (A discussion of the complex phenomenon of city shrinkage is in chapter 8.)

Russia's situation in regard to the creation and growth of cities is not just different. It is *radically* different. Never before in history has there been an urban structure shielded so thoroughly from market forces and thus allowed to misdevelop as much as Russia's in the twentieth century. Urbanization in tsarist and then Soviet Russia is examined in chapters 4 and 5, with special attention to the creation of cities in Siberia.

Connectedness

Cities' locations are primarily determined not by *natural* geography—for instance, proximity to rivers, coasts, mountain passes, and so on—but by the geography of the existing *economic structure*, notably by the existence of other cities. All but the most primitive settlements are somehow embedded in a larger economic structure. The extent to which cities grow is shaped not so much by their natural surroundings as by how well the people and businesses located there meet the needs of the larger economy. This means that cities in normal market economies grow up connected to one another from the very beginning.

This notion of "connectedness" is one of the hallmarks of a modern market economy. The efficient market economy, in order to be efficient, always seeks to reduce distance and shrink space. Only the ties of market exchange (trade) can sustain the connectedness of large cities. In large measure, they are connected only to the extent that they have *economic* reasons to be connected. This means that linkages in the Soviet planned economy were an artificial phenomenon to the extent that they were dictated by the planning apparatus and subjected to planning goals. As economic ties specific to the Soviet centrally planned economy broke down with the collapse of the USSR, cities became disconnected. Just as the value that economic activity had in the Soviet system was lost when the planning system dissolved, the connections that were justified and sustained by that planning system lost their rationale. This has left Russia's cities more distant, in an economic sense, from one another than ever before.

Transition and Space

A final reason to be concerned about the obstacles of size and distance is the continuing challenges Russia faces in building the institutions of a market economy. Nearly all observers now agree that institutions are vital for transition from the centrally planned economy to a free market economy. Nobel Prize–winning economist Douglass North has described these institutions as the "rules of the game." They are the constraints that human beings impose on themselves to reduce uncertainty as the economy becomes more complex. Primitive societies, those in which trade is local or confined to a cohesive cultural community, do not need the institutions of a modern market economy. But it is impossible to conceive of a complex economy, one based on specialization and division of labor, without strong institutions. They above all make it possible to transact with strangers. When formal institutions do not do the job of facilitating exchange, then the economy tends to revert to a more primitive level. There will be less complex exchange and less specialization. The gains from trade identified by Adam Smith will be lost. If an extended territory is to function as a single economy—that is, if it is to be able to support anonymous exchange—it must have strong formal institutions. Size and distance make it even more important that the "rules of the game" function well.

Conclusion

Russia's huge size is not a strength. It is a disadvantage that has to be overcome. Russia's land mass poses particular problems for economic competitiveness and effective governance. Population centers are spread over vast distances. As distances between cities and towns increase, physical movement becomes more difficult. Direct transportation costs increase. Information flows, the establishment of trust among market actors, and the creation and functioning of shared institutions are all impaired. In short, "being big" is a serious impediment to economic development unless a country can reduce distance and increase connections between population centers and markets.

The primary issue is not just that of Russia's physical expanse, but the *location* of people within that space and what they are close to or not close to (markets, communication routes, and so on). In Russia, it is costly to build and maintain the infrastructure to keep citizens in economic and political contact with one another and with the center in Moscow. But it is not only the vast physical space that is the problem. Russians have also located themselves poorly in "thermal" space. The uniquely cold location of many of Russia's big cities adds further costs to Russia's economic geography. The cost of the cold is the subject of the next chapter.

3

The Cost of the Cold

Problems of distance are compounded by the spread of Russia's population and economic activity across *thermal* as well as geographic space. In Europe and northern Asia, unlike most of North America, the isotherms—or lines of constant temperature—run more in a north-south direction than east-west. This means that as Russians moved east from Moscow across the Eurasian landmass, they not only increased their distance from Europe and its markets; they also made Russia colder. Today some 45 million people live and work in and east of the Ural Mountains in regions where average January temperatures range between −15° and −45° Celsius.* This imposes huge costs on the Russian economy.

It is a commonplace that Russia occupies a cold territory. Not only does its uniquely large land mass lie in an extreme high-latitude (northern) position, but very little of that territory

* We remind the reader that we cite temperatures according to the Celsius (centigrade) scale in this book. Appendix A contains a Celsius to Fahrenheit conversion chart.

enjoys any moderating influence of temperate oceans in the east and west. By nearly any conventional measure of temperature, Russia claims the distinction of being the coldest country in the world. It has twice as much territory above the Arctic Circle as Canada, ten times as much as Alaska, and fifteen times as much as Norway, Sweden, and Finland combined. Day after day, the coldest spot on the globe is usually somewhere in Russia.[1] Not surprisingly, the lowest temperature ever recorded outside Antarctica was in Russia.[2]

Perhaps even more than size, the "cold" is at the very core of popular conceptions of "Russia." Winter and snow are particularly Russian phenomena, captured in poems and novels and in the broadly recognized images on lacquer boxes—of fur-clad figures bundled against the elements, troikas or sleighs drawn by three horses, expansive stretches of birch and pine forest laden with snow, and squat wooden peasant huts built around a stove to beat back the elements. "Russia" conjures up associations of Siberia, permafrost, and vodka to warm the flesh and boost the spirits in the long winter nights. "Winter" (*Zima*) is even a place in Siberia, a small town and stopping point along the Trans-Siberian Railway from Moscow to Vladivostok. Furthermore, the onset of winter has traditionally been Russia's greatest line of defense.

Throughout its history, Russia seems to have been saved time and again by *its* winter—the "*Russian* winter." The Mongols were arguably the first and the last to execute a successful winter campaign in the Russian heartland in 1237–38, when they used frozen rivers to launch surprise attacks on Russian cities.[3] Since then the snows and the cold have trapped and entombed invaders. In 1812 Napoleon's Grande Armée fell spectacularly afoul of the Russian winter in its retreat from Moscow. Of a French force of about 600,000, fewer than 50,000 made it out of Russia along a route that extended hundreds of kilometers across rivers, forests, and plains. More troops died from starvation, epidemics, and—above all—the cold than in combat with the Russian imperial army. In September 2002, in a grim reminder of the costs of battling with the cold across the vastness of Russian territory, construction workers in Lithuania's capital of Vilnius unearthed the skeletons of as many as 2,000 of an estimated 80,000 French soldiers who succumbed there to temperatures of −20° C during the retreat.[4]

Likewise, following Hitler's invasion of the Soviet Union in June 1941, the German army, which had expected a quick summer victory, became bogged down and overextended in the winter. It was forced to withdraw from much of the territory it had captured. Subsequent winters also proved too great a challenge. In November 1942, the German Sixth Army was encircled and trapped during its siege of Stalingrad on the banks of the Volga River. Three months later, in February 1943, with its 250,000 men starving and freezing to death in temperatures of $-30°$ C, the Sixth Army finally surrendered—Germany's first major military defeat in World War II. The frozen fates of Napoleon's Grande Armée and Hitler's Sixth Army have become almost mystical invocations of two of Russia's most commonly perceived strategic assets: its size and the cold.

Geographical Fatalism

In more recent years, such glorification of the cold has been less in fashion. The imperative of competing in the world economy has focused attention on Russia's uniquely cold climate as a disadvantage. An extreme example of the pessimism this has engendered is a recent best-selling book, *Why Russia Is Not America*, by Andrey Parshev.[5] The starting point for Parshev's cleverly written tract is a map like the one shown in figure 3-1, a map of Europe showing not lines of latitude, but so-called isotherms, that is, lines of constant January temperatures. As one moves along an isotherm, the temperature remains the same. As one moves across them, the temperature gets warmer or colder.

Parshev writes of this map:

> The climate zones in Europe are located in a paradoxical manner. The climate does not get colder from south to north, but from west to east. Sometimes, even from north to south, or more accurately, from the coasts to the inland regions. Note that Leningrad is warmer than Moscow, even though it is 400 km further north. Helsinki is warmer in winter than Oryol, even though Helsinki lies 1,000 km farther north.[6]

Parshev argues that largely because of the cold climate and the costs it imposes on economic activity, Russia is fated to fail as a global competitor and thus should remain outside the world economic community. Some excerpts from his gloomy analysis are presented in box 3-1.

Parshev is fundamentally correct in many of his assertions about the disadvantages of the cold. At the same time, he wrongly assumes that Russia's coldness is an *immutable* characteristic of the country and its location.* For

(*text continues on page 33*)

---

* Parshev is also wrong because he ignores that even a cold climate can have a comparative advantage, and Russia can therefore benefit from trade with other countries. The tragic irony of Parshev's final recommendation is that if Russia were to follow his advice to withdraw from the world economy, it would be immeasurably worse off. However, this is not to say that Russia's comparative advantage lies in its current economic structure—a structure that includes *location*. The reason Russia is not competitive is precisely that its leaders insist on producing the same things in the same old locations instead of looking for true comparative advantage on a nationwide scale.

Figure 3-1. *Parshev's Isotherm Map*

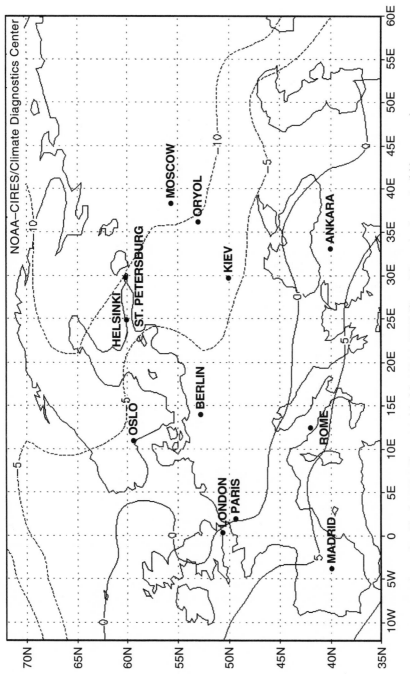

Source: Custom plot produced by the GFDL Climate Model of the NOAA-CIRES Climate Diagnostics Center. Available at www.cdc.noaa.gov.

Box 3-1. *Andrey Parshev's "Isothermal Fatalism"*

The myth of Russia's raw materials wealth:
"It's been said that we have a lot of raw materials. That's a myth, or to speak plain Russian, it's a lie." [p. 58]

The resources may be physically present, but they cost too much to extract. Take, for instance, gold:

"In most of our gold deposits the cost of mining the gold is greater than the value of the reserves. What was advantageous to mine in the Soviet economic model does not attract investors today. Today's 'investors' are simply spending the investments once made by the Soviets." [p. 62]

Such "reserves" may as well not be there. No one wants most of them:

"Those [Russians] who think that the ultimate depth to which our country can fall is that it will turn into a 'raw materials appendage' of the West are incorrigible optimists. Comrade patriots, it's time to end your illusions. We can become a 'raw materials appendage' for 5–10 years at the most. But even our pensioners plan to live a bit longer than that!" [p. 67]

The myth of cheap Russian wages:
A calculation of all the hidden subsidies needed to make Russia livable would show that Russian labor is not that cheap. If the subsidies were eliminated, the formal wage would have to be high enough to cover what otherwise was compensated in the form of social benefits, and other amenities:

"In sum, our people's wages have always been rather high by world standards. The proof of that statement is the fact that they are alive. Simply surviving under our conditions is expensive." [p. 93]

The prospects for investment:
"We cannot and will not, in any manner, by any means, attract foreign investment in Russian industrial production." [p. 23]

"In the competitive struggle for investments, if the game is played by the rules of the free world market, almost any Russian enterprise is flagrantly fated to lose." [p. 34]

In every major category of production costs—costs of construction, of raw materials and other physical inputs, of transportation and energy, of labor, and of taxes—Russia is more expensive than, or at least as expensive as, the rest of the world.

"Therefore, *under conditions of free movement of capital, no investor, whether he be Russian or foreign, will invest his funds in the development of practically any production facility on the territory of Russia.*" [p. 95]

The issue is not lack of patriotism or corruption. Investors are just obeying the law of the market: make a profit. *"There are not, and will not be, investments in our industry."* [p. 95]

Global competition:

If Russia subjects itself to the laws of the world economy, then large parts of its economy will not survive the competition. This includes "all manufacturing industry, all marketed agriculture, and most raw materials sectors." [p. 96]

"Any production on the territory of Russia is characterized by an excessively high level of costs. These costs are higher than in any other industrial zone in the world. The simplest analysis of costs of production by categories of expenditure shows that in each category Russia loses out to nearly every country of the world, and we have nothing that can offset these extra expenses. First and foremost, this is because of the excessively harsh climate. Production—indeed, simple survival—in Russia requires more expenditure of energy. Energy costs money. Therefore, all else being equal, our production will be more expensive."

"Two consequences flow from this. First, a Russian industrial product which may be comparable to foreign products in terms of consumer characteristics will be more costly to produce and, if sold at world prices, will yield a loss, not a profit."

"Second, our enterprises are an unfavorable object for attracting capital investment from abroad. Even for our own domestic investors, foreign capital markets are more attractive." [p. 103]

The condition is permanent:

"The fact that our production is noncompetitive is no secret. The secret is that the factors causing it to be noncompetitive cannot be removed." [p. 106]

And the conclusion:

"We should just admit the real state of affairs. In my view, if we are going to create a viable state on Russian territory we need do only one thing: *we must isolate the domestic Russian market from the world market."* [p. 311]

Source: Andrey P. Parshev, *Pochemu Rossiya ne Amerika: kniga dlya tekh, kto ostayetsya zdes'* [Why Russia is not America: A book for those who remain here] (Moscow: Krymskiy Most-9D, 2000), emphasis in the original.

Figure 3-2. *"Moscow Is Just the Beginning"*

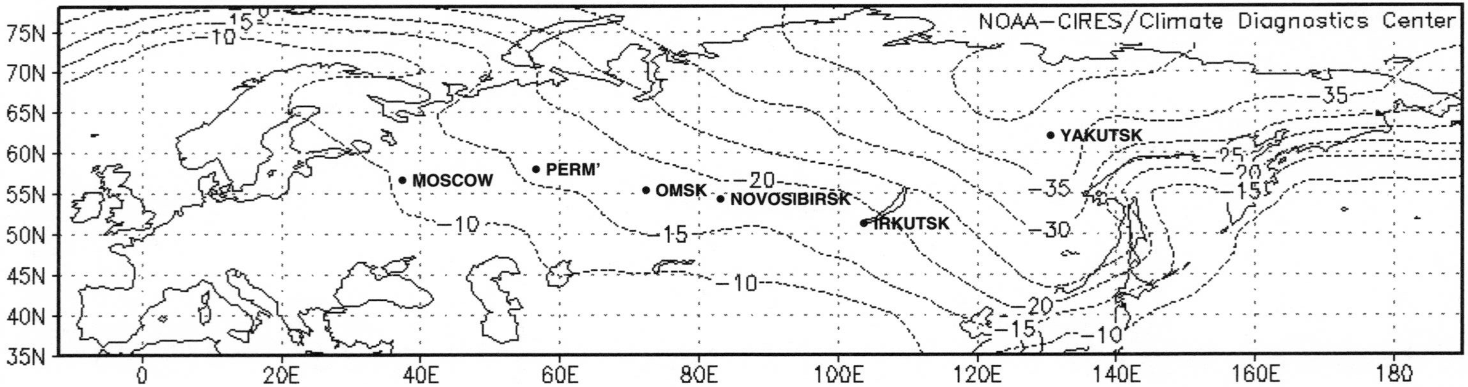

Source: Custom plot produced by the GFDL Climate Model of the NOAA-CIRES Climate Diagnostics Center. Available at www.cdc.noaa.gov.

Parshev, Russia's problem with the cold is eternal and can be fully understood by looking at the location of Moscow in thermal space. Of the several maps that Parshev presents in his book, not a single one extends beyond European Russia. In fact, however, Moscow is only the beginning of Russia's problem with the cold. An isotherm map that Parshev does not show—one that extends over the whole of Russia—makes the point (see figure 3-2). The same "paradoxical" arrangement of climate zones that Parshev describes for Europe applies to the entire Eurasian land mass. Because of the continental effect—the large distance of most of Russia to the oceans—it is movement to the east, just as much as to the north, that lowers temperatures. And, for Russians, there is much more room to the east than to the north.

Figure 3-2 illustrates that a traveler who began in Moscow and proceeded due east would, without ever moving farther north at all, enter progressively colder and colder zones. By the time the traveler approached Russia's Pacific coast, that person would not only have covered nearly 7,500 kilometers but would also have traversed a temperature range of more than 20° C. The difference between Russia and the United States in this regard is striking. To move westward from, say, New York City in the same manner would bring the traveler into regions in the center of the North American continent that are colder than New York, but not by much—about five degrees or so in January. And, at the end of the journey, there would be the Northern California climate—nearly 10° C warmer than at the start. Table 3-1 compares temperatures as one moves due east across Russia from Moscow and due west across the United States from New York. At about the point where the American temperatures have hit bottom and begin to rise again—around 2,000 kilometers into the trek—the Russian temperatures are just beginning to make a serious plunge. Russia offers thousands and thousands more kilometers of distance and another 10–15° C of cold.

Figure 3-2 and table 3-1 raise the question of why, if Moscow is so cold relative to western and central Europe, anyone would think of building a string of large cities in much, much colder and more remote areas than Moscow. After all, the conclusion of the previous chapter is that it is not important how much of Russia's land mass lies in far-away, cold space. What counts is how much and what kind of economic activity is conducted in those regions. Parshev ignores the fact that population distribution, and hence a country's cold, is the result of human choices.

Ironically, one of the serious scholars whom Parshev cites extensively, historian Leonid Milov, offers a clear statement that Russia's problems with the cold are attributable to something more than just objective, geographical causes. Milov's own historical research was devoted to studying how climate

Table 3-1. *Kilometers and Degrees: Crossing the Continents*

Distance in km from Moscow/ New York	Russian cities on the 55th parallel	Jan. temp. (° C)	U.S. cities on the 40th parallel	Jan. temp. (° C)
0	Moscow	−10.3	New York	−0.7
500	Kazan'	−13.2	Pittsburgh	−3.2
1,000				
1,500	Chelyabinsk	−16.8	Peoria, Ill.	−5.7
2,000			Lincoln, Neb.	−5.9
2,500	Omsk	−18.6		
3,000			Salt Lake City	−2.2
3,500	Tomsk	−18.8		
4,000				
4,500	Bratsk	−22.7	Eureka, Calif.	+8.8
5,000				
5,500	Chita	−26.2		
6,000				
6,500	Ekimchan	−32.7		
7,000				
7,500	Nikolayevsk-na-Amure	−23.5		

Source: Authors' database. See appendix B.

and location shaped Russia's early social and economic history. However, as he notes in the foreword to his recent magnum opus, *The Great Russian Ploughman and the Specific Features of the Russian Historical Process*, in the twentieth century it seemed as though geographical reality was disregarded entirely.[7] Soviet policymakers did not merely ignore the cold in their economic planning; they actively challenged it. To acknowledge that cold has costs would be "bourgeois" defeatism, they said. Obsessed with the idea that scientific communism could "storm all fortresses," including those of nature, Bolshevik leaders defiantly put people in places and constructed their buildings in ways that made no sense:

> With time it was as if Soviet people completely forgot about our climate: they began to build buildings out of glass and to design and build residential housing with thinner walls and with huge windows that covered nearly whole walls, something that required excess expenditures of energy in its various forms, not to mention the costs of the infrastructure of the nation's economy.[8]

Even Milov misses a crucial point, however. Contrary to Milov, the Soviet "people" did not forget how cold a country they lived in. What they did not and could not do was respond to the cold in a sensible way, for two reasons. The first was that the Soviet command-administrative economic system concealed a large part of the costs from them, by means of artificial (nonmarket) prices and hidden subsidies on heat, power, and other inputs. This meant that there was no mechanism to signal the true cost of the cold in terms of its effects on productivity. Second, even when people did recognize the costs— in terms of simple human comfort if nothing else—they were often prevented from reacting in the obvious manner: choosing a warmer location. In a market economy, a business person does not start a company in a location with clear disadvantages of climate if it is not evident that other locational advantages will compensate for the cold. Nor will a worker who has a choice take a job in a near-unbearably cold place unless offered substantial extra pay and benefits (and many will refuse to take such jobs at any wage). In the Soviet Union, with no private ownership of capital and many restrictions on residence and job choice, the option of responding to the cold by choosing warmer locations was limited. Thus both the artificial pricing system and the constraints on mobility served to conceal the true costs of the cold. Even today, the residual effects of the Soviet system hide the truth.

The Cost of Cold

That Russia does pay some penalty, in human comfort and economic efficiency, for its cold climate seems clear. The question is, how great a penalty? Answering that question raises others. First, how extensive is the cold; how can a nation's cold be measured in an economically relevant way? Second, what economic cost does a country incur per unit of cold? Finally, how much of Russia's cold is "excess" cold? That is, how much is due to allocative mistakes of the past, and how much was the unavoidable result of Russia's geography?

In short, the questions are: How cold is Russia? How much does cold cost? How much of the cost was avoidable in the past (and perhaps is remediable in the future)? These three distinct questions have been tackled in a project called the "Cost of the Cold," based at the Brookings Institution's Center on Social and Economic Dynamics (CSED) and Pennsylvania State University's Department of Economics. A summary of some of the findings so far follows.

Measuring Cold: TPC

Traditionally, studies of the effects of temperature on economic activity use territorial aggregations of climate variables—for instance, an "average

Box 3-2. *Constructing "Temperature per Capita" (TPC)*

To illustrate the concept of "temperature per capita" (TPC), imagine a country with three regions, with varying populations and different mean January temperatures. The TPC is simply the average of the regions' temperatures, weighted by their relative population shares. For example:

Region	Population	Mean January temperature (° C)	"Person-degrees" (population times temperature)
A	4	−14	−56
B	11	−8	−88
C	15	−2	−30
Country total	30	—	−174

TPC = Total "person-degrees" divided by total population = −174/30 = −5.8 degrees

national temperature" that is the mean of recorded temperatures equally spaced across the country. For economic studies, however, this is inadequate. What is important is the temperature of places where people actually live and work. As one member of the "Cost of Cold" project writes: " Using territorial temperature aggregations the countries of northern Europe—Sweden, Norway, and Finland—appear to be cold. In fact, in these countries the population is concentrated along the coasts and in the south, where temperatures are not significantly different from the rest of Europe. The same is true for Canada, where most people live along the southern border."[9]

As an alternative to the territorial temperature aggregations, the Brookings–Pennsylvania State project has proposed a simple index called "temperature per capita," or TPC, which is a population-weighted measure. For the current research on the effects of the cold, the TPC is based on mean monthly temperatures for January, the coldest month. The calculation of TPC is illustrated in box 3-2. Details on the concept of TPC are in appendix B.

TPC allows comparison of the temperature of one country with that of another in an economically meaningful way. For instance, Canada's territory lies in a northerly range that is similar to Russia's. But as we noted in chapter 2, Canada's population distribution is very different, with a much larger proportion of the total population living in the southernmost part of the country. Is Russia then colder than Canada? By how much? For that matter, is Russia colder than other northern countries such as Sweden?

Table 3-2. *TPCs of the United States and Three Northern Countries, around 1930*

Country and year	TPC (° C)
United States, 1930	1.1
Sweden, 1930	−3.9
Canada, 1931	−9.9
Russia, 1926	−11.6

Source: Authors' calculations. See appendix B.

An even more useful application of TPC is to track a single country's temperature evolution over time. Seen from the standpoint of its TPC, a country can become warmer or colder not only because of global warming or cooling, but because of shifts in population across isotherms. If a country's territory offers a range of temperature zones, its TPC could theoretically rise or fall if people moved to warmer or colder regions. It is thus meaningful to ask, for instance, whether Russia today is colder than it was in 1917.

Table 3-2 and figure 3-3 show how TPC data answer such questions. Around 1930—as the country entered the period of central economic planning—Russia was already "economically colder" than not only the United States but also Sweden and Canada (table 3-2). It was more than a degree and a half colder than Canada and well over seven degrees colder than Sweden.

What is particularly noteworthy is the contrast between Russia and the other countries in the subsequent period. Figure 3-3 compares Russia with Canada, a country fairly close to Russia in climate and size. Russia's TPC declined steadily in the Soviet era, ending up a full degree colder by 1989, while Canada's TPC rose by more than one degree in the same period. If there are indeed extra costs associated with cold temperatures (a fact we will show), then Russia's TPC evolution in the twentieth century makes little sense from a development perspective.

Pinpointing the Problem

A further use of the TPC concept is to identify which specific regions of a country are most responsible for its overall temperature. By decomposing the aggregate index of coldness, we can find each location's contribution to overall national or regional TPC. Associated with every region is a quantity of "person-degrees"—the product of its temperature and the number of people who live there. Hence, a very cold place inhabited by only a small number of people may be less important than a somewhat warmer (but still cold) location with a large number of people. Table 3-3 attempts to identify

Figure 3-3. *Russia and Canada: TPC Trends in the Twentieth Century*

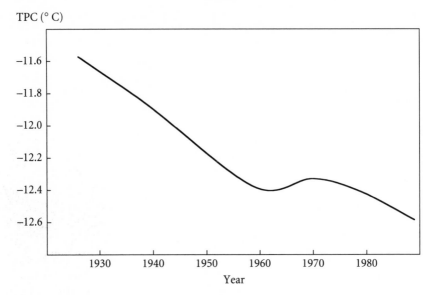

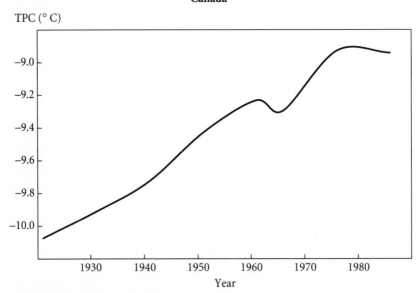

Source: Authors' calculations. See appendix B.

Table 3-3. *Who's Responsible for Russia's Coldness? Leading Negative Contributors to Russian TPC*
Population in thousands

	City	Location (federal district)	Population	January temperature (° C)	Percentage of cold[a]
1	Novosibirsk	Siberia	1,399	−19	5.2
2	Omsk	Siberia	1,149	−19	4.3
3	Yekaterinburg	Urals	1,264	−16	3.2
4	Khabarovsk	Siberia	607	−22	3.0
5	Irkutsk	Siberia	590	−21	2.7
6	Yakutsk	Siberia	196	−43	2.7
7	Novokuznetsk	Siberia	799	−18	2.7
8	Ulan-Ude	Siberia	370	−27	2.6
9	Krasnoyarsk	Siberia	875	−17	2.5
10	Noril'sk	Siberia	235	−35	2.4
11	Chelyabinsk	Urals	1,083	−15	2.3
12	Tomsk	Siberia	601	−19	2.3
13	Chita	Siberia	307	−27	2.2
14	Samara	Volga valley	1,275	−14	2.1
15	Perm'	Urals	1,011	−15	2.1
16	Barnaul	Siberia	577	−18	1.9
17	Ufa	Urals	1,089	−14	1.8
18	Komsomol'sk-na-Amure	Far East	293	−23.5	1.6
19	Kemerovo	Siberia	490	−18	1.6
20	Bratsk	Siberia	279	−23	1.5

Source: Authors' calculations. See appendix B.
a. The relative contribution of each city to the difference between Russia's urban TPC (all cities with populations of 10,000 or more) and the temperature of Moscow (−10° C).

the "worst offenders" in the low Russian TPC. It is based solely on cities and asks the question: How much does each of these cities contribute to lowering Russia's national TPC from a benchmark of −10° C?* The right-hand column in the table gives the answer.

* The national temperature being considered here is the TPC of the Russian population residing in cities with populations of 10,000 or more. The −10° C benchmark was chosen partly for convenience and partly because it happens to be the mean January temperature of Moscow and generally of the central part of European Russia. Changing the benchmark temperature would alter the results of the exercise. In general, choosing a warmer benchmark gives more weight to a city's population size than to its temperature in determining its negative contribution to overall TPC.

We can see that no single city is the problem—even the biggest negative contributors, Novosibirsk and Omsk, together account for less than 10 percent of this reduction of TPC below −10° C. However, as a group these cities are quite significant. To put their importance in perspective, note that there are a total of nearly 1,300 cities with populations of over 10,000 in Russia, home to almost 100 million people. What table 3-3 says is that of all these urban areas, the twenty listed account for over half of the drop in Russia's urban TPC below −10°.

Also note the diversity of the list in both range of temperatures and range of populations. Since the product of temperature and population is the significant factor, the cities fall into three broad categories: (1) relatively small but extremely cold cities (Yakutsk, Ulan-Ude, Noril'sk, Chita); (2) very large, although not terribly cold—for Russia—cities (the Urals and Volga valley cities of Yekaterinburg, Chelyabinsk, Samara, Perm', Ufa); and (3) cold and large cities (the two big "culprits," Siberian capitals Novosibirsk and Omsk).

Table 3-3 is useful to keep in mind as we move to the question of the actual cost of cold. It is a list dominated by the cities of Siberia. That is the real source of Russia's cold. Still, we are reminded that the problem does not end with Siberia. Yekaterinburg, Chelyabinsk, Perm', and Ufa are all in the Urals, and Samara is on the Volga River. What they have in common with one another and with the two biggest Siberian cities on the list—Novosibirsk and Omsk— is that they are exactly the so-called second-tier cities discussed in chapter 2. (See table 2-2, "Largest Russian and U.S. Cities." Of the thirteen cities below Moscow and St. Petersburg on that list, eight appear again on table 3-3 among the biggest contributors to the cold.) In chapter 2 we argued that the second-tier cities were "too small" to fit the Zipf distribution of city sizes. But from the present discussion we see clearly that if they were to grow, it would lower Russia's TPC even further. In that sense they are already "too big." Looking at the issues of city size and city location (temperature) in combination begins to suggest the real magnitude of Russia's challenge of spatial reallocation. A "normal" Russia would be expected to have several cities in the population range of two to four million people. At present it has none. However, the list of candidates for those bigger second-tier cities should *not* include Novosibirsk or Omsk or even Yekaterinburg. Russia's metropolitan future should lie in the west, in the relative warmth—in European Russia, not in these large Siberian cities.

The Question of Cost

Two categories of costs are associated with the cold. The first is the direct costs. Cold reduces the work efficiency of both humans and machines. It causes damage to buildings, equipment, infrastructure, agriculture, fishing, and human beings (including deaths). The second is adaptation costs. Human beings can, and do, take measures to protect themselves and their economies from the cold. But the adaptation itself is costly. The expenditures of energy for heating, the extra materials (and special materials) that are used in the construction of buildings and infrastructure—in general, all the money and effort that goes into protecting or at least buffering society from the cold—are costs of the cold. While it is not always possible to separate the two types of costs, direct costs and adaptation costs, a full accounting must look at both. To date, no one has conducted the kind of comprehensive research that could say what the total effects of cold are on *any* economy, much less for Russia specifically. Two strains of research offer partial answers, however. One is cold regions engineering, which looks primarily at direct costs. The other is the research on the effects of global climate change, which looks also at adaptation costs.

Direct Costs: Cold Engineering Research

Cold regions engineering research studies the effects of cold on specific activities, such as mineral extraction, construction, and military activity in far northern regions. These detailed but narrow studies often place less emphasis on cost than on pure engineering requirements. This is particularly true of studies by the U.S. military, since the tasks they investigated were cases in which "the job had to be done" no matter what the cost. The issue was to determine the technical limits and the critical material and personnel bottlenecks that had to be overcome in order to arrive at the optimal organizational approach. Despite the lack of emphasis on cost, the results of the cold regions engineering research are valuable as systematic presentations of how cold weather lowers productivity.

In a 1986 paper, Gunars Abele, of the U.S. Army's Cold Regions Research and Engineering Laboratory, synthesized data from various surveys from the construction industry and the military that indicate the effect of cold weather on the productivity of people and machines.[10] Figure 3-4 shows the drop in efficiency for manual and equipment tasks involved in typical construction or repair work as the air temperature drops from below freezing to −30° or −40° C. Below −40° C any manual work becomes nearly impossible, and even construction equipment is rarely used. To express how the reduced efficiency translates into increased work effort (in terms of time) required to perform construction or repair work in cold weather, Abele introduced a "cold-environment factor" (F). The baseline value ($F = 1$) represents the time needed to perform the task under ideal weather conditions (around +10 to +15° C for manual tasks and above +5° C for equipment tasks, with no wind or precipitation). The cold-environment factor rises as adverse weather affects work efficiency. Figure 3-5 shows

Figure 3-4. *The Effect of Temperature on Manual and Equipment Tasks*

Efficiency (%)

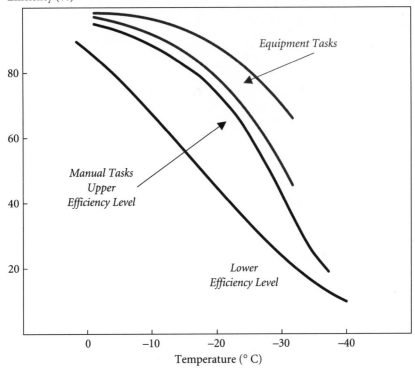

Temperature (° C)

Source: Gunars Abele, "Effect of Cold Weather on Productivity," in *Technology Transfer Opportunities for the Construction Engineering Community*, Proceedings of Construction Seminar, February 1986 (U.S. Army Cold Regions Research and Engineering Laboratory).

the cold environment factors for manual (F_m) and equipment tasks (F_e). For instance, at −25° C, the standard time for each manual task would have to be multiplied by 1.6, and the time for each equipment task by about 1.3. At −30° C, these ratios rise to over 2.1 (manual) and 1.6 (equipment), and so on.

Note that the negative effect of cold temperatures *increases* as the temperatures drop, a counterintuitive result that figures 3-4 and 3-5 illustrate. One might suspect that once the thermometer has fallen far below freezing, "another degree or two" would make little difference. Figure 3-5 shows that in the range of −25° C to −30° C, the slowdown effect for each additional degree of cold is nearly seven times as great as in the −10° C to −15° C range for equipment tasks and over 4.5 times as great for manual tasks.

Figure 3-5. *Cold Environment Factors at Various Temperatures*

Cold environment factor

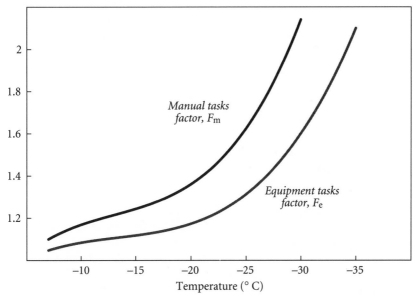

Source: Gunars Abele, "Effect of Cold Weather on Productivity," in *Technology Transfer Opportunities for the Construction Engineering Community*, Proceedings of Construction Seminar, February 1986 (U.S. Army Cold Regions Research and Engineering Laboratory).

Figure 3-5 shows reduced efficiency due solely to temperature and disregards the effects of other climatic conditions such as wind and snow. Wind, in particular, is a serious complicating factor for manual tasks in cold weather. The severity of the wind-plus-cold effect, relative to the pure temperature effect, can be seen by noting that even at −15° C, a wind of twenty miles per hour (thirty-two kilometers per hour) will produce a manual cold environment factor in excess of 4.0—in other words, quadrupling the time necessary to perform a task.[11]

Finally, in accounting for the adverse effects of cold on manual tasks, Abele looks exclusively at the physical limitations of cold. He expressly disregards any negative psychological or motivational effects of working in extreme cold.

What emerges from the cold regions engineering literature is a picture of an economic environment that is dangerous, costly, and unpredictable. Cold alters the properties of materials, leading to more accidents and breakdowns. It reduces the ability of human beings to work efficiently and safely. Many precautions must be taken to avert serious damage to property and loss of life. Many of the studies raise the question of whether it is worth it at all to continue work in these regions, especially during winter months. But even though the engineering literature provides a cautious can-do attitude to settling and living in cold regions, there is no systematic attempt to measure the costs associated with living and building in cold climates. To find such cost estimates, we must turn to recent studies spurred by concern over climate change.

Adaptation to Cold: The Case of Canada

Responding to a general concern over the consequences of global climate change, Canadian government agencies in the 1990s attempted to estimate the costs that Canadians incur in adapting to their climate. The problem, researchers found, was that although adaptation does occur, it is rarely accounted for and sometimes barely recognized as having taken place. As they wrote:

> Adaptation to present day climate is the result of a slow accumulation of policies and practices that protect people and property and allow economic and social activities to continue with a minimum of loss or disruption. Adaptation costs are thus 'built-in' to routine expenditures and budgets.
>
> Because Canada is a modern industrialized country, it has sophisticated systems which enable Canadians to continue their activities in all but the most extreme weather conditions. Most Canadians take these systems for granted, and indeed believe that the Canadian climate does not much affect them (aside from providing a perennial topic of conversation!). In fact, these systems are so taken for granted that their effectiveness and desirability are seldom evaluated.[12]

To begin to fill in the gaps, the researchers focused on the sectors of the economy that are most susceptible to climate effects: transportation, construction, agriculture, forestry, water supply and use, household expenditures, emergency planning, and weather forecasting. (They subsumed energy costs under the appropriate sectors.) Table 3-4 shows their cost estimates.

What Is Missing?

The total figure that the Canadian researchers arrived at is quite large, roughly 1.7 percent of the country's gross domestic product (GDP). This is about the size of the annual output of Canada's agricultural sector. Nevertheless, they caution that it is probably a significant underestimate. For one thing, although more than half of the costs they record are public expenditures (paid by government), the researchers limited themselves to looking only at public expenditures at the national level. No spending by subnational governments is included. Second, the only private adap-

Table 3-4. *What Canada Spends in a Year to Adapt to Its Cold*
Millions of 1990 Canadian dollars per year[a]

Sector	Main activities	Cost of climate adaptation
Transport	Snow and ice removal on roads and runways; road, railroad maintenance; marine ice breaking	1,657.3
Construction	Designing to environmental loads	2,000.0
Agriculture	Heating fuel, research, crop insurance	1,329.6
Forestry	Fuel	402.6
Water	Infrastructure	767.3
Household expenditure	Fuel and heating	5,296.4
Other	Emergency planning, weather services	200.2
Total, all sectors		11,653.4

Source: Authors' calculations based on Deborah Herbert and Ian Burton, "Estimated Costs of Adaptation to Canada's Current Climate and Trends under Climate Change," unpublished paper (Toronto: Atmospheric Environment Service, 1994).
   a. Canada's GDP in 1990 was approximately $700 billion.

tation spending the researchers estimated was for residential heating. The substantial costs of extra clothing, home construction, and private transportation are left out. Finally, one of the biggest adaptation costs of all—the higher wages that workers demand as a so-called compensating differential for working in adverse conditions—is also left out of the Canadians' calculations. The researchers accurately note that "a more exhaustive survey would certainly yield a significantly higher adaptation cost estimate."

Further, the Canadian report is only about *adaptation* costs. It does not attempt to estimate what we referred to above as *direct* costs of cold. As much as Canadians spend on climate adaptation, it does not prevent all climate damage. Thus, in addition to the omitted categories of adaptation costs mentioned above, a comprehensive account would need to include at least two main categories of direct costs: (1) the impact on productive activities ranging from agriculture, forestry, and fishing, to manufacturing, and so on; and (2) the impact on human health and mortality.

Even if the Canadians' study included additional cost categories, their approach would leave us short of the data needed to answer the question we posed earlier: What is the cost of cold *per degree of TPC*? That is, we have an (admittedly incomplete) estimate of the total amount of money spent

Table 3-5. *What Extra Cold Would Cost the U.S. Economy Each Year*
Billions of 1990 U.S. dollars

Activity	Costs per ° C
Heating	4.9
Health impacts	14.8
Agriculture, forestry, fishing	14.4
Wages	16.2 [10.3-34.4]
Human life	16.0
Total	66.3 [60.4-84.5]
Cost as percent of GDP	1.14 [1.04-1.46]

Source: Authors' calculations based on Thomas Gale Moore, *Climate of Fear. Why We Shouldn't Worry about Global Warming* (Cato Institute, 1998); and Thomas Gale Moore, "Health and Amenity Effects of Global Warming," *Economic-Inquiry*, vol. 36 (July 1998), pp. 471–88.

by Canadians to cope with their cold climate. But how would these costs increase or decrease as TPC changed by one degree, plus or minus? The Canadian experts' data and findings do not allow us to proceed further in answering that question. Fortunately, a valuable effort that uses a per-degree cost approach and incorporates the missing categories of costs was made in a U.S. study conducted three decades ago, when most U.S. government and independent experts were concerned about global *cooling*, not global warming.

United States: The 1970s DOT Study

In the early 1970s, the U.S. Department of Transportation sponsored a series of conferences to study the effects of climate change on the economy and on human well-being. This study, in which researchers were commissioned to study the effects of a cooling of 2° C, is the only one that explicitly looks at the costs of cold for the U.S. economy. In addition to the costs of damage to (reduced value of) the economy's production sectors such as agriculture, forestry, and marine resources, and the extra costs of residential and industrial heating, specialists provided estimates of the costs to human health and comfort. The health costs included expenses for physicians' services, hospital visits, and drugs. Separately, they estimated the number of excess deaths that could be attributed to the cold. Finally, they looked at the cost to human beings of living and working in cold temperatures as expressed in differences in wages among urban areas in the United States.[13]

The DOT work was brought to the renewed attention of at least a small circle of readers by an iconoclastic study on the effects of global warming by economist Thomas Gale Moore in 1998.[14] Table 3-5 summarizes the findings from the DOT study, supplemented by Moore's efforts to update some of the data.

The total amount—roughly $60 billion–85 billion—can also be translated into a percentage of total economic activity in the United States. America's GDP in 1990 was about $5,800 billion. Thus for the U.S. economy the cost of a single extra "degree of cold" (the additional costs to the economy if national TPC were reduced by one degree) would be roughly 1.0–1.5 percent of GDP in a year. This is a quite large cost, especially if it were to be incurred repeatedly over several years. For instance, an American economy that would normally expect to grow at an average of 3 percent per year over a fifteen-year period would sacrifice about *35–50 percent of that cumulative growth for a one-degree decline in TPC.*[15]

How Applicable to Russia?

These findings apply to the U. S. economy. Are they relevant for Russia?

There are many problems involved in comparing anything to do with the U.S. and Russian economies, but we can mention two major issues of relevance here. The first is the relationship between the gross cost of the cold in the two cases and the efficiency of measures taken to adapt to the cold. The second issue is the very different range of temperatures at which the costs of the cold would have to be assessed in Russia and the United States.

With respect to the first: if one spends a dollar in the United States to adapt to the cold, what is the payoff in reduced damage or direct costs? What is the return to one dollar similarly invested in Russia? An area where this is particularly relevant is assessment of the health and mortality costs of the cold. Americans spend huge sums to protect their health and treat their illnesses of all kinds, including those possibly caused by the cold. Russians clearly do not spend as much, even as a share of their much lower national income. That lower spending (and consequent lower level of health care) presumably leads to higher mortality rates. The United States is estimated to suffer 16,000 excess deaths per degree of cold. Prorated for population, that would imply about 9,000 annual excess Russian deaths per degree of cold. But do Russians die from cold at the same rates as Americans?

Then there is the issue of the economic value of each life lost. Cost-of-life calculations, though commonly used by economists, are controversial enough as it is. They are based on estimations of what an individual could have been expected to earn over the remainder of his or her working life. (Those lifetime earnings are taken as the value of a person's contribution to the economy.) This means that we would have to adjust for Russians' expected longevity as well as their specific earnings structure.

In sum, trying to adjust the U.S. findings on cost of the cold for Russian conditions may not be particularly productive. It would be wise to use the American results only as a very general indicator that cold in any temperate or cold country undoubtedly has costs. However, to determine precisely what those costs are, Russia would need to make special studies.*

Another good reason to have specific research for Russia is the second reservation we expressed earlier about applying U.S. results to Russia, namely that the countries' temperature ranges differ so much. The U.S. estimates are for the cost of a degree of cold at the current U.S. TPC, which, of course, is considerably warmer than Russia's. The issue here is that the cold-cost function is nonlinear. The magnitude of the effect will not be the same at −12° as at +3° or at +4°. But how much different would it be? Cold engineering suggests that at least some of the costs associated with the cold are greater per degree at lower temperatures. Recall from the discussion above, for example, that a drop in temperature from −25° to −30° has an effect on human and machine efficiency that is several times worse than one from −10° to −15°.

An even more serious consideration is what happens when the thermometer drops below certain critical cold thresholds that trigger massive and disastrous materials failures. For most of the populated world, the extreme cold thresholds are, fortunately, not relevant. Russia is different. Furthermore, nowhere are these critical thresholds more of a daily reality for more people than in Siberia. It is not surprising that the most systematic

---

* Note why we do not consider applying the results of the Canadian study to Russia. We are looking for the "penalty" imposed on today's Russian economy by nonmarket location decisions of the past. The figure of 1.7 percent of GDP that the Canadian researchers estimated as the amount Canada spends on adaptation to its cold is emphatically not such a penalty for excess cold. Indeed, if we assume that location decisions are efficient in Canada, then Canada has no excess cold. The reason is that if location decisions are efficient, adaptation costs are, by definition, offset by the value of locational advantages in cold climates (for instance, presence of raw materials). In the absence of nonmarket regional policy, the net costs of adaptation are zero. Thus the 1.7 percent of Canada's GDP represents gross costs only. (Of course, it is not true that all location decisions in Canada are efficient. Still, it is reasonable in our view to treat the Canadian case as a real-world approximation of efficiency.) What can we say about Russia in this light? We know Russia is colder (has a lower TPC) than Canada. We would therefore expect its gross costs to be larger as a percentage of GDP. We also know that Russia's location decisions are not efficient. Hence, its net cost of adaptation to the cold is not zero. In other words, it pays more for having people and industries in cold locations than it gains because of locational advantages. Nevertheless, we cannot claim that all of Russia's cold costs are net costs. Surely the presence of some people in cold places is economically justified—the question is how many. All of this further underscores the point made above: there needs to be a careful, independent per-degree TPC estimate of the cost of the cold *specifically for Russia*.

Table 3-6. Cold Thresholds in Siberia

Temperature (° C)	Effects on standard Soviet machinery
−6	Internal combustion engines require pre-start engine heaters
−10	Destruction of some standard metal dredge components
−15	High-carbon steels break; car batteries must be heated; first critical threshold for standard equipment
−20	Standard compressors with internal combustion engines cease to operate; standard excavator hiltbeams break; destruction of some tower crane components, dredging buckets, and bulldozer blades
−25 to −30	Unalloyed steels break; car-engine space, fuel tanks, and oil tanks must be insulated; frost-resistant rubber required; non–frost resistant conveyor belts and standard pneumatic hoses break; some cranes fail
−30	Minimum temperature for use of any standard equipment
−30 to −35	Trestle cranes fail; some tractor shoes break
−35 to −40	Tin-alloyed steel components (ball bearings, etc.) shatter; saw frames and circular saws stop work; all compressors stop work; standard steels and structures rupture on mass scale

Source: Adapted from Victor L. Mote, *Siberia: Worlds Apart* (Boulder, Colo.: Westview Press, 1998), p. 22; in turn derived from Yu. M. Dogayev, "Ekonomicheskaya effektivnost' novoy tekhniki na Severe" [Economic effectiveness of new technology in the North], *Nauka*, no. 36 (1969), pp. 29–31.

study of the cold thresholds has been made by Russians—for the purpose of determining whether Siberian regions needed machines of special design or whether standard machines could somehow be modified through the addition of special parts made of cold-resistant steels. A compilation of the behavior of machines at various Siberian temperature levels gives a harrowing picture (see table 3-6).

Table 3-6 suggests that there is a "seismic" component to very cold temperatures: extreme discrete events have the effect of an earthquake. They may occur only very rarely, but when they do occur the effects are disastrous. This suggests that it is not just the mean temperature that is important; the variance also matters. To try to analyze this "extreme temperature" component of the overall temperature profile of a location, we created the notion of a "cold decile." The cold decile is the coldest 10 percent of all temperatures (daily means) in the period recorded, and the cold decile cutoff temperature is the upper bound of that 10 percent. For instance, a cold decile cutoff temperature of −20° C means that there is a one-in-ten chance that the temperature will fall to −20° C or below. Our research suggests that in most of Russia the cold decile cutoff value is roughly 10 degrees lower than the mean. In other words, at any given mean January temperature it can be expected that 10 percent of the time the mean daily temperature will actually be 10 degrees below the monthly mean. For instance, the city of Omsk in Siberia has a January mean of −19° C. On average, however, for three days each January, the million-plus residents of Omsk will see the thermometer drop below −29° C. (And, of course, there is a smaller, but still real probability of even lower temperatures.) Omsk is only the beginning. It lies in the warmer part of the Siberian temperature range. The real cold comes farther east.

The Extraordinary Cold of Siberia

In 1983 geographer Victor Mote wrote a piece that is a veritable catalog of the insurmountable barriers to living and working in Siberia. Even when they are able to operate, he wrote, both machines and humans are less productive, not to mention the frequency of conditions under which they simply do not work. The number of breakdowns of standard equipment, owing to rupturing and wear, is three to five times greater in Siberia than in more moderate regions. Because of the cold, standard mining and excavation machinery may be used for only three to four months a year in northern Siberian tin and gold operations. Even the much-vaunted Soviet rotary excavators may not be employed between November and March. Without appropriate garages and engine heaters, standard Soviet motor vehicles are left running in bitterly cold weather, even when they are not on the road. Lacking quality antifreeze and hydraulic fluids, Siberian equipment operators often add vodka to the respective reservoirs and cylinders.[16]

Because of this, Siberia claimed far more of its share of Soviet construction machinery than even its high rates of development would warrant. When the equipment would inevitably and frequently break down, the Soviet approach was simply to cannibalize some equipment to use as spare parts for others. In the late 1960s, the extreme cold regions claimed "30 percent of all Soviet trucks, 37 percent of the bulldozers, 35 percent of the excavators, 33 percent of the tower cranes, 62 percent of the drilling equipment, and 64 percent of the tracked prime-movers." Mote notes that these percentages undoubtedly went up in the 1970s and into the 1980s.[17] Human beings were affected even more than machines: "There is a noticeable drop in labor productivity for outdoor work when temperatures fall below 0° C. . . . Once the temperature drops to −20° C, warm-up breaks of 10 minutes per hour for each seven-hour work day are imposed, which may result in work losses of up to 73 percent. In an average year, total

Box 3-3. *Siberia: Should Anyone Even Live There?*

"In terms of the geographic extent of problematic environments, the physical-geographic constraints to the development of Siberia easily transcend those in Canada and Alaska. . . . The obstacles are so great that one wonders why Siberia should be developed for permanent settlement at all. In fact, in the USSR there has been a long-standing debate over the appropriate means to settle Siberia. Initial investments are enormous and returns are limited. Construction costs range from two to three times the country average in the relatively developed areas near the Trans-Siberian Railroad to four to eight times the normal in remote centers of extraction accessible only by air, winter road, or summer boat. One-third of the investment capital consists of infrastructural costs (communications, services and amenities), which often exceed basic industrial outlays in temperate developed areas by a factor of ten. . . . [L]abor costs run 1.7 to 7 times above the norm. Finally, with equipment costs well above the country average, repair and maintenance expenses are also high. . . . [T]he annual costs of all repairs are 25 to 30 percent of the total value of the equipment now utilized in the North. Capital repairs on some units actually exceed the value of the individual machines."

   Victor L. Mote, "Environmental Constraints to the Economic Development of Siberia," in Robert G. Jensen, T. Shabad, and A. Wright, eds., *Soviet Natural Resources in the World Economy* (University of Chicago Press, 1983); footnotes omitted.

losses to cold comprise 33 percent of all possible working time in the Soviet North."[18]

Therefore, in Siberia more people were needed to perform the same tasks. It was estimated that owing to the labor intensity of the Soviet style of exploitation of the cold regions, in the late 1960s, for *each* permanent worker in the "Soviet North" nearly *ten other people* were required to live there: the worker's family and the various categories of associated support personnel.* All in all, Mote speculated, "one wonders why Siberia should be developed for permanent settlement at all" (see box 3-3).

What if Russians Had Behaved like Canadians?

So far we have established the following: Russia is cold, even in the rigorous economic sense of having a low TPC; Russia became colder in the twentieth century; and the decline in TPC was costly. What now remains is to see

---

* In the Soviet period, the term "the North" was an administrative term applied to all Arctic and sub-Arctic territories extending from European Russia through Siberia to the Far East, as we will discuss at length later in the book. See appendix C.

whether Russia's costs were avoidable, that is, whether Russia's allocation of its economy in thermal space was indeed a *mis*allocation. To answer that question, Pennsylvania State economist Tatiana Mikhailova performed an innovative simulation to see how different Russia would have looked if it had been a market economy rather than a Soviet centrally planned economy.[19]

Mikhailova writes: "While we can almost certainly infer that the Soviet system deviated from the optimal path of spatial development, the extent of the distortion is unknown until a counterfactual path—a spatial development pattern that market forces would have produced—has been derived." In her paper, Mikhailova uses econometric techniques to simulate how Russia might have developed if market forces had operated. She writes: "The idea for the simulation exercise is simple: I use Canadian behavior as a benchmark of the spatial dynamics in a market economy but apply it to Russian initial conditions and endowment." In other words, Mikhailova studies the way Canadians distributed their population over the territory during the twentieth century in relation to where they began and what resources there were and where they were located. This establishes a pattern of spatial dynamics and its dependence on initial conditions. Substituting Russia's own initial conditions, she can then infer where Russians would have ended up if they had "behaved like Canadians."

Why the choice of Canada?

> [Because] there is no other country in the world closer to Russia in climate and size. Both economies possess and export abundant natural resources. Less obvious, but also important is the fact that both Russia and Canada at the beginning of the century had (and still have) vast undeveloped amounts of land. Russia was still effectively expanding east, and Canada colonized its west. Neither country seemed to be in long-run spatial equilibrium, but they were "moving in similar directions."

Mikhailova presents a range of estimates to account for two further important adjustments in the comparison between Russia and Canada. The first is the effect of World War II, which had devastating effects on the population and infrastructure in the western part of Russia and led to evacuation to the east of a large part of industry. The second effect is the difference in birth rates in populations in various regions of the Soviet Union. Even after these adjustments, her conclusion is unambiguous:

> The present allocation of population and industry in Russia inherited from the Soviet system is far different from that which would have occurred in the absence of Soviet location policy. It is colder and further to the east.

Namely, the eastern part of the country is noticeably overpopulated compared to the counterfactual market allocation, while the western part experiences a relative population deficit. The excess population in the Siberian
and Far Eastern regions ranges from 10 [million] to 15.7 million people
according to various estimates.[20]

As we now know from the TPC exercise, that excess population in the
east means that Russia also has "excess cold" and "excess cost." The TPC of
Mikhailova's counterfactual, Canada-like Russia of 1990 would have been
as much as 1.5 degrees warmer than the real Russia's actually was by the
end of the Soviet period. Because there is a cost of cold, the locational
structure bequeathed to Russia by the communist planners represents a tax
on today's economy. How big a tax? With Mikhailova's estimate of the
amount of Russia's "excess cold"—up to 1.5 degrees of TPC—we might
seem to be tantalizingly close to answering our original question for this
entire section: What does the cold cost Russia? As we noted earlier, however, we lack a solid estimate of the cost per degree of excess cold for Russia. The U.S. estimate cited in table 3-5 was around 1–1.5 percent of GDP
per degree. Dare we simply say that Russia pays at least that much, and
probably much more, and then calculate accordingly that its total cost is at
least $1.5 \times 1–1.5 = 1.5–2.25$ percent of GDP a year? As tempting as it is to do
that, we think there are too many unresolved issues. The fact remains that
a full accounting of Russia's "cost of the cold" is a major task that remains
to be done. In appendix D, we outline a research agenda.

From "Virtual" to Real History

Tatiana Mikhailova's simulation was an economist's version of so-called
alternative or virtual history.[21] It is now time, however, to turn to real history.
Russia really did develop and populate its vast Urals and Siberian regions. It
really did build cities that are bigger and colder than anywhere else in the
world (see appendix E for more on this). The next two chapters will examine the broad sweep of tsarist and Soviet history to show how and why it all
happened. Concluding our chapters on size and cold is a brief case study of
the twentieth-century history of two cities whose fates illustrate how different the Russian development path was. Duluth, Minnesota, and Perm', in
Russia's Urals, are remarkably similar in their cold and relatively remote locations. They both were the object of grand industrial aspirations in the early
part of the twentieth century.

Duluth, Minnesota

In the early 1900s, Duluth, Minnesota, was one of the fastest growing cities in the United States. Between 1900 and 1910, its population jumped from 119,000 to 211,000.[22] Located near one the world's most productive iron mines and at the west end of Lake Superior, Duluth seemed poised to become one of America's leading metallurgical centers. The city's economic future appeared even brighter in 1915 after the United States Steel Corporation decided to construct a $20 million plant there. Predictions that Duluth would surpass Pittsburgh, Chicago, and Detroit as America's iron and steel capital were commonplace.

However, contrary to expectations, Duluth never became a metallurgical giant, for reasons of simple market economics. Duluth's distance from major iron and steel markets and an extremely cold climate eventually made it less competitive in the American and global marketplace than other similar cities in the United States. Within a few years, its dwindling markets and declining production showed that, far from becoming America's next great industrial center, Duluth was serving as a textbook example of what was to be christened "locational maladjustment."

In their now classic 1937 case study of Duluth, two economic geographers, Langdon White and George Primmer, highlighted the hidden costs associated with the city's location. First, cold winters increased steel production costs. The long-term mean January temperature in Duluth is $-13.9°$ C. But on average there is a 1-in-10 chance that January days will fall to $-22°$ C or below. In a climate with such extremes, equipment has to be specially modified to prevent water supply lines from freezing and to ensure that machinery continues to function. Second, Duluth had higher labor costs—again a result of the cold climate, which necessitated a cost-of-living adjustment.[23] Finally, Duluth was at a competitive disadvantage relative to other American steel centers owing to its distance to markets and the higher transportation costs this entailed:

> The successful location of iron and steel plants is largely a matter of transportation costs, but not, as is so commonly assumed, of freight charges on raw materials only. Transportation charges on finished steel to the point of consumption are equally, if not even more, significant. It is here that Duluth's weakness and Detroit's strength become apparent: Duluth, situated in a region where farming is the chief occupation, obviously requires little steel; Detroit, capital of the automotive industry, is the largest consumer of high-finished steel in the world.[24]

Figure 3-6. *Cold Temperature Profiles of Duluth and Perm', Mean January Temperatures (° C), 1948–89*

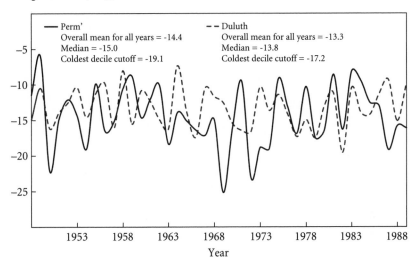

Source: Authors' database. See appendix B.

From the very beginning of its existence as an industrial center, Duluth was never in a position to become a leading producer of iron and steel. It was simply too cold and too far from the principal markets. The market clearly communicated this fundamental fact to both producers and consumers. As a direct result, Duluth's economic and population base shifted after the 1930s, and it stopped growing. Today fewer than 250,000 people live in metropolitan Duluth (the Duluth-Superior MSA), not many more than in 1910.

Perm', Russia

Like Duluth, Perm' in Russia began the twentieth century in relative obscurity. In 1923, with a population of 67,000, it was Russia's thirty-first largest city. But in the next ten years, it tripled in size. By 1939 it was the thirteenth largest city in the country. Its rapid growth was the result of the development of the Soviet defense industry. A dozen huge defense enterprises (with up to 30,000–40,000 employees in each) were located in Perm' in three distinct phases between the 1930s and the 1960s.[25]

Perm' is an even colder place than Duluth (see figure 3-6). Its mean January temperature is a degree or so lower, and it experiences even more extreme low-temperature days. (In eight of the forty-two years covered in

Figure 3-7. *Twentieth-Century Population Growth, Duluth and Perm'*

Population

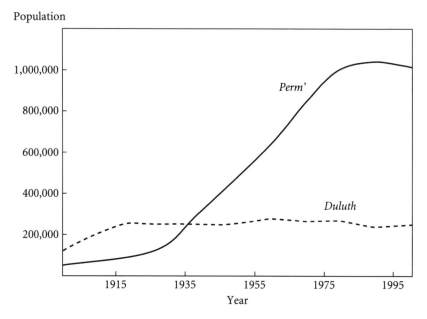

Year

Source: Authors' database. See appendix B.

figure 3-6, Perm's average January temperature was below −18° C; Duluth had only one year that cold over the same period.) Perm' also shares Duluth's remoteness. Its location in the Ural Mountains places it far from customers elsewhere in Russia, as well as from those abroad. In contrast to Duluth, however, the market was never allowed to send signals that Perm's cold climate and remote location were a disadvantage for either industrial production or population growth. Transportation, climate, and labor costs were never factored in as Soviet central planners and defense-industry specialists built and expanded the arms plants in the city. Consequently, whereas Duluth's population topped out at well under 300,000 before the 1930s, Perm's was just taking off at that point. It eventually reached more than one million people. By 1970 the Soviets had ended their final defense buildup phase in Perm'. From then on, its growth slowed considerably, and in the 1990s it finally stopped altogether as the new post-Soviet government radically demilitarized its economy. But by then Perm' was already four times as big as Duluth had ever been (see figure 3-7).

Perm' now stands as one of Russia's frozen dinosaurs, the world's fifth coldest city with a population of over a million people, bereft of the rationale that built it to such proportions in the first place.

4

Geography Is Not Destiny

Russia's problems of distance and cold are not simply the consequence of its physical geography. Its population distribution is the result of deliberate government policies. Before the Russian Revolution, the tsars encouraged migration to newly annexed territories and built military outposts and towns on the Russian Empire's frontier lands. In the Soviet period, communist planners moved large numbers of people across the Ural Mountains to settle Siberia and exploit its resources for the state. Territorial conquest, Soviet industrial and urban planning, and forced migration, not nature, have shaped today's Russian Federation.

With its harsh climate, huge territory, long distances, and remoteness, Russia seems, as Andrey Parshev has suggested, doomed to face frequent poor harvests and high transportation costs for raw materials and finished goods. But geography is not destiny. In fact, the Russian Federation of today is not at all the Russia of yesterday—the Soviet Union, the Russian Empire, or "Old Muscovy." Like most other countries, Russia's shape and extent are the product of time. Moreover, as discussed in the preceding two chapters, the most important factor in determining economic development is not so much territorial configuration—the location or the size of a country's territory—as where people live within that space and how they are connected to one another.

The spread of Russia's population from the enclave of Kaliningrad in the west to Vladivostok in the east is a relatively new phenomenon. Russia has been shaped first by conquest, then by patterns of migration and settlement, often explicitly directed by the state. Large-scale Russian settlement in Vladivostok and the Russian Far East was made possible only with the seizure of territory from China in the 1850s and the construction of the Trans-Siberian Railway in the 1890s. Likewise, Kaliningrad was wrested from Germany by Stalin in World War II (the city used to be Königsberg, the old East Prussian home town of Immanuel Kant). Its former German inhabitants were displaced, and Russians were moved in. It is the process of territorial expansion and then the relocation of population across this geographic space that have created the Russia we know today with all of its related economic and political challenges. While Russia's physical location per se has not changed much for several centuries, the borders of the state and the distribution of population within those borders have changed quite dramatically—especially over the past one hundred years.

Five Centuries of Territorial Expansion

The modern Russian state grew from the small Duchy of Moscow after the defeat of the Mongols in the fifteenth century. For the next five centuries its territory grew in great fits and bursts as Moscow's rule extended across a Eurasian landmass with relatively few geographic impediments. When expansion eventually brought it up against another major power, Moscow resorted to war to acquire territory. In the sixteenth century, Moscow reabsorbed Russian principalities that had fallen under the control of the Kingdom of Lithuania. This was followed by military expeditions to the middle Volga region, to the northern shores of the Caspian Sea, and into the foothills of the Caucasus Mountains. Peasants looking for new farming land, roving bands of Cossacks, and hunters seeking valuable furs for markets in Russia and Europe also made their own forays across the Urals and into Siberia, reaching as far as the Amur River and the Sea of Okhotsk in the

Far East.* Moscow's rule followed. In the seventeenth century, Moscow seized large sections of modern-day Ukraine and the Baltic coast after wars with Poland and Sweden.

In the eighteenth century, Peter the Great and Catherine the Great became renowned throughout Europe for their expansionary zeal. After his defeat of Sweden in the Great Northern War in 1721, Peter brought the Baltic region firmly under Russian control. His conquests were complemented some fifty years later by Catherine. She incorporated huge swathes of Polish territory—including Warsaw—after partitioning Poland with her fellow monarchs ruling Prussia and Austria. She also rolled back indigenous Turks to establish Russian rule on the northern shores of the Black Sea, on the Crimean Peninsula, and around the Sea of Azov. In addition, Catherine pushed into the northern reaches of the Caucasus Mountains. The complete conquest of this region dragged out until the end of the nineteenth century, as successive Russian tsars gradually annexed the lands of modern-day Georgia, Armenia, and Azerbaijan from the Ottoman and Persian empires and as Russia's army became bogged down in a series of "Caucasian wars" against the peoples of the most isolated of the mountainous regions. In this entire period, the appetite for expansion was so great that, between 1550 and 1800, Russia was conquering territory at an average rate of 35,000 square kilometers *every year* (an area equivalent in size to the modern Netherlands).[1]

In the nineteenth century, there was still more territory to be had. Russia wrested Finland from Sweden, gaining control of the entire eastern shore of the Baltic. From the 1860s to the 1890s, the empire began to expand south and east across the Eurasian steppe (prairie). This brought it into Muslim Central Asia, a region of independent but weak Muslim statelets contested by Great Britain as the buffer zone for its imperial holdings in the Indian subcontinent. As a result of all this conquest, by 1900 Russia's frontiers ran west from Moscow to the Baltic Sea and to the territory around the cities of Kiev and Warsaw. They extended south to the Black Sea and to the borders of Ottoman Turkey and the Persian Empire in the Caucasus. From there they stretched across the Caspian Sea, through Central Asia, and to the border with Afghanistan. Finally, they spread east across the Ural Mountains and Siberia to China and the Pacific Ocean. The consolidation

---

* Cossacks are "free warriors" or peasants turned warriors—multiethnic raiding bands that roamed the Eurasian steppe outside the jurisdiction of regional states. At first primarily Turkic in origin, by the sixteenth century Cossack groups with significant Slavic elements had formed. The term Cossack derives from the Turkic word "qazaq," meaning free man.

of control over Siberia and the Pacific coastline represented the last phase of Russian imperial expansion.*

The twentieth century turned out to be a tumultuous time for the Russian state, filled with territorial ebbs and flows thanks first to war with Japan in 1905, then World War I and the Russian Revolution. After the collapse of the Russian monarchy, the new Bolshevik government painstakingly pieced the remnants of the empire back together, creating a new state, the Union of Soviet Socialist Republics (USSR). Even though it did not include some of the empire's former possessions (Finland, Poland, and the Baltic states), the USSR was still the largest territorial state on earth. World War II and the defeat of Nazi Germany then allowed the USSR to advance into the heart of Europe. By 1953 and the death of Soviet leader Josef Stalin—who was every bit as covetous of new lands as Peter the Great and Catherine the Great— almost every piece of Russian imperial territory had been regained in one form or another. New satellite states had also been created. The Soviet Union and the Soviet bloc after World War II represented the ultimate achievement of Russian territorial expansion at any point in history.†

What explains this incredible drive for territorial possession? Was it simply the sheer vastness of the Eurasian steppe, the lack of geographic impediments to expansion, and a penchant for territorial acquisition? Was it conquest for conquest's sake? Or was there something more? Some of the explanations offered by scholars bring us again to the tricky issue of geography as destiny—this time the location of Moscow, the "Old Muscovy" of the sixteenth century, which was, in fact, less than propitious. Muscovy was located in the north of Eurasia, in the forest belt. This put it on the outer fringes of Europe's cultivatable land.

---

* In this whole period, one of the few territories that the Russian state relinquished was Alaska, which Russian settlers had begun to occupy in 1784 after moving across the Bering Strait. Alaska was used as a base from which to establish Russian trading posts in the American Pacific Northwest. These eventually stretched as far south as San Francisco. Alaska was also a launching pad for what proved to be a failed trading foothold in Hawaii in the 1820s. Perhaps surprisingly for a state that now sprawled across such a vast territory, Russia eventually considered Alaska a bridgehead too far. In 1867 Russia sold it to the United States for $8 million.

† After World War II, Poland was brought back into Russia's military, political, and economic sphere of influence, along with states like Czechoslovakia and Hungary that had never previously come under Russian authority. The Baltic states were reannexed and became republics of the Soviet Union. Galicia and Bessarabia were seized from Poland and Romania, and Tuva from Mongolia. The southern portion of the island of Sakhalin, lost to Japan in 1905, was retaken, and the Kurile Islands, which had been ceded to Japan in an 1875 treaty, were annexed.

The Quest for Fertile Soils

Russian historian Vasiliy Klyuchevskiy, American historian Richard Pipes, and British historian Dominic Lieven have all concluded that from the sixteenth to the early twentieth century, the Russian state's seemingly inexorable territorial expansion was driven by the difficulties of conducting large-scale cultivation around Moscow.[2] Lieven notes that "so long as the Russians were confined to the forest regions and poor soils well north of the steppe they could not generate the population or wealth to make true empire possible."[3] At the beginning of his landmark book on the tsarist state—*Russia under the Old Regime*—Richard Pipes makes a similar assertion.[4] The early Muscovite Russian state had to contend with a growing season of only four to five months a year. This was in sharp contrast to a growing season of six months a year in the Eurasian steppe south of Muscovy, and eight to nine months in western Europe. This meant that if its population had continued to be concentrated around Moscow, Russia would not have been able to generate sufficient agricultural surplus to spur economic development, population growth, and ultimately the development of a major European state.[5]

Certainly, the historical record shows that Muscovy did have low agricultural yields in the sixteenth century and a relatively small population—compared with its European neighbors, including France and Germany—of six to twelve million.[6] This changed dramatically once Moscow's rulers embarked on a process of territorial acquisition in almost every direction. By the midpoint of the eighteenth century, the population had begun a phase of rapid growth. It quadrupled from around 17–18 million in 1750 to 68 million in 1850.[7] In the seventeenth and eighteenth centuries, thanks to the territorial conquests from Sweden, Poland, and the Turks, Russia acquired the *chernozem* or "black-earth belt." This is an expanse of fertile agricultural land stretching across the Eurasian steppe from modern Ukraine, north of the Black Sea, through the middle and lower Volga regions of today's Russian Federation, to the Ural Mountains.* The conquered territory was immediately divided and distributed as land grants for cultivation to prominent generals, diplomats, and families close to the tsarist household. It was also parceled out to monasteries and opened to Russian peasant colonization. By the early twentieth century, around

---

* Average January temperatures in the heart of the *chernozem* region range from −2° C in Odessa and Krasnodar to −6° C in Rostov and −9° C in Voronezh, which makes it somewhat warmer than Moscow (−10° C).

eighteen million people (a number equivalent to Russia's entire population in 1750) were on the move in search of new agricultural land. The Russian government had also set aside large sums in its annual budget to provide resettlement assistance to migrants.[8]

Tsarist statistics do suggest that this extensive migration into the steppe with its fertile soils and longer growing season provided the major boost to Russia's population growth. According to imperial Russian records, from 1809 to 1887, the acreage under cultivation in Russia rose by 60 percent.[9] Between 1858 and 1897, the population of European Russia nearly doubled, rising from 68 million to 125 million.[10] Although Russian grain yields per hectare always remained low, more and more land was settled and brought under cultivation, making it possible in turn to support and feed more and more people. In the 1860s, the largest proportion of Russia's population increase occurred in rural areas in the central provinces (Old Muscovy) and in the new lands of the black-earth belt.[11] The core black-earth regions had the heaviest concentrations of population and a greater proportion of large farms than the rest of Russia. They also had a large number of fast growing towns and cities (including Kharkov, Voronezh, Kursk, and Saratov). In sum, the acquisition of new territory beyond Muscovy and a corresponding shift in the distribution of Russia's population would seem to have overcome the initial constraints of geography and Moscow's original location. Unfortunately, however, the story does not stop there. In the late nineteenth century, Russia's inhabitants continued to move. This time, they moved into territory with a much harsher climate and even poorer soils than Old Muscovy—across the Ural Mountains and into Siberia.

An "Embarrassment of Space"

By the 1880s, there were almost no "virgin lands" left in the black-earth belt to expand into. Russia's growing population strained the land already under cultivation. The country appeared to be running into the constraints foreseen at the end of the eighteenth century by Thomas Malthus in his famous 1798 essay, "On the Principal of Population."[12] Malthus predicted a global population explosion that would rapidly outstrip the capacity of the world's agricultural land to provide food resources. He set the tone for European political thinkers in the nineteenth century contemplating population growth and existing territorial capacity. In the half century preceding World War I, most European countries were in search of ways to cope with the prospect of overpopulation. If they could not expand their territory through annexation or colonization, they hoped to adjust to, and accommodate, the growth of population. The range of options included encouraging emigration, increasing agricultural productivity, and, in some cases, initiating public education programs to curb reproduction (which Malthus himself had suggested). Germany, Great Britain, Belgium, and the Netherlands effectively refuted what came to be known as the "Malthusian fallacy"—that population was destined to outstrip resources—through the introduction of intensive agriculture methods and rapid industrialization. Other European countries, such as Austria-Hungary, Italy, and Ireland, promoted the emigration of their excess rural populations—primarily to North America. Between 1870 and 1914, some 25 million people migrated abroad.[13]

Russia, however, had another option. Its "embarrassment of space" meant that it still had territory within its own borders to be exploited.[14] It therefore opened up the lands beyond the *chernozem* belt in the Ural Mountains and southern Siberia for settlement and cultivation. The vast Eurasian steppe was, in effect, Russia's own "North America." As Richard Pipes notes in his other seminal work, *The Russian Revolution*, "[Russia's] citizens did not migrate abroad." Instead, "they preferred to colonize their own country."[15] This was significant because it meant that, in the nineteenth and early twentieth centuries, Russia was continually able to cast off Malthusian constraints through territorial expansion. It could give its population growth free rein.*

Malthus had written in 1798 that population growth was driven by access to land and food. In his essay he observed, in reference to North America (although he could easily have been writing about Russia at this juncture): "It has been universally remarked that all new colonies settled in healthy countries, where there was plenty of room and food, have constantly increased with astonishing rapidity in their population. . . . A plenty of rich land, to be had for little or nothing, is so powerful a cause of population as to overcome all other obstacles." Malthus further mused that "when acre has been added to acre, till all the fertile land is occupied, the yearly increase of food will depend upon the amelioration of the land already in possession. . . . But population, could it be supplied with food, would go on with unexhausted vigor, and the increase of one period would furnish the power of a greater increase the next, and this without any limit."[16] In accordance with the Malthusian line of thinking, a country could have too many people if it had a small territory. But it could never have *too much*

---

* In fact, of course, Russia needed to cast off its "Malthusian constraints" only because it was not increasing its productivity. Only dysfunctional economies need to rid themselves of excess population.

territory, especially if this territory could also be cultivated in such a way as to provide an adequate food supply for its population. In this case, its population would continue to grow. This latter case was certainly Russia's lot. The vastness of Russia's territory, in spite of its poor soils, meant that more land could be brought under cultivation to compensate for this deficiency. As a result it could sustain more people, albeit at a relatively low level of subsistence and without the production of a huge agricultural surplus.

Indeed, the availability of new lands seemed even to absolve Russian farmers from embarking on more intensive methods of agriculture to increase productivity. Given the marginal nature of Russian land beyond the black-earth zone, this was just as well. Intensive agriculture was both difficult and costly. Throughout the nineteenth century, intensive agricultural investments produced little notable increase in returns.[17] It was always considered cheaper, easier, and more desirable to allow Russian peasant farmers to move on to new land than to encourage them to invest in and improve cultivation of the old. As a result of the excess of land, therefore, extensive development became the hallmark of Russian agriculture—and later of Soviet industry as well. When one plot of land was exhausted or maximum productivity had been reached, there was always somewhere else to move on to. Smaller European countries like Belgium and the Netherlands never enjoyed the "good fortune" of endless space.

"Terra Nullius" and the Imperative of Permanent Settlement

Overcoming Muscovy's poor soils and bringing more land under cultivation were not the only reasons for shifting population across territory in Russia. In the imperial age before World War I, perceptions of possession and prestige were as important as geography and the specter of Malthusian overpopulation. To hold on to a territory—especially one as vast as Russia's—it had to be "peopled." From the eighteenth to the early twentieth century, territory with sparse population or indigenous hunter-gatherers was viewed as "empty land" or a *terra nullius*. This meant that it could be conquered and colonized by a European Great Power. One of the most celebrated cases of the invocation of *terra nullius* was the British Empire's application of the idea to legitimize its claim to the sovereignty and ownership of Australia around 1770. The British government declared Australia to be "practically unoccupied," although it did recognize Aboriginal rights to land ownership within the British-held territories. Over the next two centuries, British and other European settlers also used the concept of empty lands to justify the forceful displacement of Australia's native population to make way for intensive farming and mining operations. The idea of *terra nullius* was enshrined in Australian land law until 1992.[18]

The same idea of *terra nullius* that drove the colonization of Australia from the eighteenth to the twentieth century also shaped the way in which Russian tsars and other European rulers thought about their territory in the nineteenth century. The concept of *terra nullius* was endowed with two different, but conflated, meanings. In the first, it referred to any stretch of land not controlled by a recognized European state.[19] This applied to most of the Eurasian land mass until the Russian Empire laid claim to it. In its second meaning, it referred to territory on which no land was "owned" or legally possessed. This implied that there had to be a permanent population living and working on the land for states to establish their sovereignty over it and to deter others from trying to take it.[20] The second meaning lay at the heart of disputes between Aborigines and British and European settlers in Australia. Aborigines, like native peoples elsewhere in North America, Africa, and Eurasia, did not establish permanent agricultural settlements on their ancestral lands. Although they certainly used and lived off the land, they also tended to roam across relatively large territories. Europeans regarded all this as tantamount to physical abandonment of the land or at least as a rather loose association with the land. As a result, as the Russian Empire moved across Eurasia, Russia's rulers were quick to establish military outposts and build towns, as well as to encourage peasant cultivation on all the new territory they acquired. In this way they established possession, demonstrated permanent settlement and use, and could thus ensure the sovereignty of the Russian state over this vast territory.

Land and Great Power Prestige

The possession of land also came with considerable international prestige, as discussed in chapter 2. By 1900 the acquisition of territory for economic and political ends had become the object of state interaction. European countries' status as Great Powers was explicitly seen as dependent on their ability to establish colonies. Most European states considered it their Great Power "obligation" to acquire territory.[21] Ideas prevailed in imperial thought that all empty territories and smaller states would eventually be subsumed into ever greater empires, leaving only a handful of independent powers. It would be these independent powers, the empires or Great Powers, that would determine the outcome of world events. Indeed, the German commentator Otto Hintze noted in 1907: "The fight for Great Power status is the true essence of the imperialist movement in the modern world. It is not a question, as in ancient times, of one power dominating the world, but of the selection of nations that are to take a leading part in world affairs."[22] Russia was by no means a small state. It had every desire to take a leading part in world affairs. And it wanted to remain a Great Power. Territory was very much associated with the idea of Russia's being "Great," and Russian rulers kept on acquiring it.[23]

The largest of all these territorial acquisitions was Siberia, a veritable treasure chest of minerals and natural resources, but also the least populated and the most difficult for the Russian state to possess in the imperial sense. Siberia was the ultimate *terra nullius* when the Russian state first moved into it. It was an uncharted terrain, inhabited by indigenous hunter-gatherers and nomadic populations who lived off the land, but were not seen to "use" it in the sense that Europeans would have described use before 1900.[24] It was, therefore, vulnerable to being deemed "unoccupied," and the Russian state had to put down permanent roots. Initially, the tsars did not attempt to populate Siberia in any significant way. They simply exploited its resources at the margins. However, with the imperative of imperialism in the nineteenth century to establish clear possession, this approach changed.

The settlement of Siberia is a central element in explaining the evolution of Russia's contemporary problems of "size" and "cold," and it will be discussed in detail in the next chapter. The development of Siberia underscores that geography need not be destiny. This enormous territory was peopled through compulsion and coercion and also by conscious choice. In the Soviet period, the deliberate policies of communist planners located people, cities, and industry within Siberia and in the adjacent territories of the Ural Mountains and the Russian Far East.

The creation of cities in Siberia in the Soviet period is an especially important issue. The tsars, in their conquest of Siberia, were content with nominal control of this huge territory—pushing excess population out of rural areas in European Russia and establishing a series of small towns and permanent settlements between the Ural Mountains and the Pacific Ocean. They did not seek to develop or urbanize it on a large scale; they would certainly not have had the resources to do so if they had tried. In fact, urbanization in Russia as a whole is a specifically Soviet rather than a tsarist phenomenon. The location and concentration of people and economic activity in a particular set of cities across Russian territory became possible only under the Soviet Union, when the communist government, through the imposition of central planning, was able to allocate resources to collect people into cities.[25]

Table 4-1. *Leading Cities of the Russian Empire, 1860s*

Rank	City	Population	Modern location
1	St. Petersburg	539,000	Russia
2	Moscow	399,000	Russia
3	Odessa	121,000	Ukraine
4	Kishinev (Chisinau)	104,000	Moldova
5	Riga	98,000	Latvia
6	Saratov	93,000	Russia
7	Tashkent	80,000	Uzbekistan
8	Vil'no (Vilnius)	79,000	Lithuania
9	Kazan'	79,000	Russia
10	Kiev	71,000	Ukraine

Source: Chauncy Harris, *Cities of the Soviet Union* (Chicago: Rand McNally, 1970).

Urbanization in Russia

In imperial Russia, a combination of the absence of an agricultural surplus to support urban life, serfdom, the scattering of the rural population, and the increasing distance between settlements as Russian territory expanded meant that towns and cities took a long time to develop. As late as the eighteenth century, only 3–4 percent of Russia's inhabitants lived in urban centers. Settlements were referred to by a range of different terms. There were no specific criteria for a particular designation, and most "urban" centers hardly deserved the name. They were often little more than overgrown rural settlements linked to agriculture rather than to industry and services.[26] Indeed, most residents of Russian cities were landowners and peasants who grew their own food.[27] Tsarist cities had to be self-sufficient in produce from their immediate agricultural hinterland since there were no additional supplies from elsewhere in the country to be relied on. Their populations were thus often not permanent inhabitants, but transitory migrants, constantly on the move back and forth between the city and the countryside in search of basic staples. In 1914, for example, peasants who retained ties to their home villages accounted for 70 percent of St. Petersburg's population.[28] Russia's cities began to grow only after the emancipation of the serfs in 1861, which freed people from their legal ties to landlords and particular parcels of land.[29] Table 4-1 shows the Russian Empire's largest cities in the 1860s.

The other major urban areas of Russia were located around Moscow and the Upper Volga Basin (Kostroma and Yaroslavl') and along the Dnepr and Don Rivers in what is today Ukraine and southern Russia:

Yekaterinoslav (which is now Dnepropetrovsk in Ukraine), Lugansk, Novocherkassk (now Rostov-na-Donu), and the Voronezh region. Not a single one of these cities was in either the Ural Mountains region or in Siberia. Furthermore, as table 4-1 shows, of the ten largest cities in the Russian Empire in the 1860s, six are now in fact *outside* the modern Russian Federation—specifically, to the west and south of it.

After the emancipation of the serfs, the real spur to urbanization came when Russia began to industrialize in the 1880s and 1890s. Foreign capital and foreign entrepreneurs, merchants, and financiers flooded into Russian cities, increasing the empire's urban population to about 18 percent in 1914.[30] As in the 1860s, most of the fastest-growing cities in 1914, with the exception of St. Petersburg and Moscow, are today outside the borders of the Russian Federation: Riga, the capital of Latvia; Kiev, the capital of Ukraine; Odessa and Dnepropetrovsk in Ukraine; and Baku, the capital of Azerbaijan. The Russian Empire reached its peak of urban growth between 1914 and 1916, during World War I. Six million peasants, war refugees, workers, and troops moved into Russian cities on the eve of the Revolution, swelling the number of urban dwellers to 28 million.[31] Richard Pipes notes that this trend was almost entirely reversed during the Revolution and subsequent civil war, when Russian cities were devastated by famine and their inhabitants fled to the countryside. Between 1917 and 1920, around five million people left Russian cities. St. Petersburg (then known as Petrograd and later Leningrad) lost two-thirds of its population, and Moscow lost about half.[32] Once they had consolidated power, the Bolsheviks had to reverse this massive deurbanization and rebuild St. Petersburg and Moscow in addition to other principal cities. In this they were certainly successful. By 1989 and the last Soviet census, the Russian Federation's urban population had risen to 74 percent of the total population.[33]

Urbanization was an imperative for the communist government. In 1917 the Bolsheviks had effected a supposedly urban-based, proletarian revolution in a largely agrarian state. Peasants accounted for around 80 percent of the population, and most city dwellers still had their roots in the countryside. Immediately after the Revolution, having used the peasants' desire for land to mobilize them in revolt against the tsars, the Bolsheviks were eager to cast off those rural peasants. They intended to create, by force if necessary, a "real" urban proletariat. The early period of the USSR was marked by a virtual war of the city against the countryside. It was waged by the state and led by slogans about industrialization and urbanization. The war was finally won by Stalin in the 1930s, when the peasants and the rest of Russia's rural population were collectivized into huge state farms or settled in villages.

From the middle of the 1920s to the outbreak of World War II in 1941, the urban population of Russia grew dramatically—6.2 percent annually.[34] This was larger than any other increase in Russian history and one of the fastest urbanizations in world history. It was promoted through extensive migration from rural areas to cities, shaped by decrees on the importance of population resettlement and a Soviet government focus on rapid industrialization, and also effected by the extraordinary expansion of the prison camp system as a tool for colonization (as the next chapter will show). But even as the Soviets pursued their unprecedented drive to expand the number and size of cities, their bias against market forces meant that some of the Russian Empire's most vital urban regions were actively targeted for decline. American economic geographer Chauncy Harris pointed out that many of the largest, fastest-growing cities during the tsarist period were no longer in that category in the Soviet Union by the 1960s. He described the fate of Odessa as a prime example:

> Odessa, the port on the Black Sea, was the third largest city of the Russian Empire for the last half century of tsarist Russia. It grew from 121,000 in 1867 to 631,000, 550,000, or 500,000 on the eve of World War I, according to various estimates. Indeed of all the large cities in European Russia, it had according to Rashin the highest rate of increase during the period 1811–1914, when it increased its population 45-fold (from 11 [thousand] to 500 thousand).[35]

As Harris notes, Odessa was not the administrative center of a tsarist Russian province (*guberniya*). Its rapid growth can be attributed primarily to market-related economic factors, most notably its location on the Black Sea: Odessa "grew with the booming trade in wheat from the hinterland in the Ukraine based on expanding grain production in the Russian black-earth steppes, the construction of railroads capable of cheaply transporting the grain to export ports, the development of ocean shipping for bulk commodities, and the rise of markets in Western Europe."[36] After the Revolution, new priority was given to building up the interior regions of Ukraine and elsewhere in the USSR. Central planning and an emphasis on creating Soviet economic autarky cut Odessa off as a major trading port with Europe. The city's population dropped. Although it later resumed its growth, Odessa never again achieved the status it had in the tsarist era. In the course of a few decades, it had gone from the fastest-growing

Table 4-2. *Growth of Russian Cities in and East of the Urals, 1897–1989*
Ranked by 1989 population; populations in thousands

Year	1897	1926	1939	1959	1970	1979	1989
Novosibirsk	8	120	404	885	1,161	1,312	1,392
Yekaterinburg	43	140	423	779	1,025	1,211	1,298
Omsk	37	162	289	581	821	1,014	1,148
Chelyabinsk	20	59	273	689	875	1,030	1,107
Ufa	49	99	258	547	780	978	1,078
Perm'	45	121	306	629	850	999	1,040
Krasnoyarsk	27	72	190	412	648	796	870
Barnaul	21	74	148	303	439	535	602
Khabarovsk	15	52	207	323	436	528	601
Novokuznetsk	3	4	166	382	496	541	581
Irkutsk	51	108	250	366	451	550	577
Kemerovo	a	22	137	289	374	462	511
Tomsk	52	92	145	249	338	421	473
Ulan-Ude	8	29	126	174	254	300	353
Chita	12	64	121	172	241	303	323
Komsomol'sk-na-Amure	a	a	71	177	218	264	315
Bratsk	a	a	a	43	155	214	256
Yakutsk	7	11	53	74	108	152	187
Noril'sk	a	a	14	118	135	180	175

Source: *Naseleniye Rossii za 100 let (1897–1997): Statisticheskiy sbornik* (Moscow: Goskomstat Rossii, 1998), pp. 58–63; G. M. Lappo, ed., *Goroda Rossii: Entsiklopediya* (Moscow: Bol'shaya Rossiyskaya Entsiklopediya, 1994), various entries.

a. There was either no settlement at all in the city's present-day location (for instance, Noril'sk until 1921, Bratsk until 1955) or only a small settlement of fewer than 3,000 residents.

commercial center in Russia to the city with the slowest growth rate of all large Soviet cities.[37]

Until the devastation of World War II, western Russia and Ukraine remained the main centers of city growth.[38] But World War II, like the Russian Civil War before it, had a ruinous impact on this urban development. More than 1,700 cities, towns, and villages were destroyed in the war, and serious damage was inflicted on other important urban centers, all in European Russia and Ukraine.[39] At the end of the war in 1945, Soviet urban planners shifted their focus to the Volga region of the Russian Federation, the Urals, and Siberia.[40] Beginning in the 1950s, cities in and east of the Ural Mountains became the loci of fast-growing population and industry, and many Siberian cities became major urban centers for the first time. These were the cities that by the 1970s had grown to become what table 3-3 identified as the "worst offenders" in lowering Russia's TPC over the Soviet period. Table 4-2 revisits the list of cities presented in table 3-3 to show when and how they grew from small towns and tiny imperial outposts of the tsarist era to cities of several hundred thousand and more.

The results of this effort to build up giant cities east of the Urals—and the consequent resettlement of Soviet population to these cities—have left today's Russia with some of its biggest challenges. Although the tsars made some mistakes in their own town and city development, they had little scope for the kind of monumental errors that came with the Soviet regime's development of Siberia.

5

Siberia—Plenty of Room for Error

The settlement of Siberia in the twentieth century and the mass movement of people and industry into this vast region by communist central planners lie at the root of Russia's contemporary problems with the cold and distance. For the Soviets, the exploitation of Siberia's rich natural resource base and the location of giant factories, mines, power stations, and cities across its territory were the culmination of efforts to transform the old agrarian Russian Empire into a modern industrial state. They viewed the conquest of Siberia—industrializing and urbanizing some of the world's most inhospitable territory—as one of the USSR's greatest achievements. The huge costs of this massive enterprise began to be apparent to the planners themselves only in the 1970s and 1980s. Today's Russia has to pay those costs.

In spite of the difficulties its climatic conditions pose for development, Siberia, like "the cold," has for several centuries been synonymous with the very image of Russia and tied to conceptions about its future. American historical

SIBERIA—PLENTY OF ROOM FOR ERROR

geographer Mark Bassin describes how Siberia has variously been seen by Russian intellectuals and political thinkers as both a "treasure" and a wasteland, a colony and a frontier, a source of inspiration for new reforms and native virtue, and as part of Russia's historical legacy. In the late eighteenth and nineteenth centuries, the exploration and development of Siberia and the evolution of European Russia's relationship with this vast land played a role in shaping a sense of Russian national identity. Siberia came to embody the success of Russian exploration and development. The intrepid Russian Cossacks who first reached the distant Kamchatka Peninsula and the shores of the Pacific Ocean were, for example, lauded by the great Russian poet Alexander Pushkin. Siberia was the source of undiscovered wealth and of new territory and also of old folk tradition and ritual. All these images have persisted until today. Siberia is valued as an "energy colony" and natural resource reserve to be exploited by other parts of the country and as the "untamed frontier" and "New World" savior for the rest of Russia.[1]

Consider, as illustrations of these ideas, the words of Russian author Alexander Solzhenitsyn from the 1970s:

The Northeast [Siberia] is a reminder that Russia is the northeast of the planet, that our ocean is the Arctic, not the Indian Ocean, that we are not the Mediterranean nor Africa and that we have no business there! These boundless expanses, senselessly left stagnant and icily barren for four centuries, await our hands, our sacrifices, our zeal and our love. . . . [W]e should be directing our forces and urging our young people toward the Northeast—that is the far-sighted solution. Its great expanses offer us a way out of the worldwide technological crisis. They offer us plenty of room in which to correct all our idiocies in building towns, industrial enterprises, power stations, and roads. Its cold and in places permanently frozen soil is still not ready for cultivation, it will require enormous inputs of energy—but the energy lies hidden in the depths of the Northeast itself, since we have not yet had time to squander it.[2]

Thirty years later, similar ideas echoed in a report by the elite Russian think tank, the Council on Foreign and Defense Policy (CFDP):

Siberia and the Far East are formative territorial and resource-rich parts of modern Russia. From the time of M. V. Lomonosov it was considered obvious that the eastern territories of Russia would "increase her strength (*mogushchestvo*)"; at the start of this millennium it has become no less obvious that Siberia and the Far East are not only Russia's "strength," but her very destiny (*sud'ba*). . . . For the European part of Russia, disintegration [the separation of Siberia from the Russian Federation] would mean not only the loss of markets, but, most important, an enormous loss of resource and territorial potential that has saved the European part from catastrophe more than once (for example, during World War II).[3]

With its allusion to Mikhail Lomonosov, the eminent Russian scholar of the eighteenth century, the CFDP emphasized the links between Siberia and Russia's past, present, and future. Indeed, as late as the 1980s, a statement attributed to Lomonosov predicting that Russia's future wealth would be tied to Siberia adorned the walls of science classrooms in Russian schools. The link between Russia's prosperity and Siberia was presented as a scientific prediction akin to Copernicus's assertion that the earth revolved around the sun. It would come true because it was destined to come true, just as the citation from the CFDP above suggests.

Although Russia extended its sovereignty over Siberia relatively early,* the age of significant settlement in Siberia is, in fact, only about a century old—dating to the 1890s. Siberia has been a rich and attractive delicacy for the Russian state, but one that has also been extremely hard to swallow. For centuries, the region east of the Ural Mountains served as a major geographical and ecological barrier to mass migration. Would-be settlers were blocked not by the mountains themselves—which are relatively low for "mountains"—but by the *cold*.

The cold, the harsh and inhospitable climate of Siberia, with its extremely short growing season and long winter nights, meant that the region was largely the domain of hunter-gatherers and nomadic peoples until the nineteenth century. Only with the advent of the Trans-Siberian Railway in the 1890s and the technological advancements of the Soviet Union in the twentieth century was Siberia's interior opened up to large-scale settlement and industrialization. All of this would also have been impossible without access to an abundance of low-cost fuel from Siberia's own vast gas and coal reserves, which were exploited in the 1930s—and especially after World War II—to fire the huge power stations that kept people's homes warm and lit in the long, cold, dark Siberian winter. Energy and heat were, and still are, essential elements in the settlement of Siberia. Furthermore, underscoring the state's difficulty in absorbing and settling Siberia, the language of conquest has consistently been used to describe the process of incorporating these cold and inhospitable lands into Russia's territorial fold. Russian sources refer to the *osvoyeniye*, or conquest, mastery, and assimilation of Siberia.

---

* Russia negotiated its first official border in the region with China in 1689, through the Treaty of Nerchinsk.

Siberia as Resource Frontier

As the idea of conquest suggests, the development of Siberia was from its earliest origins very much a mercantile colonial enterprise. Siberia was a source of valuable furs—fox, sable, and squirrel among others—essential in the cold Russian winters and much prized in Europe, as well as of salt and precious minerals. Hunters, Cossacks, and entrepreneurs chasing their fortune established the first outposts in the fifteenth century, followed by peasants fleeing serfdom in the central provinces of Russia and seeking refuge and free land in Siberia. Until the late nineteenth century, however, the numbers of settlers were always small. Beginning in the seventeenth century, other methods of settlement were also adopted when Siberia became the tsars' prison. For the next three centuries, Siberia played the dual role of resource frontier and penal colony.[4]

The first Russian movement across the Ural Mountains into Siberia was a logical progression from the exploitation of mineral and forest resources in the "Russian North."* By the seventeenth century, revenues from the rich fur trade not only covered the costs of administering Siberia, but also furnished a substantial share of Russia's total state revenue.[5] Thanks to the fur trade, Russia was the center of its own economic system, in effect "a separate Russian world economy."[6] The bulk of the permanent population in Siberia was the inhabitants of small towns, forts, and scattered settlements. These people engaged in hunting, trapping, and trading in furs, with some others involved in mining. Groups of peasant farmers and their families were also concentrated in western Siberia. The easy rewards of the fur trade lessened the incentive to develop either mining or agriculture. Consequently, the population remained low.[7] In 1700, in addition to the indigenous peoples of Siberia, there were only about 200,000 Russian settlers across an area more than twice the size of Europe. For most of the next century, the population of Siberia remained largely rural and scattered in small villages. Fewer than 10 percent of the population lived in towns, and of this small number about half were tied to military service.[8] The first towns in Siberia—Tyumen', Tobol'sk, Tomsk, Yakutsk, and others—not surprisingly developed around the fur trade

---

* In the tsarist period this was essentially the northern forest belt of Europe—stretching away from Moscow toward the Baltic and the White Seas, encompassing the old cities of Pskov and Novgorod, eventually the new capital of St. Petersburg, and other remote settlements such as Vologda and Arkhangelsk. It should not be confused with the Soviet North, referenced in chapter 3 and discussed in appendix C.

Siberia as Tsarist Penal Colony

The mercantile impulse for development dissipated with the decline of the fur trade in the eighteenth century. But interest in Siberia peaked again when the Russian state formally turned the region into its place of exile and as Russian political thinkers began to pick up on the ideas of European imperialism in the nineteenth century. The Russian state first began to deport criminals to Siberia in 1648. By 1729 it had become the official place of state exile for political prisoners. In 1762 edicts were passed allowing landlords to deport their rebellious serfs to Siberia. In 1763 a similar edict applied to convicted prostitutes, and another, in 1800, to Jewish citizens of the Russian Empire who had failed to pay their taxes. In 1800 the population of Siberia rose above one million people, thanks in part to the influx of prisoners and exiles. After the Decembrist Rebellion of 1825—led by officers of the Russian guards regiments—revolutionaries, political insurgents, and other opponents of the tsarist regime were dispatched from St. Petersburg, Moscow, and other cities of European Russia in increasingly large numbers. In 1891 an estimated 50,000 Russian political exiles, 5,000 of their wives and children, 100,000 Polish insurgents, and 40,000 criminals lived in Siberia.[9]

As the number of exiles began to swell the population, the tsars also began to think seriously about how to develop Siberia administratively. In the early 1820s, for example, Tsar Alexander I's chief adviser, Mikhail Speranskiy, was charged with thinking about ways to overcome the defects in Siberia's governance, including "excessive distances from the local points to the various headquarters of the administration"; the lack of a local nobility, which meant the appointment of governors who could not be effectively controlled or supervised; and the region's sparsely settled and small population, which frequently resulted in "too much bureaucracy for the number of residents."[10]

In spite of the state's shift toward deportation and penal settlement in Siberia, the region still retained appeal as a frontier and a place of opportunity, especially given the absence of serfdom, its vast tracts of land, and rich fishing and hunting. Many Russian imperial thinkers were also critical of the state's tendency to view Siberia as a penal colony. In the 1890s, Nikolay Yadrintsev, for example, called for the "free colonization" of Siberia. He insisted that this, rather than the tsarist policy of exile, would bring massive population growth and stimulate economic productivity, just as colonization had done in Australia, the United States, and Canada.[11] Even the Decembrists who were sent into exile in Siberia referred to it as the "Second New World." Siberia, they believed, could rely on its vast stores of natural wealth and available land to ensure that "honest enterprise and effort on the part of its citizens would be justly and amply rewarded," just as it was in America.[12] A celebrated Russian revolutionary of the nineteenth century, Alexander Herzen, drew a parallel between Russia's experience in Siberia and America's westward expansion. In a letter to his Italian contemporary Giuseppe Mazzini, Herzen argued that Russians, like Americans, had tamed the primeval expanses of the frontier regions by expanding across the reaches of the continent. He compared Siberian colonists to the first Americans who had home-steaded on the North American plains.[13]

Settling Siberia

Indeed, Russian settlers did move into Siberia in ways that echoed the home-steaders of America. From 1800 to the outbreak of World War I, in the same period that the Russian state was dispatching its opponents and criminals across the Ural Mountains, nearly five million Russian settlers migrated into Siberia of their own free will—and for the most part unauthorized and at their own expense.[14] Siberia, in effect, did become the Russian Empire's "North America." It drew surplus and desperate rural population in search of cheap or free land away from the overcrowded agricultural areas west of the Urals. Between 1871 and 1916, more than 40 percent of internal migrants in the Russian empire were settling in Siberia.[15] In nineteenth-century Rus-sia, internal migration was subject to numerous restrictions; mostly it was open, or officially extended, only to those who already owned property and had the means both to fund their relocation and to acquire land and equip-ment.[16] This did not, however, deter people without such means from mov-ing. Thanks to this migration and a high rate of natural increase among settlers, Siberia's population began to grow quite rapidly in contrast with preceding periods.[17]

The process of settlement in Siberia received a major boost from the Trans-Siberian Railway. The construction of the Trans-Siberian began only in 1891, and it was not fully completed until 1917, the year of the Russian Revolution. However, the first major section from Moscow to Chita (east of Lake Baykal near the border with Mongolia) was finished in 1899. In addition, a spur line running through Harbin in Chinese territory to the Pacific Ocean connected Chita to Vladivostok in 1903. Between the tsarist cen-suses of 1897 and 1911, one million people migrated to Siberia by train.[18] Given its desire to establish and consolidate Russian control over this vast area and a growing imperative to secure its borders with both China and an increasingly assertive Japan, the tsarist government soon began to encourage this migration. It also offered a degree of resettlement assistance, including a travel allowance, medical and subsistence aid, and a low migration tariff, equal to one-third of the cost of passage in a fourth-class train compartment.[19] The colonization of Siberia became an official government project under the agricultural reform programs of Russian prime minister Pyotr Stolypin. The goals were to relocate "surplus" population from European Russia and to increase the amount of land under cultivation.[20] Most restrictions on migration were removed in 1904, when the property requirement was lifted. By 1917 the population of Siberia stood at about ten million.[21] Siberia had become the most popular destination for migrants within the Russian Empire.

The Land of Last Resort

Although the relatively rapid rate of migration into Siberia and consequent population growth seem to indicate that the region had considerable appeal to Russian settlers, this increased settlement of Siberia came only *after* settlement in the black-earth belt, the *chernozem*, had largely reached the saturation point. Settlers in Siberia in the late nineteenth and early twentieth centuries came predominantly from the increasingly overcrowded rural regions of western and central Russia and the black-earth belt.[22] Siberia may have been a land of opportunity, but it was also a land of necessity and, for many, the land of last resort. The bulk of migrants faced poverty and potential starvation in their home regions, which were subject to frequent harvest failures and epidemics. It was a case of go east or perish. A government investigation of migration in this period concluded that all rural migrants should be permitted to migrate if they so chose, given the crisis in the Russian countryside.[23] However, the difficulties of distance and climate were still not easily overcome. Migrating to Siberia was always a daunting prospect.

The great American explorer George Kennan, in his book on his travels in Siberia, describes how Russians would kiss the soil by the designated marker between Europe and Asia in the Ural Mountains to bid farewell to the motherland as they embarked on the long, cold trip east (box 5-1).

Even today, those who live in the farthest reaches of Siberia and the Russian Far East refer to European Russia as the *materik*—mainland. Throughout the tsarist period, settlement in Siberia remained limited and constrained. The greatest concentrations of population were always in western Siberia, relatively closer to the center, where the climate was milder.[24] (Average January temperatures in western Siberia are in the −15° to −20° C range. In eastern Siberia, they reach −30° C and below.) Elsewhere, larger-scale settlements

---

Box 5-1. *George Kennan: "Across the Siberian Frontier"*

"On the second day after our departure from Ekaterinburg, as we were passing through a rather open forest between the villages of Márkova and
Tugulímskaya, our driver suddenly pulled up his horses, and turning to us
said, "Vot granítsa" [Here is the boundary]. We sprang out of the tarantas and
saw, standing by the roadside, a square pillar ten or twelve feet in height, of
stuccoed or plastered brick, bearing on one side the coat-of-arms of the
European province of Perm, and on the other that of the Asiatic province of
Tobólsk. It was the boundary post of Siberia.

No other boundary post in the world has witnessed so much human suffering, or been passed by such a multitude of heart-broken people. More than
170,000 exiles have traveled this road since 1878, and more than half a million since the beginning of the present century. [. . .] As the boundary post is
situated about half-way between the last European and the first Siberia etape,
it has always been customary to allow exile parties to stop here for rest and
for a last good-by to home and country. The Russian peasant, even when a
criminal, is deeply attached to his native land; and heart-rending scenes have
been witnessed around the boundary pillar when such a party, overtaken, perhaps, by frost and snow in the early autumn, stopped here for a last farewell.
Some gave way to unrestrained grief; some comforted the weeping; some knelt
and pressed their faces to the loved soil of their native country, and collected
a little earth to take with them into exile; and a few pressed their lips to the
European side of the cold brick pillar, as if kissing good-by forever to all that
it symbolized. [. . .]

After picking a few flowers from the grass at the base of the boundary
pillar, we climbed into our carriage, said 'Good-by' to Europe, as hundreds
of thousands had said good-by before us, and rode away into Siberia."

Source: George Kennan, *Siberia and the Exile System*, vol. 1 (London: James R.
Osgood, McIlvaine & Co., 1891; reprint: Praeger Publishers, 1970), pp. 50–54.

---

developed in close proximity to the lines of communication back toward central Russia. Ten years after the construction of the Trans-Siberian Railway
began in 1891, the population of the cities connected by the railroad grew
rapidly. In contrast, older Siberian towns that were distant from the line experienced a rapid economic and demographic decline.[25]

Settlement remained particularly marginal and tenuous in the Far East—
the territory bounded by the Pacific Ocean and the Amur River. Although
most tsarist statistics for migration cover Siberia and the Far East together,
construction of settlements of any significance in the Far East began only in

the 1850s. The territory along the Amur River was under constant dispute with China. It was not until 1858–60 that Russia effectively annexed approximately 644,000 square kilometers and established the Amur River as the official frontier with China. The Russian Far East at this time had a population of only 15,000 people.[26] The state undertook significant effort to attract settlers to this remote region. Migrants to the Far East were exempted from conscription as early as the 1860s as an inducement.[27] In 1883 the state began to fund transportation for settlers to the Far East and to specifically target farmers from western Ukraine, which was experiencing a particularly acute "land hunger."[28] Nevertheless, the region always suffered from a far smaller rate of settlement than the rate—voluntary or punitive—in Siberia. By the time of the tsarist census of 1897, the population of the Russian Far East barely exceeded 300,000.[29] Most of those people were concentrated in the Primorsk region close to the Pacific Coast.[30]

At the end of the tsarist period, the interior of Siberia beyond the hinterland of the Trans-Siberian Railway was barely charted, let alone settled. Ultimately, the large-scale settlement and, eventually, the urbanization of Siberia were simply not possible under the tsars. As the preceding chapters have shown, the costs of peopling, exploiting, and maintaining such a vast, cold area are too onerous for market forces. In spite of the centralized and administrative nature of the imperial state, the tsars were basically market oriented. They were also usually cash strapped, heavily indebted, and running the empire on a shoestring.[31] Only the Soviet Union—a totalitarian state with coercion at its core, with its highly centralized control of production and redistribution of resources, and with absolutely no sense of cost—could really conquer Siberia. It was the communist planners and secret police in Moscow who moved people out of European Russia in large numbers into the cold and across vast distances to settle Siberia. It was the Soviet state that then built cities, kept them heated by tapping into the energy resources of the region (the rich reserves of oil and gas and seams of coal), and supplied them by transporting goods thousands of kilometers by train along the Trans-Siberian Railway, by ship down the Siberian rivers, and finally by plane and helicopter to the remotest settlements.

The Soviets Open Siberia

Soviet planners with their eyes on Siberia's resources were assisted in their "conquest" by the technological advancements of the 1920s–1930s. Ships capable of breaking through the ice flows were developed, opening up the "northern sea" route through the Arctic Ocean from Murmansk to

Vladivostok. The first complete journey along this route in a single season took place in 1932, giving European Russia a direct link with the Russian Far East. Subsequently, the Soviets were able to extend the northern sea route down the great rivers of Siberia—the Ob', the Yenisey, and the Lena—by constructing a series of ports. This offered access to and the development of communications with the interior of Siberia for the first time. In the 1930s–1940s, the large-scale exploitation of Siberia's natural resources was finally made possible. By the 1950s, the USSR had begun to mine the coal basins of northern Siberia and had tapped rich deposits of nonferrous metals, including copper, tin, zinc, lead, silver, gold, platinum, and mercury. In the 1960s and 1970s, they also brought into production oil and gas fields in western Siberia, and later in eastern Siberia and the North; these offered additional possibilities for industrial development and settlement.

As the Soviets developed Siberia's resource base, they laid branch lines from the Trans-Siberian Railway to connect key regions with the rest of the USSR. They built new Siberian cities and encouraged new settlers to move out to them. As early as October 1924, the Soviet government passed a decree on the importance of relocating population to develop the resources of the USSR. They initially offered a number of inducements to settlers willing to move to Siberia and the Russian Far East, including tax reductions, postponement of military service, coverage of transportation costs, and loans— all very similar to tsarist policy.[32] One of the most interesting exercises in promoting settlement in the region in the Soviet period was the creation of Birobidzhan, a region on the Amur River in the Far East, which was established as a homeland for the Jews of the USSR in the 1920s. The Birobidzhan experiment (box 5-2), which lasted for thirty years, illustrates the difficulties of getting large numbers of people to relocate to Siberia and the Russian Far East, even with a rather elaborate array of inducements.

In spite of incentives and experiments like the "Soviet Zion," ultimately Siberia could never attract enough people in the early decades of the Soviet Union to fulfill the ambitions of communist planners for its development. Methods other than voluntary or ideologically inspired settlement became necessary. In order to exploit Siberia's resources fully, the Soviet government began to develop the Siberian penal system to levels previously unimagined by the tsars.

The GULAG

After seizing power in 1917, the Bolsheviks delivered a reprieve to tsarist-era political prisoners in Siberia and elsewhere. Soon, however, the new regime

Box 5-2. *Birobidzhan*

Beginning in 1928, the Soviet government attempted to settle Russian Jews in farming collectives in the Far Eastern region of Birobidzhan. According to the 1926 Soviet census, there were 2,672,000 Jews in the USSR.[a] In the second five-year plan of 1933–37, Soviet planners set the ambitious population target of 300,000 in the region, half of which they intended to be Jewish.[b] Birobidzhan was touted as a new socialist, Jewish homeland, a "Soviet Zion," and in 1934 was officially designated the Jewish Autonomous Region within the Russian Soviet Federative Socialist Republic.

In spite of the appeal of an explicit place of their own within the USSR—having been confined in the tsarist period to restricted areas of Ukraine and Belarus—Soviet Jewish settlers who were inspired to relocate to Birobidzhan left almost as quickly as they moved in, especially in the first five years of the project:

1928	950 arrived, 600 left
1929	1,875 arrived, 1,125 left
1930	2,560 arrived, 1,000 left
1931	3,250 arrived, 725 left
1932–33	11,000 arrived, 8,000 left

The height of activity and settlement in Birobidzhan was reached after Nazi Germany's invasion of the USSR in 1941, but the region never had more than 50,000 Jewish residents (out of a total population of 114,000). In 1958 Soviet leader Nikita Khrushchev declared the project of Jewish resettlement in Birobidzhan a failure, which he blamed on "Jewish individualism."[c]

If by "individualism" Khrushchev meant the desire to exercise free choice, he was undoubtedly right. By normal measures, Birobidzhan is close to unlivable. Its mean January temperature is −22° C, and it is quite arguably located in "the middle of nowhere." Jews in the USSR preferred to face discrimination and limited employment opportunities in European Russia (and, later, to emigrate entirely) rather than to live and work in a remote corner of the Russian Far East. The more recent history of Birobidzhan bears out this conclusion. By 1979 the Jewish population had dropped below 10,000 (barely more than 5 percent of Birobidzhan's total population) and continued to decline thereafter.[d] Between 1989 and 1996, 7,500 Jews left the region, mostly for Israel, reducing the Jewish population in Birobidzhan to 1,500.[e] This is less than 0.5 percent of the total Jewish population of Russia today.

a. *Narodnoye khozyaystvo SSSR, 1922–1982* (Moscow: Goskomstat, 1982), p. 33.

b. Robert Weinberg, *Stalin's Forgotten Zion. Birobidzhan and the Making of a Jewish Homeland: An Illustrated History 1928–1996* (University of California Press, 1998), p. 43.

c. Martin Gilbert, *Russian History Atlas* (MacMillan, 1972), p. 135.

d. *Rossiiskiy statisticheskiy yezhgodnik 2000* (Moscow: Goskomstat), pp. 55, 67.

e. Lev Krichevsky, "Remote Russian Community Is Losing Last of Its Jews," *Jewish Telegraphic Agency*, 6 September 1996. At www.jewishsf.com/bk960906/iremote.htm.

found that a lack of capital, machinery, equipment, and other resources was impeding the implementation of its planned massive industrialization campaign. Only labor seemed to be in ample supply. The communist leaders initially assumed that a voluntary, contractual system of labor would be sufficient to draw the urban unemployed and peasant labor out to Russia's most undeveloped regions. However, it did not take long to realize that the voluntary system would not work. Unemployment in the Soviet Union was effectively eliminated by 1930, greatly reducing the incentive to go east. Increasingly, as soon as peasants confronted the reality of living even in the Urals, not to mention in Siberia, they violated their contracts with enterprises and returned west. But still faced with the imperative of meeting the harsh production quotas of the first Soviet five-year plan, local enterprise directors themselves demanded that they be given access to the pool of labor just beginning to be made available with the penal camp system. Historian James Harris describes, for instance, how the Urals Metallurgical Trust in 1931 sent an urgent telegram to the oblast labor department complaining that out of the 2,700 recruits they had received that year, 1,000 had already left.[33] Harris goes on:

> Enterprise managers did not see any immediate prospects for creating sufficient conditions to keep recruits on the job. They tended to see the solution to the problem in . . . using forced labor for those jobs with particularly harsh conditions, from which the rate of "leakage" (*utechka*) was especially high. This was the basis for demands for the expansion of the camp system. For example, the above telegram from the Urals Metallurgical Trust argued that "the transfer of a labor colony (to the Nedezhdinskiy plant) would solve the problem" of the need to continue housing construction in the middle of winter. Peasants were less likely to run away when they were being watched by armed guards.
>
> By the late 1930s, forced labor was used in all major industries in the Urals.[34]

The labor camp system had been launched in 1929 by a government enactment ordering the notorious police ministry—the OGPU, or Unified State Political Directorate—to establish a network of corrective labor camps for the express purpose of colonizing "the least accessible and most difficult to develop" regions of the country and exploiting their natural resources. The camps would be placed in "Siberia, the North, the Far East, and in Central Asia." At the time of the original 1929 order, the handful of prison camps in the USSR had a population of about 23,000 inmates.

Less than five years later, half a million Soviet citizens—all persons who had received a prison sentence of three years or longer—were in the GULAG.[35]*

The GULAG and its pool of slave labor became fundamental tools in Soviet industrialization. As Anne Applebaum describes in her history of the GULAG, Solovetskiy, the first camp of the GULAG system, was run on an "eat-as-you-work system" in the late 1920s. This became the model for how prison camps could be made self-sufficient and even run as apparently profitable state enterprises.[36] Throughout the GULAG system, prisoners, specifically maintained as laborers, facilitated the exploitation of timber and mineral resources in remote areas that lacked a significant population base. They also developed vital infrastructure and key industries in areas, including places in European Russia and around Moscow.[37] Projects carried out by prisoners under the GULAG system extended across the region east of the Urals. They ranged from the construction of the north Siberian railway (carried out in temperatures of −55° C and later abandoned) to the building of the Baykal-Amur main railroad line stretching to the Russian Far East. One of the largest GULAG undertakings was centered in the gold mines of the Kolyma Basin, an area almost equivalent in size to Ukraine, and part of the *Dal'stroy*, or Russian Far East Construction project, which was run in many respects like a "business conglomerate," separate from the rest of the GULAG system.[38]

The exploitation of the Kolyma gold mines is one of the classic examples of the great human cost underlying Russia's economic modernization and the development of Siberia. Forced to work in temperatures as low as −50° C, prisoners in Siberia were prohibited in 1938 from using fur in their winter clothing; only wadding was allowed. Canvas shoes were introduced in the penal system to replace felt boots. Allotted food rations were also barely enough for survival. According to historian Robert Conquest, the prevailing mindset in the NKVD (the People's Commissariat of Internal Affairs, which ran the GULAG from 1934 to 1946) was that "since the prisoners were not expected to withstand the winter's rigors, it was unnecessary to keep them strong," and there were always more prisoners to replace those who succumbed.[39] Other sources indicate that for every ton of Kolyma gold that was extracted, 700–1,000 lives were lost in the process.[40] Soviet planners regarded the slave labor pool as virtually inexhaustible.

* The term GULAG is an acronym based on the name of the department within the Soviet internal affairs ministry that ran the camp system, the Main Directorate of Camps (_Glavnoye Upravleniye LAGerey_). The official name of the directorate underwent twelve changes from its creation in 1929 until its dissolution in 1960. The acronym GULAG remained until the end.

Figure 5-1. *Peak GULAG Populations in Cities and Towns of the Soviet Union, 1923–60*

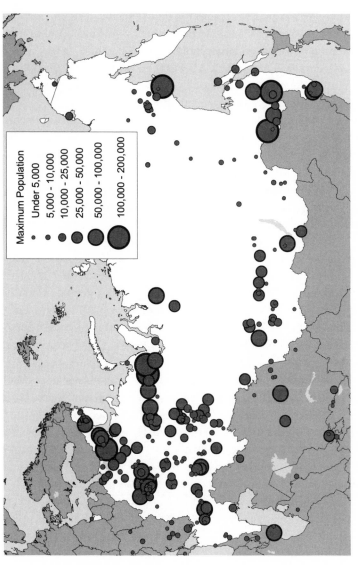

Source: Calculated from data in M. B. Smirnov, *Sistema ispravitel'no-trudovykh lagerey v SSSR 1923–1960: spravochnik* (Moscow: Zven'ya, 1998).

Note: Circles indicate the peak GULAG population in each location (city or town) over time. When there was more than one camp in a single location, the population is the maximum combined camp population in the location at a single date.

Stalin's great purges of the late 1930s and the zealous efforts of NKVD chief Nikolay Yezhov brought ever increasing numbers of prisoners into the GULAG system. In 1936 alone, the number of GULAG camps increased from thirteen to thirty-three. By April 1938, the total camp population exceeded two million people. The numbers declined during the war years but rose again after 1945, as postwar economic development plans demanded even more forced labor. From mid-1949 to mid-1953, the camp population remained at around 2.5 million. Throughout that period, roughly half of the people condemned to the GULAG had been imprisoned for crimes no more serious than theft.[41]

At its peak in the late 1940s and 1950s, the GULAG accounted for an estimated 15–18 percent of all Russian industrial output and industrial employment.[42] The Far Eastern *Dal'stroy* project alone housed fifty-two surface gold mines [*priiski*], five underground gold mines [*rudniki*], five gold extraction factories, seven tin mines, eleven tin enrichment factories, twenty-five electrical power plants, and numerous additional enterprises and facilities.[43]

Soviet statistics deliberately masked the fact that the achievements of the USSR's industrialization campaign were based on slave labor. Forced labor camps in the GULAG system that exceeded 3,000 or 5,000 people (depending on location) were classified as towns. This meant that to the outside observer, regions like Siberia were experiencing unprecedented population as well as industrial growth.[44] In their book on prison labor in the USSR, David Dallin and Boris Nikolaevsky note that forced migration was an essential component in this population growth—underscored by the fact that the fastest urban growth was recorded in the Russian North and the Far East, where most of the labor camps were located.[45] Even after their release, prisoners still contributed to the population growth of regions like Siberia. On the completion of their sentences, former prisoners were given a new provisional status of "special migrant." As such, they were legally prohibited from relocating or moving back to their original homes. Everyone who passed through the GULAG system east of the Urals became part of the "migration" wave that swept through Siberia and the Far East, whether they liked it or not.[46]

The GULAG's impact was by no means limited to the most remote and sparsely populated areas. One attempt to depict the regional impact of the GULAG is the map in figure 5-1, which shows the location of GULAG camps and their peak populations over time. As figure 5-1 indicates, some of the largest camps were located in European Russia. It was in the east, however, that the GULAG shaped Russia's development the most. Every one of the large cities of the Ural, Siberian, and Far Eastern regions was a beneficiary of the deployment of forced labor between 1929 and 1953. Take, for instance, the case of Khabarovsk, one of the Russian Far East's major cities since the mid-nineteenth century. In 1938 Khabarovsk's population was around 200,000. At the same time, it was surrounded by four major GULAG camps with a total inmate population of more than 300,000. That massive camp labor force was deployed to build various branches of the Siberian railroad lines.[47] The prisoners built factories to produce materials for additional construction projects in and around Khabarovsk (including in Birobidzhan). They laid roads, worked in the nascent fishing and timber industries, and built infrastructure in support of the shipping traffic along the Amur River.[48] Today Khabarovsk has a population of more than 600,000 and, as was shown in table 3-3, makes the fourth largest negative contribution to Russia's temperature per capita (TPC).[49]

World War II Relocation of Industry and the Virgin Lands Campaign

Another major turning point for Siberian development was World War II. Although Soviet planners had already begun to build factories in Siberia in the 1930s, the 1940s saw the deliberate relocation of Soviet industry and economic activity. Key factories were moved from European Russia to the regions east of the Volga and into the Ural Mountains and beyond with the explicit purpose of putting them beyond the reach of invading German forces. From July until November 1941, immediately after the German surprise attack on the USSR in June, more than 1,500 factories were moved east from cities like Leningrad (St. Petersburg), Moscow, and Kiev. Of these factories, 244 were moved to western Siberia and 78 to eastern Siberia. Cities like Omsk and Novosibirsk became major recipients of new industry.[50] Siberia was thus reconceptualized as a strategic redoubt: its vast territory placed it far away from European Russia and the possibility of a conventional attack across the weak western front.

Further spurs to Siberian development came in the decades after the war with the "Virgin Lands" campaign, promoted by Nikita Khrushchev. Between 1953 and 1961, Khrushchev launched a campaign to increase grain cultivation on the southern steppe in what is today northern Kazakhstan. He also targeted marginal lands stretching into Siberia between the Volga and the Yenisey Rivers. By 1956, 35.9 million hectares (88.6 million acres)—an area equivalent to the total cultivated land of Canada—had been brought under intensive cultivation. Some 300,000 Soviet citizens had been permanently resettled in new farming regions.[51] The majority of these settlers were young ethnic Russians and Ukrainians who were recruited as agricultural pioneers or dispatched under work programs. The Virgin Lands program was officially ended in 1970 after it proved too difficult to sustain crop yields.* But many of the settlers stayed nonetheless. By the 1970s, in both rhetoric and design, Soviet central planners were bent not only on cultivating virgin lands but also on building major cities and specialized extractive industries in Siberia. It was a massive project—a Siberian industrial utopia—that was intended to take the Soviet Union up to the eve of the twenty-first century.

The Siberian Industrial Utopia

For the most part, the motivations for the development of specific industries and the location of cities in Siberia and the Russian Far East remain mysterious, but what rationale can be gleaned from Soviet planning documents suggests that a number of factors were at work. Communist economic planners sought to develop the territory and to move people there not because it was Siberia but because of the availability of resources—the oil, gas, diamonds, gold, and other precious metals. The goal was to make the Soviet Union self-sufficient in strategic resources, especially after 1929, when the USSR was isolated from the rest of Europe and its access to outside resources was deliberately blocked by western governments fearful of the contagion of communism. Other related rationales, concepts, and theories were also developed by planners: moving industry closer to sources of raw materials and energy to minimize transportation; equalizing the level of economic development across the USSR; and eventually increasing specialization and large-scale development in specific territorial regions.[52]

Military planners had strategic concerns in mind in seeking the development of Siberia, more akin to the basic desires of the tsars—to simply "secure, hold, and, in some manner, settle that huge and, to varying degree, vulnerable part of national territory."[53] Finally, Soviet politicians tasked with engineering and mobilizing society in the relatively less coercive era of the 1960s–1980s stressed the ideology of conquering new lands to increase the strength of the Soviet state with slogans and propaganda. In general, there was no single, *regional* plan for developing Siberia. Only after the fact was the effort formulated in this way. Central planners, military strategists, and Soviet ideologues all had their reasons for turning to and focusing on Siberia. In fact, they all fed one another's utopias.

One of the more curious ideological motivations behind industrial planning in Siberia was the so-called "Engels dictum"—Friedrich Engels's con-

---

* In some of the Siberian centers of the Virgin Lands program, such as Tomsk on the Ob' River, snow lay on the ground for around 180 days of the year, drastically shortening the growing season.

tention that large-scale industry should be "freed from the restrictions of space" and be equally distributed within and across a socialist country:

> Large scale industry . . . has thereby to a considerable extent freed production from the restrictions of place. . . . Society liberated from the barriers of capitalist production can go much further still. . . . The abolition of the separation between town and country is therefore not utopian, even in so far as it presupposes *the most equal distribution possible of large scale industry over the whole country.* It is true that in the huge towns civilization had bequeathed us a heritage to rid ourselves of which will take much time and trouble. But this heritage must and will be got rid of, however protracted the process may be. [Emphasis added][54]

The Engels dictum was seized upon by Soviet economists, especially those concerned with the confluence of economics and state security. By the late 1950s, it had become a major factor in important Soviet circles, including in the military academies. One of the most explicit references to the concept enshrined in the Engels dictum can be found in the writings of General Andrey Lagovskiy, one of the first military economists in the USSR and the founder of the Military Economics Department of the Soviet General Staff Academy (see box 5-3).[55]

Siberia and the Russian Far East were certainly territories that the tsars had left undeveloped in terms of industry. At the same time, their remoteness from Europe and the efforts to relocate industry away from the western front and thus from attack in the 1940s suggested that they should become a focus of industry for security purposes. Security and the importance of increasing the defense capabilities of the USSR gave a new twist to the Engels dictum. To that end, Siberia, the Russian Far East, and the Pacific coastline were heavily built up from the 1960s to the 1980s to support defense industries. Major military and naval installations were located there to defend Soviet territory against possible attack from China. By the 1980s, approximately 25 percent of Soviet ground forces, a similar percentage of the Soviet Union's air force, and about 30 percent of Soviet naval capacity were based east of the Urals. The heightened sense of Siberia and the Russian Far East as the military redoubt also fueled earlier ideas of ensuring autarky in metals and other strategic resources, which were now essential to the defense industries based there after World War II. All of this meant the increased exploitation of Siberia's rich mineral deposits.[56]

This concoction of motivations for development placed Siberia and the Russian Far East at the forefront of Soviet planning. But on the basis of the Engels dictum, and General Lagovskiy's elaboration on it, in a country as vast

Box 5-3. *General Andrey N. Lagovskiy on "The Geographical Location of Productive Forces"*

"The geographical location of productive forces, and above all of heavy industry, as the leading sector of the economy and the basis of the nation's defense capability, has enormous political, economic, and strategic significance in contemporary conditions. [...]

In contemporary conditions the components of a highly developed economic base, especially industrial enterprises, should be located on the country's territory in such a way as to have the most favorable conditions for their operation in wartime.

In the socialist countries, on the basis of planned (proportional) development of the economy, the productive forces are located in a fundamentally different manner than in the capitalist countries. In the latter, as is well known, production is located where it brings maximum profits for the monopolies.

The uneven and irrational location of production in the capitalist countries is apparent from the fact that industry spontaneously develops in those regions where it brings the quickest and greatest profits. This means that it is usually concentrated in a small number of centers of the metropolis. Meanwhile, vast territories of the borderlands of the country and the colonies remain totally undeveloped in terms of industry. . . . Tsarist Russia was a prime example of inefficient location of industry from the point of view of the overall state interests. [...]

The Great October Socialist Revolution, which eliminated the capitalist mode of production in our country, also put an end to irrational location of new construction of industrial enterprises. In the process of construction of socialism, the ugly legacy of capitalist location of productive forces was gradually liquidated, although it has not yet been completely overcome."

Source: Andrey N. Lagovskiy, *Strategiya i ekonomika. Kratkiy ocherk ikh vzaimnoy svyazi i vzaimnogo vliyaniya* [Strategy and economics. Brief outline of their mutual ties and mutual influence] 1st ed. (Moscow: Voyennoye izdatel'stvo Ministerstva oborony Soyuza SSR, 1957), p. 107.

as Russia it would certainly "take much time and trouble" to ensure a distribution of large-scale industry or economic development equal to European Russia across a territory as enormous as Siberia and the Russian Far East. In fact, it would likely be impossible. This prospect, however, did not deter Soviet planners, although they did eventually modify Engels's dictum to try to achieve a distribution of productive forces that was more *even* rather than equal.[57] Lagovskiy and other Soviet planners like him came to believe that locating industry in remote regions alongside mineral resources would, in fact, enhance the value of Soviet industry. Remoteness and cost were not issues in this line of thinking. As Lagovskiy made clear in the extract from his book above, the very fact that they were not issues was the primary advantage of the Soviet system. Time, or rather the length of it, was also not a deterrent. The concept that industry should be dispersed across the vastness of Russia and Siberia for ideological and security reasons, enshrined by Lagovskiy in 1957, persisted well into the 1980s.[58] Most of the plans formulated for the construction of industry had extremely long time horizons.

Planned "Cities"

Cities in Siberia were an important feature of these plans. The cities were developed in tandem with industries to provide a fixed reserve of labor for factories, mines, and oil and gas fields. They were also designed according to a descending geographical and functional hierarchy to maximize the exploitation of strategic resources. Cities were planned as bases, or concentration points for social infrastructure, and as supply or residential centers for extractive industries in isolated areas. In western Siberia, for example, major cities along the Trans-Siberian Railway, such as Tomsk, Novosibirsk, Omsk, and Tyumen', were first-order cities in the hierarchy—primary social and supply centers with concentrations of infrastructure, intended as focal points for a larger geographic area. Farther from the Trans-Siberian, smaller cities like Surgut and Nizhnevartovsk had similar functions on a lower scale, acting as base cities for workers in distant Arctic gas fields. Even smaller settlements and seasonal mining camps or oil and gas fields were dependent on the closest city for a variety of services, including the provision of long-term housing for their families.[59]

In many respects, however, the planned cities in Siberia were not really cities as we might think of them. They were less social or economic entities than physical collection points, repositories, and supply centers—utilitarian in the extreme. Cities were functional mechanisms for "storing," funneling through, and directing labor and supplies for the huge planned industries of the region. Their size and municipal profiles, including population mix and infrastructure, were designed in relationship to specific industrial enterprises. They were thus built to suit the needs of industry and the state, not the needs (apart from the most basic), or desires, or preferences of their populations. Indeed, primary responsibility for planning and constructing infrastructure in these cities came under the jurisdiction of the particular Soviet economic ministry responsible for the enterprise the city was designed to serve—with very few responsibilities assigned to the municipal governments. In many

cases, if there were shortfalls or delays in regional investment funds, the min-
istries would simply divert resources earmarked for the development of social
infrastructure in the cities to the respective industrial facilities, leaving housing stock and urban amenities underfunded.[60]

The Siberian Development Boom

In the 1970s and 1980s, Siberia and the Russian Far East dominated Soviet
regional development programs. This development was boosted by the intensive exploitation of oil and natural gas reserves in western Siberia, which
began around 1964. By 1985 western Siberia had become the largest energy-
producing region in the USSR, and massive long-term industrial projects
were planned for the whole of Siberia. These included the construction of
the world's largest aluminum plant at Sayan, a huge dam on the Yenisey River
at Sayan-Shushenskoye, the completion of the Baykal-Amur rail line (BAM),*
gigantic power plants in the Kansk-Achinsk Basin, and the opening up of the
coalfields of the Kansk-Achinsk Basin to create the USSR's largest coal supplier, among others. Analysts were astounded by the magnitude of the projects
and by the scale of investment that would be necessary to carry them out. As
geographer Robert Taaffe noted in reviewing these initiatives, "There has
never been a period in Soviet history when as many major developmental
projects were carried out in a large economic zone."[61] Of these huge Siberian
construction projects, some of the largest (including BAM and the Tyumen'
oilfields) were located in the harshest climatic zones in the North. Between
1976 and 1980, the North accounted for 36 percent of all Soviet investment
channeled to Siberia, although its population, at 3.5 million, accounted for
only about 12 percent of the total population of Siberia. Given the climate in
the North, the scale and cost of regional projects imposed considerable strain
on the Soviet construction industry.[62]

By the 1970s, analysts both inside and outside the Soviet Union had
begun to note and to question the high costs of developing Siberia. According to Soviet statistical information, average construction costs in Siberia

---

* The BAM railway was originally launched in the 1930s as a GULAG project to provide an
alternative route to the Trans-Siberian, to which it runs parallel but approximately four hundred kilometers to the north. (In fact, the Baykal-Amur Corrective Labor Camp, or Bamlag,
with 200,907 prisoners in 1938, was the single largest forced labor camp in the history of the
Soviet Union.) The BAM project was abandoned by Stalin and resumed under Brezhnev in
1974. Construction of the almost 3,200 kilometers of rail line was completed in 1986 (with the
exception of some tunnels). Since 1989 BAM has been the principal route for freight transportation from European Russia to the Far East.

and the Far East were then running more than 50 percent higher than in European Russia, with higher costs for related inputs such as labor, installation, maintenance, and transportation.[63] It also cost the state 18,000 rubles per worker to bring a new migrant laborer out to Siberia, including the related infrastructure for living support. Bringing on a new worker in European Russia, in contrast, cost 5,000–7,000 rubles.[64]

Costs were high not only for the state to develop the region, but also for the workers who moved there. Soviet statistics showed that the cost of living in Siberia and the Russian Far East was 35–50 percent higher for workers than elsewhere in the Russian Federation. However, the higher wages and other supplements increased workers' incomes in these regions by only 15–20 percent over those in European Russia.[65] Real incomes for workers in Siberia were ultimately not higher than in European Russia. The relatively low rate of investment in urban housing and other infrastructure by the state compounded the hardships Siberian workers faced.[66]

The investment that flooded into Siberia, including capital, labor, materials, and foodstuffs, was largely "uncompensated inflow from west of the Urals." Some regions, especially those in the more "temperate" western and southern parts of Siberia, were less heavily subsidized than others, but the Far East and the North proved to be a particular drain on resources.

Magadan oblast on the Pacific coast, for example, had 75 percent higher per capita consumption than the oil region of Tyumen', where the labor force was more mobile and directed toward shift work, with laborers' families remaining behind in base cities. The military installations in the Russian Far East were a further sinkhole for regional investment, requiring heavy importation of supplies from outside the region.[67] With the Soviet economic slowdown of the late 1970s, maintaining economic development in Siberia became a major challenge.

The Monumental Mistake

By the 1980s, Siberia and the Far East were offering an extremely low return on the massive investment made in the exploitation of their resources. Many huge construction projects were left incomplete because of "frequently unrealistic appraisals of the availability of resources, equipment, and supplies" or were postponed indefinitely.[68] The planned large-scale development of the Russian Far East, which had been last on the agenda, was "pushed further into the future."[69] At first, the problems were seen to be the result of disproportional and incoherent planning, ineffective management, and poor coordination. But by the reformist era of the late 1980s under Mikhail Gorbachev, the problem was seen to be Siberia itself as well as the efforts to develop it. Criticism of the giant outlays in Siberia became commonplace in Soviet planning circles. Planners in Moscow "sought to subordinate the development of Siberia to the needs of the European economic core" and gave up on the "hope for self-sustained growth in this century."[70] Gorbachev's economic adviser, Abel Aganbegyan, for example, decried the "gigantomania" in Soviet industrial projects, which undermined economic objectives, while Soviet defense industry analyst Andrey Kokoshin pointed to increased spending on the creation of new defense enterprises in distant regions, which were "from the economic point of view . . . unjustified."[71]

Regional analysts and planners in Siberia mounted a fierce rearguard action. They would try, in fact, to justify continued high investment rates by pointing to the value of the commodities produced in Siberia—especially oil and gas—on world markets, the dependence of European Russia on Siberian natural resources and energy supplies, and the immense economic potential of exploiting the region's riches.[72] But it was still apparent that these valuations favoring Siberia could never factor in all of the associated costs of bringing the region's commodities to market. Indeed, by 1989 the industrialization of Siberia was beginning to seem not like a great utopia but a monumental mistake. The Siberian enterprise was, in any case, brought to a screeching halt by the collapse of the Soviet Union in 1991 and the beginning of Russia's macroeconomic reforms in the 1990s.

The fact that the effort to industrialize Siberia was a huge mistake is clear from the discussions of the unique set of problems related to Russia's size and the cold in chapters 2 and 3. But in the final reckoning, the scale of the mistake could have been much worse. The utopian schemes concocted in the 1960s and 1970s were intended to set Siberian development on a path that would have taken it as far as 2000.[73] This was a long-term project of gigantic proportions. The Siberian utopia was stopped by resource limitations, not lack of imagination. In the 1980s, the ultimate constraint was not insufficient investment capital, as the discussion above might suggest (after all, the USSR was pumping money into Siberia at a phenomenal rate for about fifteen years); it was *people*. The Soviet system of the post-Stalin era could not induce or cajole enough people to move to Siberia to carry out this giant enterprise.

The Manpower Problem

Comparatively early in the Soviets' grand Siberian project of the 1960s, planners ran up against what they called the "manpower problem in

Siberia." As long as the GULAG had been in operation, manpower had not been an issue. From 1926 to 1939, the Urals region and areas to the east had experienced a population boom. But of course very little of the migration had been voluntary. Forced resettlements and deportations accounted for the lion's share of incoming residents. Once the GULAG was dismantled in the late 1950s and restrictions on the relocation of former prisoners were lifted, there was a massive wave of out-migration. Soviet officials had to devise a system of amenities—including the granting of freedom of movement within Siberia—to stem the tide of out-migration. But this system proved ineffective. In the 1960s, S. G. Prociuk wrote that when given a choice, many settlers opted to "exchange the cold and unfriendly taiga for the rich sunny steppes of the North Caucasian region."[74] The pull of warmer regions was strong even among relatively recent volunteer settlers. As Prociuk noted, "The great majority of [Siberian] workers leave their positions before the expiration of their contracts; in Krasnoyarsk kray, for example, no more than 12 percent of newly recruited workers finished their contracts, the others leaving their jobs prematurely."[75]

Soviet survey data from the period offered some insight into the factors motivating out-migration from Siberia. They included low wages, professional discontent, unsatisfactory living conditions, insufficient cultural activities, and the desire to be closer to family members in European Russia.[76] It was widely recognized that living conditions were better in other parts of the country. The Don and Kuban' areas of eastern Ukraine and southwestern Russia, where the climate was relatively mild and the cost of living considerably lower, drew many workers out of the Siberian frontiers.

To try and solve the problem, Soviet planners initially launched a campaign to draw "unproductive labor," principally housewives, into the factories. According to Prociuk, this new policy became "some kind of escape ladder for the confused Soviet labor specialists, who suddenly found themselves faced with the impossibility of reverting to the Stalinist methods of deportations that helped to colonize Siberia in 1937–52."[77] This grand strategy ultimately proved ineffective, however. Housewives were generally ill-suited for the dangerous, labor-intensive work associated with Soviet-style mining and refining of nonferrous metals. While the share of women workers in nonferrous metallurgy did jump to 24 percent in 1962, they could not fill the mounting labor gap.[78] As a result, planners had to turn increasingly to higher wages and other incentives for workers in Siberia. But even with this system in place, "the manpower problem in Siberia" continued to be a headache for the Soviet government until its collapse in 1991.

"Too Few People"

The basic fact was that, given the unattractive nature of life in Siberia, Russia simply did not have the population to match its gigantic projects. Siberia had to compete with other Soviet frontier regions such as Ukraine's Donbass coalfields, which were also being developed in this period and which had more to offer in terms of climate and amenities. When the GULAG was in operation, convict laborers required very little support in terms of resources allocated to their maintenance. They lived in flimsy barracks, survived on the most basic of food rations with minimal clothing, and certainly required no social amenities. They needed only a handful of guards from the NKVD to keep them working and under control. With the demise of the convict labor system, however, people came to work and settle in Siberia with their families. They demanded more extensive support and supply systems—housing, foodstuffs, heating, schools, and so on—which in turn required people to maintain them. (As noted in chapter 3, the ratio of auxiliary personnel and dependents to permanent workers in the Far North in the late 1960s was ten to one.)

In sum, in the absence of extreme coercion, the labor required to exploit resources in the harsh living and working conditions of Siberia was going to be very expensive. The correct response would have been to use technology that drastically reduced the number of workers needed. The Soviet planners moved in exactly the opposite direction. They wanted to continue the Stalin-era approach of bringing in massive amounts of cheap labor using very low technologies. But without coercion, it could not work. There were two reasons why the planners were so unwilling to appreciate the implications of what they saw as a "labor shortage." First, in the Soviet system planners essentially saw labor as just another objective factor of production that they could "deploy" and allocate in the same manner as they did metal or gas or cement. They could never quite accept the idea that labor is people, and that people have a free will. Second, Soviet leaders were conditioned by Russian history to think in terms of a limitless population.

Most Soviet industrial and urban planning was based on completely unrealistic expectations of Russia's population growth. The opening up and development of the Soviet Union's territory, and thus of Siberia, were predicated on the implicit notion of limitless population. In spite of its rapidly growing population before World War I (with an increase of around one million annually by 1900), Russia had never really faced Malthusian constraints on its population thanks to the vastness of its territory. As it entered the twentieth century—with the immensity of Siberia stretching before it—

there was no sense that Russia could ever run out of space and, thus, no conceivable limit to its population. It was widely expected that its population would keep on growing. As German chancellor Theobald von Bethmann-Hollweg exclaimed in 1914: "The future belongs to Russia, which is growing and growing and growing."[79]

In constantly acquiring territory and encouraging people to migrate, the tsars set the scene for Siberia's extensive development. But the tsars' goal had been simply to put people—not huge cities or vast industries—east of the Urals. It was the Soviets' goal of industrializing Siberia that set Russia on its warped trajectory in the twentieth century. Paradoxically, the Soviets could not populate and at the same time industrialize Siberia as, contrary to all expectations, Russia's population growth *did not* continue unchecked. It took some time for this fact to become apparent as even seemingly major set-backs to population growth were quickly overcome. For example, the upheavals of World War I, the Revolution, and civil war saw the population drop dramatically. Collectivization and the purges of the 1930s similarly retarded growth. World War II was a further blow. In each case, however, Russia's population bounced back. After World War II, from about 1950 to 1960, the population growth curve was even steeper than before. For a Soviet planner contemplating the future in the late 1950s and early 1960s, there was no reason to think that the extensive notions of developing Siberia and turn-ing it into the new frontier of Soviet industry would not bear fruit.* By 1970 Russia's population total was close to back on track with what might reason-ably have been extrapolated from the growth rates of 1900. Soviet planners could easily have foreseen Russia's population hitting 180 million or 190 mil-lion by 2000.† Unfortunately, all projections and extrapolations proved deceptive and unrealistic. In fact, by 1970, although the total population numbers looked good from a planner's perspective, Russia's population growth had already slowed dramatically. In 1992, as figure 5-2 shows, the population began to decrease. Russia began to follow the mature population

---

* Furthermore, even World War II had not slowed Siberia's development. During the war the instrument of the GULAG provided a targeted population to maintain levels of production, even at a time when the overall Russian and Soviet population was in decline. Deported peoples, including Poles and Ukrainians, and prisoners of war, boosted the GULAG labor force. Stalin did not have to worry about people volunteering to go out to Siberia; he just moved them out.

† In addition, Soviet planners would not have been constrained anyway, even if the popula-tion of Russia were in decline. They were projecting on the scale of the Soviet Union, not just of Russia. In their minds, they had considerably more flexibility than we are assigning here in our focus on the Russian Federation. They thought they would be able to move skilled workers from Ukraine, or Belarus, or other parts of the USSR out to Siberia. They were not limited to workers from Russia in thinking about the industrialization of Siberia.

Figure 5-2. *Russia's Population, 1897–2002*[a]

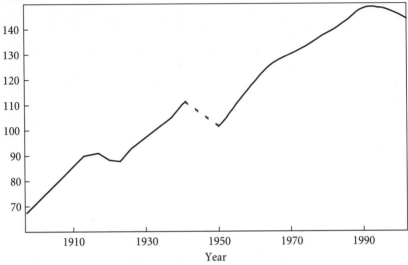

Population in millions

Source: Data for 1897–1997 from *Naseleniye Rossii za 100 let (1897–1997)* (Moscow: Goskomstat Rossii); data for 1998–2002 from Goskomstat annual data.
  a. Figures reported represent population on the territory of the present-day Russian Federation.

patterns of other industrial states. Thanks to the age structure of the population and a reduction in fertility, the previously high birthrate declined. In
addition, the rapid rate of Soviet industrialization and urbanization, with
all its related stresses, began to take its toll. Russia had already, in the 1970s,
begun to show the increased mortality from poor health related to heavy
industrial pollution, alcoholism, smoking, and industrial accidents that
became a demographic feature of the 1990s.
  As natural population growth slowed and the number of people declined,
there were limits to how far the labor force could be squeezed. Thus in the
1970s and 1980s, even with the majority of working-age women included in
the work force, there were simply not enough people to develop Siberia
in the ambitious way that Soviet planners envisioned: with huge cities across
the region, giant factories, enormous dams and power stations, vast mines,
the world's longest railway lines, and so on. Although the largest of the
Siberian cities were already in place, the planners' utopian schemes saw
them continuing to grow as more workers would flood into Siberia. But
workers did not flood in.

The high costs of living in Siberia, combined with the poor housing and lack of amenities (thanks to the consistent diversion of funds from urban infrastructure to industry), encouraged many migrants to leave for other developing regions in the Soviet Union, such as Ukraine.[80] Although the population of Siberia was considerably younger than in most areas of European Russia, and this boosted birthrates to relatively high levels, by the mid-1980s migration losses outstripped work force gains from natural increase.[81] As in the case of Birobidzhan, people would move into Siberia, stay for a while, and move out, leaving planners' dreams unfulfilled.

"Lost Cities"

What Soviet planners did leave behind in Siberia, however, was an economic structure with high levels of settlement and with specialized, mostly extractive, industry in some of Russia's—and therefore the world's—remotest regions. The settlements and industries were for the most part not linked to one another, and, in any case, the distance between them was excessive. Not a single city or region in Siberia could be considered economically self-sufficient. Consider as a vignette the unfortunate case of Mirnyy in Siberia's Sakha (Yakutiya) region. In August 1958, Soviet planners held a conference to outline a development strategy for the economy of northern Siberia. They identified diamond mining as one of the priority industries for investment expansion. As a result, in 1959 they launched a massive construction project in the diamond-rich region of western Sakha (Yakutiya) to build a new city, Mirnyy, which would serve as the center of the new industry. A highway was planned to connect Mirnyy to the nearest port, Muktuya (now the city of Lensk), 204 kilometers away on the mighty Lena River. Fixated solely on the physical presence of diamonds in the ground, the planners unfortunately failed to consider (or perhaps chose consciously to ignore) the constraints of Yakutiya's climate and the remoteness of the planned city and port. As Constantine Krypton observed as early as 1960:

> Muktuya itself is cut off from the outside world in wintertime, for there is no highway between Muktuya and the nearest railway station in Ust' Kut (the southern gate to the Yakut A.S.S.R.). Trucks sent from Ust' Kut to Muktuya must travel 1,120 kilometers along the frozen Lena [River] under extremely difficult and sometimes dangerous conditions. At the present time, transportation to and from the diamond-mining center [in Mirnyy] is chiefly by airplane.[82]

The highway from Mirnyy to Lensk that the planners had promised in 1958 was not completed until 1982. It remains impassible in winter. Today Mirnyy still has diamonds. But they (like Mirnyy's population of 37,000 people) are cut off from export markets by a frozen river, an impassible road, and an absent rail link. The town's only tenuous connection to the outside world is air transportation—itself vulnerable to weather-related delays and ruptures.

Huge industrial cities and "lost towns" like Mirnyy in Siberia have put Russia in an entirely different league from other developed states. The problems of Russia's Siberian legacy are rooted not in the vastness of the territory per se, nor in the fact that there are people there—as they were under the tsars in scattered towns and settlements—but in the fact that there are huge cities and massive enterprises and extractive industries all across the territory. The attempt to follow even a modified version of the Engels dictum, and to try to spread productive forces throughout Siberia to achieve a more equal level of economic development in every region of the Russian Federation, resulted in a monumental misallocation of resources, not in a boost to Soviet or Russian production. Engels in his writings had more compact European states like Germany or Great Britain in mind. His idea was to distribute manufacturing industry more evenly across historically settled areas. Soviet planners were carrying this economically dubious notion a giant step further in the wrong direction. They wanted to evenly populate vast unsettled areas. They were thwarted in their efforts when population resources proved to be neither infinite in number nor costless to relocate. The Russian people were both finite and quite costly to keep in Siberia's cold.

Solzhenitsyn asserted in 1974 that Siberia and the Russian Far East "offer us plenty of room in which to correct all our idiocies in building towns, industrial enterprises, power stations and roads." In the final reckoning, it became clear that the exact opposite holds true. Siberia offered plenty of room for more idiocy and error in territorial allocation of people and industry than ever before in history. For more than fifty years, the Soviets built towns, industrial enterprises, and power stations (although often not roads) in places where they should never have been.

6

Disconnected Russia

The single most distinguishing feature of Siberia's development is the prison system, the GULAG. It is the epitome of the "unfree" nature of Russia's distribution of population. But this lack of choice in location and, thus, of freedom of movement in Russia is not simply a feature of Siberia or of the Soviet Union. It is rather the culmination, or the most extreme form, of coerced population movement and location within Russia dating to the tsarist period and the Russian Empire. It was dictated by the imperative to populate rapidly expanding space, to work the land, and to exploit its resources.

Today, the dislocation of population across geographic and thermal space and the paucity of physical and economic connections between population centers are the greatest impediments to Russia's future development. Russia's spatial distribution of its population and its consequent "disconnectedness" have not only economic but also political disadvantages. Physical and personal connections among

populations provide an organic basis for personal and group ties and ultimately for economic, political, and social cohesion. At the simplest level,
distance is an obstacle to democracy. Political thinkers from Alexis de
Tocqueville in the early nineteenth century to Robert Putnam in the
late twentieth century stress the importance of association and social trust
in the development of democracy. They link these attributes, at least in
part, to the physical proximity of the participants through face-to-face
contact.[1]

An Unfree Distribution of Population

In democratic development, space—or distance—per se is not the real
problem, however. This is illustrated by contrasting the examples of the
United States and the Russian Federation. How do two of the largest countries in the world territorially, with so many geographic attributes in common, differ so starkly from one another in their political development?
The answer, in part, is that it is not the size of the territories that is critical,
but rather the way in which those territories were settled in the past and
remain settled today. In the United States, settlement from the eastern
seaboard across the plains to the west and the Pacific Coast was the result
of free choices of individuals (the use of slave labor in some of the original
colonies and in southern states notwithstanding). Russia, in contrast, was
characterized by a distinctly unfree distribution of its population, both in
terms of settlement within European Russia and when the population
began to move east of the Urals into the cold of Siberia and toward Russia's
own Pacific Coast. This has made the development of liberal democracy and
a fully functioning free market economy in Russia extremely difficult since
the collapse of the Soviet Union.

Throughout history, Russians have been severely restricted in their ability to live in places they want to live in for the purposes of improving their
welfare and of associating with whom they choose, socially, politically, and
economically. In modern free market economies, the single most important
factor determining people's choice of residence is jobs. Location is an
attribute of the job—for many people an extremely important one. In Russia
and in the USSR, job choice was restricted. In the tsarist period, social
class was a restrictive factor. Individuals were assigned to particular social
categories that generally prescribed where they could live and the professions
they could engage in. In the Soviet era, many people—especially those with
higher education—were directed to work in specific enterprises or government institutions. That job assignment (referred to as *raspredeleniye*—

literally, "distribution" or "allocation") predetermined the individual's city of residence, the neighborhood, even the specific apartment. In the USSR, citizens were also assigned to membership in the second-most important social organization, the enterprise (the first was the household, or extended family). Thus, instead of belonging to the ever-expanding social networks that are typical of a democratic society, Russians in the Soviet period were members of a couple of very small, mostly self-contained social networks, the family and the production or labor collective [kollektiv]. Beyond these personal networks, their identity was as "Soviet citizens"—subjects of the central state. Association in the community, the city, the region—not to mention in ethnic or religious communities—was not permitted to have much meaning. In the Soviet period, especially under Stalin, "narrow local interests," including regional, ethnic, and religious identities, were seen to be in competition with the state. They were fought against and in some cases stamped out, often brutally.

In the tsarist, Soviet, and post-Soviet periods in Russia's history, the top priority of every Russian government has been control of the territory and of the population, not the maximization of the freedom and welfare of individuals (nor even the economic development of the state).* But this priority on control has also posed a major dilemma for Russian governments. Because of Russia's vast size there has always been a trade-off between control of territory and control of the population. In Russia, controlling territory has always meant inhabiting it, populating it, and exploiting it, which required spreading people out across huge distances. The population centers were consequently so remote that they were well beyond the easy physical reach of the Russian capital and the seat of government. The population therefore became increasingly difficult to control for purposes of levying taxes or even ensuring social order. Historically, this dilemma was resolved by fixing the rural population in place and tying it to the land through serfdom and the peasant commune, or mir; and by using cities as administrative tools. That is, most cities in Russia did not grow as voluntary associations of free individuals, as havens from the arbitrary power of the ruler, as was the case in western Europe.[2] Rather, the cities were the centers of that very "unfreedom."

* Discussion of the state's controlling territory and population in this context refers to the state's efforts to control its citizens' lives and to determine what they do and where they live within its territory, not to the state's efforts to protect itself from outside encroachment or attack.

Fixing Population in Place: Serfdom and the Mir

In the early stages of Russian history, the tsar's power was dependent on levying armies and waging war and thus on raising revenues through taxes and other methods to support those armies and wars. Wealth came from the land, that is from agriculture and natural resources (whether in the form of furs and forest products or metals and minerals). This meant that it was imperative to control the land that represented the deposits of wealth, in the case of natural resources, or from which the wealth sprang, in the case of fertile agricultural land. As long as land was the source of wealth, labor was needed to exploit it. As long as labor was scarce relative to land, as it certainly was early in Russia's modern history, then immobility—the fixing of the rural population in place to work the land—was critical. Without the immobility of labor, it would be impossible to create the basic agricultural surplus that underpinned state revenues and the economy. In a country as large as Russia, stretching into the Eurasian steppe land, there was always somewhere the peasant farmers could flee to escape the reach of the state or the landlord and to perform labor for themselves instead of working for the state or for someone else.

As a result the state had to create, or use, a mechanism that could exert some authority over peasant farmers, keep them in one spot (as far as possible), exploit their labor, and tax them. Serfdom was one of the resulting instruments, binding peasants to the person of the landlord, who, in essence, managed the land for the state in key agricultural areas. Serfdom was, in fact, a relatively modern version in Russia of more ancient forms of slavery elsewhere in the world.[3] It was not codified until the seventeenth century, and its advent was very much tied to the imperative of extracting value from the land. Although not all peasants in Russia became serfs—that is, directly and personally owned by a specific landlord—all peasants were eventually bound to the land that they farmed and subsisted on.[4] This bondage to the land was effected through another social institution, the collective unit called the *mir* or *obshchina*. This was the agricultural peasant community or commune, which was based on joint ownership of arable and grazing land.[5]

Peasants were registered through the *mir* for the purposes of performing labor or military services and for paying taxes. This resulted in a phenomenon of almost extreme localism or commune focus for the bulk of Russia's population in the tsarist era—illustrated quite aptly by the fact that the first term for the peasant commune, *mir*, also means in Russian "the world." (*Obshchina* translates more directly as community or society.) For many Russians, the *mir* really was the world—their world—insofar as it

contained or constrained their interactions. Before the Russian Revolution, about 80 percent of Russia's population fell under the category of
"peasants" (krest'yane) as far as the state was concerned. Most of these
retained ties to their rural communes for the purposes of state service and
taxation even if they no longer farmed and lived in towns or cities.[6] Peasants
were also obliged to petition the mir every time they wanted to leave the
community for an extended period of time as well as to obtain permission
to live and work outside their commune. It was not until 1906, barely a
decade before the Russian Revolution, that peasants were allowed to move
freely away from the land and the commune and to seek work and permanent residence where they wished.

Cities as Administrative Tools

Towns and cities became administrative tools for controlling the people
living outside the mir and for mediating interactions between the state, the
individual, and the communal unit. Because of the rapid rate of Russian territorial expansion, commercial and trading cities to serve the surrounding
agricultural area had little time to develop in most of the newly incorporated and settled regions. As a result, the tsars resorted to administrative fiat,
creating towns and cities in the territories they conquered or in regions
where Russians settled. These towns and cities were explicitly developed as
centers for collecting the population to control and mobilize them, mili-
tarily and economically. Cities became an administrative tool of the Russian
state as early as the sixteenth century.

Before Muscovy established itself as the dominant power in the Russian space, independent "city-states" had emerged in northwest Russia—
Novgorod, Pskov, and Smolensk in the twelfth to fifteenth centuries—in a
manner similar to cities elsewhere in medieval Europe. The cities were
strongholds, market towns, and important trading posts, situated on key
river or land routes. Beginning in 1487, however, with Moscow's conquest
of Novgorod, these cities were all suppressed as independent commercial
and political centers. From then on, city growth was tied to the strengthening and militarization of the centralized Russian state. Towns and cities
in imperial Russia were planned military-administrative outposts. Many
cities, such as Arkhangel'sk, Voronezh, Saratov, and Samara, were directly
founded by state fiat. The imperative to wage, finance, and win wars turned
towns into elements of the state military structure as well as sources of state
revenue. Towns and cities were collection points for direct taxes and for
indirect taxes on trade and alcohol. In the seventeenth century, town

administration and the collection of taxes came under the jurisdiction of the local military commander, the *voyevoda*, who also oversaw and replicated the functions of elected town officials.[7] Although some large urban centers with significant population and commercial activity developed more "organically" and were not linked to the military command, they were often not designated as cities by the imperial capital.[8] As historian Marc Raeff notes about imperial Russia:

> The empire was divided . . . with little regard for geography, historic social bonds, or effective economic connections. In order to provide the necessary administrative centers, new cities were created by fiat [decree] out of villages, though some lip service was given to their potential economic functions as trade centers. But this economic potential was evaluated from the point of view of imperial connections, not on the basis of local and regional patterns of trade.[9]*

Town and city development was a major feature of Catherine the Great's provincial reforms in 1775–85, in which she set the criteria for a "village," designating some specific villages as cities and some cities as the capitals of certain districts. Ultimately, she endowed cities with a very limited degree of self-government in the City Charter of 1785. But the rulers in the Russian capital of St. Petersburg always remained reluctant to permit cities, provinces, or any administrative entity real forms of self-management. In essence, a legally designated urban center had a specific set of taxes imposed on it, but it received very few privileges.[10] This same kind of approach to controlling and circumscribing the activities of the population for taxation and military purposes rather than with the aim of improving the people's welfare was also evident on a larger, regional scale. Like cities, Russia's regional administrative divisions were planned from the top down, without much attention to historic social bonds or economic connections. In the early eighteenth century, Peter the Great created the first administrative districts, dividing Russia into ten provinces, or *gubernii*, for military, financial, and judicial purposes. He appointed governors to supervise them and

---

* In the United States, too, many cities, especially those on the frontier, began as military forts. They later became economic towns. As discussed in chapter 2, the history of a city's creation matters only insofar as one thinks about initial settlements as seeds. That is, government action sows many seeds in establishing forts and outposts, thus creating many candidates for true cities over the course of time. But economics usually selects the "winners," that is, the seeds that grow. In Russia, in contrast, administrative (government) decisions have continued to prevail throughout its history, even up to the point of directing the growth of cities with populations of over one million.

to report directly to him.[11] Catherine the Great subsequently reformed these provinces by breaking them up into smaller entities. Catherine also established criteria for a region to be considered a *guberniya*: it must contain a town or city center and at least 300,000 men available for conscription.[12] Except for a few minor changes under her son and successor, Paul, Catherine's regional divisions were maintained until the Russian Revolution in 1917.[13]

There were periodic attempts to inject more efficiency into regional administration through various experiments in local self-governance. These included the *zemstvo* (land assembly) reforms of the 1860s, which envisaged the creation of elected boards at the provincial and district level, with representation from local peasants, townspeople, and gentry; the boards would employ professional staff to oversee the provision of local services including education, health care, roads, and emergency food supplies.[14] In the last decades of Imperial Russia, following the revolutionary upheavals that tore across Russia after defeat in the 1904–05 war with Japan, there was also a brief and failed flirtation with constitutional monarchism and parliamentary democracy (the post-1905 Duma experiment). This attempted to give the broader population a role in electing deputies from their regions to an all-Russian parliament with legislative functions. However, in the period between 1906 and 1917, four separate Dumas (parliaments) were convened, with increasingly stringent executive control over them and rapidly dwindling powers. The experiment was eventually swept away with the Bolshevik Revolution.

Bolshevik Slogans and Soviet Cities

After 1917 the Bolsheviks essentially faced the same dilemmas as the tsars regarding how to control the population on a larger scale than the basic household or communal unit across such a vast territory. During the October Revolution, Lenin and the Bolsheviks were able to mobilize the population through the use of primitive, basic slogans that appealed to readily identifiable interests. Bread for the workers, land to the peasants, and no more war (in reference to bringing an end to World War I): these slogans all resonated at a time when there was widespread hunger, a shortage of arable land, and an unpopular war. They were sufficient to rally the population in support of a new regime. In the Soviet period, after the unbridled anarchy of the Revolution and the Civil War, mobilization for the fulfillment of obligations to the new Soviet state was initially (from the 1920s to the 1950s) effected through force and also through ideological motivation with reference to the Communist Party and its tenets. This meant more liberal use of slogans. Inspirational propaganda campaigns promulgated by political *komissars* in the new Soviet armed forces and *agitprop* brigades that traveled around the USSR also exhorted the population to build a brave new communist world.* They encouraged mass membership in the Communist Party of the Soviet Union (the CPSU) and its affiliated institutions.

To control the population, the new Soviet state, once again, fixed people into specific places of residence in cities or rural settlements and specific places of work in the enterprises or agricultural collectives that they were assigned to for labor purposes. Towns and cities were also used as administrative tools. Soviet cities were designed to facilitate their residents' service to the state, not to foster social connections. As noted previously, they were artificial, formalized, functional, and ultimately utilitarian. The newly planned Soviet cities, those built up after World War II in the Urals, Siberia, and the Russian Far East, emphasized this by being designed on a huge scale. Heating, electricity, and water supplies were all generated or processed to serve entire districts or blocks of buildings. Likewise, food and clothing stores, public services, and amenities (kindergartens, schools, cinemas, sports facilities, even parks and other green space) were all assigned proportionally to new city districts to accompany large blocks of housing. If you saw one Soviet city, you had seen them all.

The most peculiar Soviet cities were the ones shaped by the massive defense-industrial complex (known by the acronym VPK, for *voyenno-promyshlennyy kompleks*); see table 6-1. Nearly every one of the big Urals and Siberian cities was primarily a VPK city—a status that dictated their remote locations. This remoteness in turn contributed to their eventual "nonconnectedness." These cities were also notably few in number and distinctly large—for reasons, once again, proceeding from their administrative, noneconomic function. Defense industries were concentrated not because it was efficient to have many defense plants close to one another to save costs in shipping from supplier to client, and so on; and not even because they came under the jurisdiction of the same ministry. Rather, the main reason appears to have been that once a city was designated as a defense city, it was subject to a special security and political regime. This was a costly insti-

Agitprop is the Russian acronym for the Agitation and Propaganda Section [*otdel agitatsii i propagandy*] of the Communist Party apparatus from 1920 to 1934. Those sections were responsible for working out policies for all aspects of domestic and foreign propaganda, conducting activities to win mass support for party policies ("agitation"), and organizing cultural activity.

Table 6-1. *Top Russian Defense Industrial (VPK) Cities, Late 1980s*
Thousands, unless otherwise indicated

Number of defense industry employees				
Absolute numbers	As percentage of total civilian labor force	City	Population, 1989	Population rank (among all cities)
>300	10–15	St. Petersburg (Leningrad)	5,024	2
200–250	5–10	Moscow	8,972	1
	20–30	Nizhniy Novgorod	1,438	3
150–200	25–35	Kazan'	1,094	9
	25–35	Perm'	1,091	10
	20–30	Novosibirsk	1,437	4
	20–30	Yekaterinburg (Sverdlovsk)	1,365	5
	20–30	Samara (Kuybyshev)	1,254	6
100–150	30–40	Izhevsk	635	17
	30–40	Tula	540	29
	20–30	Voronezh	887	16
	15–25	Ufa	1,078	11
50–100	10–20	Omsk	1,148	7
	10–20	Chelyabinsk	1,142	8
	10–20	Rostov-na-Donu	1,019	12
	10–20	Krasnoyarsk	913	14
	10–20	Saratov	905	15

Source: Clifford G. Gaddy, *The Price of the Past: Russia's Struggle with the Legacy of a Militarized Economy* (Brookings, 1996), table 9-4.

tutional arrangement, even if the cost was not measured in money. The scarce resource was reliable and competent political leaders—the regional first secretaries. Once a VPK city was designated, the more efficient use of that scarce resource (the personnel) was to place a new defense industry there rather than to set up the corresponding infrastructure in a city that had previously not hosted a defense plant. There was an "economy of scale" in the security realm. In the planners' minds, there was possibly also the logic of keeping all these provincial cities roughly the same size in order to reduce their potential political weight within the Russian Federation. There should be no rival to the political center, Moscow.[15]

Moving beyond cities, the Soviets also divided the territory of the USSR into administrative units. Just as in the tsarist era, these had little relevance to economic linkages and everything to do with the needs of the centralized state (although they did have some relationship to the historic incorporation into the Russian Empire of territories with different, non-Russian, ethnic groups). The USSR was split into fifteen national "union republics," including the Russian Federation.* And the Russian Federation itself was further subdivided into a complex descending hierarchy of republics, *krays*, *oblasts*, and *okrugs* with their own designated "capital." The Russian Federation became an unwieldy patchwork of eighty-nine regions (or "subjects of the federation"), each with different status and privileges depending on its place in the hierarchy.[16]

In many respects, the administrative nature of cities and regional entities aside, the Soviet system was quite effective in creating social connections across the territory of the USSR. The homogeneity of state symbols, political institutions, education, physical structures, household goods, forms of entertainment, and language, among other things, across the Russian Federation and the Soviet Union, engendered a sense of shared experience and of belonging to a common, unified Soviet state. Social connections were enhanced through common participation and service in institutions like the youth organizations of the "pioneers" and the Komsomol, in subbotniks,† and universal conscription for all Soviet males into the armed services. With the collapse of the USSR and the demise of the CPSU, however, the system lost its discipline and cohesion. The social connections of the Soviet era were eroded, beyond the most personal networks. Today, although the vertical links between the state and the population are still there, the common bonds of citizenship—of participating in a single, homogeneous entity of institutions—have ruptured as diversity has burst in. Although the Russian population is still in its Soviet-era locations, in the same cities, towns, and villages, the horizontal local community and regional social and political (as well as physical and economic) connections are missing. In large part this is because the Soviet system never allowed them to develop or actively prevented them from developing.

---

* The other fourteen union republics are today the independent states of Armenia, Azerbaijan, Belarus, Estonia, Georgia, Kazakhstan, Kyrgyzstan, Latvia, Lithuania, Moldova, Tajikistan, Turkmenistan, Ukraine, and Uzbekistan.
† Subbotniks were days of voluntary labor service performed on a Saturday (*subbota*); tasks might include cleaning up in a city district or picking vegetables on a collective farm.

New Post-Soviet Connections—Rearranging the Federation

The lack of horizontal connections has left post-Soviet Russian governments with the dual dilemma of how to create effective governance on a federation-wide scale and how to devolve authority to regional and local governments. Local governments have only a vertical political relationship with the state, are physically disconnected from one another, and have no experience of self-management. Most important, without the Soviet system their regions and municipalities have no economic basis for existence and no natural connections. Since the 1990s, the Russian government has, in essence, attempted to create a democratic system of governance and a free-market economy across a state with an unfree distribution of population, with predictably complicated results.

In these attempts the government has focused primarily on strengthening the vertical relationship between regions and the state rather than on trying to encourage the development of horizontal relations among regions. This is in large part because early efforts to promote democratic governance and regional autonomy in Russia in the 1990s were eventually seen among the Russian political elite in Moscow to have done nothing more than erode the vertical relationships within the federation and result in political and economic disorder. They were also seen to raise the possibility that the Russian Federation would follow the Soviet Union down the path to dissolution. This was especially the case after Chechnya's declaration of independence at the end of December 1991 and after signs of dissent emerged in other national republics.[17]

Fears of disintegration were heightened in February 1992, when a federal treaty designed to create a new agreement on power sharing and fiscal authority between the federal center and its eighty-nine administrative units was rejected by both Chechnya and Tatarstan and criticized by republics such as Sakha (Yakutiya) and Bashkortostan.[18] Russia's oblasts, the basic nonnational administrative units, subsequently protested what they saw as the special privileges accorded to the federation's national republics in the treaty. They demanded equal treatment, including increased authority over local economic and political issues. After the federal treaty, the 1993 Russian constitution marked a further attempt at delimiting powers between the center and the regions. The chapters dealing with the respective authorities of the federation and the administrative units were submitted to the republics and regions for approval in a referendum in December 1993. But a number of republics that had initially signed the federal treaty now rejected the constitutional provisions on the basis that they violated the original provisions of the treaty. In the wake of these rejections, and to prevent its relations with the regions from falling into legal limbo, Moscow began to conclude bilateral treaties with key republics.

The first of these treaties on "Delimitation and Delegation of Authority" was signed between the federal government in Moscow and Tatarstan in February 1994. It set off a flurry of other bilateral treaties with key regions, including Sakha (Yakutiya), the heart of Russia's diamond industry; Bashkortostan, a major oil-producing republic; republics neighboring Chechnya in the North Caucasus; and regions such as Perm', Irkutsk, Kaliningrad, Yekaterinburg, Nizhniy Novgorod, St. Petersburg, and the Leningrad oblast.[19] By 1998 the Russian federal government had concluded treaties with more than half of the individual subjects of the federation. The last such agreement, signed on June 16, 1998, was with the city of Moscow itself.[20]

Although many of the special provisions of these treaties were never really implemented or honored by the federal center, Russia's regions did try to take matters into their own hands. They proceeded to initiate and implement legislation that was at odds with federal law. They adopted protectionist economic policies, levied tariffs on goods from other regions crossing their territory, and refused to remit tax revenues to the central government. Individual regions also independently developed new communications infrastructure with little thought as to how it would connect to broader systems or could be coordinated with efforts in neighboring territories. A typical result was a new road in one region that ended abruptly when it reached the border with another region.[21]

In addition, regional leaders became separate centers of authority in their own right, often challenging the president and government on policy decisions. Perhaps the most notorious example of this was Yevgeniy Nazdratenko, the governor of Primorsk kray in the Russian Far East. Nazdratenko constructed a virtual fiefdom around himself with deft and blatant use of patronage and favors. He defied the attempts of President Boris Yeltsin to rein him in and then engaged in a protracted power struggle with Vladimir Putin soon after Putin became president. With flagrant disregard for the central government's attempts to reform the Russian power sector and introduce market pricing for regional utilities, Nazdratenko insisted on keeping electricity prices below cost for consumers in the region. He thereby sparked a major energy crisis during the winter of 2001, when utility companies cut off power to households and public buildings, including schools and hospitals. The federal government responded by dispersing emergency funds, which were promptly diverted and embezzled by regional officials, seemingly with Nazdratenko's tacit encouragement, triggering a further crisis. Putin eventually succeeded in forcing the governor's resignation (moving him temporarily to a "holding position" in the Russian fisheries ministry), but not without a great deal of effort and public excoriation, which transfixed the Russian press and Russia analysts for several months.[22]

By the end of the 1990s, the government in Moscow had already concluded that the federation's subjects had been afforded too much power (from the government's perspective at least). The regions were in danger of becoming individual strongholds, increasingly disassociated from the center as well as from one another. As geographer Grigory Ioffe and his colleagues noted, the "systematic attempts of regional authorities to fence off their respective areas from the rest of the country" simply exacerbated the already acute fragmentation of Russia.[23]

In the eyes of Russian government leaders, however, the underlying problem was not the spatial misallocation of Russia's population and its consequent economic "disconnectedness." It was, they insisted, an inefficient and "irrational" system of territorial administration left over from the Soviet period. The consensus in Moscow was that people were fine where they were (this was never questioned), but the Russian Federation's "subjects," its constituent administrative units (the lines of jurisdiction on the map), were irrationally divided up and thus disorganized rather than organized. They were too numerous to manage and coordinate effectively from the center. They were too small (with an average population of less than two million) to be self-sufficient and too asymmetrical to facilitate a rational and streamlined system of federal governance. The fact that—thanks to the vagaries of the Soviet administrative hierarchy—tiny territorial units and those with large territories but minuscule populations enjoyed status and privileges similar to larger or more populous regions was a particular problem. More uniformity, Russian leaders believed, would provide the basis for administrative efficiency.

Putin's Federal Districts

Throughout the 1990s (and even before the actual dissolution of the USSR), a debate raged among elites in Moscow over how to contract and consolidate subjects into fewer, larger units. One of the earliest suggestions, by Russian constitutional scholar Oleg Rumyantsev, was to reorganize the federation into twenty new administrative units. These would be based on the model of Germany's historic, semi-autonomous provinces, or *Länder*—even though there was nothing particularly historic or even rational, from an economic point of view, about most of Russia's administrative units. President Boris Yeltsin also proposed the creation of eight to ten new regions as part of his election platform in 1990.[24] In contrast, regional leaders outside Moscow, such as President Mintimer Shaymiyev of Tatarstan, pushed for a bottom-up approach to federal governance, giving the existing regions even more economic and political autonomy from the center rather than reorganizing their administration. In addition, in the 1990s, regional leaders created eight interregional economic associations, some with overlapping membership, to try to stimulate the missing horizontal connections between regions and to promote trade and economic growth.[25]

The conclusion that the vertical axis of the administrative system was broken and needed to be fixed was a major factor in compelling Vladimir Putin to tackle the issue of territorial-administrative reorganization as one of his first initiatives after being elected president in March 2000. In May 2000, Putin created seven federal districts (*federal'nyye okruga*), or superregions, each bringing together roughly a dozen regions, and each headed by a presidentially appointed "plenipotentiary representative" (*polnomochnyy predstavitel'*, or polpred). The seven designated capitals of the federal districts were intended to become real regional centers for the subordinate territories. Within the districts, the polpreds were made responsible for ensuring that the regional leaders complied with federal laws and budgetary policies, for developing and implementing programs for social and economic development, and for collecting statistical and economic data from all the regions for the central government.[26] Putin's explicit intentions were to rationalize the system, increase administrative efficiency, restore and strengthen the "vertical of power" (*vertikal' vlasti*)—or the administrative connections between the center and the regions—and to rein in the regions and their leaders politically and economically.[27] Putin's new federal districts and the polpreds were all variations on old themes. Once again, the creation of the districts in 2000 represented an attempt to impose order and rationality on an inherently irrational system through an administrative fiat that took its cue from the needs of the center rather than from conditions in the regions. As table 6-2 shows, the new federal districts still vary in size of territory and population. However, they are much more uniform than the underlying regions.[28]

Despite the passage of centuries, the great upheavals in its history, and frequent attempts at territorial division and reorganization, Russia has tended to keep the same patterns of administration from the imperial period through the Soviet era to the present day. The motivation for these policies has been largely the same: to control people's location and to mobi-

Table 6-2. *Russia's Federal Districts, 2002*

Federal district	Capital[a]	Number of regions contained	Territory (000 km²)	Population (thousands)
Central	Moscow	18	651	37,991
Northwestern	St. Petersburg	11	1,678	13,986
Southern	Rostov-na-Donu	13	589	22,914
Volga	Nizhniy Novgorod	15	1,038	31,158
Ural	Yekaterinburg	6	1,789	12,382
Siberian	Novosibirsk	16	5,115	20,064
Far Eastern	Khabarovsk	10	6,216	6,687

Source: Population data are preliminary 2002 census results as reported in *Interfax Statistical Report*, no. 18 (2003). All other information from *Rossiyskiy statisticheskiy yezhegodnik* (Moscow: Goskomstat Rossii, 2001), pp. 40–43.

a. Seat of presidential representative [polpred].

lize them for taxation and other state purposes. In July 2002, for example, in a step reminiscent of Catherine the Great's attempts to consolidate rural settlements and establish criteria for villages, the Russian government announced that it was considering merging several rural and urban populations of fewer than 1,000 people to create larger administrative units for the purpose of introducing systems of local self-government.[29] Analysts of Putin's administrative reforms have also noted other continuities. The seven new federal districts are intended not only to promote economic development and good governance, but also, as in the past, to streamline the relationship between the center, the military and security forces, and regional elites in preparation for any prospective internal instability or military intervention.[30] Indeed, ever since Peter the Great created Russia's first administrative divisions, Russian and Soviet civil administration has always conformed to the basic military-oriented divisions of the state.

Peter created his *gubernii* to sustain the imperial state's military structures—at a time when between 80 and 85 percent of the state budget was consumed by military expenditures—by establishing rational units for managing conscription as well as ensuring tax collection.[31] The governors of Peter's provinces had close ties with the military. Likewise, Putin's federal districts have considerable overlap with the military districts established in Soviet times.[32] Moreover, five of the seven polpreds appointed in 2000 had backgrounds in the military or security service.[33] With the exception of former Russian prime minister Sergey Kiriyenko, who was appointed to head the Volga Federal District, none of the seven polpreds had administrative experience or expertise in complex political and economic issues. In fact, in a manner similar to the selection of tsarist governors and Communist party secretaries, Putin's polpreds were selected on the basis of their personal connections and loyalty to the president. Appointment of regional governors by the center, rather than their election at the regional level, was the norm in Russia for centuries and has become so again. The tsar appointed the governors in the imperial period, and the Communist Party's central leadership appointed the regional party secretaries as heads of administration in Soviet times. Putin's predecessor, Boris Yeltsin, also appointed presidential representatives and the heads of administration in certain key Russian regions in the 1990s until direct elections were introduced for all high-level posts in the Russian Federation in 1996.[34]

Attempts such as Putin's federal district experiment to reorganize the Russian Federation's administrative structure and thus create more efficient government as well as promote economic competitiveness seem more likely to fail than to succeed in the absence of an organic basis for building connections. Without organic connections there are no natural reasons for linkages among communities and regions. Linkages and cohesion have to be imposed from the outside, from above. Vertical power has to be instituted and strengthened when horizontal connections do not exist. If, however, cities and the hinterland around them made economic sense—if economic motivations had determined where people were located—then rational political ties and administrative structures might be a natural outgrowth. Economic connections are essential for real political connections to develop. They, in turn, make local self-governance possible. Unfortunately for Putin in 2000, he was working with cities and regions that were designated and located by Gosplan, the Soviet central planning agency, not by natural economic forces and the free movement of the population. He was forced to work with what he had. Ultimately, the federal districts created in 2000 are simply another effort to create artificial connections across Russian territory.[35]

In this larger context, only Moscow works as a place and a mechanism for fostering normal connections. It is the exception that proves the rule. Moscow embodies the notion of "the market" in the true sense. It attracts and has attracted people to live and work there on a voluntary basis.[36] It is the connected place in Russia as well as connector to the outside world. It is also the new frontier in post-Soviet Russia, the place of jobs and opportunity, and an attractive place to be in terms of relative temperature and amenities. In spite of the Soviet-era giant, impersonal housing projects on the outskirts of Moscow and in some of the central areas, Moscow is also a "real" city, with a long history and a sense of communal identity.[37]

Forcing Artificial Connections and Appealing to the Past

Beyond Moscow, in the absence of natural economic connections and with the added burden of inadequate physical connections, the Russian government—like the early Bolshevik and Soviet governments before it—must constantly intervene to bring the economy and the population together to ensure the allocation and provision of essential resources and to promote economic and political interaction. Historically, in the absence of natural economic connections, the government has resorted to forging artificial connections through administrative fiat, ideological exhortation, and co-ercion to mobilize Russia's population and resources for economic and political ends. The allure of such top-down approaches remains strong today. By the end of 2002, Putin had systematically restored a number of old Soviet-era symbols of significance for different social groups and insti-tutions—including the Soviet anthem and the red star (the symbol of the Soviet Red Army)—to emphasize the state's solidarity with important seg-ments of Russian society and to boost public morale.[38] The Kremlin had also flirted with the shades of a leadership cult as another method of mobi-lization. This was manifested (if not entirely managed by the Kremlin) in the publication of a series of popular books about Putin's life, the creation of a youth movement, "*Idushchiye vmeste*," inspired by the president, a number of mass outdoor events such as rock concerts to rally youth behind the government, and the encouragement of a pop song—"I Want a Man Like Putin" [*Takogo kak Putin*] by an all-girl group—praising Putin as the ideal "boyfriend." Other oddities included the naming of cafes and food-stuffs, including a new variety of tomato, after the president.[39]

Such popular appeals are unlikely to enhance the vertical connections between the state and the population. Nor can they substitute for the miss-ing horizontal connections among the population itself across Russia's vast space. Instead, they form part of a long line of attempts to galvanize into action a disconnected economic, political, and social system. Instead of con-tinually appealing to the past and resurrecting its symbols to create artificial connections between the state and its citizens, the only solution to Russia's current predicament is somehow to undo the past, to roll it back. This means migration, shrinkage, and reconnection. As we will see in the next chapter, very little of this was achieved in the 1990s.

7

Taking Stock: How Much Has Changed?

Since the collapse of the USSR, migration, economic development, and technological advancement have not dramatically changed the population profile of the Russian Federation. In spite of targeted programs to move people from some of the most remote and marginal regions in the so-called northern territories, migrants have, for the most part, simply relocated elsewhere in the Urals and Siberia. New means of communication, such as the Internet, have also done little to create new connections or shrink the distance between population centers.

Many observers of Russia (both in the West and in Russia itself) argue that, in fact, over the past decade Russia *has* begun to self-correct and to address and redress the misallocations of the Soviet past. This, they say, has taken place in three key areas. First, there is increasing migration, specifically from the areas in the Russian Far East and the North that were most overemphasized in Soviet planning. Second, new communications technologies have been developed.

Third, economic growth has taken place in European Russia, and specifically in Moscow.

On the first point, some analysts have described how in the 1990s the transition to a market economy started to change Russia's economic geography, as Russians began to move from areas in the North and the Far East toward the south and west (European Russia). "The eastern regions of Russia are emptying out," and everyone is heading west.[1] Freed from the strictures of the Soviet era, Russians are voting with their feet and moving closer to Europe and warmer climes and thus reconcentrating and reconnecting. Many of these analysts identify the North as the real problem area for Russia—in its climate, its remoteness, and the consequent depth of its economic crisis. This is the most extreme of the extremes, and here, too, there has been positive change—people moving away. The total population of the area designated by the World Bank as the Russian North decreased by more than 14 percent between the censuses of 1989 and 2002. Eight of the fifteen northern regions lost more than 20 percent of their population, and two—Magadan and Chukotka—lost a staggering 53 percent and 66 percent, respectively (see table C-1 in appendix C.).[2] In November 2001, the Russian Ministry of Federal Affairs and Nationalities and Migration Policy reported that more than one million people had left northern regions (more loosely defined) since 1991.[3]

On the second point, Russian observers argue that while people are on the move in Russia and the North is shedding its population, new technologies are shrinking distance for those who remain in Siberia and the Russian Far East. The electrification of the Trans-Siberian Railway (completed in 2002), the expansion of regional airline routes with the deregulation of the Russian airline industry, and telecommunication breakthroughs—including the spread of personal computers, the Internet, and cellular phones—have all transformed the Russian Federation in the 1990s. They have brought Russians into closer and faster communication with one another as well as with the outside world. In an August 2001 article, recounting a trip through Siberia, for example, Washington Post senior correspondent Robert Kaiser noted the presence of cyber cafes in most of the places he visited. "Thanks to the Internet," he asserted, "Siberians are fully part of the modern world, no longer cut off from European Russian and foreign countries, as they were for nearly four centuries. Now they are plugged into information sources all over the world. . . . Siberians no longer feel stuck in a forgotten corner of the globe."[4]

Finally, many people see the undoubted and dramatic transformation of Russia's capital, Moscow, as the indicator of economic growth and improvement in European Russia. It points the way forward for the ultimate transformation of the rest of European Russia, if not for the Russian Federation

120   TAKING STOCK

as a whole. Moscow has become the major center of growth in the service sector and the "new economy" in Russia and has thus attracted the bulk of foreign direct investment. Moscow's relatively booming economy has also, since 1993, attracted the majority of internal migrants. Today Moscow is Russia's migration magnet, drawing waves of migrants from all over the former Soviet Union. Preliminary data from the 2002 Russian census indicate that the city's population has risen to 10.4 million permanent residents—a figure exceeding previous official government estimates by nearly two million.[5] The census also recorded three million "nonresidents" or unofficial residents in Moscow, bringing the city's total population to 13.4 million.[6] This would put it at around 9 percent of the total population of the Russian Federation.

In short, as a result of this combination of migration, relocation of people from the North, new technologies, and the growth of Moscow in the 1990s, Russia's problems with a dislocated and misplaced population seem to be finally on their way to resolution. Unfortunately, however, on closer scrutiny, not all of these data point in a positive direction. We would argue that Russia is not, in fact, self-correcting as a consequence of the changes that occurred in the 1990s. Change has come slowly and often with dubious results.

Migration in Russia is a complex phenomenon. The problems of the North are extreme, but not unique. The impact of new technologies is debatable. And Moscow, rather than serving as a beacon of development for the rest of Russia, is the exception that proves the rule. Moscow is neither a replicable experience nor capable of being a source of trickle-down benefits to the rest of the country. Instead of lighting a way forward, its growth illuminates the problems of the Russian Federation. Moscow has everything that Russia as a whole does not have (including a concentration of all new technologies and infrastructure). The major question is how the rest of Russia can develop in relation to Moscow.

Russia on the Move?

Migration statistics do show that in the 1990s Russians began to move away from the coldest areas of the Russian Federation and generally to migrate within the country. That is, people relocated and continue to relocate. The Russian government, for example, estimated that in December 2002, 27 million people, or about 20 percent of the Russian population, had changed residence at least once since 1991.[7] However, analysts of Russian migration, like World Bank migration expert Timothy Heleniak, have pointed out that for a country of around 145 million, 27 million people changing their location over a ten-year period is not such a large number.[8] Heleniak also notes that migration in Russia actually peaked in the early to mid-1990s, immediately after the Soviet-era restrictions on migration were lifted with the abolition of the internal passport system in 1993. It has since tapered off quite dramatically.[9]

Beyond the question of whether or not Russians are really becoming mobile, the most important question to ask about migration statistics is not only where people move *from*, but also where they move *to*. The fact that many people would move from the coldest and most marginal areas of the North and the Far East—as soon as the government removed Soviet-era restrictions on migration and ended the massive subsidization that made life bearable—was obvious. But the answers to the questions of where they have moved to—and where they *can* and *will* move to in the future—and *who* actually is moving are much more complicated. This is quite evident in migration and population growth in Russia's southern regions in the 1990s.

Migration to southern Russia, which shows up clearly in Russian government statistics, would seem to indicate a positive development in Russia's economic geography as people move to warmer and potentially more productive places. In fact, the North Caucasus region—part of Russia's Southern Federal District—was one of the major recipient regions for migration in the Russian Federation in the 1990s. However, the growth in population in this region is not unambiguously good news for Russian economic development. It has, in fact, masked some rather negative underlying realities.

Migration from Desperation: The North Caucasus

The North Caucasus region extends across Rostov oblast and Stavropol and Krasnodar krays. It also encompasses the seven autonomous republics of Dagestan, Chechnya, Ingushetiya, North Ossetiya, Kabardino-Balkariya, Karachayevo-Cherkessiya, and Adygeya. The region accounts for about 2 percent of the territory of the Russian Federation and in 1989 had a population of 13,183,860, or about 8 percent of the Russian population. The North Caucasus could qualify as Russia's "sunbelt." Its winters are especially mild (ranging from +2° C in January in Sochi to –6° C in the city of Rostov-na-Donu), and it is home to some of Russia's premier holiday destinations, like the coastal resort of Sochi and the spa towns of Kislovodsk and Pyatigorsk. But it is hardly a "boom region" economically.[10] The North Caucasus is predominantly agrarian with an emphasis on food processing and agricultural machinery manufacturing. In the early 1990s, it accounted for almost one-quarter of Russia's agricultural output.[11] While there has been some growth in private-sector industries related to the transit and shipping of goods—including oil and petroleum products through the region's Caspian and Black Sea ports—the North Caucasus is, in fact, a region in social and economic distress rather than one enjoying economic growth or political consolidation.[12]

In the Soviet period, the North Caucasus was heavily dependent on Moscow for subsidies. Since the dissolution of the USSR, it has been riven by interethnic conflict and social dislocation: two wars in Chechnya since 1994, war in 1992 between Ingushetiya and North Ossetiya, and simmering tensions in other ethnically divided regions.[13] Ethnic Russians and others have fled the autonomous republics—especially Chechnya, Ingushetiya, and Dagestan—for Krasnodar and Stavropol krays. There has also been an influx of refugees from conflicts in other former Soviet states, including Armenia, Azerbaijan, Georgia, and Tajikistan. In fact, most of the migration into the North Caucasus can be accounted for by economic migrants or "forced migrants" from the South Caucasus and Central Asia. Migration into this region comes mostly from *outside* Russia, not within. It is not the result of Russians' relocating from cold and distant places in the North and the Russian Far East.

Migration into the North Caucasus is reminiscent of Haitian and much Central American immigration into the United States. Migrants have come to the North Caucasus region out of desperation, fleeing a far worse economic and political situation in a nearby region. The weather and the nature of the land in the North Caucasus are significant factors in shaping migration decisions. The mild climate of the region is more conducive to human survival, and the availability of agricultural land with a relatively long growing season makes it easier to eke out an existence through subsistence farming. Many migrants are attracted by the opportunity to obtain small plots of land.[14] They are also able to find basic accommodation like barns or abandoned buildings. While such dwellings would not meet the simple survival test of a harsh winter farther north or east, they are adequate for the warmer winter temperatures in the North Caucasus.

By 1998 the population of the North Caucasus region had increased by more than four million to 17,707,000 people—now equivalent to about 12 percent of the population of the Russian Federation—making it one of the most densely populated regions of the Russian Federation.[15] In some part, this increase in population was due to a high rate of natural increase of population in some of the autonomous republics with predominantly non-Russian populations. But the bulk of growth was most certainly due to migration.[16] In 1998, for example, the North Caucasus received 248,000 migrants, with many of these migrants settling in rural areas rather than in towns and cities, because of the prospects for seasonal labor and menial jobs on regional farms. In fact, the rural population of the region increased to almost 45 percent in

1998 from 43 percent in 1989. Such a shift in population distribution from urban to rural runs entirely contrary to migration patterns in other modern societies and underscores the point that urban areas in the region are not generating a sufficient number of new jobs to accommodate new migrants.[17]

Indeed, many of the migrants moving to the North Caucasus in the 1990s were also urban dwellers displaced from other settings and taking up more primitive occupations in rural areas. Rather than representing the movement of elites or urban professionals in search of closer connections to the market, migration to the North Caucasus has taken a more primitive form. It is more reminiscent of the tsarist-era flight of peasants from pressures at the center in search of land than of twenty-first-century patterns of migration from rural to urban areas.

Furthermore, in the North Caucasus, migration has increased the social and economic strains on one of the most fragile regions of the Russian Federation. It has not boosted the region's productivity. On all economic indices in 1998, for example, including per capita incomes, average wages, purchasing power, and unemployment, inhabitants of the constituent parts of the North Caucasus fell well behind the Russian national average. There was also a notable increase in poverty rates over the course of the 1990s.[18]

"Emptying Out" the North

Concerning the North and migration, there is an equal degree of ambiguity and complexity. However, the idea that Russia's problems will be solved by simply relocating population from the most remote settlements in the northern territories and the Far East to other places within the broader region east of the Urals has been enshrined in Russian government policy. It also tends to shape international thinking about the issue of reconnecting Russia. This thinking has been bolstered by the fact that the North is a vast place geographically but has a relatively small population, and certainly faces a range of difficult economic circumstances.

The North is something of a variable construct in Russia (see appendix C for amplification). Statistics on the North often cover different sets of regions at different times and for different purposes. In Soviet planning literature, more than 60 percent of the territory of the Russian Federation from the Barents Sea in the west to the Bering Sea in the east was actually classified as the Far North. According to the World Bank's definition of the North, which we use in this book, in 1989, 6.7 percent of the Russian population lived within the confines of the North.[19] This is a small percentage of population given the size of the territory, but it is also extremely *large* compared with the 1 percent of population living in similar areas in western countries with significant land above the Arctic Circle.

Initial settlements in the North were created in the 1930s (see chapter 5) in response to the perceived size and value of the region's physical assets—its rich and often rare mineral reserves.[20] Like most mining and extractive industries in the Soviet period, the resources of the Russian North were first exploited using forced labor and the GULAG system. The North later became a major destination and priority area for migrant labor in the 1970s and 1980s on the basis of the huge construction projects and industries planned there. Today, however, the North is an especially "disconnected" place, even for Russia. There are few roads and railways to provide connections between settlements or between the North and the rest of Russia, apart from those built by GULAG inmates to serve the region's mines and factories. Most supplies must be flown in from European Russia or brought in by ship or barge along the region's river system. Basic communications are made even more problematic by the fact that sixty thousand settlements in the North have no phone lines at all.[21] In fact, Russia's current litmus test for a territory's official classification as part of the broadly defined North is: *partial to complete inaccessibility for 180 days or more per year.*[22]

According to Konstantin Dotsenko, acting head of the Economic Development and Trade Ministry's department for the North in 2000, this definition generally encompasses any area without a railroad.[23] In areas of the North where settlements can be reached only by river transportation (or, of course, by helicopter), inaccessibility may also be complete for most of the year. The Taymyr autonomous region above the Arctic Circle in Krasnoyarsk kray is an example of this inaccessibility. The chief economist of the Taymyr region, Viktoriya Morozova, noted in 2000 that some settlements are only accessible one or two weeks of the year when water levels of the Siberian rivers are high enough for navigation.[24] In other areas of the North, such as Magadan, high water has brought unique problems for residents.

In March 2001, rising ground waters forced residents of one subsection of the Magadan metropolitan area to evacuate their homes. According to a report from the Russian news agency ITAR-TASS, ground waters had gushed to the surface, enveloping the district's houses and transforming them into ice blocks. The Russian journalist's account paints a vivid picture of the extraordinary measures city officials had to take to combat the ice invasion:

A number of houses in the settlement Snezhny, Magadan region now look like huge blocks of ice. Ice is even filling some rooms in the houses up to the ceiling. The ground waters keep rising to the surface. Their flows envelop houses and turn to ice, transforming human dwellings into ice houses. . . . The city mayor has ordered temporary resettlement of the inhabitants of the ice houses to hostels and unoccupied apartments in the city regardless of their ownership. . . . Bulldozers have been rolled out to crash ice onto the streets but more water keeps coming to turn the settlement into a huge ice town.[25]

Russian regions officially classified as "northern" by the Russian government today qualify for federal subsidies. These come in the form of fuel and food deliveries during the winter months, which are supervised by the State Committee for the Northern Territories. Russian sources assert that each resident of the North costs the Russian state four times as much in subsidies as a "regular citizen" living in European Russia.[26] Nevertheless, federal subsidies for the so-called northern deliveries are also seen as inadequate to the needs of the North. In 2001 Valentina Pivnenko, chair of the Russian Duma Committee on Problems of the North and Far East, assessed the cost of the northern deliveries at $685 million, but federal budgetary outlays fell far short of that figure, totaling only about $224 million.[27] This imposes considerable strain on meager regional budgets. In Taymyr, as just one illustration, Morozova, the chief economist, estimated in 2000 that the region had to use its own funds to cover as much as 60 percent of the costs of its winter fuel and food deliveries.[28] Bridging the shortfall between federal government subsidies and actual costs has led to some creative and desperate measures by regional authorities. In 2002, for example, officials in the Siberian city of Irkutsk, facing the prospect of trying to meet the mounting costs of winter fuel, began to sell state-held stakes in local businesses to Russian energy suppliers in return for forgiveness of fuel debts.[29]

To sort through all the various and often conflicting estimates of spending on the North, in 1998 World Bank staff attempted a calculation of the total extra costs incurred by the Russian public finance system in supporting the Far North compared with the rest of Russia. They included both explicit expenditures (expenditures by both regional and federal budgets and by so-called extrabudgetary funds) and implicit expenditures in the form of various tax and other arrears. The bottom line was that Russia was spending a staggering 2–3 percent of its GDP per year during the period 1995–97 to support the population of the North.[30]

As fuel debts have mounted, food has become prohibitively expensive in the Russian North. In August 2002, while the average monthly cost of a minimum basket of foodstuffs in Russia was reported to have actually fallen in some regions of European Russia—and stood at 955 rubles for the country as a whole—it peaked in the most marginal regions of the northern territories and the Russian Far East. In Anadyr in Chukotka, foodstuffs were more expensive than anywhere else in the Russian Federation at 2,823 rubles. Anadyr was followed by Petropavlovsk-Kamchatskiy on the Kamchatka Peninsula (1,762 rubles) and nearby Magadan (1,601 rubles). In contrast, the average food basket in Moscow cost 1,244 rubles and in St. Petersburg, 1,047 rubles.[31] In this respect, the Russian North distinguishes itself from other remote and cold resource regions in the United States, Canada, and Scandinavia. While food costs in a city like Anchorage, Alaska, for example, might be higher than in a large southern U.S. city like Los Angeles—and costs of living in Anchorage and other Alaskan cities may be relatively high in comparison with the United States as a whole—they do not exceed—in fact are considerably less—than the costs in the most expensive of American cities, like New York.[32]

Beyond the problems of covering the costs of annual winter fuel and food deliveries, investment capital for the revitalization of industry and state support for the upkeep of municipal infrastructure in the North is almost completely lacking. According to regional government estimates, for example, in 2001 even the most advanced region of the North—the Barents region in the west, around the port-city of Murmansk—required at least $70 billion just to modernize its outdated industrial stock.[33] Across all the northern territories, housing stock and municipal infrastructure (including gas and water pipelines) were in an advanced state of disrepair. In addition, oil production and other extractive industries dominate the northern economies. There is little activity in manufacturing and little prospect for the stimulation of new industrial development in the most distant regions—especially as production costs in industry run between 20 percent and 30 percent higher than elsewhere in Russia.[34] While Murmansk has benefited from its proximity to Scandinavia, with some degree of foreign investment from Sweden and other countries, other regions of the North that are much farther away from Europe and from European Russia have attracted virtually no foreign investment other than loans from financial institutions like the European Bank for Reconstruction and Development (EBRD).[35] The North has thus seemed to be in particularly desperate straits since the collapse of the USSR and in need of drastic intervention. This came in 2001, in the form of a World Bank program.

The World Bank and "Northern Restructuring"

In June 2001, in response to Russian government appeals to assist it in addressing the problems of the North, the World Bank approved a four-year,

$80 million pilot program.[36] The goal of the program was to help with the resettlement of some of the poorest Russians (especially pensioners and families with young children) living in "nonviable" northern territories as well as with the economic restructuring of the North. The "northern restructuring" project was launched in the summer of 2002, after a year of preparations and some wrangling between the World Bank and the Russian government over its terms. For its initial phase the project leaders selected three towns and cities in regions close to the Arctic Circle: Susuman in Magadan oblast, Noril'sk in the Taymyr autonomous okrug, and Vorkuta in the Komi republic—centers of gold mining, nickel processing, and coal mining, respectively.*

In these regions, the objectives of the program were to offer financial support for those wishing to relocate on a voluntary basis; to finance the demolition of dilapidated housing stock and infrastructure; to aid the local governments in modernizing the management of municipal services for the remaining population; and to assist the federal government in Moscow in deregulating the regional economy. The project provided for the relocation of more than 27,000 people: up to 6,000 people from the Susuman district, up to 15,000 from the city of Noril'sk, and 6,500 from Vorkuta. Those eligible for relocation would receive allowances, including housing certificates for purchasing apartments in other Russian regions, and the costs of train or plane transportation for their families and belongings. Prospective migrants would also be provided with information on relocation opportunities, including housing availability, employment, and social services in potential recipient regions.[37] The recipient regions were not specified in the terms of the pilot program, as people were given the right to choose their destination, but press reports indicated that they would all be on "the mainland" (*materik*).[38] In the parlance of the North, however, the mainland does not refer solely to European Russia, but simply to somewhere more "connected." This could very well be another—but larger—northern or Siberian city, such as Krasnoyarsk, that can be reached by railways, roads, or regular airline routes, and not intermittently by helicopter or ship.

The towns selected in 2001–02 for population relocation in the World Bank program, Susuman, Noril'sk, and Vorkuta, are all good examples of settlements located in places they would never otherwise have been but for the "northern dreams" of Soviet planners (and the nightmares of ordinary Soviet citizens). The settled, industrialized North is the GULAG's ultimate gift to modern Russia, and all three towns and cities are either former labor camps or an agglomeration of camps (see box 7-1).

---

* Although Noril'sk is located in Taymyr, it technically falls under the direct administrative and economic jurisdiction of Krasnoyarsk kray.

Box 7-1. *The North—The GULAG's Gift to Russia*

A handbook produced in 1998 by Russia's Memorial group on the GULAG offers a complete and detailed record of the activity of the camps in the cities of Susuman, Noril'sk, and Vorkuta gleaned from the records of the NKVD, MVD (Ministry of the Interior), and other Soviet government agencies.[a]

Susuman was created in September 1949 as part of the NKVD's notorious *Dal'stroy* construction empire, which was intended to open up the resources of the Russian Far East. The Susuman camp was established to mine a series of gold deposits as well as tin ore, to carry out the necessary construction of processing facilities, and to provide labor for the mines. Closed in December 1956, Susuman had more than 16,000 prisoners/laborers at its peak in 1951.[b]

Noril'sk consisted of a series of labor and construction camps that operated from June 1935 to August 1956. The early numbers of prisoners were small, around 1,200 in October 1935, but swelled to a peak of 72,500 in 1951. The camp construction brigades built the giant Noril'sk Nickel foundry, the city of Noril'sk itself, most of its basic municipal infrastructure, and other small processing factories that served Noril'sk Nickel. Camp labor extracted and processed local resources including gold, cobalt, platinum, and coal; produced cement; and provided the labor pool for a whole range of local industries.[c]

Vorkuta had eleven camps surrounding it at different times. Some were created specifically to mine isolated ore deposits near the Arctic Circle in the 1930s, to construct railway lines, roads and port facilities, and to provide labor for factories. One of the largest camps, created in May 1938 and operating as late as January 1960, mined coal along the Pechora River, processed molybdenum, and constructed roads and housing. It had a peak prison population of almost 73,000 in 1951.[d]

In a 2001 article on the development of Vorkuta, written just after the announcement of the World Bank resettlement and restructuring program, journalist and GULAG historian Anne Applebaum noted: "Although even the

As elsewhere in Siberia and the North, migrants were quick to move away from places like Vorkuta as soon as they were given the opportunity to do so. The World Bank project simply gives this movement an added boost. The question remains, however, Where are people moving to when they leave the remote settlements of the North? Have they, in fact, moved out of the region entirely to warmer, more productive parts of the Russian Federation—is *everyone* really "heading west" as observers have asserted? Unfortunately, although there are some migration statistics that can help to track who moves from where to where, it is impossible to get a complete picture. It is, how-

tsars had known about the region's enormous coal reserves, no one had managed to work out precisely how to get the coal out of the ground, given the sheer horror of life in a place where temperatures regularly drop to –30 or –40 in the winter. . . . But Stalin found a way—by making use of another sort of vast reserve . . . prisoners."[e]

Applebaum further observes that the prisoners' "subsequent existence was maintained only thanks to the Soviet Union's inability to calculate things like 'cost' and 'profit.'" In the 1960s and 1970s, following the closure of the GULAGs, Vorkuta was turned from a labor camp into a typical Soviet city, with a population of 200,000. It was made attractive through the construction of a range of social amenities (kindergartens, sports facilities, museums) and provision of higher wages for those working in the coal mines to compensate for the harsh climate. Nevertheless, seventy years after the arrival of the first prisoners, Vorkuta is now in decline. "Slowly, Vorkuta will contract, and then Vorkuta may well disappear, sinking back into the tundra from where it so recently emerged."[f]

a. M. B. Smirnov, ed., *Sistema ispravitel'no-trudovykh lagerey v SSSR: spravochnik* (Moscow: Zveniya, 1998).

b. See "102. Zapadniy ITL Dal'stroya (Zaplag, Zapadnoye GPU i ITL, Zapadniy ITL USVITLa)," in Smirnov, *Sistema*, p. 224.

c. See "257. Noril'skiy ITL (Noril'lag, Noril'stroy)," in Smirnov, *Sistema*, pp. 338–39.

d. See, for example, "49. Vaygachskaya Ekspeditsiya OGPU (Vaychagskiy OLP)," pp. 179–80; "64. Vorkutunskiy ITL (Vorkuto-Pechorskiy ITL, Vorkutpechlag, Vorkutlag, Vorkutstroy)," pp. 192–93; and "104. Zapolyarniy ITL i stroitel'stvo 301 (Zapolyarlag, Polyarniy ITL)," pp. 225–26, in Smirnov, *Sistema*.

e. Anne Applebaum, "The Great Error: On the Wretched Folk Who Refuse to Leave the City Built on the Bones of Stalin's Victims, Vorkuta," *Spectator* (28 July 2001), pp. 18–19.

f. Ibid.

ever, possible, as in the case of the North Caucasus, to get a glimpse of the profile of migration into a recipient region, which suggests that not many people from the North moved to southern Russia in the 1990s.

TPC and Russian Migration in the 1990s

However, if, indeed, Russians are moving in large numbers to warmer places—even if this is not in southern Russia, but elsewhere in European Russia—then we would expect to see a positive change in the country's population-weighted average temperature, or TPC (see appendix B). The news here is not encouraging. Figure 7-1 shows what has happened with the TPC of Russia's major urban areas. For the ten largest cities, the TPC has barely budged in the ten years since the end of communist rule and central economic planning (in fact, there has been a slight cooling).* While there was a more significant warming of the TPC of the 100 largest cities—from −12.43° to −12.30°—this is, recall, over a ten-year period. It is still far from the rate that would be necessary to truly correct the overall misallocation of Russia's urban population. Furthermore, it is worth noting that the change for the one hundred largest cities was due almost exclusively to a slight downsizing of one single city, Noril'sk. Noril'sk, which happened to be city number 100 on the list through 1995, lost around 3,000 people in 1996 and therefore dropped off the list. That was enough to show up on the chart in figure 7-1. Meanwhile, the other big negative contributors to Russia's TPC—places like Novosibirsk, Omsk, Yekaterinburg, Khabarovsk, and the others listed in table 3-3, for instance—did not downsize relative to the total urban population of Russia.

Most analysts assume that Russian migrants in the 1990s have followed the same trends as in other parts of the world—moving from the "frost belt" (or in this case the "permafrost belt") to the "sunbelt." But, in fact, the evidence from TPC points in a somewhat different direction. Most Russian migrants in the 1990s did not make it as far as the sunbelt. Instead, they moved from the permafrost to the frost belt—in other words, from extremely cold places to other, somewhat less cold places. They moved out of the most remote villages and small towns and cities in the North and the Far East to larger settlements, often in the same region. They also moved to cities in the Urals and western Siberia (the regions that attracted most of the tsarist era migrants from European Russia before Soviet planners began to push people out to the extremes), including cities like Irkutsk, Yakutsk, Krasnoyarsk, Omsk, Novosibirsk, Chelyabinsk, Perm', and Yekaterinburg. Of these cities, however, only Krasnoyarsk experienced steady population growth in this period. Yakutsk fluctuated from growth to decline and back to growth, and the others ended the decade in decline. In most cases, in-migration was still not sufficient to stem the processes of natural population decrease thanks to an aging population.

As discussed earlier, Russia's real problem with the cold climate (with having economic activity in places that are too cold) lies not in the relatively small

---

* The two biggest changes, the drop in 1993 and the rise in 1998, are easy to explain. In 1993 Ufa (January temperature of −13° C) ousted Saratov (−11° C) as number 10 on the list. In 1998 Kazan' (−13° C) replaced Chelyabinsk (−15° C).

Figure 7-1. *Temperature per Capita (TPC) of Major Russian Cities, 1991–2000*

TPC (° C)

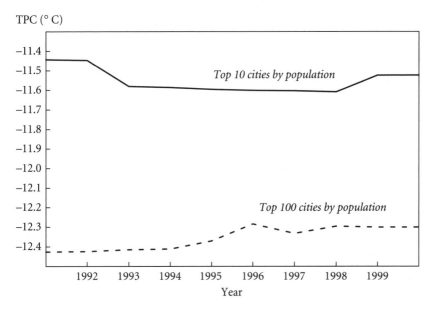

Source: Authors' calculations. See appendix B for definition of TPC.

population and industrial centers of the North, but in the *large cities* of the region and those of western Siberia and the Urals. A relocation of population that produces an influx of migrants from the North to the cities listed above—all major offenders in their negative contributions to Russia's TPC (again, cf. table 3-3, "Who's Responsible for Russia's Coldness?")—does not solve Russia's problems resulting from the "cold." Russia has not really "warmed up" in any appreciable way. Indeed, Krasnoyarsk, the Siberian city that experienced population growth in the 1990s, is one of the top ten offending cities in its negative contribution to TPC, with an average January temperature of –17° C.

In addition, the problems faced by the northern territories are reflected across the whole of the region east of the Urals. The North is not unique, as many have claimed. Its problems of cold, remoteness, and economic decline are by no means exclusive, just more extreme. Central and regional government statistics paint an increasingly bleak picture of Siberia as a whole, as mines have closed, industries have shed workers, and uncontrolled retail prices have contributed to increased costs of living. Unemployment has soared in Siberia—increasing by more than 38 percent, for example, in the first half of 2002 over the same period in 2001—with some regions such as

Chita east of Lake Baykal and Tuva on the border with Mongolia particularly hard hit.[39] To make matters worse, in July 2002, Russia's fledgling Green Party came out with a list of Russia's most polluted cities: Kemerovo, Magnitogorsk, Novokuznetsk, Omsk, Cherepovets, and Khabarovsk.[40] With a sole exception (Cherepovets), all are industrial centers in, or notably east of, the Ural Mountains. Migration and population shifts within this region will do little to relieve the pressure on services or the environment or to increase its productivity.

In sum, the changes in TPC since 1991 indicate that although Russia is "warming up," it is doing so only extremely slowly—in part because of the places that Russians move *to*. Although there was a small warming of Russia due to migration in the first half of the 1990s, the time of the most dramatic phase of out-migration from the North and Far East, the warming rate has slowed remarkably since then. At current rates, it would take more than one hundred years for Russia's TPC to get back to where it was in 1926—before the Soviets' forced exodus from European Russia to and across the Ural Mountains began.

Shrinking Distance through New Infrastructure?

Unfortunately, there has also not been a great deal of progress in shrinking the physical distance between cities in the 1990s. Although the decade did see a boom in construction and infrastructure development, much of the construction was more regionally focused than transregional in nature. And, as we have already noted, shrinking distance and reconnecting the Russian economy is not simply a question of upgrading infrastructure, but also of reconcentrating population.

Regional airlines, such as Siberia Airlines, have emerged to meet the growing demand for faster connections between European Russia (mainly Moscow) and the country's scattered cities east of the Ural Mountains. During its peak summer season, Siberia Airlines, for example, offers three hundred flights to fifty different destinations per week.[41] In December 2002, the Trans-Siberian Railway also finally became fully electrified, thus completing a seventy-four-year-old project to allow electric-powered (and therefore faster) trains to run the entire line.[42] In addition, in 2002 the Russian government announced the projected completion of a highway from St. Petersburg to Vladivostok in 2004 that will allow trucks to transport cargo across Russia in about ten days.[43] Several Russian regions have also seen some growth in housing construction, although this sector has experienced numerous fluctuations throughout the decade stemming from Russia's economic situation and fed-

Figure 7-2. *Housing Construction in Russia, 1970–2002*

Thousands of square meters

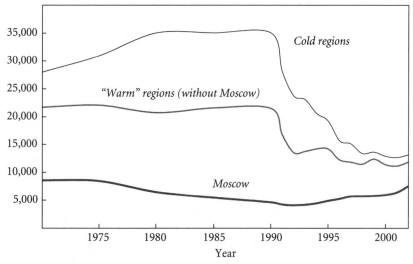

Source: Data on housing completions in 1970-2000 from *Rossiyskiy statisticheskiy yezhegodnik, 2001*, pp. 441–42; in 2001 from *Interfax Statistical Report*, no. 7 (2002); in 2002 from *Interfax Statistical Report*, no. 7 (2003).

a. Cold regions are those whose TPC is colder, and warm regions those whose TPC is warmer, than the Russian national TPC.

eral funding for construction.[44] The vast majority of this housing growth, however, is concentrated in Moscow (see figure 7-2).

Moscow has also commissioned a third ring road to be built around the city at a cost of nearly $100 million per kilometer.[45] Likewise, the construction of a new ring road in St. Petersburg was launched in 2003 to coincide with the three-hundred-year anniversary of the city.[46] Construction has been completed on two new Moscow metro stations, and other new stations are under way both above and below ground.[47] Similarly, Omsk, Chelyabinsk, Krasnoyarsk, Ufa, and Kazan' have all broken ground on new city subway systems of their own.[48] All of these developments, however, have done little to reconnect Russia, even though some of them may have improved communications or the prospects for migrants' finding housing in some cities. Especially in the North, even large cities like Noril'sk are still served only by airlines (or ships in the summer). They have no railways or major highways linking them to the rest of the country, while airline tickets remain prohibitively expensive for most people in remote cities.

Russian geographers and economists continue to see Russia's main economic problems today as linked to the distance between the country's main urban areas and the paucity of communications infrastructure among them. In the words of Grigory Ioffe and a team of Russian scholars writing at the end of the 1990s, Russia is a "fragmented space." Its territory "comes to resemble an archipelago: scattered pockets of intensive land use and vibrant economic life in a sea of social stagnation and decay."[49] Ioffe and his colleagues describe how "the sheer size of the country, its uneven population distribution . . . and high 'friction' of distance due to a low rate of private car ownership and an inadequate road system reinforce the mutual separation of population clusters and enhance their potential to develop differently and to remain different from one another."[50] Cities in Russia, they argue, are "oases in rural vastness"; they are largely unable to extend their influence and services into the space between urban centers or to act as centers of gravity and transmitters of goods, services, and information for the country as a whole.[51] Across the Russian Federation, the hinterlands or zones of immediate influence around towns and cities tend to be small. Even 150 kilometers from the largest cities of Moscow and St. Petersburg, there is "a sense of remoteness" and "the perception of living in the middle of nowhere [which] belies the actual proximity to those population centers."[52] Ioffe claims that the territory that finds itself cut off from communication with a population center, or "torn apart by distance," accounts for two-thirds, or ten million square kilometers, of the Russian Federation.[53]

Shrinking Distance through New Technologies?

In the absence of physical highways and new rail and air routes, the development of the information superhighway in the 1990s has generated great expectations in Russia. Many see new communications technologies and the Internet as the means of reconnecting Russia internally and with the outside world. However, like the development of physical infrastructure and the Russian construction boom in the 1990s, most of these new technologies have simply served to enhance the position of Moscow as the ultimate connector within the Russian Federation rather than to connect Russia's scattered cities.

Cellular phone use did rise dramatically in Russia in the 1990s, helping overcome the limitations of the country's decrepit land-line system. But the new communications network extends only to major cities, mainly in European Russia. While Moscow and its surrounding area are saturated with cellular providers, the regions beyond the Urals have very limited coverage. In fact, cell phones are displacing land-lines to the disadvantage of the majority of the population. Wealthier segments of the population, and wealthier regions, benefit as a traditional public-sector service is neglected.[54] According to the website of MTS, one of Russia's largest cell-phone service providers, using a phone in the Yekaterinburg, Novosibirsk, Omsk, and Rostov oblasts, in the Altay region, in Krasnodar and Khabarovsk krays, and in the republics of Adygeya and North Ossetiya-Alaniya (both in the North Caucasus) requires activating their international roaming service, as well as the national roaming service.

In addition, while computer use expanded from an almost negligible percentage of the Russian population in 1991 to around 25 percent of the population in 2001, the reach and impact of information and communication technology in Russia remained limited in 2000–2002.[55] For the most part, this was the result of a lack of telecommunications infrastructure, as well as of a particularly low number of personal computers, four per one hundred inhabitants. In spite of a rapid rate of growth over previous years, Internet use also remained relatively low: just over 4.3 million regular (as opposed to occasional) users in early 2002.[56] It too was a phenomenon of major cities—with inhabitants of Moscow and then St. Petersburg dominating access.[57] Outside the home there were few Internet access outlets available to the public, apart from cyber cafes and some post offices. Of Russia's 40,000 post offices, however, only 2,200 offered Internet access in 2002, and during a Russian government survey in September 2002, only a total of 240,000 people actually accessed the Internet at these post offices (not even 0.2 percent of the Russian population). Only a handful of these post offices with Internet access were outside big cities or in rural areas.[58] Beyond post offices and cyber cafes in many Russian towns and cities, would-be Internet users in Russia largely logged on at their places of work, as well as at universities and schools.[59] In short, ten years after the collapse of the Soviet Union, although there has obviously been considerable progress, Russia is still waiting to become electronically connected across cyberspace as well as connected across physical space.

Stemming Migration through Technology

One of the main arguments in favor of promoting these cyber and electronic connections in Russia has been that this will allegedly stimulate the development of new high-tech industry in Siberian cities. Turning Siberia into "Cyberia" will thus, it is argued, help stem the exodus of people from these cities as well as from the more marginal areas of the region by linking their populations to the rest of the Russian Federation and the world. The

---

Box 7-2. *Bringing High-Tech to North Dakota*

In a July 2002 commentary on the decline of rural America in the *Washington Post*, Joel Kotkin, the author of a book on "The New Geography: How the Digital Revolution is Reshaping the American Landscape," wrote: "Decline, depopulation and a slow passing are not inevitable. They can be forestalled and reversed by a change in policy—a change that seeks to reinvigorate rural areas not by subsidizing the existing economy and elites but by finding ways to lure new energies and industries, and to encourage the most energetic local population, particularly young people, to remain." He argued that in the United States, federal government subsidies for rural economies should be channeled to "targeted venture funds, development grants and assistance for building technical infrastructure . . . and new telecommunications technology that allows . . . communities to participate in the global information economy."

Kotkin noted that in the 1990s some small cities in many "less-favored agricultural areas" in the United States—such as Sioux Falls, South Dakota, Iowa City, Iowa, and Bismarck and Fargo in North Dakota—transformed themselves into centers for high-tech companies. He further suggested that smaller communities in the hinterlands of these cities could also become "hubs of new economic activity."

Source: Joel Kotkin, "The Decline of Rural America. If We Let Rural America Die, We Shall Lose a Piece of Ourselves," *Washington Post*, Sunday, 21 July 2002, Outlook Section, Commentary, p. B1.

Internet and other telecommunications breakthroughs have been seen as mechanisms that will bring information, goods, and services into Siberia. Given the preponderance of skilled workers, especially the concentration of researchers and scientists in the old, closed, Soviet nuclear cities, some optimists see Siberia as a potential Russian version of California's "Silicon Valley."[60]

Siberia is not the only cold and remote place in the world that has dreams of a high-tech future. Consider a similar idea for stimulating new economic growth in the American plains states (box 7-2). But, like the proposal to convert U.S. federal farm subsidies into subsidies for high-tech businesses, the proposals for "Cyberia" or a "Siberian Silicon Valley" absolutely depend on an inflow of federal Russian government funds. The availability of such federal resources in Russia, however, is scarce. Even if they were in good supply, it seems unlikely that a cyber cafe in every town and city in Russia, Internet access in every rural post office and school, or an influx of new technology industries into Siberia would be sufficient to promote economic development and keep the existing population in place—especially in places where they should not even be in large numbers from the point of view of economic geography.

Even in the United States, predictions that the Internet and new technology would stem rural depopulation, or in fact encourage people to relocate to more remote areas in search of work, have not been borne out. In a November 2002 interview with the *New York Times*, for example, Microsoft founder and philanthropist Bill Gates noted that—in spite of his own and others' expectations and desires —his 1995 prediction that the Internet would halt the exodus from rural America had yet to come true: "I thought digital technology would eventually reverse urbanization, and so far that hasn't happened."[61] While Mr. Gates's charitable foundation endowed more than 95 percent of public libraries across America with free Internet access in the 1990s, many of the rural areas that the libraries serve continued to lose population.[62]

The Importance of Physical Connections

The fact remains that, in spite of the advantages of electronic connectivity, physical connections are still important at the beginning of the twenty-first century—as are standards of living and quality of life. Being plugged in to information sources all over the world does not make Siberia or the Russian Far East, or even the remotest areas of the United States, very desirable places to live. It may make life a little more bearable, but it does not increase the average January temperature of a city like Novosibirsk. Nor does it bring in basic foodstuffs and consumer durables to a place like Anadyr or Magadan or decrease the physical distance between Khabarovsk and Moscow. Siberian entrepreneurs, for example, still have to fly all the way to Moscow to purchase and bring in supplies.[63] Only certain jobs can be performed over the Internet. Mining and manufacturing cannot be conducted remotely. Clearly, Russia still has a long way to go before expanding communications links mitigate the constraints of distance. In the meantime, remote and cold regions remain just that—remote and cold—and unattractive to new migrants.

In the United States, comfort and convenience of place—so-called locational amenities—are more important than ever, especially for those Americans who have been described as the "creative class." They are precisely the people who populate the high-tech Silicon Valleys and Research Triangle Parks. Economist Edward Glaeser has spoken of the shift from the producer to the "consumer city" in the new American economy: "As important as the production side is, the future of most cities depends on their being desirable places for consumers to live."[64] In the United States, places like San Francisco will always have a competitive advantage over places like Detroit (not to mention Fargo). And in Russia, Moscow will always have a competitive advantage over Novosibirsk, and, in fact, over almost any other city in Russia.

The continued importance of physical connections reinforces Moscow's centrality in the Russian Federation. Moscow's growth in the 1990s was not a sign of what was or could happen elsewhere in the Russian Federation. What makes Moscow work is what the rest of Russia lacks—communications, connections, services, growth in new technologies and new industries, new housing, and so on. In keeping with the old adage "all roads lead to Rome," most roads and other forms of communication in Russia lead to or run through Moscow. To stress again, the attractions and growth of Moscow do not mean that Russia has changed. Moscow was always the most connected city in the entire territory once encompassed by the Soviet Union. It has become more so with the demise of the USSR. It really is, in the words of Russian geographer Vladimir Kaganskiy, "the state within the state," or "the capital outside the country."[65] As Kaganskiy notes, "The border between the Russian Federation and Moscow is stronger and more noticeable than perhaps most of the state borders of the Russian Federation."[66]

The 1990s—Ten Years of Slow Change

In conclusion, during the 1990s, there *were* some positive changes in Russia's inherited economic geography. A number of programs were initiated, including those supported by the World Bank, that were intended to help move people away from colder remote areas and to facilitate their migration elsewhere. And by the end of the decade, in 2000–02, important members of the Russian government's economic team, such as Prime Minister Mikhail Kasyanov and Economic Development Minister German Gref, were also expressing concern about the burdens that maintaining Siberia imposes on the Russian economy. They were either reluctant to support the status quo or openly opposed to putting more central government resources into the region, preferring to let it sink or swim on its own resources.[67] However, the sound policies were, and still are, rare. And even when they are adopted, they may have dubious results—like "Far North" relocation programs moving people into the larger cities in the region east of the Urals, rather than out to warmer, potentially more productive places in the west. Meanwhile, local leaders in Siberia have, not surprisingly, resisted the Moscow government's efforts to downsize or cut off the subsidy spigot (see chapter 8)—evoking the idea that "When Siberia is healthy, Russia is healthy."[68]

Overall, the pace of change in Russia has been too slow to reverse the processes of relocation of population and industry that moved people out into the cold and disconnected them over the course of the twentieth century. People in Russia continue to want to move. The fact that people have already migrated from regions east of the Urals underscores the very point of the argument that they should not have been there in the first place. As Anne Applebaum stated in her article "The Great Error," these people were uprooted to work in "factories and workshops designed to support a civilization which never should have been transplanted to this uninhabitable place."[69]

The problem now, the error of the Russian government today, is that it wants to keep most of these transplanted people in place or to move them to places of the government's choosing. The Russian government does not really want people to move freely, to Moscow or anywhere else in the Russian Federation. The mindset of the Russian political elite and the population—the prevailing attitude toward Siberia as a central element in the development of the Russian state—has become as great an obstacle to moving forward as the physical and objective challenges of reversing the misallocations of the past. Minds are not impervious to change, but they are difficult to change.

8

Can Russia Shrink?

If Russia is to be governable and economically viable, it needs to "shrink" itself—not by divesting territory but by organizing its economy differently. The objective is to reduce distance and create new connections. People will need to migrate westward on a large scale, and the large cities in the coldest and most remote regions will have to downsize. The barriers to self-correction, however, are considerable. So far, mobility and migration to European Russia have been constrained by restrictions on settlement in Moscow; by the absence of significant economic growth, new jobs, and housing in other towns and cities; by inadequate social safety nets; by the population's own reluctance or inability to move; and by the pull of subsidies in specific regions. In addition, there is no historical precedent for the shrinkage of cities on the scale that will be required in Russia. As a result, changing Russia's economic geography will be a costly and wrenching process, even if it will eventually put Russia on the right path of development.

Relocation and resettlement programs like the World Bank program for "Northern Restructuring" can do little to help people move away from Russia's harshest and most undesirable regions if there are no real options for migrants in the places they can move to. In fact, "emptying out the North" might actually mean increasing the difficulties for migrants and local and federal government elsewhere. Although many Soviet-era restrictions on migration have been removed, and the Russian government claims that the population is becoming increasingly mobile, relocation is still not an easy matter in the Russian Federation. And subordinating people's desires for the good of the state remains one of Russia's greatest problems.

The legacy of Russia's imperial and Soviet history is the imperative to constrain and direct the movement and location of population. The irony of Russia's physical geography is that its huge territorial space encouraged people to move, while the Russian government did not necessarily want them to move, or wanted them to move to a particular part of the territory. It, therefore, had to try to stop them. Although all states have problems in keeping tabs on their inhabitants, controlling and constraining voluntary mobility is a particular hallmark of the Russian state, precisely because of its unique size and, thus, the potential for people to hide and escape detection.[1]

Obstacles to Mobility and Migration

Today people are still not really free to move in Russia (although they obviously do), and it is not at all clear that the Russian government realizes the importance of actively helping people to migrate. Russia's demographic crisis fuels fears of the depopulation of strategic areas like the Russian Far East and Siberia that border China (an issue we will discuss further in the next chapter). There is a parallel fear of concentrating more population in Moscow, thus exacerbating the phenomenon of the capital city's becoming a "state within a state." In addition, many people stay and also want to stay in the Urals and Siberia in spite of all the disadvantages of living there. But one of the primary obstacles to full mobility and migration is the persistence of Soviet-style residency restrictions in Moscow and other cities that are attractive to migrants. In spite of the formal abolition of the Soviet residency permit system, cities still try to discourage migration for fear that municipal services and welfare systems will be overburdened.

The Propiska System

Government intervention to control population flows in Russia dates back at least 150 years. In the late nineteenth century, the tsarist regime issued internal passports to regulate the processes of urbanization and migration. Although the Bolsheviks abolished this system when they came to power in 1917, internal passports were reintroduced in 1932 along with a mandatory *propiska*, or residency permit. Soviet citizens were required to register their place of residence with the local police in order to receive their *propiska*. It became a criminal offense, punishable by fines or even imprisonment, to live at any other address. Presenting one's *propiska* was a prerequisite for securing employment, getting married, attending school, obtaining social services, or purchasing tickets for travel within the Soviet Union.

Although the policy was initially presented as a means of protecting the Soviet population and of guaranteeing the necessary distribution of labor and resources within the planned economy, the *propiska* was clearly used to promote other political agendas. For example, a number of societal groups were consistently denied *propiski*, including former convicts, dissidents, and members of certain ethnic groups like the Roma.[2] In an effort to further control migration, some cities in the Soviet Union were deemed "closed cities." These urban areas were either completely closed to in-migration or contained enterprises that were administratively restricted from expanding. In both cases, *propiski*—or rather, the refusal to issue *propiski* for residence in these cities— were the mechanism by which the "closed cities" policies were enforced.[3] "Closed cities" included those with significant and sensitive defense enterprises or research facilities, such as Gorkiy (Nizhniy Novgorod) and the nuclear cities of Siberia, which were also often not marked on maps.[4] In addition, in the 1950s and 1960s, Soviet urban planners became concerned about the impact on the USSR of trends in the West toward increasingly large cities. They attempted to prevent the development of so-called "city-giants" by trying to cap the population of large Soviet cities at 250,000–300,000.[5]

In the Soviet period, the *propiska* system was never quite as rigid as Soviet planners intended it to be. Many people found ways to circumvent it. Migrant workers to Siberia and the North from the 1960s through the 1980s, who would have been registered in these regions, often left for other areas of the USSR or returned to their original homes. There was also a great deal of movement from rural regions into cities throughout the USSR. Nonetheless, Soviet citizens considered the internal passport and the *propiska* systems as particularly onerous barriers to geographic mobility. In Soviet surveys carried out in 1989–90, 76 percent of people polled sought the abolition of the *propiska* system.[6] In the late 1980s, restrictions on migration were actually enforced more strongly than in earlier phases, especially migration into cities like Moscow and the capitals of other Soviet republics.[7]

When the Soviet Union finally collapsed in 1991, there was a great deal of pent-up mobility and capacity for migration still within the system. The *propiska* system was technically abolished after the new post-Soviet Russian constitution was adopted and ratified in December 1993. Article 27 of the constitution states: "Everyone who is lawfully present on the territory of the Russian Federation has a right to freedom of movement and to choose his place of stay and residence." Nevertheless, there have been subsequent attempts to restore a form of the *propiska* regime. Residence restrictions persist in more than one-third of Russia's eighty-nine regions—despite the fact that the Constitutional Court of the Russian Federation has ruled these practices unconstitutional on several occasions.[8]

Personalized Social Safety Nets

In the Soviet era, many people were either forced to move as prisoners in the GULAG or migrant workers or forced to stay in one place thanks to the *propiska* system. In the post-Soviet era—in spite of the great potential for out-migration from the most undesirable regions of Siberia, the North, and the Far East—people, when given a choice and allowed to exercise free will, have often chosen *not* to move. The reasons are more complex than simply the constraints imposed by the residual restrictions on mobility.

Many of those who moved to the North, Siberia, and the Russian Far East in the 1970s and 1980s have, in essence, become stuck there. Those who moved later in the 1980s, who did not establish firm roots, and who still had links with other regions, moved out in the 1990s as part of the initial wave of out-migration that shows up in statistics. For the older generation there is often nowhere to move back to, nor is there even the possibility to move somewhere new. Yevgeniy Rupasov, an administrator for a pilot program of the World Bank's Northern Restructuring Project for Russia, pointed out in a July 2002 interview: "In the late 1980s, some of the richest people were in the North. Today they have become the greatest victims. Fifteen years ago, they could return to a better city than they came from, buy a flat, a dacha, a car and furniture. Now their savings have been burnt, and they are stuck without money." In a similar interview one retiree in the former GULAG city of Susuman noted ruefully: "We're under arrest here."[9] A vivid illustration of this phenomenon and the difficulties of migration was provided by the impressions of German journalist Michael Thumann from a trip through Siberia in 2000 (box 8-1).

Normal economic theory would suggest that an increasing discrepancy in living standards and job opportunities between colder, Siberian regions

Box 8-1. *"A Farewell to the End of the World"*

Yevgeniy Janssen, an eighty-year-old ethnic German from Ukraine, was deported to a camp in Zakamensk in Buryatiya during World War II to work in a wolfram mine. The camp was later converted into a town to support the local mines and processing factories. Today, Zakamensk's wolfram production has collapsed, the town has been abandoned, and the bulk of its population has gone. Janssen and his wife live in a tiny wooden house on the outskirts of the town in the middle of an allotment full of potatoes, cabbages, tomatoes, and cucumbers. He uses his meager pension to buy seeds and survives on the produce of his plot. There are no shops left in Zakamensk, only a few kiosks selling basic staples and a smattering of consumer goods. Janssen and other inhabitants were offered the chance to move to other cities, but many simply could not afford to go. One young woman, Elena, who found herself trapped in Zakamensk with her family, notes that she and her husband could not sell their apartment to buy a new one elsewhere—it was worth nothing—and they could not find new jobs. She said: "We have no other chance to survive. . . . We are chained to this apartment."

The town of Sarylakh in Sakha (Yakutiya) grew up around a gold mine. As in Zakamensk, most of Sarylakh's inhabitants have moved away, in some cases to the nearby city of Ust'-Nera. The city itself is poorly supplied. Basic staples—butter, bread, meat, and milk—have become prohibitively expensive. Fruit has disappeared from the local shops. Life has become "dependent on whatever happens to be available." One of Ust'-Nera's former residents, Gennadiy Kumachenko, moved there relatively late in 1978. When the gold mines closed, Kumachenko moved back to his hometown in Ukraine where he still had relatives, but he could not find work. Now he returns in the summer months to Sarylakh, to work in a mine that has been reopened on a seasonal basis. He lives in an abandoned apartment in the town. Throughout Sakha (Yakutiya), nineteen mining towns like Sarylakh have been designated as "settlements without prospects for the future" and have been "liquidated." In the region around Ust'-Nera, including the population of the city itself (11,000), only 19,000 people remain. Every summer, a further 1,000 people (often former residents like Kumachenko) travel to the region as migrant workers.

Source: Michael Thumann, "Dossier: Abschied vom Ende der Welt" (Dossier: A Farewell from the End of the World), *Die Zeit*, 31 December 2000.

and those in western Russia will induce westward migration. But reality is likely to be the opposite for many people: continued decline in the eastern economy will tie them even more tightly to their current locations. The situation is reminiscent of that during the Soviet Union's campaign to "liquidate" tens of thousands of rural villages in the 1960s. Like today's far northern settlements, those villages were labeled "lacking prospects for the future" [*besperspektivnyye*]. Some of their residents were persuaded to leave, while others—the very poorest—were often left behind because they could not afford to abandon their plots or their family networks. History tells us that migration follows these family and social networks. People have to feel reassured by a social safety net.

The fact that the North, Siberia, and the Russian Far East became home for millions of people in the Soviet era has a very definite set of implications with the decay of Russia's social welfare system in the 1990s. Those who find themselves stuck are the most vulnerable and the oldest members of the population. For them, even if they had the resources to move elsewhere, finding themselves in a new location, but far away from their remaining social networks of family and friends, has serious consequences. Sociologists, scholars, and reporters visiting the most marginal regions of the Russian Federation over the past decade have chronicled the efforts of its citizens to survive in the face of dwindling resources. They have noted how these efforts result in binding people even more tightly than before to a particular place.

Nancy Ries of Colgate University, for example, describes the survival mechanisms of teachers, health-care workers, and other state employees "whose wages are very often low and often not paid," pensioners on low fixed incomes, and factory workers in "large but stagnant enterprises, where wages are low, often in arrears, and often paid 'in kind.'" Ries writes that for "most of these people, the entire decade of the 1990s has meant steadily and dramatically declining purchasing power, combined with a decline in social welfare provisions from the state (health care, child care, housing, energy, transport, and subsidies, paid vacations, etc.)."[10] With purchasing power depleted and subsidies gone, the food that people can produce themselves in small family plots or can obtain from family and friends has become one of the mainstays of life.[11] As a result, "Self-sufficiency—extreme 'localism'—has become the logic of survival for millions of people. This is not the localism of decentralized markets. In many cases families simply have no *access* to markets, whether or because they live in isolated villages, far-flung regions, or the war-ravaged North Caucasus where there are no regularly functioning shops, or because (most commonly) they have no cash."[12] Many people—like Michael Thumann's Yevgeniy Janssen (box 8-1)—do not want to move from their existing family plots or their sources of food, no matter how poor this plot of land might be, if there is no guarantee of a similar means of sustaining themselves elsewhere.[13]

Access to means of subsistence, therefore, plays an important role in shaping relocation decisions. In cases where this subsistence is tied to an industrial enterprise, rather than just to a plot of land or an apartment, retaining or securing these ties becomes particularly important. As Nancy Ries writes:

> Even marginal attachment to an even marginally functioning enterprise can mean the difference between minimal subsistence and the desperation of being truly on one's own. Among other things, enterprises can (variously) provide: access to plots for potato growing and other farming; subsidized or free electrical, heat, water supply . . . in the absence of wages, goods to be bartered . . . or direct distribution of foodstuffs [and] membership in a mutually sustaining network or group.[14]

One of the clearest examples of the importance of an individual enterprise in shaping relocation decisions is Noril'sk Nickel, in Noril'sk—one of the cities targeted by the World Bank's Northern Restructuring Project in 2001–02 for resettlement assistance. In spite of its isolated and undesirable location and harsh climate (with average January temperatures of −35° C), Noril'sk, number ten in the ranking of Russian cities making negative contributions to Russia's TPC, has actually proved attractive to migrants from within and outside the Russian Federation (box 8-2).

"Serfdom" for Migrants

Noril'sk has proved appealing to migrants not because of the availability of new jobs or the attractions of the city itself, but because of Noril'sk Nickel's relatively generous social subsidies. But where else would people like to move to in Russia? In most cases, not where the Russian government might like— such as to the central regions of European Russia that have suffered from demographic decline and are beginning to face a labor shortage. As Russian prime minister Mikhail Kasyanov, for example, noted in a presentation coinciding with the drafting of a special government program for children living in the North: "Many people who have lived here in the North just do not want to move to the central parts of Russia, they sometimes say they would like to live in the country's south or in the southern parts of these northern territories [where the larger cities are located]."[15]

But even if migrants are agreeable to moving to the locations selected or preferred by the government, access to residence permits and housing persist as major constraints on relocation, if not as deterrents to migration. Migrants to new regions in the Russian Federation compete with long-time residents who are already fighting for access to scarce housing. British journalist Andrew Jack, in a July 2002 *Financial Times* article, noted, for example, that apartments "earmarked for residents from the North have been constructed elsewhere, only to be appropriated by local authorities seeking them for their own population."[16] The reality facing many migrants to even the most desirable locations in Russia is illustrated by the plight of some people who, having moved from Kazakhstan to an area near Moscow, found themselves living in old or abandoned buildings like refugees (box 8-3).

No Russian Boomtowns beyond Moscow

In the case described by the *Moscow Times* in box 8-3, migrants found a semblance of work near Moscow. But finding alternative or new employment in recipient regions has proved to be a considerable problem for most would-be migrants. Beyond Moscow, there are few cities in the Russian Federation with a solid or growing employment base—hence the reason Noril'sk has seemed so attractive. Clearly, few people would be willing to move from Siberia and the North, no matter how difficult the circumstances there, to face unemployment in an unfamiliar place in European Russia without the provision of a formal social safety net.

The true performance of Russian enterprises remains a puzzle, owing to hidden subsidies and so on.[17] However, one relatively good indicator of future viability is the way regions are judged by foreign investors, who are far less likely to be swayed by political considerations. Overall levels of foreign direct investment in the Russian economy remain pitifully (and perhaps undeservedly) low. But more important for our purposes is the regional breakdown. Here, the dominance of Moscow is unmistakable. In the past five years, the city of Moscow and the surrounding region have accounted for close to 40 percent of all foreign funds into Russia in the form of investments in physical capital. The St. Petersburg area is far behind, with less than 9 percent (see table 8-1).[18]

The conclusion from this review of enterprise growth and foreign direct investment is that Moscow is essentially the only "boom town" in Russia— with a considerable gap between Moscow and other Russian cities, including St. Petersburg. It should, therefore, be attracting migration, just as it is. Migration to Moscow is a sign of the development of a market economy and the positive pull of economic forces. Unfortunately, however, throughout both its

(*text continues on page 151*)

Box 8-2. *Noril'sk and Relocation in the Russian Federation*

Noril'sk Nickel is one of the world's largest metal companies, producing, in addition to nickel, one-third of the world's palladium, a quarter of its platinum, and one-fifth of world copper.[a] The company employs thousands of people—including a significant contingent of prison labor—in the metals foundries and also as geologists, miners, and support workers in electricity production, regional transportation, housing, education, and local hospitals.[b] It remains, in the words of one official, "an island of communism."[c]

In stark contrast to businesses in other single-enterprise cities, after the collapse of the Soviet Union and the subsequent privatization of the company, Noril'sk Nickel continued to pay higher wages (six to ten times the national average) and provide and support social services in the city of Noril'sk (including housing subsidies, supplementary pensions, and school allowances). This has attracted thousands of migrants from around the region, as well as from elsewhere in Russia and the former Soviet Union, including Azerbaijan, Kazakhstan, and Ukraine.[d]

In 2001, according to official Russian government statistics, the city of Noril'sk had a population of approximately 235,000 people. It also had a reported 35,000 additional "unofficial" (unregistered) residents.[e] New migrants were flooding in to such an extent that, in March 2001, the city mayor, Oleg Budgarin, and the general director of Noril'sk Nickel, Dzhonson Khagazheyev, appealed to the Russian minister for emergency situations, Sergey Shoygu, to cap migration by restoring the Soviet-era travel restrictions (Noril'sk was a restricted zone for settlement until 1990). They claimed that this was to prevent "criminals and terrorists" from entering the city, but their appeal primarily referred to the strain that an influx of migrants was imposing on "the effectiveness of state and local social programs and enterprises."[f] The mayor subsequently complained that (like elsewhere in the North) "maintaining nonworking people here is four times more expensive than on the 'mainland.'"[g] Noril'sk's request that the Russian government restrict migration was accepted. On November 25, 2001, entry restrictions were imposed. Would-be visitors to the city were required to obtain an invitation and special permission to visit before being able to purchase an airline ticket.[h]

Under the terms of the World Bank's Northern Restructuring Project and other initiatives, the city of Noril'sk wants to reduce its population by 160,000

by 2010. Noril'sk Nickel has already reduced its work force from 125,000 in 1996 to 60,000; it hopes to reduce it even further, to perhaps as low as 50,000 workers, to increase productivity.[i] Meanwhile, however, the company continues to support not only the city of Noril'sk but much of the surrounding region. As one western reporter visiting the region put it in August 2001: "In Soviet years, development of the Far North was organized, and there was a sense that the state could be relied on, but over the last decade, as the state has seemed to be following the Marxist principle of withering away, Noril'sk Nickel has filled the gap, taking a greater hold on the region than any Soviet party boss could have dreamed of."[j]

a. Cited in Geoffrey York, "Even Prosperous Russian Towns Yearn for Soviet Rule. Noril'sk Could Have Barred Fortune-Seekers under the Old System," *Globe and Mail* (Canada), 24 July 2001, p. A3.

b. Russian geographer Vladimir Kaganskiy claimed that as many as 3,000 convicts from local prisons worked at the Noril'sk Nickel combine in 1997. See "Chto takoe 'Noril'skiy Nikel,' " in Vladimir Kaganskiy, *Kul'turnyy landshaft i sovetskoye obitayemoye prostranstvo* (Moscow, 2001), p. 238.

c. Colin McMahon, "Siberian City Balks at Reform: Old-Style Subsidies Keep Town Alive, to Russia's Dismay," *Chicago Tribune*, 20 June 2001, p. 3.

d. Sharon LaFraniere, "A City Built by Stalin Chooses to Stay Frozen in Time," *Washington Post*, 25 May 2003, p. A29.

e. "Russia Closes Its Northernmost Industrial Center to Foreigners," *BBC Monitoring*, 24 November 2001.

f. "Noril'sk Asks for Travel Restrictions," *Moscow Times*, 14 March 2001, p. 4.

g. Aleksei Tarasov, "Svoi i chuzhiye. Noril'skiy promrayon zakryvayut dlya inostrantsev," *Izvestiya*, vol. 75, 26 April 2001, p. 2.

h. Robyn Dixon, "Russian City to Ban 'Outsiders': Authorities in Noril'sk Say Decree is Aimed at Curbing Crime and Drug Problems," *Los Angeles Times*, 9 November 2001, p. 30A.

i. McMahon, "Siberian City Balks at Reform"; LaFraniere, "A City Built by Stalin"; York, "Even Prosperous Russian Towns Yearn for Soviet Rule"; Robert Kaiser, "Siberia Diary: Noril'sk, Stalin's Siberian Hell, Thrives in Spite of Hideous Legacy," *Washington Post*, 29 August 2001, p. C1.

j. Tara Warner, "Building a Home in Russia's Far North: Subsidies and High Wages Lure Some to a Harsh Arctic Land," *Russia Journal*, 24–30 August, 2001.

Box 8-3. *"Migrants Live as Serfs South of Moscow"*

"When agronomist Anna Samusenko left Kazakhstan for Russia two years ago she felt relief. Now she would live with her own people, speak her own language and put her skills to good use reviving Russian agriculture. But her dreams have come to nothing. Although she found work on a collective farm south of Moscow, she is treated little better than a serf. [. . .] Samusenko, 52, and her family live in an abandoned office on the run-down *Leninskoye Znamya* (Lenin Banner) collective farm in Sharapovo. She guards the barns and takes care of the calves, which means carrying 1.7 tons of fodder every day, for wages that work out to 83 kopeks, or about 2 cents, per hour. [. . .] Without Russian citizenship or local registration—the farm says it's too expensive to get her a *propiska*—she has no rights, no way to complain to the authorities and nowhere to go. [. . .]

"There are dozens of families in Samusenko's situation in Sharapovo alone and 700 elsewhere in the Chekhov district, said Lilia Makarova, who heads the regional migrants organization *Svet*. It was founded last fall and unites 1,300 families from the Chekhov, Istrinsk and Podolsk districts and the towns of Lyubertsy and Klin, all in the Moscow region. Five to 10 new members join each week, she said. [. . .] The migrants, many of them ethnic Russians, come to the Moscow region from Moldova, Kazakhstan, Kyrgyzstan, Uzbekistan and Tajikistan. Some were invited by farm directors who placed newspaper advertisements promising registration, housing and jobs, Makarova said. Others, like Samusenko, just left everything and fled, hoping for support in their fatherland. But most were deceived, Makarova said. Those who invited them housed them in nonresidential buildings like *banyas* [bathhouses], abandoned schools, laundries, or office buildings. Few get registered. They are afraid to leave the farms, cannot get free medical help, cannot vote and as outsiders they are subject to regular abuse and humiliation."
[. . .]

"The *Migratsiya*, or Migration, information agency estimates there are 8 million ethnic Russian migrants in Russia. Only 800,000 people received the status of a 'forced migrant' from Russian migration authorities before coming to Russia, which gives them the right to apply for local registration. Most did not manage to get the proper papers or did not even know how to get them.
[. . .]

"'We have 12,000 official forced migrants from former Soviet republics in the Moscow region,' Viktor Lopyryov, head of the Moscow regional branch of the Nationalities and Migration Ministry, said in a telephone interview. . . . 'Many of the migrants have a higher education and professional skills, but they work at the lowest-paid jobs or receive miserable pensions because they lack documents.'"

Source: Yevgenia Borisova, "Migrants Live as Serfs South of Moscow," *The Moscow Times*, 17 July 2001, p. 1.

Table 8-1. *Moscow's Domination of Foreign Direct Investment (FDI), 1998–2002*

Region[a]	Percentage of total national FDI, 1998–2002
1 Moscow (city and oblast)	39.2
2 Sakhalin	12.3
3 Krasnodar	11.9
4 St. Petersburg and Leningrad oblast	8.8
5 Tyumen'	3.1
6 Samara	2.7
7 Novosibirsk	2.7
8 Sverdlovsk	2.4
9 Kaluga	1.5
10 Volgograd	1.2
11 Orenburg	1.1

Source: Authors' computations using Goskomstat data from *Interfax Weekly Reports*, nos. 11 (1999), 12 (2000), 12 (2001), 11 (2002), and 12 (2003).
a. The remaining regions each account for less than 1.0 percent of total FDI. Collectively, their share is 13.2 percent. The total dollar amount of FDI in 1998–2002 was $20.0 billion.

Soviet and recent history the government has frequently intervened to restrict in-migration and to curb Moscow's growth. Moscow may be Russia's migration magnet, but Russian authorities have consistently, and often futilely, tried to repel migrants.

Restricting Moscow's Growth

From the very beginning of the Soviet regime, state planners sought to limit Moscow's population. The internal passport and *propiska* system of 1932 was designed not only to control internal migration in the USSR, but also to prevent a massive influx into the Russian capital. In 1935 the Communist Party Central Committee tried to cap Moscow's population at five million, but in the aftermath of World War II, postwar reconstruction efforts drew more and more villagers from surrounding areas to Moscow.[19] By 1965 urban migration rather than natural increase accounted for the lion's share of Moscow's population growth. As Harvard scholar Timothy Colton notes in his seminal work on Moscow, "From 1965 to the late 1980s, roughly 85 percent of Moscow's demographic gain stemmed from a mass influx from Russian towns and villages—movement of the kind debarred by the master plan."[20] Clearly, the *propiska* system did not function as effectively as Soviet planners had hoped. Colton highlights four shortcomings of the *propiska* system that contributed to Moscow's population gain, including marriage by residents to nonresidents, the evasion and bribery of passport police, personal connections to large enterprises and other Soviet organizations, and special labor permits granted to outsiders. This latter group became collectively known as *limitchiki* (or those outside the administrative "limits" or quotas for labor).[21] *Limitchiki* often took jobs that Muscovites were unwilling to fill in construction or custodial services. But once employed they were usually quick to move ahead and secure more prestigious positions, thereby fueling demand for more outside workers.

In 1971, alarmed by Moscow's extraordinary growth, the municipal authorities, the *Mossovet* and *Gorkom*, enacted a new plan for Moscow's development. Their underlying assumption was that city growth had to be checked in order to improve the living conditions of Moscow's working population. As a result, the new city plan fixed the population limit at eight million. It called for stricter enforcement of the *propiska* regime and placed limits on job creation to check the increase of *limitchiki*.[22] In spite of these projections and constraints, however, employment jumped by more than one-third in every labor sector except manufacturing between 1965 and 1980. Enterprise directors stepped up their demands for *limitchiki* accordingly. The lack of coordination between local enterprise directors, city officials, and central planners enabled thousands of new *limitchiki* to pour into Moscow, effectively undermining the 1971 plan.[23]

The situation was similar in the 1980s. In 1985 the problem of Moscow's unchecked growth fell into the hands of the newly appointed Central Committee secretary (future Russian president), Boris Yeltsin. In September 1987, Yeltsin persuaded the Politburo to decree an indefinite ban on *limitchiki*.[24] But the new population targets proved, once again, completely unrealistic. Colton writes: "[The plan] posed a population quota of 9.5 million for 2000 and 10 million for 2010; [but] even those figures would require a two-thirds slackening of population growth."[25]

For a brief period, it did seem possible that population growth would slacken. Natural processes negatively affected Moscow's demographic situation. In the late 1980s, low birth rates combined with increasing mortality gave the city its lowest growth in the postwar period. After the collapse of the Soviet Union, negative net migration during the disarray of the early 1990s further aggravated the situation. In 1992 and 1993, Moscow experienced its first net decrease in permanent residents since Stalin's purges of the mid-1930s.[26] This trend was, however, short-lived. From 1993 to 1994, the net migration rate per 10,000 people increased from –6 to +12.[27] It has continued to climb ever since, in spite of continued efforts to enforce residency permits. As in Soviet times, efforts to curb Moscow's population growth have proved fruitless. Indeed, preliminary data from the 2002 census indicate that Moscow now has more than thirteen million inhabitants (both permanent and unofficial).[28]

The Propiska System Lives On

In spite of numerous legal challenges in the 1990s, residency within Moscow is still governed by a version of the propiska system.[29] Like Boris Yeltsin before him, Moscow's mayor, Yuriy Luzhkov, has personally spearheaded the effort to preserve the Soviet-era policy of restricting residency, citing the risk of untrammeled migration's overwhelming city services and undermining security. After a series of apartment bombings in Moscow in the summer of 1999—linked by the Russian government to Chechen rebels—residency permits were explicitly tied to efforts to combat terrorism. In September 1999, Luzhkov decreed that visitors to Moscow would have to submit to questioning and obtain new residency permits within a three-day period.[30] In addition, Moscow's police effectively barred nonresidents from entering the capital, and the Moscow city government later passed an emergency measure calling for the deportation of all those who had failed to register for the new residency permits.[31] Immigration control points were established at Moscow's railway and bus terminals, while vehicles entering Moscow on the major highways into the city were searched with greater frequency.[32]

Luzhkov's attempts to restrict migration into Moscow were given a further boost in 1999–2002 by an influx of refugees from the renewed war in Chechnya, which erupted in the wake of the apartment bombings. Of the estimated three million "nonresidents" in Moscow in the preliminary data from the 2002 census, as many as two million were reported as originating in the Russian North Caucasus and in the South Caucasus states of Armenia, Azerbaijan, and Georgia.[33] In July 2002, new regulations on the "Legal Status of Foreign Nationals" were introduced, ostensibly to combat the risk of further terrorist acts, but they were widely viewed as an effort to stem and reverse the tide of migration from the Caucasus. These regulations initially stipulated that a "migration card" be issued to all foreigners (citizens of countries other than Russia) entering the country.[34] However, the seizure of a Moscow theater by a group of Chechen terrorists in October 2002 led directly to calls for even tougher enforcement of the existing restrictions on the residence of Russian citizens migrating to the capital. In a speech in

November 2002, Mayor Luzhkov declared that Moscow and other large Russian cities "must have" a "mandatory residence-registration system" like the *propiska* system "to ensure security and prevent terrorist acts."[35]

All this continues to complicate the efforts of migrants to move to new places of their personal choice within the Russian Federation—especially to Moscow, the one city that offers real opportunity of housing and employment in the Russian Federation. Russians need to be able to move freely for Russia to develop. If people are stuck in place, there is no competition and no incentive for development without coercion. At the same time, however, mobility itself initially has negative consequences: the movement of people and businesses away from towns and cities means a decline in both population and services. In Russia, if people were allowed true freedom of movement, Moscow's growth would likely continue, while population decline would be dramatic in some cities and regions.

The Dilemma of Mobility: Shrinkage

Russia's biggest challenge is not that it could face the depopulation of relatively small cities and of towns and villages in the remotest regions of the North that have already shed population and been targeted for out-migration by the Russian government and the World Bank. The greatest problem is the huge Urals and Siberian cities, those with populations of several hundred thousands, or even in excess of one million, like Novosibirsk, Omsk, Yekaterinburg, Khabarovsk, and Irkutsk. These are all the major offenders from the point of view of negative contribution to TPC. As we have argued in this book, they need to downsize. Much of their population needs to move west to relieve the current burdens on the Russian economy. Unfortunately, although population and urban settlement patterns in developed countries have changed quite dramatically since World War II, there is no parallel for such a relocation of urban population on this kind of scale. Really big cities tend not to shed truly large numbers of population and shrink. In fact, shrinkage would be a huge problem for Russia, even if it is necessary to the future of the Russian economy.

In general, there is a fixation on growth in modern economies. Shrinkage, or negative growth, is generally perceived as a bad thing, although this is not always the case. There are also plenty of examples of emphasis on the benefits of shrinkage, or "downsizing," in modern economies. This can apply in cases ranging from staffing of departments to hiving off entire lines of business in order to make the whole more productive. However, the principle of healthy downsizing does not apply to large cities. In the recent history of the

United States, for example, city shrinkage is extremely rare. Despite a popular perception of a crisis of declining cities, Americans know very little about the phenomenon of downsizing very large cities, those comparable in size to Russia's industrial dinosaurs. Indeed, looking at the population of U.S. cities over the two-hundred-year period 1790–1990 reveals that although big cities may have declined in population size, in most cases the immediate areas surrounding the cities (which are also included in the metropolitan statistical area or MSA) have actually grown. This trend is explained by the flight of population from a decaying urban core to new suburbs, which first became noticeable in the 1950s and has continued since. The trend has created concern about how suburban sprawl is changing the face of America, but it has not resulted in city shrinkage.[36]

Data from recent U.S. censuses remind us of the facts. Of the approximately one hundred major U.S. cities (MSAs)—those with total metro area populations of half a million or more—no more than four lost population in the twenty-year period from 1980 to 2000. The largest of these happened to be the one that shrank the most—Pittsburgh. The Pittsburgh metro area is a large one, nearly 2.5 million people. But relative to Russia's challenge, there was not much shrinkage: only an 8.3 percent loss over the twenty-year period. Most important, the period of intensive loss was relatively brief. Pittsburgh lost nearly 7 percent of its population in the 1980s. That rate slowed considerably in the 1990s, and it may have been reversed in the past few years (see table 8-2).

There are also instances in the United States where economic downsizing rather than suburbanization has significantly altered a city's landscape— creating an extraordinary population shift. This has occurred in so-called "company towns," which are much more likely, by definition, to be adversely affected by the economic downsizing of their primary industry. Lacking other options for gainful employment, the residents must often move elsewhere in search of work. One example is Rome, New York, where, between 1990 and 2000, the town's population dropped from 44,350 to 34,950 (a 21 percent decline) after the closing of Griffiss Air Force Base.[37] However, given that company towns in the United States tend to be smaller in population to begin with than other towns and cities, dramatic declines in their population do not significantly alter the U.S. urban profile. Box 8-4 contains an illustrative piece on U.S. company towns.

Elsewhere, in Europe, there has also been some shrinkage of small settlements and single-enterprise towns. This has occurred in postindustrial settings as countries have made the transition from an emphasis on heavy or extractive industries to light manufacturing and service industries. For

Table 8-2. *U.S. Metropolitan Statistical Areas of over 500,000 People with Negative Population Growth, 1980–2000*

	Pittsburgh, Pa.	Youngstown-Warren, Ohio	Buffalo-Niagara Falls, N.Y.	Scranton-Wilkes-Barre-Hazleton, Pa.
Census population				
1980	2,571,223	644,922	1,242,826	659,387
1990	2,394,811	600,895	1,189,288	638,466
2000	2,358,695	594,746	1,170,111	624,776
Percentage change				
1980–90	−6.9	−6.8	−4.3	−3.2
1990–2000	−1.5	−1.0	−1.6	−2.1
1980–2000	−8.3	−7.8	−5.9	−5.2

Source: For 1990–2002 population data: U.S. Census Bureau; for 1980 population data: Demographia Demographic Brief, U.S. Metropolitan Areas: Population from 1900, available online at http://www.demographia.com/db-usmetfr1900.pdf.

example, in Great Britain, a policy of shrinkage was actively pursued by the government after World War II in mining villages of the English coalfields, which were deemed no longer viable after the closure of the coal mines. Some former mining settlements were given the designation of "Category D," which essentially meant that a no-investment policy was applied to accelerate the socioeconomic and physical decline of these settlements and encourage the out-migration of the most active groups.[38] In addition, since the reunification of Germany, many industrial cities in East Germany that were built up around major enterprises under communist central planning after World War II have also now declined. One of the best examples of these is the town of Hoyerswerda in Saxony, where the population has decreased from 75,000 to 45,000 over the past decade (a shrinkage of 40 percent) with the downsizing of the town's massive power plant, the primary employer. Hoyerswerda was heavily developed and expanded from an initial population of 8,000 in the 1960s, in a manner similar to Soviet cities in and east of the Urals. Many of the workers at the power plant and inhabitants of Hoyerswerda who have left the city have relocated to western Germany.[39]

Likewise, rural towns and villages have shrunk across Europe and North America. Rural-to-urban migration is a centuries-old phenomenon and one that continues even in industrialized societies. Marginal or difficult-to-sustain areas such as the U.S. and Canadian plains states continue to depopulate. In the 1990s, for example, 65 percent of counties in the American "Great Plains" lost population at a time when the population of the United States, overall, grew by 13 percent.[40] In most cases natural increase of population turned into a natural population decrease as the youngest and most productive residents moved out in search of employment opportunities in bigger cities and other regions. In Russia, too, this phenomenon continued during the Soviet period as people moved from rural areas to cities to bolster the industrial work force. And, as we have already discussed, small towns and villages in remote regions of the Russian Far East and North have shrunk since the collapse of the Soviet Union. In fact, already between 1979 and 1989, 977 towns in Russia experienced an absolute decline in population—roughly one-third of Russia's urban centers—while some towns vanished altogether.[41] Between 1989 and 1994, the largest number of declining towns was in the northwest, in the central regions around Moscow, in the Urals in Sverdlovsk and Perm' oblasts, and above the Arctic Circle. Most were centered on forest products, textiles, or mining—all industries in decline—and the general population shrinkage was attributed to the overall population decline and consequent urban slowdown in Russia, beginning in the 1970s.[42]

In spite of all these examples of shrinkage, however, the most notable feature of all of them is that they occur on a relatively small scale over time. When significant declines are recorded, they take place in small or medium-size cities. In general, in modern times *large* cities do not shrink on a massive scale, and they certainly do not "empty out." This would be unprecedented. Throughout the world, cities are organic. They are robust. They adapt. There is a permanence to cities. They can grow and they can stagnate, population can move and relocate within the metropolitan area. But it is very hard for them to shed population. The reason is that they have evolved to play a role in a larger economy. These roles do not usually change drastically and suddenly. Cities and their citizens have time to adjust to new conditions and survive.

Of course, one can imagine catastrophic events such as wars. Russia has also historically seen its cities shrink as the result of World War I and World War II, as well as during the upheavals of the Russian Revolution and the Civil War. But one of the most remarkable empirical examples of the resiliency of cities is Japan after World War II.

The Permanence of Cities

The story of what happened to the war-ravaged cities of Japan after World War II provides a vivid illustration of cities' permanence and their resistance to downsizing in cases where the shocks are temporary and noneconomic in

Box 8-4. *Company Towns in the United States*

"The town of Hershey, Pa., no doubt breathed a sugared sigh of relief earlier this month when a county court blocked a proposed sale of Hershey Foods on the grounds that selling the candy maker might cause the community 'irreparable harm.' Rural Coudersport, Pa., knows this fear well: its largest employer, the giant cable operator Adelphia, declared bankruptcy in June. But that is the ever-present threat confronting the 'one-company town,' that smaller American town or city whose identity and economic future is so intertwined with the large business headquartered there. (Sometimes, of course, a place outgrows its dependence, if not its ties; Battle Creek, Mich.—a.k.a. 'Cereal City'—will always be a Kellogg town, even if in recent years the Japanese car-part manufacturer Denso has become Battle Creek's largest employer.) Shown here are some other one-company towns—some familiar, some less so—whose fates are bound up in the big business done there:

1. Phillips Petroleum, Bartlesville, Okla. Pop.: 34,748. Local employees: approx. 2,400.

2. Leggett & Platt, industrial-materials maker. Carthage, Mo. Pop.: 12,668. Local employees: 2,169.

3. Wal-Mart, discount retailer. Bentonville, Ark. Pop.: 19,730. Local employees: 20,000.

4. Tyson Foods, meat processor. Springdale, Ark. Pop.: 45,798. Local employees: approx. 3,200.

5. Maytag, appliance maker. Newton, Iowa. Pop.: 15,579. Local employees: 4,000.

6. Pella, window and door maker. Pella, Iowa. Pop. 9,832. Local employees: approx. 3,000.

7. Hormel Foods, meat processor. Austin, Minn. Pop.: 23,314. Local employees: approx. 2,100.

8. Lands' End, catalog retailer. Dodgeville, Wisc. Pop.: 4,220. Local employees: 4,354.

nature (that is, not related to the role of cities in the national or international economy). Economists Donald Davis and David Weinstein studied the effects of allied bombing, a campaign they described as "one of the most powerful shocks to relative city sizes that the world has ever experienced."[43] The United States targeted sixty-six of Japan's cities for massive and systematic bombing, which had devastating effects. Bombing destroyed almost half of all structures in cities—2.2 million buildings. "Two-thirds of productive capacity vanished"; 300,000 people were killed; 40 percent of their populations were rendered homeless. "Some cities lost as much as half of their population owing to

9. WorldCom, communications carrier. Clinton, Miss. Pop.: 23,347. Local employees: approx. 900.

10. Whirlpool, appliance maker. Benton Harbor, Mich. Pop.: 11,182. Local employees: approx. 2,700.

11. Kellogg, cereal producer. Battle Creek, Mich. Pop.: 53,364. Local employees: 1,650.

12. Dow Chemical, Midland, Mich. Pop.: 41,685. Local employees: approx. 6,000.

13. Mohawk Industries, carpet maker. Calhoun, Ga. Pop.: 10,667. Local employees: 2,793.

14. J. M. Smucker, fruit-spread maker. Orrville, Ohio. Pop.: 8,551. Local employees: 660.

15. Adelphia Communications, cable operator. Coudersport, Pa. Pop.: 2,650. Local employees: 1,500.

16. Corning, optical-fiber and cable maker. Corning, N.Y. Pop.: 10,842. Local employees: 5,200.

17. Hershey Foods, candy maker. Hershey, Pa. Pop.: 12,771. Local employees: 6,200.

18. Smithfield Foods, pork producer. Smithfield, Va. Pop.: 6,324. Local employees: 4,511.

19. Timberland, boot and clothing maker. Stratham, N.H. Pop.: 5,810. Local employees: 730.

20. L. L. Bean, catalog retailer. Freeport, Maine. Pop.: 1,813. Local employees: 1,600."

Source: J. R. Romanko, "The Way We Live Now: The One-Company Town. The Big Business of Small Towns," *New York Times Magazine*, 22 September 2002, p. 20.

deaths, missing, and refugees." "We find that, in the wake of destruction, there was an extremely powerful recovery. Most cities returned to their relative position in the distribution of city sizes within about fifteen years." That is, post-war growth in the bombed cities was much faster than in the others, resulting in their catching up to their previous positions in the size hierarchy of cities. The typical city completely recovered its former relative size within 15 years following the end of World War II. Most remarkable of all were the cases of Hiroshima and Nagasaki. The official data (and they were most likely underestimates) were that the nuclear blasts killed no fewer than

Figure 8-1. *Postwar Recovery of Hiroshima and Nagasaki*

Log of Population

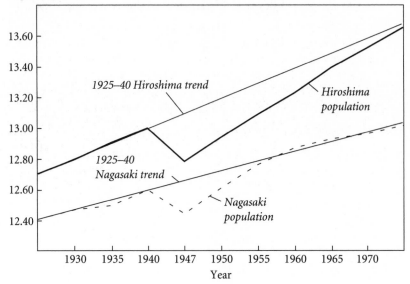

Source: Donald R. Davis and David. E. Weinstein, "Bones, Bombs, and Break Points: The Geography of Economic Activity," Working Paper 8517 (Cambridge, Mass.: National Bureau of Economic Research, October 2001), figure 2.

20.8 percent of the population of Hiroshima and 8.5 percent in Nagasaki. Yet even those cities regained their previous relative size—Nagasaki within only ten years and Hiroshima within thirty (see figure 8-1).

In Russia, too—with the exception of the war periods—cities have had a particular permanence.* Indeed, until the 1990s, they were unique in the *artificial* nature of this permanence. Although there were sixteen instances of shrinkage of cities with populations of over 100,000 in the United States between 1980 and 2000, the only city over 100,000 in Russia that shrank sharply at the end of the 1980s (by just under 11 percent) was Magadan. This is one of the remotest and most difficult Russian cities to live in, in the North, and its rate of shrinkage has slowed since the mid-1990s.[44] As already discussed, Russia has a long history of administrative or planned cities. In the

---

* The most extreme case of city "shrinkage" in Russia since the collapse of the USSR has been the capital of Chechnya, Groznyy, which has dropped from a population of approximately 400,000 in 1989 to just over 220,000 in 2002, after two rounds of devastating civil war since 1994.

Soviet era, cities were not allowed to adapt on their own or to change with shifts in the global economy—especially those in the Urals and in Siberia. Unlike Canada and the United States, where settlements in remote and cold places either reached a maximum growth or tended to downsize naturally over time (all in spite of the seeming attractions of their natural resource base or their traditional industrial importance), in Russia, government interventions prevented this from happening. In the Soviet period, cities underwent phases of growth planned and implemented by the government. They were then prevented from shrinking as their population was locked in place (except for the natural shrinkage resulting from decreasing birthrates and an aging population, which the Russian government was not able to prevent).

Obstacles to Downsizing Old Soviet Cities

The two facts that large cities in general tend not to shrink and that large Soviet cities were never allowed to shrink—or even halt in their growth when perhaps they should have—constitute bad news for a Russia today that needs to downsize some very large cities to bring itself into line with broader global economic trends. Imagine shrinking a Noril'sk, for example, if the nickel foundries were to close—a city of 235,000 people, of whom currently around one-third are employed at Noril'sk Nickel. Or shrinking Novosibirsk, the number-one offender in its negative contribution to Russia's TPC, a city of almost 1.4 million people. Hoyerswerda, the shrinking city in eastern Germany, had a population of well under 100,000 people and lost 30,000 people over a decade. Imagine a 40 percent shrinkage in Noril'sk, with around 90,000 people leaving, or more than half a million people leaving Novosibirsk in the same period. Where would they go? And what would happen to the cities when they left?

If Russian policymakers do decide to take the recommendations of this book to heart and to pursue a program for downsizing Urals and Siberian cities, given that the only examples of shrinkage in other countries are smaller settlements, the prospects are daunting. Consider the discussion by Witold Rybczynski (box 8-5) on the problems of downsizing American cities. Rybczynski's piece is, in fact, the only contemporary article that discusses the problems associated with the shrinking of large cities in any detail, because the phenomenon is so rare.

Rybczynski points out that even if a city shrinks in terms of the size of its population, its physical area remains the same. As a result, basic services have to be maintained even as people depart, while a decreasing population leads

Box 8-5. *Downsizing Cities*

"Two things happen when a city loses population. The reason for the first is that although a city is often said to be shrinking, its physical area remains the same. The same number of streets must be policed and repaired, sewers and water lines maintained, and transit systems operated. With fewer taxpayers, revenues are lower, often leading to higher taxes per capita, an overall deterioration of services, or both. More people depart, and the downward spiral continues.

"The reason for the second is that urban vitality has always depended on an adequate concentration of people. In 1950 the average density in cities like Detroit, Cleveland, and Pittsburgh was more than 12,000 people per square mile; by 1990 it was around 6,000 or 7,000—a dramatic decline. The reality is even worse than it sounds, because the decline was not distributed equally across the city, and certain areas experienced much more dramatic reductions.

"Without sufficient concentrations of people, not only is the provision of normal municipal services extremely expensive but urban life itself begins to break down. There are not enough customers to support neighborhood stores and services, or even to provide a sense of community. Empty streets become unsafe, and abandoned buildings become haunts for drug dealers and other criminals. A national study of housing abandonment found that the 'tipping point' in a neighborhood occurred when just three to six percent of the structures were abandoned. Vacant lots and empty buildings are more than just symptoms of blight—they are also causes of it. Central cities of metro areas that have aggressively expanded their borders face these problems too, even if the cities have a broader and richer tax base.

"The first need of a city whose population has declined radically is to consolidate those neighborhoods that are viable. Rather than mounting an ineffectual rear-guard action and trying to preserve all neighborhoods, as is done now, the de facto abandonment that is already in progress should be encouraged. Housing alternatives should be offered in other parts of the city, partly occupied public housing vacated and demolished, and private landowners offered land swaps. Finally, zoning for depopulated neighborhoods should be changed to a new category—zero occupancy—and all municipal services cut off. Efforts should be made to concentrate in selected areas resources such as housing assistance and social programs.

"Inevitably consolidation would involve the movement of individuals and families from one part of the city to another. . . ."

Source: Witold Rybczynski, "Downsizing Cities: To Make Cities Work Better, Make Them Smaller," *Atlantic Monthly*, vol. 276, no. 4 (October 1995), pp. 36–47. Available online at www.theatlantic.com/issues/95oct/rybczyns.htm.

to the decay of urban life. The solution is to try to relocate and consolidate population in viable city districts and to demolish those districts that cannot be maintained. This seems plausible in an American city where services are provided on a building-to-building or neighborhood-to-neighborhood basis, but in the case of Russian cities built on such a large scale during the Soviet era, this is a far more difficult proposition. All indications in the Russian case suggest that any projects like the World Bank's Northern Restructuring Project, which seek, eventually, to regroup people in shrinking northern Russian towns and cities and improve the efficiency of services in consolidated districts, will face serious problems. There will be high opportunity costs because of the peculiarities of Soviet centralized heating and power systems and other utilities.

In the Soviet era, the big defense cities in the Urals and Siberia were all built on a scale to accommodate a population of 1 million to 1.4 million people. This scale in itself was dictated by the engineering constraints of the giant power generating and centralized steam distribution systems used to light and heat housing—an obvious imperative in Siberia. There was a set Soviet model for power and heating infrastructure, including a certain size oil refinery linked to a certain size power and heating plants.[45] Cities with populations of around one million people would be powered by four to five power plants, some operated by the municipal government, others by individual enterprises, and each serving a major segment of the city. As we have noted before, Soviet cities were not designed to be flexible in their infrastructure and to adapt to changes in population size. They were built to a certain size for a certain purpose. Everything was meant to fit together. Power and heating utilities, sanitation, apartment blocks, schools, hospitals, and so on, were all designed on a district-wide and city-wide basis.[46]

Those cities built in the Soviet era are, in fact, from the point of view of their municipal systems more like an agglomeration of huge individual factories with single power and heating supplies and water and sanitation units. The indivisibility of municipal infrastructure thus makes it extremely difficult to simply cut off individual apartments, a totally empty building, or a depopulated neighborhood from the basic systems. Relocating population within the city and cutting off services would require shutting down and dismantling an entire power plant complex manned by huge teams of people that keep it operating and constantly repaired and maintained.[47] In two of Siberia's nuclear cities, Seversk and Zheleznogorsk, for example, three aging military nuclear reactors slated for decommissioning have had to remain in operation simply because the heating systems in apartment blocks in these cities are entirely dependent on them. New generating stations are not in place and are not likely to be in the near future. In the words of a local journalist: "At present the stopping of these reactors will automatically paralyze life in Seversk and Zheleznogorsk."[48]

Power generation, electricity supplies, and heating are all huge drains on municipal budgets in Russia in general and in the Urals, Siberia, and the Russian Far East in particular.[49] Heating systems are largely one-two pipe, constant open flow, direct distribution systems, often operating above ground, with significant thermal loss and few means of detecting leaks. Seventy percent of all residences in Russia are linked to centralized direct heating systems. Heat distributed from the plants through a series of substations serves a building or group of buildings. The substations normally have four pipes—two providing hot water and two providing heat (transmitted through hot water or steam)—directly connecting the system to building taps or heating pipes.[50] Municipal governments are billed on the amount of heat leaving the generating plant, rather than on the basis of use. Supply temperature can be regulated only by the central boiler house or power/heating plant, which sets the temperature according to ambient temperature—the colder it is the more heat is produced. Except by opening the windows to vent excess heat, the end user cannot regulate the temperature, nor can providers measure or modulate use to reflect changes in demand.[51]

Some fixes for these systems may be possible. There has been considerable discussion of ways in which to make Russia's large cities, particularly those in very cold places, more energy efficient. The Moscow Center for Energy Efficiency, the World Bank, the Institute for Urban Economics, and many others have proposed solutions including metering, improving housing insulation, introducing measures to reduce energy consumption, and shifting over to new piped-gas heating systems to replace water or steam distribution.[52] However, proposed solutions are difficult and costly to implement on the kind of *massive* scale that would be required—and one really has to question: Would they be worth it?

New gas heating systems, for example, would require a huge overhaul of the existing infrastructure. Even sensible smaller-scale interventions such as metering would do little to address problems of downsizing or shrinkage, given the fact that the amount of heating distributed to a building or neighborhood cannot be easily regulated and scaled down. In an effort to try to enforce both payment and conservation and to relieve some of the burdens on municipal governments, the Russian federal government also proposed shifting most utility costs to the consumer (domestic and industrial) in 2003.[53] This policy innovation has the potential to be politically explosive, because Russian sociologists suggest that as much as 60 percent of the population will be unable to afford market value for their utilities, and those who do not pay their utility bills cannot simply be punitively disconnected on an individual basis.[54] Buildings have to be cut off from utilities in totality. If, for example, a factory fails to pay its utility bills and gets cut off, then the whole district surrounding it, including apartments and hospitals, also gets cut off from electricity, heat, and water. This is a phenomenon that has been repeated across the Russian Federation in the past several years and has become almost a fact of life east of the Urals.[55] In terms of conservation, as things currently stand, the structure and design of distribution substations and pipes within buildings limit the benefits of reducing energy consumption: "any attempt to limit heat flow through a given radiator would affect heat flow to others in that vertical series, unless a bypass were installed. Uneven heat distribution within buildings results in overheating in the 'upstream' units, prompting the well practiced response of 'heat venting' via open windows."[56] In addition, in the case of city shrinkage, if people moved out of buildings, per capita costs would simply increase rather than decrease for the remaining consumers, adding to their burdens.

In general, the bulk of the housing stock in Russia is in need of structural repair and replacement. The Soviets built housing largely to a standard design, which made renovation difficult, costly, and frequent. Special cold-resistant steels and aluminum, essential for regions like Siberia, were shortage items in the Soviet period and rarely used in construction.[57] And in spite of an abundance of timber and a long native tradition of building wooden housing on a small scale to withstand the cold, Soviet planners built housing on a large scale and of concrete. Little attention was given to insulation and energy efficiency in the Soviet period, when cost and conservation were not a major issue. One recent idea has been to bring in energy-efficient housing technology from places like Canada and Scandinavia. Indeed, in the 1990s, an entire model Canadian village was imported into Siberia and fully assembled (box 8-6). Although Canadian companies are pitching the construction of 10,000 new individual housing units across Russia from Moscow to the Russian Far East by 2005, it is clearly not feasible to reconstruct housing to Canadian or other cold-weather standards on a large city–wide scale.[58]

Overall, the power generation (and thus the electricity and heating) system in Russia remains largely unreformed and prone to crisis. Although most of it is integrated through Unified Energy Systems (UES), Russia's power utility monopoly, the situation in the Russian Far East is particularly challenging. Here, the regional system is cut off from the national grid,

Box 8-6. *Canadian Village Imported to Siberia*

"An almost exact replica of a Canadian Arctic village exported to Siberia gives the concept of mail-order shopping a new dimension. The $25-million prototype will give the Russians the benefit of Canadian cold weather technology in a near-instant town.

"The Canadians are delivering the new village, named Sakha, complete with paved roads, utilities, water and wastewater treatment plants, civic buildings, a school, a general store, a fire station and 40 three-story houses. 'The Russians came over and picked specific facilities from Arctic communities and housing developed by the territorial housing corporation,' says Ray Karst, a principal of architect-engineer Ferguson, Simek and Clark, Yellowknife, Northwest Territories. 'They wanted a design-build team, so we brought in Clark-Bowler Construction, Edmonton, as general contractor.' The contract for the village with Sakha Vneshstroy, a local government entity, was signed in January, 1992. Completion is set for October [1993]. More than 4,400 tons of material for the mostly stick-built village has been shipped by freighter and barge. Ninety Canadian workers also made the trip.

"Everything but the concrete fire station is highly insulated light wood-frame construction. 'For the Siberians, who build summer cottages of wood and everything else in concrete and masonry, this was quite new,' says Bill Gibelhaus, a Clark-Bowler partner.

"Drywall and prefabricated windows are also novelties, as is a cold porch, an entry vestibule that shuts out cold air and snow.

" 'There is much we can help them with,' says Clark-Bowler partner, Andy Clark. 'Such things as wall cavities and air barriers are unknowns,' he adds.

"Steel pile foundations are sunk to permafrost levels because of soil that becomes loosened by summer temperatures that reach 104° F. 'Besides, steel doesn't rot,' says Gibelhaus. For infrastructure, a water pipe and submersible-pump system was installed by drilling 360 ft through permafrost to tap an aquifer. The town is served by a modular wastewater treatment plant. 'If the prototype is successful, the Russians will likely tender another nine villages in a few years,' says Clark."

Source: *Engineering News-Record*, vol. 231, no. 6 (9 August 1993), p. 15.

which makes it extremely difficult to deal with power shortages. As Anatoliy Chubays, the head of UES, noted at a government conference in the Russian Far East in August 2002:

The structure of the energy [power generating] system in the Far East region is completely unique, and is not replicated in any of the other regions of the country. It is constructed in such a way that only about 4 of the energy systems are actually linked to each other. These are the systems in the south of Sakha (Yakutiya), in the Amur oblast, in Khabarovsk kray, and in Primorsk kray. All the other energy systems are isolated, and operate independently from each other. And this, of course, imposes some very serious constraints on any proposals for [energy] strategies, which have to be formulated separately for every individual part of the energy system in the Far East, and also separately for isolated regions.[59]

One of these particularly isolated regions, the Kamchatka Peninsula, for example, relies entirely on electricity generated by massive local power plants operating on fuel oil. This was the ideal fuel in the Soviet period given the remoteness of the region. It was relatively easy to transport over long distances by road as well as by ship. Today, however, fuel oil has become extremely expensive. As UES spokesman Yuriy Melikhov pointed out during a power crisis in Kamchatka: "In Soviet times, no one counted expenses . . . [now] . . . oil fuel is the most expensive kind of fuel. When you include very high transportation expenses, Kamchatka has the most expensive electricity in Russia."[60] In July 2002, unable to meet its debts for fuel to the sole supplier—Russian state oil company Rosneft'—the Kamchatka branch of UES faced the prospect of having to suspend power generation entirely, plunging the region into a blackout. Regional authorities called, in response, for a new long-term regional energy development program that would include tapping into local gas resources and completely overhauling the power generation infrastructure. But the immediate problem was solved only through government intervention with Rosneft' to help restructure the region's fuel debts. In his August presentation on the fuel and power generation crisis in the Russian Far East, Anatoliy Chubays noted that cost was the primary factor in thinking about the issue. Of these costs, the price of the fuel itself might account for one-third, while transportation would account for fully two-thirds. Outside Kamchatka, other power stations in the Russian Far East are largely coal fired, with coal also brought in by rail over long distances from western and eastern Siberia.[61]

In sum, although we are advocating city shrinkage, it would seem to be an almost insurmountable task for Russia. At the same time, all the fixes to improve the situation with power generation and heating cost and efficiency also seem to lead back to high-cost interventions. The modernization of one UES rural power station serving 3,000 people in Russia alone is said to cost around $35 million.[62] Moreover, the estimated costs for simply meeting the minimum annual needs of replacement of obsolete generation capacity in the late 1990s were more than $3.5 billion, with an additional $750 million required to upgrade and improve the UES transmission network.[63] As one of our interlocutors in the Russian energy sector remarked, "It would be cheaper to move people out of these Siberian and Russian Far East cities altogether than to try to restructure all the energy and electricity supply systems, or shift some of the coal and fuel oil systems over to new gas infrastructure."[64]

Power and heating systems, and the related infrastructure, were designed to form an indivisible whole. Division and downsizing inevitably mean destruction and starting anew, while maintaining one part of the system means maintaining the whole—a genuine dilemma for Russian policy-makers. So if there are indeed technical obstacles to downsizing cities in Siberia and the Russian Far East, and if maintaining them is prohibitive, is it really conceivable that Russians could and would simply abandon certain cities altogether and relocate their populations en masse to European Russia? Can cities of several hundred thousand or even one million people effectively become ghost towns at the beginning of the twenty-first century?

What happens if Russia cannot cut the Gordian knot of its historical baggage? If Russia cannot shrink and warm up, what does this mean? Russian responses, so far, involve muddling along. The idea is to keep everyone in place and try to improve efficiency within the existing constraints. This is an unsustainable approach in the long term. Muddling along only appears to be less costly than a policy of shrinkage. In fact, it is not. Local governments will continue to demand expensive central government interventions just to maintain the status quo. Worse yet, failure to acknowledge the necessity of downsizing in the east will only increase the temptation to view Siberia as the key to Russian economic development. The Russian government has maintained a policy of redeveloping and repopulating Siberia and the Russian Far East in spite of the evident lack of financial and human resources for most of the plans put forward. In doing so, it condemns the country to a further cycle of misallocation.

9

Russia of the Mind

Beyond the concrete difficulties associated with mobility and migration and the concept of city shrinkage, the most serious obstacle of all to changing Russia's economic geography is the continued fixation on Siberia as a central element in future development. Today in Russia, there is a political imperative on maintaining and expanding Siberia's existing assets—the cities, factories, and mines inherited from the GULAG. Programs for Siberian redevelopment and policies designed to bring in migrants and immigrants to stem the decline of its population and labor force have all been put forward. Ultimately, government efforts to repopulate Siberia will create more problems than they solve. An influx of immigrants will bring new dilemmas. Government interventions will still be required to contend with the severe cold spells, frequent power outages, and floods that plague the region after every severe winter. Battling the elements in Siberia will continue to drain resources away from Moscow and other more productive areas and to imperil the region's unique and fragile ecology.

In the tsarist period, Siberia was attractive to some as a place of escape or adventure. Likewise, in the late Soviet period, scholars and scientists moved voluntarily to work in the Russian Academy of Sciences branches in cities like Novosibirsk. Here they hoped to escape from stringent Communist Party control in Moscow and to gain intellectual freedom and a degree of opportunity to do their own thing. For others who came out to work in the defense enterprises, extractive industries, and huge factories of Siberia, there was the attraction of higher wages and the opportunity to be "pioneers" on the frontier of new Soviet industrial power. Today, as we discussed earlier in the case of Noril'sk, although the value of these comparative freedoms and opportunities is gone, at the micro or household level, housing subsidies and other benefits keep people in place.

Siberia has also acquired a certain mythology for today's Russian population. The ideas of the 1970s of exploiting Siberia's vast resources and building a Soviet industrial utopia were still very much current in the 1980s, especially with the push to complete the BAM railway project, one of the last great Soviet construction achievements. Siberia and its natural wonders, like Lake Baykal, were also a favored subject of the "Village Writers" of the 1980s, who revived Russian nationalist and pastoralist themes in late Soviet literature. In short, the Soviet mythology of Siberia is a recent and vivid memory for the generation of contemporary Russian leaders who came of age in the 1970s and 1980s.

The image of Siberia became particularly politicized in the 1990s, with the revival of late-nineteenth- and early-twentieth-century theories of "Eurasianism," which offered a popular justification for Russia's unique geographical position between Europe and Asia.[1] A full-fledged Eurasianist political movement, headed by philosopher Alexander Dugin, emerged in the late 1990s, emphasizing Russia's command and control of the "North" and the lands of the Arctic (Arctogaia).[2] Based on the early-twentieth-century geopolitical theories of British scholar Halford Mackinder, Dugin's movement advocated the "self-sufficiency of [Russia's] large spaces" and increasingly dense settlement of Siberia—with the declaration that "sacred places are never empty."[3] Although the Eurasianist movement was something of a novelty act in Russian politics, it also had a not inconsiderable influence in shaping views among policymakers and analysts about Russia's dual role in Europe and Asia. Dugin himself became an advisor on "geopolitical affairs" to Russian parliamentary speaker Gennadiy Seleznov and was associated with a number of ultranationalist politicians, as well as Russian television show host Mikhail Leontiev and the right-wing newspaper *Zavtra*.[4] Eurasianist ideas were also espoused by more mainstream

Russian nationalist parties, like Unity, Fatherland–All Russia, the Communist Party, and the Liberal Democratic Party—whose members dominate the Russian Duma's Committee on Geopolitics—and were reflected in speeches by political leaders, including President Putin.[5] "Eurasianist" assertions, like "He who controls the Arctic controls the world," remain a common feature of Russian newspaper commentaries and analytical pieces on Siberia and the Russian North.[6]

In all these references and discussions, Siberia is the key to Russia's boast to straddle Europe and all of Asia. Without it, Russia would not have its reach and relevance. Even distinguished western observers like historian James Billington, the U.S. Librarian of Congress, continue to see Siberia as the essence of Russia: "Siberia is the ideal location because it has become the emotional focus of Russia's quest for a new national identity as a developing frontier civilization rather than a militant imperial power."[7]

In the 1990s, this political mythology of Siberia also became closely linked to concepts of Russian security and the fear of a demographic and geopolitical vacuum in the Russian Far East that might eventually be filled by China. Given that the region north of the Amur River—wrested from China in the late nineteenth century—was one of the last territories brought into the Russian empire and that serious military clashes broke out in 1969 between the USSR and China over disputed territory along the Amur River, these fears were not unjustified. Siberia and the Russian Far East were two of the most heavily militarized regions of Russia in the Soviet period, especially in the 1970s.[8] Today Russia's economic and demographic decline has coincided with China's economic and demographic boom. The buildup of Chinese conventional military forces has occurred at the same time that Russia's own military is in a process of abject decay, leaving Russian policymakers understandably nervous.

The threat from China in the Russian Far East; the potential influx of Chinese migrants into rapidly emptying Russian lands; and how to maintain Russia's military presence in the region have all become frequent topics of political debate in Moscow as well as in Siberia and the Far East.[9] Indeed, in many respects, contemporary Russian leaders and analysts are still grappling with the security dilemmas that have plagued Russia since the tsarist era. How does the government ensure Russian sovereignty over such a vast territory and protect it from encroachment? Does Russia's size alone still insure it against aggression? Can its territorial integrity be maintained even if large swaths are thinly populated or not populated at all? Will Russia's demographic decline mean that Siberia and the Russian Far East will once again be seen as *terra nullius*—empty lands subject to external claim and seizure?

Then there is the perennial idea of Siberia as Russia's treasure chest. The Russian press is still replete with articles extolling the importance of stimulating Russian economic growth by tapping into the resources—the oil, gas, coal, platinum metals, copper, hydroelectric potential, and so on—of Siberia and the North.[10] Resistance to deemphasizing Siberia and the North in Russian economic policy comes from the continued importance of exploiting natural resources and finding new oil and gas fields.[11] It also comes from the tendency of "oligarchs," Russia's new business leaders, and would-be Russian politicians at the federal level to carve out fiefdoms for themselves in remote, resource-rich areas so they can increase their influence at the center.

Erstwhile Russian presidential candidate General Alexander Lebed, for example, having lost the 1996 election to Boris Yeltsin, secured the governorship of one of Russia's largest—and most sparsely populated—territories, Krasnoyarsk, in May 1998. From this new and influential political base, he proceeded to clash with local industrial heavyweights and the central government before his untimely demise in a helicopter crash in April 2002.[12] Likewise in December 2000, Russian oligarch Roman Abramovich, the head of the Sibneft oil company and a major shareholder in the aluminum and air transportation industries, became governor of remote and impoverished Chukotka in the Russian Far North.[13] Since then, Abramovich has effectively replaced, if not usurped, the role of the state in the region. He has literally supported the population out of his own pocket, provoking a great deal of speculation about his intentions.[14] Life in Chukotka is particularly grim for its 78,600 inhabitants, who are spread across a huge territory—737,700 square kilometers—and have the highest costs of living in the Russian Federation, with about 75 percent of their monthly wages eaten up by food costs alone.[15] However, while Siberia offers bleak prospects for most of its inhabitants, for Russia's businessmen and politicians it remains the frontier of opportunity.

Planning for Siberia

All of this produces a heady Siberian cocktail that leads back again to the kinds of plans for Siberia's development that existed in the Soviet era. Indeed, projects to maintain and redevelop Siberia have continued unabated over the past decade—at least on paper—while economists and analysts have urged the Russian government to implement them.[16] Even some of the most grandiose schemes of the Soviet era for exploiting Siberia's vast resources have persisted as current ideas. This includes the plan, first promoted in the 1970s and 1980s, to tap the plentiful supply of water from the great Siberian rivers and transport it via a giant series of canals to irrigate the cotton fields of drought-plagued Central Asia. In early December 2002, Moscow mayor Yuriy Luzhkov purportedly sent a letter to President Vladimir Putin proposing that Russia sell "excess" Siberian water to Central Asia. He suggested the construction (with the assistance of Moscow-based construction companies) of a 2,225-kilometer canal (at a cost estimated between $12 billion and $20 billion), from the Ob' River through Kazakhstan to Uzbekistan to supplement the depleted waters of the Amu-Darya and Syr-Darya Rivers in Central Asia.[17] The original Soviet Siberia–Central Asia canal construction plan was abandoned in the mid-1980s because of the high investment costs involved. In contrast, other major Soviet canals, such as the White Sea–Onega and the Moscow-Volga canals, were built in the Stalin period using GULAG labor, with cost never considered as an issue.

In April 2002, after much lobbying by regional leaders, the Russian government approved a twenty-year "Strategy for the Economic Development of Siberia." This plan was drafted by a group of Siberian think tanks and regional associations in conjunction with the Ministry of Economic Development and Trade. The strategy (largely declaratory in nature) aimed to promote, among other worthy goals, the construction of new infrastructure and the modernization of existing transportation; to lower transportation tariffs and tax incentives to help reduce high Siberian industrial production costs; and to introduce energy-efficient technology.[18] The whole strategy was based on the hope of some additional federal and regional budget funds. In an echo of the Soviet-era "Engels dictum" (that all productive forces should be more uniformly spread throughout the country), one overarching goal of the strategy was to reduce "the difference in economic development among the regions" by restructuring the Siberian economy and generally stimulating economic growth.[19]

As might be anticipated, the basic premise of the strategy was rooted in the idea that a combination of Siberia's rich natural resources and a "good" central government plan would be the key to success. One supporter of the strategy, Leonid Drachevskiy, President Putin's polpred for the Siberian federal district, argued: "All the difficulties stemming from Siberia's geographical position and harsh climate are offset by the tremendous wealth of its natural resources. All that is needed from the state is a systematic approach to the solution of Siberia's problems." Drachevskiy noted that given sufficient opportunity to secure international investment, Siberia could in fact fund its own development. In addition to its resource base, Siberia was bolstered by its "science-intensive technologies," its Academy of Sciences research centers and defense enterprises, its machine-building plants, its forestry complex, and its transportation routes to Europe and Asia. It would simply "be enough," Drachevskiy declared, "if the government showed some attention to the region."[20]

Unfortunately, simple "attention" from the Russian central government to Siberia is unlikely to be enough. And in spite of the fact that Drachevskiy and many others in Russia have asserted that all Siberia needs is "a new, focused regional policy" to succeed in its development, Siberia will need far more than a plan if the aspirations to redevelop its current economic profile are to be realized.[21] As Russian policymakers and analysts themselves have acknowledged, it will once again take heroic and costly measures on the part of the central as well as the regional governments to rebuild existing infrastructure, increase energy efficiency and supply, and create a single economic system. Resources to accomplish these goals are in extremely short supply. Indeed, this very issue was the focus of a high-level debate in Vladivostok, during a presidential visit to the Russian Far East in August 2002. As part of the visit, President Putin convened a meeting of central government and regional leaders to discuss the social and economic problems of the Far East Federal District.[22] Once again, a development policy was seen as the starting point (and one had been requested by the president in August 2000 for the region). However, Viktor Khristenko, the Russian deputy prime minister in charge of regional economic policy, also noted that the Russian government would have to set priorities and admit that some parts of the region, especially the north with its harsh climate, would be difficult to redevelop. Khristenko recommended, in response, that the Russian government concentrate its efforts on the south of the region.

At the end of the Vladivostok meeting, President Putin concluded that "the problems in the region are far greater than the number of solutions" and the Far East's potential could be fully realized only with "intense effort." President Putin went on to assert:

> [The Russian Far East] is that very part of the Russian Federation where we will have to undertake policies that are no longer in fashion [elsewhere]—that is preferential policies. We can't do anything about this, and if we try to do something else then we will never succeed—indeed, we have not been able to historically. The preferential tariffs we have today for the railways, for electrical power, for investment, for the whole range of government support—these preferential policies will have to be retained, and they will be retained.... The plans for developing the Far East region ... are without any exaggeration on a large scale and grandiose. We need to strive to ensure that they are realized.[23]

In spite of President Putin's pronouncements, development plans for Siberia and the Russian Far East have languished in their grandiose elaboration on paper with little prospect of implementation.

More Warm Bodies for Siberia

One of the primary problems noted by Russian government officials at the August 2002 Vladivostok meeting is that all these large-scale and grandiose redevelopment projects for Siberia also require labor—and labor that is far in excess of the current population pool in Siberia and the Russian Far East. As Viktor Ishayev, the governor of the Far East oblast of Khabarovsk, declared at the meeting, "We will not conquer the Far East if we do not create a permanent population."[24] Concerning its inherited Soviet economy—rather than the portion of its economy that is viable under market economic conditions—Siberia today faces a critical labor shortage in the same way that it did in the late Soviet period, in the 1980s. It does not have sufficient people willing to work in harsh conditions for extremely low pay to keep failing enterprises and mines afloat, let alone to build the proposed new infrastructure.

As a result, keeping people in place and bringing more people into Siberia and the Russian Far East (even as the existing population tries to move out) have become major themes for Russian politicians in the region and in Moscow. In an earlier speech in Siberia, in February 2001, President Putin noted: "In recent years the population of most of our Siberian regions has been steadily declining. People are leaving. They are leaving because they simply see no future for themselves. The demographic imbalance between the European part of Russia and the Trans-Ural regions—which is bad enough as it is—has exacerbated in recent years. . . . We have to substantially raise the migration attractiveness of our Trans-Ural regions."[25] Similarly, in an interview with the Russian press in July 2002, former Russian prime minister Yevgeniy Primakov (once again echoing the "Engels dictum") asserted that one of the main problems facing Russia was "the unevenness in the distribution of population across Russia's territory. There is a 'vacuum' in the Far East, in East Siberia. But a vacuum always fills itself."[26]

But how, in fact, will this perceived vacuum fill itself? Again, as Viktor Ishayev admitted at the August 2002 meeting in Vladivostok, "[the Russian Far East] did not develop on a commercial basis. It developed because it was fulfilling a geopolitical, geostrategic mission, which the state and the government always imposed. People came to live here not because they really wanted to, because it was warm here, because there was plenty to eat, or because it was

comfortable. It was a mission. That's why people came. That's why they conquered the Far East."[27]

Ishayev's statement once more brings us full circle to exhortation and
compulsion. Indeed, the idea that the Russian state should explicitly direct
labor to certain areas and industries, rather than allow the market to decide
(by giving people a choice), remains deeply rooted in Russian political
thinking. At the Vladivostok meeting, although both Deputy Prime Minister Khristenko and President Putin noted in their presentations that the
usual axiom for people in selecting their place of work and residence in a
market economy was "you should work where it is most efficient and live
where it is most comfortable," they both stressed that there should also be
another imperative for people in Russia: "You should serve wherever the
state's interests require it." In fact, Putin went so far as to assert that as
Russia's commander-in-chief, it was up to him to decide "who serves
where."[28]

Although President Putin and other Russian leaders may still assert the
importance of a sense of mission and serving the state's interest, since the
1990s Russians have more readily responded to the pull of market/economic
forces in leaving Siberia and the Far East when they could. As experts like
the World Bank's Timothy Heleniak have indicated, in the period 1989–2001,
there was a significant degree of migration within the region. More than
12 percent of the population of the regions defined by the World Bank as the
Russian North (see appendix C) moved out of these remote areas—even
though many of these migrants, as noted in chapter 8, were not able to relocate out of Siberia completely.[29] As analysts have noted, the most dramatic
burst of migration was in 1992, immediately after the collapse of the Soviet
Union. While the pace of out-migration has waned as the political barriers to
mobility have been reintroduced and as it has become increasingly difficult
to relocate elsewhere in the Russian Federation, the very fact that such a mass
exodus did occur in the early 1990s was a strong and accurate market signal. It demonstrated that much of production in this part of the country is in
decline. This signal should have been noted by regional authorities and the
central government, but unfortunately it was not.

The end of Soviet-era subsidies was one of the major factors behind the
initial exodus. As we have already discussed, labor was a heavily subsidized
factor of production in Siberia and the Russian Far East until the collapse of
the USSR. Wage supplements were only a minor part of these subsidies. The
nonwage benefits provided by the Soviet state, independent of the particular enterprise for which people worked, were far more important for all residents of the region. These ranged from low prices for electricity, heat, and

housing to virtually free airplane travel back to European Russia. When this subsidization was reduced in the early 1990s, workers in Siberia and the Russian Far East did not find themselves compensated by higher cash wages and thus faced a massive real wage cut. Many responded as might have been expected—they left not just the enterprise, but also the region. This was a natural consequence of the loss of central government subsidies. With the exception of Noril'sk Nickel, almost no enterprise in the region was productive enough to be able to pay its employees a cash wage sufficient to compensate for the lost subsidies.

In economic terms, when workers cannot be paid enough to induce them to stay and they leave a factory, it should be a signal about the value of the capital (the factory). In Siberia and the Russian Far East in the 1990s, however, the "owners" of capital—the factory directors, the oligarchs who acquired Russian industrial assets, regional leaders, and ultimately the federal government in Moscow—did not receive, or at least did not understand, the implicit message from the out-migration that this capital was, in fact, less productive (more costly) than it appeared to be. The factory directors as well as the government all had a political commitment to uphold the value of the capital. The full-blown version of this scheme of maintaining the pretense of value in nonviable enterprises was described as Russia's "virtual economy."[30] Nowhere was the scheme more widespread than in the Urals and Siberia regions. Yet even there a problem arose. While political connections among enterprises and the government could ensure that the game was played by some in transactions between enterprises and between enterprises and the governments ("virtual" prices and "virtual" tax payments), many workers simply did not feel compelled to pretend that the "virtual" wages they were receiving were real. Labor was imbued with a free will; workers left the factories.

Thus there was an eventual imbalance between physical capital, the factories and machines on the one hand, and the workers on the other. Labor became the scarce factor. Indeed, labor would have been even scarcer had it not been for all the constraints on mobility in the Russian labor market. As we discussed in the last chapter, many people remain trapped in Siberia and the Far East. They are unable to relocate because of residence restrictions in the most desirable destinations, the underdeveloped Russian housing market, and the enduring importance of personal safety nets (household plots, social networks, and all the other coping mechanisms that have helped Russians survive the upheaval of the 1990s). Consequently, factories in Siberia were able to retain some portion of their former labor force in spite of all the negative incentives—although those who remained also tended often to be the least productive as well as the least mobile of the workers. They are those with the fewest skills and the poorest prospects for relocation.

Replacing Migrants with Immigrants

While they still fail to admit that factories and entire industries east of the Urals are increasingly unproductive, owners and regional authorities now see addressing the problem of scarce labor as the solution to restoring and defending their value. Without production, industrial assets would indeed seem worthless, and without labor there can be no production. However, given its limited ability to compensate for the lost subsidies of the Soviet era in the form of higher wages, how can the Russian government make Siberia and the Russian Far East attractive to labor? Can migrants from elsewhere in Russia or the broader region really be encouraged or inspired to move east of the Urals again? Should this be done by decreasing the attractiveness of everywhere else, or by emphasizing the negative features of other regions, as some Russian analysts have suggested?[31] Or should it be done by making it even more difficult than it is already for people to move to Moscow or to other European parts of Russia?

Encouraging ethnic Russians living in other republics of the Soviet Union to return to Russia to replace the lost labor force east of the Urals was initially seen as one solution to the problem of Siberia's declining population. At the dissolution of the USSR, approximately twenty-five million ethnic Russians lived beyond the borders of the Russian Federation. In 1992 members of this diaspora and other former Soviet citizens were granted the right under the new Russian citizenship law to "return" or to immigrate to the Russian Federation, provided they established their Russian residence and applied for citizenship before 2000.[32] However, as in the case of migration within the Russian Federation, there was an initial burst of migration to Russia from other former Soviet republics immediately after the break-up of the USSR, which peaked in 1994 and then tapered off significantly.[33] Of the twenty-five million ethnic Russians registered outside the Russian Federation in the last Soviet census (1989), only three million have actually returned to Russia since then, with the bulk moving from Central Asia and Ukraine. The majority—twenty-two million—have, in fact, chosen not to relocate. They are now unlikely to do so, given the passing of the 2000 deadline.[34] Timothy Heleniak and other migration experts conclude that this "migration momentum seems to have nearly exhausted itself."[35]

Since Russians from the diaspora no longer seem likely to return in large numbers, the Russian state and regional authorities have begun to flirt with the idea of immigrant labor—importing workers from outside Russia—to compensate for scarcity in places like Siberia. Indeed, immigration is already a reality in Russia, not just a prospective fix. However, as elsewhere in Europe, it has also become one of the most contentious issues of the early twenty-first century. Immigrant labor seems more likely to lead to increasing problems in Siberia than to solutions.

Officially, there are only slightly more than 200,000 immigrant workers in Russia today.[36] But experts estimate that there are an additional 3 million to 3.5 million illegal foreign workers in the country—about 5 percent of the national labor force.[37] More than 90 percent of all immigrant workers in Russia are employed in jobs that are low in skills and prestige and require heavy manual labor. Like immigrants in other developed economies, they work in jobs that native Russians reject because such jobs are dirty, difficult, or in remote locations. Nearly one-third of these foreign workers are in western Siberia and the Russian Far East, where they work predominantly in markets, on farms, and in construction. In the Far East, foreign workers are reported to account for over half of the labor force of some construction enterprises; in northern Tyumen' oblast, they account for up to 70, 80, and even 90 percent.[38] In Siberia, immigrant workers from Central Asia have become a major part of the regional work force, fleeing an even more dire situation at home.[39]

Central Asians in Siberia

Today there are approximately half a million Tajik and a similar number of Kyrgyz immigrant workers in Russia. Many have sought jobs in the produce markets, enterprises, and construction industries of western Siberia, especially in the Yekaterinburg and Novosibirsk regions. They are attracted by salaries that are relatively low by Russian standards but high for workers from these two impoverished Central Asian states.

There are now so many Kyrgyz citizens working permanently in Russia that in 2002 the government of Kyrgyzstan requested and received permission to set up a consulate in Yekaterinburg to deal with their needs—a "first" in the new post-Soviet relationship between the Central Asian states and the Russian Federation. In December 2002, a Kyrgyz government delegation was also dispatched to Russia's Volga region and Siberia to meet with Kyrgyz migrant workers and assess their living conditions.[40] Direct flights

180 RUSSIA OF THE MIND

between the Kyrgyz capital of Bishkek and Yekaterinburg and Novosibirsk, as well as bus and rail routes to Siberia from Kyrgyzstan across Kazakhstan, have all increased in number and frequency. Western Siberia is seen as relatively "close" for Kyrgyz workers, who also have historic associations with the territory of the Altay region in southern Siberia.

The interaction with the Siberian economy is having a significant impact on Kyrgyzstan's economy and creating multiple interdependencies. Kyrgyz businesses are procuring and producing goods especially for the Siberian market, including foodstuffs and cheap clothing using Central Asian textiles. Kyrgyz "shuttle traders" also often buy cheap products in neighboring China for resale in Siberia. Kyrgyz consumer goods have proved highly competitive with comparable Russian products, given the high cost of living in Siberia and the difficulties and costs of "importing" consumer goods over the long distances from European Russia. Central Asian sociologists predict that since most Central Asians speak Russian and are willing to work for low wages, Kyrgyz and other similar immigrant workers will soon become a mainstay of the Siberian economy. It is unlikely, however, based on the relative proximity and ease of transportation, that workers from Central Asia will travel as far as the Russian Far East in search of work, so this will likely remain a phenomenon of western Siberia.[41]

Bringing in the Chinese?

Many Russian analysts have lauded Central Asian and other Asian immigrant labor as the answer to Siberia's asserted labor shortages. The members of the prominent Council on Foreign and Defense Policy, for example, asserted in a June 2001 report on Siberia and the Far East:

> The only way to prevent the depopulation of the huge Siberian and Far Eastern territories is through immigration, which is also the only way to improve the sex and age structure of the population. Given that immigrants are already arriving from the Asian-Pacific region, principally from China, this immigration should be seen as socially significant and should be welcomed by the state. . . . Given that Chinese immigration . . . is inevitable, a targeted information and propaganda campaign should be organized to change public opinion, calm its fears of "the yellow peril" and form a positive image of Asian immigrants.[42]

The council's reference to Chinese immigration raises some interesting issues. In fact, Chinese immigration is not as significant as thought, despite the fears of some Russian politicians about a mass influx of Chinese workers and would-be settlers in the Russian Far East and declarations by regional officials that hundreds of thousands have already poured across Russia's borders with millions more from China's "overcrowded" northern provinces poised to follow.[43]

In the 1990s, some Russian analysts claimed that as many as 2.5 million Chinese migrants were living and working in Russia. Even the most conservative estimates put the figure at 200,000—a twenty-fold increase since 1989, when only 11,000 ethnic Chinese were recorded in the entire USSR.[44] In contrast, official Chinese government figures put the number of Chinese citizens working across the entire territory of the former Soviet Union (not just Russia) in 2002 at around 300,000. Opinion surveys of Chinese migrants in Moscow, as well as in the Far East cities of Khabarovsk and Vladivostok, indicate that very few of these migrants seek to remain in Russia on a permanent basis.[45] The perception of Chinese migration into Russia's Far East far outweighs the reality.[46] But this misperception of waves of Chinese moving across Russia's borders also leads right into the heart of a backlash against nonethnic Russian immigration across the Russian Federation—which has become increasingly acute on the popular level.

As Timothy Heleniak has concluded from his work on migration in the Russian Federation, Russia's anti-immigration lobby is "in the ascendant."[47] While some Russian policymakers call for more foreign workers as replacement labor for Siberia and the Russian Far East, most insist that Russia has been flooded with too many foreigners since the collapse of the USSR. They have pushed for more restrictions on refugees and immigrants as well as more stringent citizenship requirements.[48] The Russian Federal Migration Service, set up in the early 1990s to encourage and manage migration, was abolished in 2000 and folded into the Interior Ministry in May 2002. In December 2002, the Russian State Duma began debating a new draft national migration policy, first drawn up in 1998, that would impose controls on both legal and illegal immigration.[49] In addition to contending with attempts to exert more political control over immigration, foreign workers in Russia have already had to face blatant exploitation by regional employers as well as harassment from local authorities and populations. In 2002 there were several reports of racially motivated murders of immigrant workers from Central Asia.[50] One of the more astounding examples of the exploitation of illegal immigrant labor from Central Asia was revealed in a Russian radio report in November 2002 (see box 9-1).

The popular and political backlash against immigration aside, the use of illegal immigrants as "slave labor" on a Siberian vegetable farm raises one major question that remains unanswered in Russian discussions of migration

Box 9-1. *"Uzbek Slaves Freed from Russian Vegetable Farm in Siberia"*

"Police in Novosibirsk have freed fifty slaves from Uzbekistan who had spent six months working on a vegetable farm. Before the frosts came, they were virtually living in the open air. Details from our correspondent Aleksandr Yerakhtin.

"[Correspondent:] The freed slaves say that at first it appeared as if they were being recruited for work. Last spring a woman from Novosibirsk visited Fergana and Namangan, where she took on a fifty-strong group of Uzbeks to cultivate carrots. They were promised pay of one hundred dollars a month. The vegetable farmers got onto a bus and were taken to Novosibirsk. En route their documents were taken from them, apparently for processing.

"On arrival, it became clear that the work was out of town, virtually in the open air. They put up a bivouac of sorts in the field and there they lived. They were not paid the money they had been promised. They were mostly fed on peas. The Uzbeks quickly realized their plight and that without money or documents it would be very difficult to get back home. The majority did manage to get away and found fellow-countrymen at the town markets. The last six slaves were moved by the entrepreneurs and put to work in a warehouse, sorting vegetables, which is where they were freed by the Novosibirsk police.

"I was told by the press service of the regional police that two overseers were arrested in the operation. Both are students, one at law school. An inquiry is under way."

Source: Radio Mayak, Moscow, in Russian, 1200 GMT 21 November 2002.

and the labor shortage in Siberia—does Siberia, in fact, really have a labor shortage? We suggest that it does not. Instead of seeking labor, or slaves, that can put up with wages low enough to make either private farms or the existing industries profitable, Russian policymakers need to focus their attention on trying to create new productive industries that can employ the current Russian labor force at a decent wage level, without compulsion—and probably not in Siberia. Unfortunately, Russia is trapped by trying to maintain the apparent value of the physical assets it inherited from the Soviet Union—the legacy of the GULAG.

The GULAG's Legacy

At the beginning of the twenty-first century, Russia finds itself battling with the dilemma of what to do with its resources in cold, remote regions and how to address the sunk costs of infrastructure, cities, and factories built by the GULAG and gifted—passed on—by Stalin to his successors. The resources located in the ground in Siberia—oil, gas, diamonds, gold, and so on—are safely deposited there until they are exploited. It costs nothing to leave them lying there untouched (one possible exception: the costs of defending the territory). However, the "gift" of the GULAG prisoners to modern Russia is not the resources themselves, but the infrastructure that (perhaps) makes the exploitation of these resources worthwhile. Russians today would be unlikely to create most of the extractive industries and enterprises they have inherited in Siberia given high labor costs and market prices of other inputs. But the assets are there. They are already built and in operation. The sunk costs cannot now be saved by abandoning these GULAG assets, and the infrastructure must be maintained. While it may be profitable to exploit some of Siberia's resources today, thanks to the sunk costs of the GULAG, this does not mean that it will necessarily be profitable tomorrow, given future capital investment costs that will grow over time, probably exponentially. Profitability, capital and operating costs, and sales revenues were never a factor in driving the decision to build a factory under the GULAG system. But they are factors in its operation today.

Even if Central Asians and others are willing to come to Siberia to work for lower wages than ethnic Russians to escape unemployment and poverty at home, they are still coming to work in unproductive industries in cities like Yekaterinburg and Novosibirsk, as well as others farther afield in Siberia and the Far East. These are cities that were built up in the Soviet period on the basis of central planning rather than economic principles. As a result, the foreign workers are effectively being used to sanction the continuation of factories that would otherwise not survive under market conditions.[51] They are also being used to bolster declining and ultimately doomed heavy and extractive industrial sectors. Once immigrants are brought in to work in these industries—especially if they are given long-term work permits and ultimately residency and citizenship—they are likely, in a decade or so, to find themselves stranded in Siberia as the industries disappear beneath them. Russia could then face the kinds of problems experienced by other European countries such as Great Britain after World War II, when the government encouraged immigrant workers to come to fill low-paid, unskilled jobs rejected by domestic workers. In the British case, South Asian immigrants were brought in to keep already unprofitable textile factories in production in cities in northern England that were heavily dependent on the industry for employment. The British textile industry subsequently collapsed, leaving second- and third-generation immigrant families trapped in decaying urban areas with little prospect of new employment. In 2001 several former textile towns in northern England were wracked by social upheaval and riots attributed to the high rates of unemployment, deprivation, and frustration among postwar immigrants.[52]

If formal immigrant labor proves difficult to sustain, then illegal immigration or even "slave labor" may become the only means of keeping some industrial sectors in production given their lack of profitability. Indeed, in spite of the demise of the GULAG, the use of Russian state-sanctioned forced labor is still alive and well today in the Russian Far East thanks to North Korea.

North Korean Slave Laborers in the Russian Far East

When the reclusive North Korean president, Kim Jong Il, met with Russian president Vladimir Putin in August 2001, he made his journey to Moscow a public relations tour of sorts, traveling by train with several stops along the way. The trip made headlines, but it also resulted in several articles exposing the continued use of North Korean slave labor in the Russian Far East. According to a *Wall Street Journal* article by Claudia Rosett, North Koreans began filtering into Russian logging operations in the late 1960s, when a deal was struck between Leonid Brezhnev and Kim Il Sung. "Russia supplied the remote, inhospitable forest land, plus the fuel and transportation. North Korea shipped in the lumberjacks, rotating them through in three-year stints, accompanied by North Korean security agents. The two countries sold the lumber abroad for hard currency and shared the take."[53]

The collapse of the Soviet Union called into question the continuation of such camps. Weighing concerns for human rights against the need for hard currency, Russian officials opted to scale back operations—although not to dismantle the camps entirely.[54] For its part, North Korea saw the continued shipment of slave labor as a means of offsetting its Soviet-era debts to Russia. In an interview with an official from the Russian Economic Development and Trade Ministry, the *Moscow Times* discovered that the ministry "officially classifies such workers as 'exports' and calculates that they account for 90 percent of all 'goods' imported from North Korea every year."[55] In 2000 Pyongyang was reported to have relied on this method of "exports" to reduce its $3.8 billion debt to Moscow by $50.4 million.[56]

Figures on how many camps still exist are murky. Estimates put the number of slave laborers between 6,000 and 15,000. Some analysts argue that the numbers will continue to increase as more North Koreans determine that life in the camps is actually better than life in their home country, if only because workers are fed three meals a day. In her investigation, Rosett learned that some North Koreans were even bribing Pyongyang authorities for the opportunity to go work in the camps.

Masking the True Costs of Production

Slave labor and illegal migration may be a way of keeping logging operations and other extractive industries viable. Ultimately, however, they mask the true costs of production: the necessity of maintaining coercive methods and the social problems associated with the creation of an underclass within the Russian labor force without access to housing, healthcare, education, and other social services; stripped of protections; and subject to predation. Indeed, the very existence of an industrialized Siberia and the Russian Far East and the perceived need to maintain and develop these regions becomes a cause of illegal migration within the Russian Federation. It creates a demand for extremely "cheap" labor that Russians and legal immigration will not fill. Compulsion and coercion of labor seem likely to be as much a part of Siberia's future as of its past and present if Russian policymakers continue to refuse to acknowledge the region's limitations. In spite of all the evidence that Siberia and the Russian Far East cannot function as modern market economies in their existing industrial profile and with their current distribution of population, prominent Russian analysts and politicians repeatedly and consistently assert that the only solution is to bring more people in.

Consider just two recent comments: sociologist and demographer Zhanna Zayonchkovskaya, who is generally recognized as one of Russia's leading experts on migration—"The situation is now such that the big empty spaces can't be developed without topping up the population. . . . The government doesn't understand that we won't be able to develop Siberia on our own"— and Putin's polpred for the Siberian Federal District, Leonid Drachevskiy— "The whole history of our state has been a search for ways to settle and provide stimuli to settle Siberia."[57] On the final point, while settling Siberia may not in fact define the whole history of the Russian state, as we have already discussed, it has certainly been the constant pathology of the country's leadership since the 1930s. Even though ordinary Russians had to be forced into exile and dragged to Siberia through the GULAG system, or induced to go there with all kinds of elaborate incentives and subsidies once coercion came to an end, the idea of Siberia as Russia's destiny is an ideology that has been imposed from the top. Common sense and sober economic analysis have all taken a back seat to the mythologization and ideologization of Siberia for the best part of a century.

An End to the Ideology of Space

As we have tried to demonstrate in our discussions of the disadvantage of "size" and the costs of the "cold," Siberia is in fact overpopulated for its economy. Its population is almost entirely mislocated. Siberia is also misdeveloped, rather than underdeveloped. It needs to be downsized, not filled up again with people. The fundamental problem is the way that Russians have thought about and continue to think about the relationship of their state to the land. Russia has traditionally been defined by its land—the size of its territory. Everything in Russia has been thought of in spatial terms—*prostranstvo* in Russian. Space, *prostranstvo*, has spawned a whole series of theories and been seen as "by far the most important element of statehood."[58] In economic terms, however, the spatial aspects of Russian statehood are no more and no less important than anything else.

For most of its modern history, Russia has been defined more by conceptions of geopolitics than economics. It has let its physical geography overwhelm it, clinging since the tsarist period to the idea that controlling territory means putting people there. If there is a security vacuum, or if foreigners seem poised to move in, then this requires more people to move to the threatened territory. In an interview in July 2002, for example, Grigoriy Yavlinskiy, head of Russia's Yabloko Party, was quick to criticize Russia's rampant "migrant phobia," asserting in response that "Russia, which loses 700,000 people a year [in natural population decrease], will soon be unable to maintain its sovereignty in Siberia and in the Far East. That is why not migrants, but prevention of migration is the real threat for the security of Russia."[59] However, the current policies to redevelop Siberia and to target migration and immigration to areas east of the Urals are all premised on the wrong mentality. Russia does not necessarily need more people to fill up its empty spaces; it needs to have the people it already has in different places.

The Soviet-era fixation on physical assets—if you have a natural resource you need to exploit it, and if you have a factory, you must do something with it—has also led Russia astray today. The Soviets, when they embarked on their enterprise to develop the USSR and Siberia, believed they had infinite resources of land and people. The only thing they lacked was industrial infrastructure. Of these three traditional factors of production—land, labor, and capital—the Bolsheviks thought they had more than anyone else of the first two. All they needed to do was requisition the labor to create the third and to transform the USSR into an industrial economy with a uniform or even distribution of the forces of production across the entire country. Ironically for the movement that styled itself "the vanguard of the toiling masses," it turned out that labor—not capital—was their ultimate constraint.

Today this logic must be reversed. Russians need to get rid of the idea that land is the benchmark of everything in Russia and instead embrace the idea that the real benchmark is people—Russia's human capital. Labor is, today, the critical factor for every developed economy. This is especially the case for Russia, which faces acute demographic problems. Since the 1970s, Russian leaders have become increasingly worried about a sheer lack of people—of Russians simply "running out." Western demographers also predict a dramatic decline in the Russian population's numbers as well as in its general health and well-being.[60] Russia's population fell from 147 million people in the 1989 census to around 145.2 million according to the preliminary figures from the 2002 census.[61] Future population projections vary quite markedly. The U.S. Census Bureau predicts that by 2015, Russia's population will drop to 141 million.[62] According to the Russian State Statistics Committee, Goskomstat, Russia's population could drop as low as 128 million by that year. If this contraction of population continues unchecked, in the next two decades it will return Russia roughly to where it was in 1900.

But quality not quantity of population is the key to the future. The definition of "too few people" is always seen as relative to the size of the country, not to the size of the economy. From the point of view of the economy, Russia has too many people of too poor quality—unhealthy, poor, increasingly ill-educated, and lacking in skills. To improve the quality of its population, Russia needs to pull some of its most productive forces back from some of the planet's most isolated places.

Unfortunately, Russian leaders continue to cling to the idea that Russia has its weight on the international stage by virtue of its territorial size. Size is at the root of Russia's greatness. No matter what you say about Russia, it is still the world's biggest country. Russian historians and scholars have depicted the country as guided throughout the centuries by a mission of the "Gathering of the Russian Lands"—Russia's own version of America's "Manifest Destiny."[63] Putin himself has been referred to as another potential "Gatherer of the Lands."[64] However, Russia's vast territory has been its fatal flaw since the days of the tsars. It cursed the Bolsheviks and the communists and now casts a pall over post-Soviet Russia. Russia needs to stop fixating on territory and start concentrating on its people. It especially needs to stop trying to find sufficient people to "fill up" and develop the territory of Siberia—a territory that simply should not have been developed in the manner it was in the first place.

Battling the Elements—Paying for Old Mistakes

In short, it is size that got Russia into trouble in the twentieth century. Today's generation, at the beginning of the twenty-first, does not face the heroic challenge of overcoming nature and conquering new lands beyond the Ural Mountains, as their parents and grandparents were regularly called to do in the Soviet era (see figure 9-1). Instead, theirs is the tedious task of paying for old mistakes in these regions. This payment comes due every winter with increased deprivation and suffering in Siberia and the Russian Far East. In winter 2000–01, the bill seemed unusually high when temperatures plunged to as low as −57° C and held steady at −40° C for several weeks in January and February. The winter was declared "the coldest this century," a freak of nature, while Siberia itself was pronounced "colder than Siberia."[65] In actual fact, winter 2000–01 was not the coldest of the century—unless reports were referring to the twenty-first rather than the twentieth century. Temperatures routinely fall to below −50° C in Siberia. In addition, average monthly temperatures in Siberia and the Russian Far East for 1969, 1972, and 1977 were somewhat lower than the averages for 2001 according to meteorological records from Russian weather stations.[66] To underscore this point, in January 2003, temperatures once again plummeted across Russia, leading to a flurry of commentary both inside and outside the country. The British newspaper the *Guardian* summed things up appropriately: "Situation normal: Russia is frozen solid."[67]

The spring thaw after every winter of profound cold also brings with it some particular challenges—floods—with, again, one of the most dramatic examples in 2001 in Lensk in Sakha (Yakutiya) (see box 9-2).

Every Russian winter is replete with stories of cities such as Lensk that have been turned into veritable "refrigerators." All across Siberia, infrastructure buckles and crumbles under the onslaught of the cold. Towns plunge into a frozen darkness as utilities fail. People freeze to death in their icy apartments (or apartments turn into ice blocks as in the case of Magadan in March 2001) or die in the street from hypothermia.[68] The federal and regional governments frequently intervene, and this is followed by a rash of resignations as local officials find themselves unable to counter the cold with their inadequate budgets (see box 9-3).

Such stories cause Russian officials at the highest levels in the Russian Federation great frustration. In a trip through Siberia and the Russian Far East in January 2001, President Putin called for regional officials to take responsibility for failing to provide energy and heat: "We talk a lot about needed
(*text continues on page 192*)

Figure 9-1. *Battling the Elements*

A Soviet-era poster declaring "Everyone to the Battle against the Blizzard!"

Box 9-2. *Lensk—Russia's Battle with the Elements*

In May 2001, over the course of two days, a fleet of Russian supersonic SU-24 bombers dropped approximately one hundred bombs—totaling more than eighty tons of explosives—on Russia's own territory. The target: a massive natural dam, made of ice, that spanned eighty kilometers of the Lena River, one of Siberia's major waterways.[a] Backed up behind the ice dam, the Lena had risen to a high mark of 20 meters (65 feet), exceeding its normal flood level by 6.5 meters (21 feet). It inundated 98 percent of the town of Lensk, located on its banks, prompting a drastic intervention by Russia's Ministry of Emergency Situations.[b] Nearly all of the town's 27,000 residents had to be evacuated as the floodwaters swept hundreds of homes away and damaged thousands of other buildings, roads, and bridges. It was not until the bombing campaign successfully broke up the ice that the waters over Lensk began to recede. Media coverage of the heroic "man versus nature" accounts placed the blame for the disaster on the "exceptionally cold" winter of 2001, which had caused an "abnormal" buildup of ice on the Lena River. Emergency Situations Minister Sergey Shoygu announced that "Russia has never had such devastating floods before."[c]

In reality, flooding in Lensk and elsewhere in Siberia is an almost yearly occurrence. Like all the great Siberian rivers, the Lena flows from south to north. Every spring, melting snows in the south run off into the Lena, usually before the frozen northern sections of the river thaw—with predictable and often catastrophic results. The southern sections of the Lena, swollen with meltwater, cannot continue along the river's natural course and spill over the riverbanks into the floodplain. Indeed, in one of the Russian press reports that described the Lena flood of 2001 as the worst in the past one hundred years, the author—completely without irony—referred to a flood only three years previously, in 1998, when the Lena floodwaters reached seventeen meters (fifty-five feet), more than ten meters above normal and only three meters lower than the 2001 level.[d] In short, almost every year, residents in the Siberian river regions fall victim to disastrous flooding, which often requires extraordinary intervention. Each time, residents rebuild their houses along the banks of the river. In 2001 billions of rubles from federal and regional budgets were poured into humanitarian assistance and the reconstruction of Lensk. And despite the efforts of Emergency Situations Minister Sergey Shoygu to relocate the town to a less vulnerable site, Lensk was rebuilt in exactly the same location.[e]

Lensk itself is a city of considerable significance for many Russians. The city's name, like that of first Soviet leader Vladimir Lenin (born Vladimir Ulyanov), is taken from the Lena River and is a symbol of the Soviet conquest of Siberia and nature. It is the major transportation hub for Mirnyy, Russia's diamond capital and the headquarters of ALROSA, the Russian diamond monopoly. However, Lensk was never designed to withstand floods. Indeed, its airport is located too close to the river to be used for rescue missions during a flood.[f] In Soviet times, the Ministry of Transportation set aside funds every year to dredge and to deepen the riverbed in order to prevent ice dams from forming.[g]

The flood of May 2001 had a major impact on Lensk and consequences for regional and federal authorities. After being blamed for mishandling the flooding in Lensk and then encountering Russian electoral term-limit laws, Sakha's (Yakutiya) incumbent president, Mikhail Nikolayev, withdrew his candidacy from the republic's elections in December 2001. The newly elected president of the republic, Vyacheslav Shtyrov, subsequently focused much attention on the city, promising that Lensk would not experience a flood for another five years (coincidentally, the length of his term in office).[h] Furthermore, Lensk became popularly known as "Putin's city" after the Russian president visited the city to oversee its reconstruction in fall 2001 and expressed the Russian government's commitment to its rebirth and survival.

But for the people of Lensk, life has not improved appreciably with the new attention—or with the new construction. The new concrete apartment buildings that were erected to replace those swept away in the floodwaters were built in record time. They are now plagued by leaking roofs and pipes, broken-down sanitation systems, and cracked exterior walls.[i] Most of the city's apartment buildings have inadequate heating. Many residents have to place electric heaters next to their radiators to keep the pipes from freezing and bursting. One newspaper headline in December 2002 suggested that a more appropriate new name for Lensk than "Putin's city" would be "Putin's refrigerator."[j]

a. "V strane i v mire," *Vechernaya Moskva*, 16 May 2001, p. 2; "State of emergency in the Sakha Republic (Yakutiya) occurred as a result of a flood in 1998," www.yakutia.ru/~pages/win/sos/saxarespE.htm.

b. Nadezhda Popova, "Bor'ba so stikhiey prodolzhayetsya," *Nezavisimaya gazeta*, 19 May 2001, p. 2.

c. Judith Ingram, "Water Rises in Flooded Siberia City," *Associated Press*, 21 May 2001.

d. Oleg Yemelyanov, "Siberia-Inundation. Water is nearly 20 meters high in Siberian city," *ITAR-TASS Weekly News*, 18 May 2001.

e. Extracted from several articles including: Anna Badkhen, "Powerful Spring Flood Threatens Siberian City," *Boston Globe*, 19 May 2001, p. A7; Anastasiya Naryshkina, "Unikal'nyye, no ne ochen'. Luchshiye almazy ostanutsya v Gosfonde," *Vremya novostey*, 7 June 2001, p. 4.

f. Anna Badkhen, "Powerful Spring Flood Threatens Siberian City."

g. "V strane i v mire," 16 May 2001, p. 2.

h. Yelena Milashina, "Mifu–mif. Yakutiya. Lensk: Led tronulsya. Zasedaniya prodolzhayutsya," *Novaya gazeta*, 20 May 2002.

i. Yelena Milashina, "Spetsial'nyy reportazh. Yakutiya. Lensk: Led tronulsya. Zasedaniya prodolzhayutsya (okonchaniye)," *Novaya gazeta*, 27 May 2002.

j. Yelena Milashina, "Nesluchaynyy zvonok v Lensk. Kholodil'nik im. Putina," *Novaya gazeta*, 16 December 2002.

Box 9-3. *The Cold Schoolboy and the President*

On December 24, 2001, Pavel Shvedkov, a schoolboy from the city of Ust'-Kut in the Siberian Irkutsk oblast near Lake Baykal, called President Putin during a nationwide "phone-in" to complain that his school had been closed indefinitely because of the cold. He asked the President to intervene.[a] Putin declared that heating was the responsibility of the local administration but assured Pavel that the Irkutsk governor would deal with the situation. Within days, the mayor of Ust'-Kut had resigned, on grounds of ill-health, and the deputy governor of Irkutsk had promised that the school's heat would be restored.[b] It duly was, in early 2002. But by the end of 2002, Pavel's school, like much of the rest of the Ust'-Kut, was once more languishing in the cold.[c] In December 2002, a World War II veteran living in the city was found frozen to death in his apartment, in a building where the central heating system had been inoperative for fully two years and where the electricity had been disconnected indefinitely for repairs. Local officials were complaining that the city did not have sufficient budget resources to keep utilities running. And, like many other Siberian cities in the winter of 2002, Ust'-Kut sought a loan for additional fuel using municipal property as collateral.[d]

    a. Irina Len'shina, "Khoroshiy mal'chik," *Izvestiya*, 16 December 2002.
    b. *RFE/RL Russian Federation Report*, vol. 4, no. 1, 9 January 2002.
    c. Len'shina, "Khoroshiy mal'chik."
    d. Oksana Yablokova, "A Veteran Freezes to Death in Siberia," *The Moscow Times*, 17 December 2002.

structural changes in the government and its departments and we set up new structures, but nobody is taking specific, personal responsibility for the current situation . . . [I will no longer] . . . seriously accept the severe cold as an excuse."[69] In commenting on the aftereffects of extensive flooding throughout Russia in 2002 at a November 2002 meeting, Putin once again asked, "How many times do we have to repeat such exceptional algorithms of action? Even in emergency situations. In similar situations last year, the Russian federal government and its departments were forced to work out detailed coordinated plans of action. Each time, it seems that we decide to save people and property as if we were starting from scratch."[70] And, during the January 2003 cold spell, the president appeared on Russian television, publicly admonishing regional leaders by telephone for not being prepared to deal with the consequences of the predictably low temperatures.[71]

    Unfortunately, such rearguard actions against the elements are, and will be, necessary every year. Sending the airforce out to bomb the ice dams on the Lena River—extreme and exceptional as it may seem—is not and will not be an unusual occurrence. In spite of President Putin's protestations, the cold and the elements are not an "excuse" in Siberia and the Russian Far East. They are a fact of trying to maintain life there. Better planning and more competent leadership may help to mitigate costs, but heroic interventions— be they military or political—will always be the norm when a priority has been placed on saving and maintaining the Soviet-era mass-produced, mass- heated, and increasingly dilapidated towns and cities of Siberia. Local and regional politicians will remain incapable of dealing with the enormous task of powering and heating their cities, as will their successors—forced to take up their political agendas after the inevitable resignations—unless the central government intervenes to subsidize the imported fuel supplies that these Siberian cities have always relied on.

Tellingly, in the winter of 2000–01, those who weathered the cold most effectively were the residents of old-style wooden Russian housing, off the heating grid but able to resort to traditional stoves to warm their homes. Maura Reynolds of the *Los Angeles Times* noted when visiting Vladivostok in the Russian Far East during the January 2001 blackout: "Those who live in old-fashioned wooden cottages are better off because they tend to have wood-burning stoves. But . . . residents [who] live in more modern, concrete- paneled apartment blocks constructed in the last 40 years . . . are all but help- less when city utilities fail."[72] Although some hapless official can always be found accountable, the real culprit is the cold. As one resident of the Russian Far East remarked in January 2001, "A human being can get used to anything—to shortages of food, to high temperatures, to wind. The only thing that's impossible to get used to is cold."[73]

Each summer Russia's regions in and east of the Urals have to make the build-up and consolidation of winter fuel stocks their major priority.[74] The ultimate "impermissibility" for regional authorities in Russia is to cut peo- ple off from heat. As Russian economist Alexander Tsipko pointed out in a February 2001 discussion of the heating crisis in Siberia:

> It is now clear that in view of the natural climate in Russia, the "heating" question is fundamental and cannot be resolved purely in accordance with the economic climate. The truth which has now dawned on the majority of the population is that in Russia, where a significant number of people live in extreme conditions, especially in Siberia, the problem of heating cannot be the individual problem of each individual family. The heating problem is a task of national importance and cannot be farmed out, left to chance or dependent on either economic conditions or the mood and

whim of energy producers. When the health and lives of hundreds of thousands of people are at stake, bargaining over the price of coal or oil is inappropriate. In extreme or emergency conditions, the exchange value and commerce should probably take a back seat, at least for a time.[75]

Burdening Moscow and Plundering Siberia

With government intervention inevitable to keep Siberian cities heated and ice free in winter, the region will be left dependent on subsidies from the center, as well as on state action to try to increase energy efficiency, improve systems, and so on. But what this means is that Russia's overall development and growth will continue to be retarded by the need to reallocate (and thus misallocate) resources from more productive areas in the warmer west, in European Russia, to the cold and underproductive (if not entirely unproductive) east. Under this scenario, the state will remain a major player in the Russian economy as well as in politics. As Alexander Tsipko has pointed out, a laissez-faire approach would doom people in the marginal areas east of the Urals literally to physical death as well as economic disaster.

In addition, even the current success of Russia's most prosperous region, the city of Moscow, is not sustainable over the long term. It lives and prospers on the resources of the rest of the country—especially on those of the resource frontier east of the Urals and the flows of cash from the energy sector—but it also subsidizes the rest of the Moscow region and the rest of the Russian economy. Moscow cannot simply free itself from the rest of the country. Over time it will become increasingly burdened.

In the final reckoning, we should also consider not just the burdens on Moscow, but the impact on Siberia itself—a treasure chest, a jewel indeed, but a fragile ecology—of maintaining cities east of the Urals and their related industries. Siberia's ecology is in fact one of the most fragile in world, easily lost to future generations. In the Soviet period it was not so much conquered as plundered. Lake Baykal in the heart of Siberia, the world's largest and deepest body of fresh water (accounting for fully one-fifth of all the planet's fresh water), has seen its pristine water and unique flora and fauna (1,500 types of plants and animals including freshwater sponges found nowhere else in the world) threatened by a wood pulp mill that deposits its waste water in the lake. Near the Arctic Circle, permafrost has been melted with hot-water pressure hoses to facilitate construction in oil-bearing regions. Tundra, forests, and swamps have been polluted by oil spills from shoddy extraction practices in Tyumen' oblast and elsewhere in western Siberia. Radioactive material has been dumped in the rivers and lakes surrounding Siberia's nuclear cities. Giant dams and mines have torn up the landscape, and there have been no subsequent efforts to restore the surrounding land in places like the Kuzbass coalfields of western Siberia. Severe air pollution in industrial cities like Chelyabinsk, Kemerovo, Krasnoyarsk, and Noril'sk has been cited as a major public health threat since the 1980s. Indeed, almost all of Russia's most heavily polluted cities are in the Urals region and Siberia, and the Noril'sk Nickel company is seen as one of the worst offenders.[76] Unfortunately, this despoliation of Russia's avowed national treasure seems likely to continue with the abolition of the Russian State Committee for Environmental Protection along with the Forestry Administration and the transfer of their responsibilities to the Natural Resources Ministry, which occurred in 2000.[77]

10

Tearing Down Potemkin Russia

Russia needs to radically rethink its current trajectory of development. Its misallocation of population and resources will not self-correct under the influence of market forces. The political pressures to muddle along, to continue with "more of the same," and to look for technical fixes to the challenges of the cold and distance are ingrained in the system. But, more important, even if there were no political barriers to self-correction, the distortion of Russia's economic geography is too great. History is history. We cannot rewind it. And more than seventy years of Soviet rule have completely changed Russia's economic and political parameters.

As we have discussed in the preceding chapters of this book, cold and distance are costly, long-term impediments to Russia's development. For reasons of economic efficiency, Russia needs to "shrink distance and grow warmer" by having people move back to the western and southern regions of the Russian Federation and away from Siberia. An optimist might point out that this is already happening. As the market economy develops and expands opportunity, mobility, and free choice, the positive trends that began in the 1990s will continue. Does this mean that Russia will, over time, achieve an optimal population distribution and thus an optimal economic geography? The short answer is no.

Thanks to its Soviet history, Russia moved from a starting point in 1914, or 1917, or 1926 (respectively, the beginning of World War I, the Russian Revolution, or the introduction of communist central planning) to its actual position in, say, 1990, just before the dissolution of the USSR. "Virtual history"—along the lines of the exercise conducted by Tatiana Mikhailova described in chapter 3—gives us a hypothetical state, a "counterfactual 1990," that might conceivably have emerged without the Soviet intervention. However, the important point here is that although Russia did move from 1914 to the real 1990, and could theoretically have moved from 1914 to the counter-factual 1990, it cannot necessarily now move from its current state to the counterfactual 1990 given the huge gulf between these two end points. In other words, the first-best outcome that Russia could have contemplated in 1914 is no longer attainable. We have to face the facts. Russia will continue to be unique in having more people in cold and remote places than any other country in the world. This will be a permanent cost burden—a special "cold and distance tax" that the communist planners bequeathed to today's Russia. The goal, then, must be a second-best outcome, somewhere between the real 1990 and the counterfactual 1990, that mitigates this burden.

The obvious and most important conclusion from this is that Russia should not continue along its current track with a strong emphasis on the redevelopment of Siberia. Understandably, the prevailing attitude in Siberia is, "the state put us here and now the state needs to take care of us." More central government subsidies, preferential tariffs, energy-saving technologies, new infrastructure construction, and new communications are all seen as part of the solution for dealing with Siberia's problems and for bridging the gaping distances between its cities—instead of encouraging people to relocate. As American geographer Leslie Dienes has written recently, such a series of technical fixes would be extremely difficult given the magnitude of the problem, even if the Russian government were to have new resources at its disposal:

> Left to market forces, the future of millions who inhabit the bulk of Russia's vast, environmentally harsh stretches and rural backwaters appears grim. In theory, the dead space of the rural *glubinka** that interpenetrates

---

* *Glubinka* in Russian is derived from the word for "deep" or the "depths" and is used to describe remote, out-of-the-way places. It is used in the same way that Americans would use "the middle of nowhere," "the sticks," or "the boondocks."

"archipelago Russia" [the cities], in the European Urals, and perhaps
neighboring West Siberia regions can be bridged and largely brought into
the geographic mainstream *in time*. Assuming an economic renaissance
and targeted investment policy, transport and communications technology could triumph over that vacuum.[1]

Dienes concedes that such a triumph over distance seems unlikely under
any circumstances in eastern Siberia. But even in the western regions of
Siberia and in the Urals, it would require a huge amount of resources as well
as considerable time to develop the extensive network of roads, railways, airline routes, and telecommunications infrastructure that would be required
to fill that vacuum. In viewing the problem in this way, however—as the result
of a major infrastructure deficit—Dienes, like other observers of Russia,
assumes from the outset that cities in Siberia are "real" cities, which simply
need to be connected to one another to make the regional (and Russian)
economy work. As we have already discussed in the course of this book, they
are not "real" cities. Russia's fundamental problem of regional development is *not* the lack of infrastructure between these cities, but the fact that
the cities themselves should not have been where they are in the first place.
While Siberian cities might indeed become better connected in a physical
sense with the construction of new infrastructure, they would not miracu-
lously become more connected economically. Better road and rail links
would simply make it easier and more convenient (but not necessarily
immensely cheaper) to ship out natural resources and ship in fuel, food, and
other supplies—even as people in these cities remained cut off from any
meaningful participation in the Russian, as well as the global, economy.[2]

Siberian cities are artificial, mislocated cities. They are "Potemkin cities,"
to use and adapt an earlier metaphor. As the legend goes, in 1787 Catherine the Great took Emperor Joseph of Austria and King Stanislaw Ponia-
towski of Poland on a tour of her newly acquired territories around the
Black Sea and on the Crimean Peninsula. Eager to please his empress (and
former lover) and her distinguished guests with how quickly these new southern lands had been settled with Russians, General Grigoriy Potemkin, the
viceroy of the region, had a series of elaborate wooden structures thrown up
along the route that Catherine was scheduled to follow. The structures
passed for villages in the distance, adequate to fool the royal entourage,
and they passed into history as "Potemkin villages"—a term for structures
with little substance, impressive facades and shams. As far as today's Siberian
cities are concerned, it would have been better if they really were Potemkin
cities—wooden facades built for show with minimal expenditure of

resources and then dismantled when their time had passed. But Siberia's cities are not wooden facades like the historical Potemkin villages. They were built with real construction materials, they were filled with real people. Those people also believed that the cities were real and had a purpose, not that they were phony. As a result, today's Potemkin cities are extremely costly to maintain, and they will be even more costly and difficult to tear down.

Changing the Mental Geography of Russia

In thinking about "tearing down" Siberia's Potemkin cities, and thus about real change in Russia, the objective barriers to city shrinkage (discussed in chapter 8) are not the only problems. The psychological barriers to change will likely be as great, if not greater, obstacles to overcome. In the final reckoning, changing mental geography in Russia will be a prerequisite for changing Russia's economic geography. Russians will have to abandon their current ambivalent attitude toward their political identity. They speak at the same time of integrating economically with the West and of maintaining Russia's "Eurasian" profile and celebrating the distinctiveness of "Arctogaia." They cannot do both. This is Russia's primary existentialist dilemma. Russia cannot hope to achieve true economic integration with Europe while it continues to maintain and subsidize huge cities in Siberia. Russians will have to reshape their mental geography of Russia along with patterns of settlement and economic activity; they will have to stop looking for technocratic solutions that might make the situation they have, in the economic geography of "Russia of the mind," more bearable.

This means casting off the mythology of Siberia. Russians need to start thinking of the vast expanse east of the Urals as Russ*ian* but not as Russ*ia*. In thinking about Russia, and its economic geography, the locus of its heartland should be returned to the historic Muscovite core rather than Siberia. The region east of the Urals is the periphery, the outlying territory, like Canada's Northwest Territories or like Alaska in the United States—as suggested by the Russians' in the region referring to European Russia as the "mainland" [*materik*]. It must be viewed once again as a remote "resource frontier."[3] If Russia's identity continues to be associated with and rooted in its vast territory and Siberia, then Russia will not be able to move forward. Psychological change—changing Russia of the mind into Russia of reality, dismantling Potemkin Russia and turning Russia into something real—is key.

Clearly, positive change and movement in the general direction of the optimal state of the "counterfactual 1990" cannot be a wholesale reversal of the process that put people in Siberia in the first place. It took "a Stalin," that is, the use of overt force, to put people there, but Stalinist methods of compulsion to move them out again are impermissible. Policies will have to be measured and modest in their expectations. People will not move en masse, and the goal is not, in any case, to "empty out" these regions. The goal is to enable them to move closer to an optimal level of economic activity and thus of population, along the lines that one might have expected under market conditions without the massive state intervention of the Soviet period. Even without a Stalin, and even if Russians *had* "behaved like Canadians" after the Russian Revolution, we would still have expected a certain amount of increased settlement in the region east of the Urals. The problem is not that Siberia is populated, or even that its population has grown, but that it is now overpopulated. It is populated and urbanized to an extent and in a manner that could never have been anticipated if the patterns established before 1914 or 1926 had prevailed and if Russia had followed the general trends of the rest of the industrialized world (of non-Soviet, market-based economies) in the twentieth century.

Furthermore, the fact that there is general opposition by Russian political leaders to large-scale movement of people in post-Soviet Russia means that even encouraging the government and the people to think about shrinkage and migration from Siberia as solutions to Russia's economic development problems will be difficult. As we have already discussed, shrinkage of cities seems almost impossible to undertake on the scale that would be required in Siberia to reverse completely the misallocations of the past. As much as considerations of pure economic efficiency might dictate a radically different spatial allocation of Russia's population and economic activity, we have to accept what are real limitations. What, then, are viable solutions or approaches? What is the minimum that Russia should and can do to mitigate the problems? What are the principles for moving forward and the minimum list of "dos and don'ts" for the Russian government?

Maximize Mobility

As an essential starting principle, the Russian government must set as one of its highest priorities making the reallocation of resources within the Russian Federation easier. This should be done by supporting the process of reallocation rather than explicitly directing it. Reallocation means facilitating the full mobility of people and other factors of production. In addition, the Russian leadership must adopt a long-term approach to the problem, one that gives scope for adaptation. Mistakes will be part of the process. Some strategies will fail. Cities and regions that initially seem promising in terms of economic growth and attracting migration will turn out not to be (as in the case of the North Caucasus region in southern Russia, where positive population growth in the 1990s masked sharp and continued economic decline). Patience will be essential. Everything cannot be fixed at once.

A key step in facilitating the mobility of resources is to reconceptualize issues of migration and immigration. There should be no more campaigns to develop Siberia. The Russian government should not seek to repopulate Siberia. Russia does not have to live without Siberia, but Russians should not be forced, or even encouraged, to live in Siberia. Russian government policies should not focus on keeping people east of the Urals. Instead, Russian policymakers need to allow exit for those who can move out and wish to do so. Market forces will drive the process. The government should neither stand in the way nor try to direct people to specific, preselected destinations. The whole development of capitalism and market economies demonstrates that people have to be given maximum mobility, allowed to make their own choices, and permitted to experiment—even if this does mean that they make mistakes and that the government cannot control or even necessarily predict what the outcomes might be. The basic principle, then, is to maximize labor mobility. Let people move where they want to move by removing overt or hidden constraints.

Assert the National Interest

The Russian leadership will also have to be frank about the future of Russia and Siberia. It is in Russia's national interest to downsize Siberia. In trying to do so, however, the Russian government will continually run up against the problem of the power granted through Russia's evolving democratic system to regional leaders, and thus to the governors, oligarchs, and others who have based themselves in Siberia, politically and economically. They all have vested interests in preventing the central government from downgrading Siberia's political position within the federation, as well as in seeing the continuation of the subsidies and redevelopment programs for the region. Even President Putin's polpred, his representative in Siberia, Leonid Drachevskiy, was championing increased subsidies to the region at the expense of the center, rather than promoting the Russian Federation's overall interests in the region, in 2002.

Experience elsewhere—including in the United States, where the political representatives of the plains states, for example, play a major role in ensuring the continuance of massive subsidies to these regions through the annual farm bill—shows how difficult it is for governments to break through vested interests. This is especially the case when the long-term national gain is secured at the expense of their very painful (albeit short-term) loss. In this instance, members of the Russian federal government, including leaders like President Putin and his representatives in the region such as Drachevskiy, will have to place themselves above regional interests. The center must not appear biased toward the redevelopment of Siberia. Instead, it should send out clear signals that the future of Russia (and, consequently, also of Siberia) depends on a strong, integrated, and connected Russia, which will not be achieved if the government continually pumps resources—not least human resources—out of more productive areas and into Siberia.

Managing Migration

The message of the preceding chapters of this book is that the future of Russia should be based on the development of European Russia—the warmest parts of the federation, closest to important markets. It is perfectly sensible for the Russian federal government to encourage voluntary population movement in that direction. Steps in this direction on the part of the Russian government might include removing the *propiska* and similar residence constraints in cities in European Russia and focusing efforts instead on other methods of dealing with the inevitable increase of migration into Moscow. Migration should be managed, not restricted.[4]

In thinking about assisting the process of relocation from Siberia, the Russian government should also acknowledge that many people who would like to move are too poor to do so, and the worse the economic situation becomes in the region, the less they are able to move. In an ideal world, the Russian government might sponsor large-scale relocation programs—as some regional governments have done, for example, in the United States.[5] But Russia is not rich enough to finance a mass relocation, and there are not many places with new jobs. In the short term, therefore, the Russian government should embrace expanded international programs like that of the World Bank's Northern Restructuring Project. These programs should focus on helping to move people completely out of Siberia to European Russia—not just on relocating them from the most marginal settlements of the North to cities elsewhere in the region—and also on assisting the younger and most productive members of the population to move. (This is in contrast to current relocation initiatives, for instance in Chukotka, where the policy has been to prioritize the relocation of the old or infirm to places where it is cheaper to support them.) Part of the assistance process will also have to involve the provision of formal social safety nets—including a housing relocation package for migrants—to make it possible for people to break loose from their informal household safety nets. Formal safety nets, ensured by the government, would empower people to make their own decisions about what makes the most sense for them in terms of staying in or relocating from Siberia.[6]

In general, the Russian government will have to formulate a coherent policy on demographic issues, migration, and immigration (legal and illegal). In this regard, Russia has many of the same problems to contend with as the United States and other European countries. It has become a magnet for immigrants from less developed countries, who seek to fill the low-paying, low-skilled, and low-prestige jobs that its own citizens have rejected. Russia also has its own specific sets of problems, including what to do with those immigrants who have now moved to the declining areas east of the Urals. Here the government will have to try to regulate the Central Asian labor force already seeking employment in Siberia. It will have to channel these immigrant workers into viable sectors on official contracts rather than letting them fill ever-growing vacancies in moribund enterprises to keep them afloat.

Above all, Russia's migration policy needs to be fitted to a broad conception and vision of Russian development, not to desires to maintain the status quo. Russia's currently proposed migration bill is based on the precepts of the 1990s and thus on illusory trajectories for a sustainable future for Russia. It needs to be rethought in the context of a mobile Russia and a downsized Siberia. As in other industrial economies with a mature and aging population profile, Russia will continue to require imported foreign labor, especially if it can attain its goal of sustained economic growth. In this respect, Russia can learn from other countries' experiences and can make its own contributions to the international debate on the issue.

Livable Cities as Migration Magnets

Russia has one great success story, Moscow. The capital city has attracted the cream of domestic investment, in terms of physical, financial, and human capital. It is also attracting the bulk of foreign direct investment in Russia. This should be encouraged, not discouraged, but Moscow should not become the "be all and end all." The real challenge for the Russian Federation is promoting the development of the rest of the country. Here, the government needs to support and enhance processes already under way but, again, resist the temptation to push investment and infrastructure development in the direction of vested political interests. This was a general pattern in the 1990s, when certain Russian provincial cities, like Nizhniy Novgorod, were declared almost mystical places, "locomotives of reform."[7] Incentives to attract more foreign and domestic investment to these cities never quite panned out. The attraction of place was based more on the pull of powerful political personalities—in the case of Nizhniy Novgorod, of leading reformers like Yabloko Party leader Grigoriy Yavlinskiy, former Nizhniy Novgorod governor and deputy prime minister Boris Nemtsov, former prime minister Sergey Kiriyenko, and others who had a strong connection to the city and surrounding region—than on the sustainability of the local economy.

Notably, while provincial cities like Nizhniy Novgorod drew the attention of foreign governments and aid agencies in the 1990s, what they never really attracted was people: few Russian migrants moved there. It will thus be a milestone in Russia's economic development when Russian cities and regions begin to compete with one another not to attract foreign aid or Russian government subsidies, but to get ordinary Russians to move there. Another will be when Russia starts to develop its own list of the top ten most livable Russian cities to replace the current lists of the largest cities with the most services or highest rates of consumption left over from the Soviet period, or the negative lists of the least livable and most polluted cities that everyone would like to move away from if possible.[8] At present, most of the cities on the negative lists seem to be concentrated in the North and in the Russian Far East. The process of determining what the most attractive and livable cities in Russia will be, based on how many people want to move there, would signal a real revolution in Russian development.

Instead of trying to select the winners in advance, the Russian government should create a level playing field so winners can emerge on their own merits. Russia needs to get rid of its preferential economic zones and hidden subsidies for certain industries in specific regions, including in Siberia. Subsidies that are retained should be made transparent so that investors (foreign and domestic) all know the rules of the game. The guiding principle should be that investors, like migrants, can move their capital where they want it to be and not where the government thinks it should be—even if this means they move it to Moscow.

A "Leaner Approach" to Siberian Development

The current approach toward maintaining industry and existing labor patterns in Siberia must also be reexamined. British geographer Michael Bradshaw has recommended that Russia adopt a "cleaner, leaner approach to the development of Siberia and the Russian Far East"—one in which technology replaces people. Siberia specialist Victor Mote has noted that while the global economy can survive without Siberia, "Siberia will languish in isolation from the global economy."[9] In the Soviet period, central planners focused their attention on promoting and creating a natural resource autarky in Siberia. This was effected through the extraction and processing of natural resources, which in turn supplied the manufacturing industries of the USSR, and which, in some cases (oil, gas, gold, diamonds), were also produced for hard currency export to boost Soviet central government revenues. There was scant regard for the exigencies of the global economy or for the profitability of individual sectors and industries. Today Siberian industries can survive only through being connected to the global economy. And this requires adaptation—especially because of Russia's demographic crisis and the necessity to promote migration out of the region. There will have to be a shift from labor-intensive methods to labor-saving technologies and to industries that can easily shed labor or employ temporary workers.

Ironically, this may result in a renewed emphasis on extractive and energy industries in the region that can rely on (and pay the high wages to attract) outside workers on short-term tours of duty. As we have noted, cities in Siberia were created or built up in this great wilderness area to serve as labor pools for large industrial enterprises like Noril'sk Nickel. But outside the manufacturing sector, even in the 1970s and 1980s, the export-oriented energy industry in western Siberia was already cutting costs by using workers who operated from makeshift temporary settlements, while their families were permanently housed in distant "base cities" like Omsk, Novosibirsk, Tomsk, and Tyumen'.[10] In spite of the fact that wages were high in the oil-bearing regions, as elsewhere in Siberia, in the Soviet period, labor costs were relatively low. "Expedition" and "tour of duty methods" were seen as more cost effective for the state than a "stable, anchored force." In the early 1980s, about one-third of oil and gas workers in western Siberia were part of this new mobile labor force.[11] This has remained the norm in Russia's oil industry and is now beginning to be adopted by other extractive industries farther afield in eastern Siberia and the Russian Far East. It is being adopted, for instance, by gold mines in Sakha (Yakutiya) that can no longer support and subsidize the small towns that were built around them to maintain a permanent labor force.[12]

Turning Russians into Canadians

Canada could be an appropriate model for Russia to adopt for a future, viable economic relationship with Siberia. Russians should become as far as possible like Canadians in their relationship to the Siberian territory and in their techniques of resource exploitation. Canada's North is a resource base, but the bulk of the Canadian population is located along the U.S. border—that is, people are both close to markets and in the warmest areas of the country.[13] The Canadian North has been developed with an eye toward resource extraction, not settlement. According to the 2002 Canadian Census, Canada's northern territories—Yukon, Nunavut, and Northwest Territories—have a combined population of 100,000, or less than 1 percent of Canada's total population.[14] Mining is one of the primary industrial sectors in both Northwest Territories and the Yukon, and the Canadian mining industry—and northern industry in general—relies on seasonal labor.[15] Canadian labor statistics show that the labor pool shrinks during the coldest winter months and increases again in summer. Summer workers are deterred from permanently relocating by both high costs of living and the harsh climate.[16] Likewise, if we look at the case of Alaska in the United States, the region has only about 0.2 percent of the U.S. population. Its urban population is very small, with only a single city over 100,000 people, and most of its major cities are located along the coast near shipping routes, not inland. As in the Canadian northern territories, Alaska relies on seasonal and a mobile labor force as a mainstay of its economy, especially in the oil industry.

All of this would imply that if Russia adopted a similar approach to the territory east of the Urals, then we might expect to see the bulk of the population living closer to the markets of Europe in the warmer areas of the country (Europe is the analogue of the United States in applying the Canadian model to Russia). This would mean that cities in the south along the Trans-Siberian Railway and in coastal areas in the Far East would be much smaller than at present. In remote areas where key natural resources are located, settlements would be outposts, with small permanent populations and a heavy dependency on seasonal workers for the bulk of production in the summer months.

Linking the Russian Far East with Northeast Asia

Rethinking the role and potential of the Russian Far East as separate from the rest of Siberia will also be important. With the exception of the Trans-Siberian Railway and transcontinental airline routes, the Russian Far East is far removed and disconnected from European Russia. Its pole of attraction is effectively in Northeast Asia. In the August 2002 Russian governmental meeting on the future of the region in Vladivostok, Deputy Prime Minister Khristenko recommended that the government focus its efforts on promoting the development of the southern regions of the Far East, including Khabarovsk and Vladivostok. This approach makes some sense. In the southern regions along the Amur, Ussuri, and Tyumen' Rivers, proximity to China with its large population and markets may ultimately be an advantage economically, rather than the disadvantage from the security perspective that it is commonly supposed to be. Proximity to the Pacific coast and world shipping lanes offers additional economic advantages. In this regard, the port city of Vladivostok has often been touted as a "Vancouver" or "San Francisco" of the Russian Far East. But because it was a closed military city until the end of the USSR, as the headquarters of the Soviet Pacific Fleet, and very much tied to Moscow many thousands of kilometers to the west, its purported commercial potential within the immediate region has yet to be actively pursued.

The Russian Far East, however, also has some other distinct disadvantages for future development. Thanks to the influence of the ocean, the southern territory is not as cold as the north, and it is far less frigid than the interior of Siberia. But it is by no means "warm"—and certainly not in comparison with the North American port cities. Vladivostok, with its population of 600,000, has an average January temperature of −14° C, in stark contrast to Vancouver, which has a population of two million and an average January temperature of +2.7° C, not to mention the San Francisco area with its population of seven million and average January temperature of +9.2° C.

Vladivostok, in spite of its location on the Pacific, is a cold place. In the Soviet period, Vladivostok's economy was very much dependent on military-related industries and large central government subsidies tied to the strategic importance of its location on the border with China and North Korea and facing the Sea of Japan. Like the rest of the Russian Far East, its hinterland was dominated by extractive industries, especially timber, minerals, and fisheries. Given the persistent difficulties of transportation inland, and the vast distances from European Russia, all of these sectors will have to orient themselves toward Pacific region markets in the future. Consumer goods production and the manufacturing sector, however, remain grossly underdeveloped, and, as already discussed, the Far East is disconnected from the national Russian energy grid (for both electricity and natural gas) and entirely dependent on shipped-in fuel. Economic considerations dictate that, in the future, consumer and manufactured goods, as well as fuel, will have to be imported from the neighborhood rather than brought in from elsewhere in Russia. Cheap consumer durables from China are already coming across the border.

There is one potential bright spot on the horizon for the littoral regions of the Russian Far East in the development of the oil and gas resources of

Sakhalin Island. This has already attracted substantial investment from international oil giants such as ExxonMobil, Shell, and a number of Asian companies. Sakhalin offshore fields represent one of the few new energy reserves brought into production in Russia over the past decade. They are anticipated to account for up to 10 percent of annual Russian oil production by around 2010, as well as substantial production of natural gas and liquefied natural gas. Access to world sea routes, close proximity to the Chinese, Korean, and Japanese coasts, and growing demand for energy in these three countries provide a local export market for Sakhalin energy in the coming decades. In 2001, 51 percent of all foreign investment in the Russian Far East was in Sakhalin, with 83 percent of this investment in the energy sector.[17]

Although ambitious energy projects are already under way on Sakhalin, there are still some hurdles to be overcome. All offshore fields and related refining, processing, and pipeline infrastructure projects have to overcome considerable technical challenges. These are posed by the extreme winter temperatures in the north of the island, its rough terrain, a high level of regional seismic activity, and the possibility of serious environmental damage to the region's rich fisheries.* In addition, the domestic infrastructures of Japan, China, and South Korea still need considerable improvement to allow energy markets to develop and to permit their integration with Russian suppliers. While additional development projects in the region are also envisaged as the energy-based economy develops—including new port facilities and gas pipelines on the mainland, as well as an extension to the Trans-Siberian Railway down the Korean Peninsula—it is still not clear what the energy economy will ultimately support over the long term. The prospects for a Sakhalin "energy boom" should certainly not lead to more Russian government efforts to populate the Far East or even to halt out-migration, especially as the energy industry is more likely to import skilled workers for shift duty. It will be several years before local workers will be hired in significantly large numbers in support services for the oil and gas industries.[18]

The uncertainty of these prospects and the persistent regional disadvantages have led to some serious thinking on the future of the Far East. Economist Vladimir Kontorovich, for example, sees the population decline in the Russian Far East as inevitable (if not entirely desirable) and the current programs to jump-start the Far Eastern economy to attract migrants to the region as misguided. In fact, Kontorovich asserts that even a slight economic improvement in the region will "turn deferred migrants" [those

---

* Average January temperatures on Sakhalin Island range from –6° C in the south to –24° C in the north. The average January temperature in the island's capital, Yuzhno-Sakhalinsk, is –13° C.

who would like to leave the region but have not because they lack resources]
"into actual ones."[19] Discrepancies between the Far East and European Russian
regions in wages, housing, and general standards and costs of living will persist over the long term. Kontorovich argues that out-migration should be
seen as a positive development: "Population decline will boost wages in the
region, as the number of working age people approaches the number of jobs
in viable businesses. This will slow down, and eventually stop, the outflow of
the population."[20] In other words, an equilibrium of sorts will eventually
be achieved in the Russian Far East through natural downsizing, even if and
as the economic situation in the region improves.

Overall, Kontorovich recommends a program of economic contraction
in the Russian Far East, combined with efforts to connect its otherwise dispersed and weakly integrated local markets.[21] Infrastructure development
(highways to compensate for currently discontinuous rail links and unreli-
able water routes) would be targeted to connect the Amur oblast, Khabarovsk
kray, and Primorsk kray with one another, as well as with other regional centers.[22] This would integrate the region internally, although not necessarily
with the rest of the Russian Federation. Kontorovich also notes that the border with China in Primorsk kray would have to be opened to transit to a
much greater extent than at present to really facilitate trade with China's
northeastern provinces and the rest of the northeastern Pacific region.[23]
Finally, he urges that individual strategies be created for the separate Far
East subregions based on the viability of their industrial base and local
conditions instead of the large sweeping regional development programs
favored by the Russian government and regional leaders.[24]

Ensuring the Survival of Those Who Remain in Siberia

Creating realistic subregional policies and adopting Canadian and other similar methods may help to restructure Siberia's economy and provide new jobs
in productive sectors for some of the population. But what should become of
the "excess" population—those who are too old, or unskilled, or supported
by and part of the "virtual economy," who would find it hard to obtain jobs
elsewhere and whose assets in the region are worthless and cannot be sold
to finance their relocation? How can and should the government ensure their
subsistence? In this case, given the realities of the climate and the structural
disadvantages of the regional economy, fuel, food, and other subsidies will
have to be continued to make life bearable. The Russian central and regional
governments will have to accept the inevitable and contend with and plan
for these "lost generations" in the coming decades. Subsidies will have to

continue to sustain life. But they must be transparent, so that the population elsewhere in Russia, as well as in Siberia, knows who is paying for what and why. Everything has to be properly budgeted and accounted for.

New Conceptions of Security

Finally, Russia will have to think about security issues in Siberia and the Russian Far East in new ways as it contemplates the prospect of "empty lands." Analysts like Mikhail Alexseev, who have seriously looked at issues of Chinese migration in the Russian Far East, do not foresee a mass influx from China across Russia's borders. The Far East has only limited attraction for Chinese migrants who often use it to move elsewhere in the Russian Federation and even farther afield—although this could change if there is an economic turnaround and more prospects open up for temporary work and trade.[25] But given that Russia is not Canada (even if its territorial profile resembles Canada's), and, unlike Canada, it borders China and many other countries (instead of just one country, the United States) that may not always remain friendly, Russia's security provisions do need to be enhanced. This might include the creation of sensors, new rapid reaction forces, and high-tech weapons systems on Far East borders, which would replace the deployment and support of large conventional land and sea forces. It might also involve the formulation of a new international treaty with neighbors like China and the United States, which would guarantee Russia's territorial integrity and its continued sovereignty over Siberia and the Far East. The designation of Siberia as a world heritage site and specially protected territory, through a United Nations or other convention that also underscored Russia's stewardship of this unique ecological zone and all of its resources, could be part of this approach.[26]

Conclusion

Although we certainly do not have all the answers and solutions to Russia's problems, we have tried in this book to describe some of the problems and to reframe the questions that Russia has to address in the coming decades. Over the past ten years, issues related to economic reform and political development in Russia have proceeded from false premises. A new research and policy agenda for the Russian government will have to be worked out on the very different basis of the spatial allocation of Russia's population.

To do this, the Russian government will first have to acknowledge and come to terms with the origins of Siberian development and its misdevelopment in the twentieth century. As we have described in the book, a number of factors interacted to promote the settlement and industrialization of Siberia that we see today. This was not Russia's destiny. Instead, it was the combination of autarkic resource exploitation policies, notions that empty territory had to be populated to be secure, ideological precepts that dictated the equalization of productive forces across a country's territory and the building of industry in every region and locality (the Engels dictum), and national security imperatives to move defense industries away from the West and to militarize the region against incursions from the East. All of these motivations operated together and fed on one another. The key instrument in fulfilling all of these plans for Siberia was the GULAG.

Contrary to popular wisdom, the GULAG was not simply developed by the Bolsheviks to punish their enemies as part of the repressive totalitarian system they imposed on the Soviet Union. The development of Siberia was also not simply a byproduct of the GULAG. It was, in fact, its officially sanctioned goal. The labor camp system evolved explicitly after 1929 to conquer, colonize, and develop the resources of Siberia, the least accessible and most difficult area of the country. It was the GULAG that then transformed Siberia from the traditional penal colony of tsarist Russia into the flawed Soviet industrial "utopia" we see in its death throes today.

Today this means that to move in the right direction, away from its supremely misallocated starting point, Russia will require an active state policy. This does not imply that Russia should create its own version of "anticommunist" central planning to undo the policies and mistakes of the past. But it will need an interventionist approach to achieve something closer to optimum. Market mechanisms alone will not solve Russia's problems. Bold action will be required to remove the constraints and to maximize mobility.

This implies a federation-wide policy that aims to break the grip of regional leaders and oligarchs over resources and political and economic decisions in Siberia and the North—in places where people should not be, from a market economic point of view. It means a concerted effort by the government to end formal and informal residence restrictions on European Russian cities like Moscow. And it demands the creation of positive incentives, like lump-sum payments or bonuses, for those who would like to leave Siberia. One way for the Russian government to finance migration might be through the creation of a special fund generated by revenues from Siberian natural resource wealth. This special resource fund would be used not to keep people in place, but to help those who want to move but are too poor to do so.[27] Of course, none of this can work, as we have already noted, unless there is economic growth in European Russia. In some respects this is a classic "chicken or egg" scenario. It is difficult for people to move if there are no jobs or homes to go to. But the more money that is expended in keeping people in Siberia and in making life there more bearable, the less is available for investment elsewhere.

In this regard, the Russian government will also have to end some of the more dubious policies of uprooting and moving elderly inhabitants of Siberia and the North because they cost the state the most to maintain there. The government should place a priority on relocating Siberia's youth. Young people of working age could be more productive elsewhere in Russia, and in being more productive could help to subsidize pensioners in the region. In addition, although pensioners' social safety nets are closely connected to the informal, personal networks they have established over a long period of time, the young can break loose from these more easily and start again. While it may seem harsh, the challenge of maintaining the stranded elderly population of Siberia is something of a finite proposition, although it will certainly be a major focus of Russian policy for the next ten to fifteen years. Many other countries also have to deal with this problem. Dying villages populated by pensioners are a common phenomenon in postindustrial and rural settings all over Europe. In Russia this may eventually be a feature of many towns and cities in Siberia.

The general principle to bear in mind is that Russia needs to achieve, as best it can, a match between its most productive (or potentially most productive) regions and its most productive capital, including people. In contemplating this principle and in dealing with the persistent mythology of Siberia and the importance of its vast resources to the Russian economy, Siberia has to be put in its proper context. The wealth of Siberia is not Siberia's. It is Russia's wealth. It so happens that part of Russia's wealth—the bulk of its natural resources—is located in Siberia. But Siberia cannot claim this as its own, much as the oligarchs and local government officials there may want to.

This is part of Russia's problem. The lesson of successful market economies is that resources need to be put to their highest-value uses if the state and its population are to prosper. The goal is to maximize the wealth of the entire country and to do this in the most efficient manner possible by seeking a comparative advantage. All other considerations are separate from this. Many governments are concerned with trying to ensure regional equity for social, political, and ethical reasons. But there is nothing in economic thought that suggests that a region is entitled to make a major claim on revenues because the resources that generate them are physically located within its territory. While governments may choose, or be politically obligated, to support historically settled but backward regions of their countries (like northern Italy's heavy subsidization of southern Italy), Russia should not have to be so constrained. Siberia is not a centuries-old populated region. Its traditional population base was always small until the Bolshevik Revolution, and it was artificially settled and developed in the twentieth century.

As we have stressed, acknowledging these facts does not mean that Russian leaders are faced with a black-and-white choice: develop Siberia or reject it and cast it off. The resources of Siberia can be developed, but this should be done by reducing the dependency on huge fixed pools of labor and shifting to more technologically intensive methods of extraction and temporary work schemes that do not require a large permanent population or extensive urban infrastructure.

At present, Siberia's resources are developed at too high a price. Enterprises outside the energy sector cannot generate sufficient revenues to pay high wages to attract new labor or to keep the existing labor force. Instead, administrative, nonmarket, mechanisms keep people in place, by denying them the ability to move somewhere else. Siberia is, in essence, sustained by a mild form of the GULAG that first dragged people there to work and then forced them to stay. Siberia's resources can contribute to Russia's future prosperity, and the regional economy can one day be viable, but not if the Russian government persists in trying to maintain the giant Potemkin cities that communist planners left for it out in the cold.

APPENDIX A
Celsius-Fahrenheit Conversions

Table A-1. *Temperature Conversion Chart, with Mean January Temperatures of Selected Russian and North American Cities*

° C	° F	Cities	Comment
5	41	Sochi, Atlanta	
4	39		U.S. January TPC,[a] 2001
3	37		
2	36		
1	34		
0	32	Makhachkala, Baltimore	
−1	30		
−2	28	Krasnodar, Boston	
−3	27		
−4	25	Stavropol, Detroit	
−5	23	Buffalo, Toronto	
−6	21		
−7	19		
−8	18	St. Petersburg, Cedar Rapids	
−9	16		Canadian January TPC, 2000
−10	14	Moscow, Green Bay	
−11	12	Minneapolis	
−12	10	Quebec, Ottawa	Russian January TPC, 2001
−13	9		
−14	7	Vladivostok, Duluth	*(continued)*

215

Table A-1. (*Continued*)

° C	° F	Cities	Comment
−15	5	Perm', Chelyabinsk	High-carbon steels break
−16	3		
−17	1	Krasnoyarsk, Magnitogorsk	
−18	0	Kemerovo	
−19	−2	Novosibirsk, Omsk, Winnipeg	
−20	−4		Napoleon's retreat from Moscow, 1812
−21	−6	Irkutsk	
−22	−8		
−23	−9		
−24	−11		
−25	−13		Unalloyed steels break
−26	−15		
−27	−17	Chita	
−28	−18		
−29	−20		Exposed human flesh freezes within one minute when wind speed is 8 km/h (5 mph)
−30	−22		Battle of Stalingrad, 1942–43
−31	−24		
−32	−26		
−33	−27		
−34	−29		
−35	−31	Noril'sk	
−36	−33		
−37	−35		Standard steel structures rupture on mass scale
−38	−36		
−39	−38		
−40	−40		
−45	−49	Yakutsk	
−50	−58		
−55	−67		
−60	−76		Coldest temperature recorded in the winter of 2001–02 (Siberia)
−65	−85		
−68	−90		Coldest temperature ever recorded outside Antarctica (Siberia)

Source: City temperatures and TPC figures from authors' database. See appendix B. Other information from text.

a. TPC = temperature per capita. For explanation of this concept, see appendix B.

Definition of the TPC Concept and Sources of Data

The concept of temperature per capita (TPC) was introduced in Clifford G. Gaddy and Barry W. Ickes, "The Cost of the Cold," Pennsylvania State University, unpublished working paper, 2001. A theoretical argument for the use of TPC was first made by Frederick Hodder in an unpublished research memorandum dated June 6, 2001.

Definition of TPC

We formally define the TPC of country or region k as:

$$TPC_k = \sum_j \eta_j \tau_j,$$

where η_j is the share of the country's/region's total population residing in subregion j, and τ_j is the average mean temperature in subregion j. An equivalent formula is

$$TPC_k = \sum_j p_j \tau_j / P_k,$$

where p_j is the population of subregion j and $P_k = \sum_j p_j$, the total population of the country/region. The quantity $p_j \tau_j$

217

(a magnitude expressed in "person-degrees") can be thought of as the "amount of cold" in subregion *j* and is useful in thinking about the relative contributions of various subregions or cities to the entire country's aggregate cold.

Criteria for Selection of Location

The need to have both consistent temperature data and historical population data dictated our choice to use Russia's federal subjects as the subregions in computing the country's TPC. The temperature of an oblast is assumed to be a weighted average of the temperature of its major cities (all cities with a population of over 100,000). The relative populations of the cities serve as the weights.

Selection of Temperature Data

The process of selecting the temperature data for this project and some of the complicating factors involved in the process are discussed in an unpublished research memorandum by Marjory Winn, "Technical Issues in the Selection of Temperature Data for Russian Cities," Brookings, March 2002. The following discussions are excerpts from that document.

In selecting mean January temperature data for Russian cities, two data sources were tested, the Global Historical Climate Network version 2 (GHCN v2) and the Russian HydroMetCenter (Rosgidromet).

THE GHCN v2

The GHCN v2, prepared and maintained by the U.S. National Climatic Data Center (NCDC), includes mean monthly temperature data for 7,280 land-based temperature stations worldwide. Raw data from the stations were adjusted so that each station had at least 20 years of data and discontinuities were eliminated. The adjusted mean subset contains a total of 201 Russian stations. However, the period of record for each station varies considerably. For example, St. Petersburg includes data from 1850 to 1991, while Volgograd covers only 1951–70 and 1981. Such divergence makes cross-city comparisons difficult.

Another problem associated with the GHCN is the inconsistent spatial distribution of its stations. Several of the most populous Russian cities—for instance, Novosibirsk and Chelyabinsk, two cities with populations over one million—are missing. In fact, the GHCN includes data for only forty-nine of the eighty-nine provincial capitals in the Russian Federation.

The GHCN's format also makes it difficult to generate a single, accurate monthly mean temperature for a particular station. In some cases, stations employed different methods of calculating mean temperature, producing two distinct recordings. A similar outcome occurred when data were drawn from two neighboring stations (a weather station within the city and a nearby airport, for example). In such cases, each temperature data set was numbered and included as a separate time series for the same station. Thus a city like St. Petersburg included five distinct series of mean temperature data, each representing varying time periods. NCDC scientists explicitly acknowledge the difficulty the duplicates pose for researchers interested in a single monthly mean temperature for a specific city.[1]

An examination of data for cities in Russia highlights the pitfalls involved in attempting to derive a precise mean temperature using the multiple duplicates in the GHCN v2. The cases of Moscow and Perm' best illustrate the point. Temperature data for Moscow include five duplicate data sets that prove to be quite similar: the largest difference between the January monthly means of any two of the duplicates in the same year is 1.6 degrees. The case of Perm' is quite different. The Perm' data include four duplicate data sets, one of which was consistently at odds with the others. For example, in 1949 the difference in the mean January temperatures between that data set and the others amounted to over 16 degrees. Nor was that an isolated finding. The case of Perm' indicates that duplicates can and do differ significantly, raising questions about using such data to determine long-term mean temperature with a reasonable degree of accuracy.

RUSSIAN HYDROMETCENTER

In contrast to the GHCN v2, the temperature database of the Russian HydroMetCenter, an affiliate of the Russian state meteorological agency, Rosgidromet, proved much more consistent with the research needs of this project.[2] Its spatial coverage is more extensive, providing data for 82 of Russia's regional capitals. The total number of Russian cities covered is 327, and the data have been drawn from a uniform, thirty-year period (1961-1990) and presented as a single value.

As table B-1 demonstrates, the Rosgidromet data are relatively consistent with those of the GHCN v2. The mean temperature values for Russia's twenty-five largest cities vary only slightly between the two.

In view of its consistency and extensive coverage of large cities, the HydroMetCenter was selected as the primary data source for the project.

Definition of Mean Temperature

A further issue complicating the study of the effect of cold temperature is: What is meant by the daily or monthly mean temperature? This is especially relevant for the discussion of extreme events, since the mean daily tem-

Table B-1. *Comparison of Mean Temperature Values (° C) from GHCN and Rosgidromet's HydroMetCenter for Russia's Twenty-Five Largest Cities*

	City	GHCN v2	HydroMetCenter
1	Moscow	−9.2	−10
2	St. Petersburg	−6.7	−8
3	Novosibirsk	n.a.	−19
4	Nizhniy Novgorod	−11.6	−12
5	Yekaterinburg	−15.7	−16
6	Samara	−12.9	−14
7	Omsk	−18.8	−19
8	Chelyabinsk	n.a.	−15
9	Ufa	−14.6	−14
10	Kazan'	−13.7	−13
11	Volgograd	−7.9	−10
12	Perm'	−15.1	−15
13	Rostov-na-Donu	−4.9	−6
14	Voronezh	−9	−9
15	Saratov	−11.7	−11
16	Krasnoyarsk	−16.8	−17
17	Krasnodar	−0.5	−2
18	Tol'yatti	n.a.	n.a.
19	Ul'yanovsk	n.a.	−14
20	Barnaul	−17.8	−18
21	Izhevsk	−14.3	−14
22	Yaroslavl'	n.a.	−11
23	Vladivostok	−14.5	−14
24	Khabarovsk	−21.6	−22
25	Irkutsk	−21.2	−21

perature may still fail to reflect the fact that the daily low temperature may be significantly below the daily mean. Most weather stations report only the daily maximum and minimum temperatures. Hence, what is labeled the daily mean is really only an approximate mean, namely the mid-point of the maximum and minimum. Meteorologist John Griffiths notes that values labeled as mean temperatures have been calculated "in a bewildering variety of ways." He personally has unearthed more than one hundred different methods used to calculate the daily mean.[3] This implies that the mean temperature should be regarded only as a reference point in thinking about the cold with the understanding that it does not capture the full range (including duration) of daily temperatures.

APPENDIX C

The Russian North

The definition of the Russian North has varied over time. The most complete definition of the North used during the Soviet period was given by S. V. Slavin. He classified the North according to four criteria: 1) northerly location and remoteness from large industrial centers; 2) harsh climatic conditions (for example, long winters, widespread permafrost, marshiness, and so on); 3) very low population density and low level of industrialization, including a limited transportation network; and 4) high costs of construction compared with other regions of the country.[1]

As geographers in particular have noted, this Soviet definition was skewed toward economics more than geography, reflecting the predominant concerns of Soviet planners.[2] But even for economic analysis, the Soviet-era definition of the North presented problems. In certain cases, only a few rayons [districts] within an oblast qualified as part of the North. Most official Russian economic and demographic data, however, are available only at the oblast level. Consequently, it was difficult to conduct statistical analysis on the North.

The World Bank confronted the practical dilemma of defining the Russian North when it launched its so-called Northern Resettlement Project in the fall of 2000. In the

Table C-1. *Northern Regions as Defined by the World Bank*
Temperature in Celsius; population in thousands

Region	TPC[a] (° C) in 2002	1989 Population	2002 Population	Percentage change, 1989–2002
1 Kareliya republic	−10	791	717	−9.4
2 Komi republic	−15	1,261	1,019	−19.2
3 Arkhangel'sk oblast	−11.7	1,570	1,336	−14.9
4 Murmansk oblast	−11	1,147	893	−22.1
5 Khanty-Mansi autonomous okrug	−23	1,268	1,433	+13.0
6 Yamal-Nenets autonomous okrug	−23	486	507	+4.4
7 Tuva republic	−33	309	306	−1.1
8 Taymyr autonomous okrug	−28	55	40	−27.6
9 Evenki autonomous okrug	−36	24	18	−26.3
10 Noril'sk (city)	−35	175	135	−22.8
11 Sakha republic (Yakutiya)	−43	1,081	948	−12.3
12 Kamchatka oblast	−8	466	359	−23.0
13 Magadan oblast	−18	386	183	−52.7
14 Sakhalin oblast	−13	710	547	−23.0
15 Chukotka autonomous okrug	−21	157	54	−65.9
Total	−19.1	9,886	8,493	−14.1

Source: World Bank definition of the North from Timothy Heleniak, "Out-Migration and Depopulation of the Russian North during the 1990s," *Post-Soviet Geography,* vol. 40, no. 3 (1999), p. 157, fn. 5. 1989 population figures from *Naseleniye Rossii za 100 let (1897–1997)* (Moscow: Goskomstat Rossii, 1998). 2002 population figures are preliminary 2002 census figures as reported in *Interfax Statistical Report,* no. 18 (2003).

a. Temperature per capita (see appendix B).

end, the organizers of the pilot study developed their own definition, based in part on the Russian government's definition of "the Far North and regions equivalent to the Far North" and in part on recent migration data from regions with large outflows of people. The World Bank group paid special attention to issues of data compatibility. In his article "Out-Migration and Depopulation of the Russian North during the 1990s," World Bank demographer Timothy Heleniak provided a detailed footnote explaining the selection process.[3] Table C-1 gives a complete list of the northern regions included in the World Bank's definition (see also figure C-1).

Figure C-1. *Siberia and the Far North*

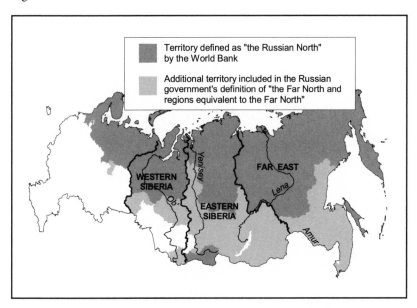

Source: See text.
Note: The territories labeled "Western Siberia," "Eastern Siberia," and "Far East" are three of the eleven economic regions [*ekonomicheskiye rayony*] of Soviet Russia and the Russian Federation before 2001. Although the economic regions had no real political or administrative meaning—they were used primarily as a way of classifying and presenting statistical data—they did roughly follow common notions of the geography of Siberia and the Far East.

Because it is both geographically consistent and compatible with regional-level data, the World Bank definition has provided the general framework for this book's inquiry into the Russian North.

APPENDIX D

An Outline for Further Research

W hat is the penalty that Russia pays for misallocation of population and industry in "thermal space"? To answer that question involves four tasks.

Task 1: Determine the optimal territorial distribution of Russia's population and industry if thermal and other costs were taken into account. Compare the difference between the actual and optimal distributions to obtain the misallocation of resources due to location.

Task 2: Translate pure (geographical) spatial allocation into distribution in thermal space. The latter can be measured by the scalar index called TPC—temperature per capita. The difference in the optimal (hypothetical) and actual allocations then translates into a difference in the TPC index.

Task 3: Calculate the cost of cold to the Russian economy for one degree's change in TPC.

Task 4: Multiply the extent of misallocation, as measured by the TPC index (task 2), by the cost per degree of TPC (task 3). This yields the aggregate cost of past spatial misallocation. (The same procedure can also be used to estimate both savings or losses from current and future changes in the TPC.)

The Brookings–Pennsylvania State University "Cost of the Cold" project has made significant progress on tasks 1 and 2. Tatiana Mikhailova has simulated what the Russian population distribution would have been if decisions had been made rationally (that is, according to market principles). Using the TPC measure, she translated her counterfactual (optimal) population distribution into a TPC effect.[1] The critical step that remains is task 3, calculating the cost of a degree of TPC. Once this is done, task 4 follows easily.

Guided by the North American studies on climate costs discussed in chapter 3, the Cost of the Cold project proposes to examine three main components of direct and adaptation costs: (a) energy consumption costs, (b) costs to human health (increased morbidity and mortality effects), and (c) amenity costs (the wage premium). The complexity of the research task is driven by the fact that none of these costs can be directly measured in Russia. That is, although they are all incurred, they are not accounted for. Some of these costs are internalized, especially by individuals and households (for instance, in the form of poorer human health or quality of life), while others are paid by different levels of government. But even the latter are rarely, if ever, separated as effects of the cold. Obviously, it is not possible to aggregate all the individual costs all over Russia in "building block" style. Hence the project will use interregional (oblast) variation in temperature and in the relevant cost variables—energy, morbidity and mortality, and wage effects —to calculate the implications of cold.

We can illustrate this indirect approach for the case of energy. Let e_j be energy use (e.g., BTU equivalent) in region j. Then we would estimate:

$$e_j = \beta_1 p_j + \beta_2 \tau_j + \sum_i \alpha_i X_{ij} + \varepsilon_j, \qquad (1)$$

where p_j is the population in region j, τ_j is the temperature in region j, and X_{ij} is the share of employment in industry i in region j. The coefficient of interest is β_2, which measures how sensitive energy consumption is to temperature. Combined with estimates of thermal misallocation, we can then estimate the excess energy costs that are due to thermal misallocation. We can use a similar methodology for health.

A complementary approach is to use panel data—that is, one would use the same variables as in equation (1), but for a series of years. Such an approach would require having annual temperature data for a large number of oblasts. This would be necessary to deal with selection issues associated with health effects.

226   AN OUTLINE FOR FURTHER RESEARCH

    The so-called amenity costs of the cold (the negative value to workers of living in cold regions) will be estimated differently. Here, the project will use a methodological approach that follows the standard labor economics literature to estimate the temperature premium in labor supply.[2] It will use data from market-economies with relatively cold regions (Canada, Scandinavian countries) and then apply those results to the Russian distribution of industry and employment.

APPENDIX E

Cities in the Cold

Because of the concentration of population, resources, and economic activity that cities represent, it is precisely the temperatures of cities that are important for the economist. Some comparative facts about Russia's and North America's coldest cities show how cold Russia's urban agglomerations are.

—The United States' coldest cities are places like Fargo (North Dakota), and Duluth, St. Cloud, and Rochester (Minnesota). But they are not particularly cold compared with Russian cities. A list of the 100 coldest Russian and North American cities with populations of over 100,000 would have 85 Russian, 10 Canadian, and 5 U.S. cities. The first Canadian city to appear on the list (Winnipeg) would be in 22nd place. The coldest U.S. city (Fargo, N.D.) would rank 58th.

—Americans are accustomed to thinking of Alaska as the ultimate cold region. It is therefore interesting to note that on that list of the coldest Russian and North American cities with populations of more than 100,000, Anchorage would be number 135, outranked by no fewer than 112 Russian cities! The explanation for this surprising result is not that Alaska isn't cold. It is. It is just that Americans do not build big cities

Table E-1. *The Coldest 25 Cities in North America and Russia with Populations over 500,000 in 2001*

Rank by temperature	City	Country	Mean January temperature (° C)	2001 population in thousands
1	Khabarovsk	Russia	−22.0	604
2	Irkutsk	Russia	−21.0	587
3	Novosibirsk	Russia	−19.0	1,393
4	Omsk	Russia	−19.0	1,138
5	Tomsk	Russia	−19.0	483
6	Winnipeg	Canada	−18.6	686
7	Barnaul	Russia	−18.0	573
8	Novokuznetsk	Russia	−18.0	565
9	Kemerovo	Russia	−18.0	487
10	Krasnoyarsk	Russia	−17.0	876
11	Yekaterinburg	Russia	−16.0	1,257
12	Tyumen'	Russia	−16.0	500
13	Edmonton	Canada	−15.3	967
14	Chelyabinsk	Russia	−15.0	1,081
15	Perm'	Russia	−15.0	1,005
16	Orenburg	Russia	−15.0	517
17	Samara	Russia	−14.0	1,146
18	Ufa	Russia	−14.0	1,089
19	Tol'yatti	Russia	−14.0	724
20	Ul'yanovsk	Russia	−14.0	662
21	Izhevsk	Russia	−14.0	650
22	Vladivostok	Russia	−14.0	599
23	Naberezhnyye Chelny	Russia	−14.0	518
24	Kazan'	Russia	−13.0	1,090
25	Nizhniy Novgorod	Russia	−12.0	1,343

Source: Authors' database. See appendix B.

there. In fact, Anchorage is the only city in Alaska with a population of over 100,000.

—For really large cities, things get even worse (see tables E-1 and E-2). The United States has only one metro area over half a million that is colder than −8° C (Minneapolis-St. Paul, Minn.). Russia has 30 cities that big and that cold.

Table E-2. *The World's Coldest Cities with More Than One Million People, 2001*

Rank by temperature	City	Country	Mean January temperature (° C)	2001 population in millions
1	Novosibirsk	Russia	−19.0	1.4
2	Omsk	Russia	−19.0	1.1
3	Yekaterinburg	Russia	−16.0	1.3
4	Chelyabinsk	Russia	−15.0	1.1
5	Perm'	Russia	−15.0	1.0
6	Samara	Russia	−14.0	1.1
7	Ufa	Russia	−14.0	1.1
8	Kazan'	Russia	−13.0	1.1
9	Nizhniy Novgorod	Russia	−12.0	1.3
10	Ottawa–Hull	Canada	−11.7	1.1

Source: Authors' database. See appendix B.

Notes

Chapter 1

1. Georgiy Bovt and Yelena Korop, "Obyknovennoye chudo Andreya Illarionova: Rossiya smozhet vyyti iz tsivilizatsionnogo tupika tol'ko cherez revolyutsiyu gosudarstvennosti," *Izvestiya*, no. 231 (20 December 2002), p. 1.

Chapter 2

1. Cited in Richard Pipes, *Russia under the Old Regime* (Scribner's, 1974), p. 84.

2. See, for example, Nikolay A. Kosolapov, "Rossiya: v chem vse-taki sut' istoricheskogo vybora," *Mirovaya ekonomika i mezhdunarodnaya otnosheniya*, no. 10 (1994), p. 15.

3. Cited in M. A. Maslin, *Russkaya ideya* (Moscow: Respublika, 1992), pp. 6–7.

4. Paul Kennedy, *The Rise and Fall of the Great Powers: Economic Change and Military Conflict from 1500–2000* (Random House, 1987), p. 195.

5. Francis Henry Skrine, *The Expansion of Russia* (Cambridge University Press, 1915), p. 1.

6. Halford J. Mackinder, "The Geographical Pivot of History," *Geographical Journal*, vol. 23, no. 4 (April 1904), pp. 421–37.

7. For example, "A Survey of Russia," *Economist*, July 12, 1997, p. S11.

8. Cited in "Mezhdometiya," *Itogi,* no. 30 (31 July 2002), p. 8.

9. William Moul, "Measuring the 'Balances of Power': A Look at Some Numbers," *Review of International Studies,* no. 15 (1989), pp. 111–16.

10. William Fuller, *Strategy and Power in Russia: 1600–1914* (Free Press, 1992), p. 278.

11. Konstantin Pleshakov, *The Tsar's Last Armada: The Epic Journey to the Battle of Tsushima* (Basic Books, 2002).

12. See Fuller's discussion of Russian strategic railway development in *Strategy and Power,* p. 440. Orlando Figes notes that in World War I, Russia's military trains could not travel more than two hundred miles a day and tended to transport horses and feedstuff for the cavalry rather than infantry forces. See Orlando Figes, *A People's Tragedy: The Russian Revolution: 1891–1924* (Penguin Books, 1996), p. 261.

13. Wolf von Schierbrand, *Russia: Her Strength and Weakness: A Study of the Present Conditions of the Russian Empire, with an Analysis of Its Resources and a Forecast of Its Future* (G. P. Putnam's Sons, 1904), p. 48.

14. Dwight H. Perkins and Moshe Syrquin, "Large Countries: The Influence of Size," in H. Chenery and T. N. Srinivasan, eds., *Handbook of Development Economics,* vol. 2 (Elsevier Science, 1988), p. 1695. One might add, however, that some of the most valuable natural resources are often found in remote locations. Their presence seems correlated with geographical features that make the areas less suitable for human settlement—deserts, mountainous regions, and so on. Space and distance, therefore, remain factors to be overcome in an economic sense.

15. James E. Vance Jr., *The Merchant's World: The Geography of Wholesaling* (Prentice-Hall, 1970).

16. Table D 75-84, "Gainful Workers, by Age, Sex, and Farm-Nonfarm Occupations: 1820 to 1930," *Historical Statistics of the United States: Colonial Times to 1970: Part 1* (U.S. Census Bureau, 1975).

17. See Richard Florida, "Bohemia and Economic Geography," *Journal of Economic Geography,* vol. 2, no. 1 (January 2002), pp. 55–71. The thesis is presented in popular form in Florida's book *The Rise of the Creative Class* (Basic Books, 2002).

18. Jared Diamond, *Guns, Germs, and Steel: The Fates of Human Societies* (W. W. Norton, 1999).

19. See Antonio Ciccone and Robert E. Hall, "Productivity and the Density of Economic Activity," *American Economic Review,* vol. 86, no. 1 (March 1996), p. 55.

20. Ibid., pp. 54–70.

21. Ibid., p. 64.

22. Facts presented in Tertius Chandler and Gerald Fox, *3000 Years of Urban Growth* (Academic Press), p. 19.

23. One recent article states that "Zipf's law for cities is one of the most conspicuous empirical facts in economics, or in the social sciences generally." Xavier Gabaix, "Zipf's Law for Cities: An Explanation," *Quarterly Journal of Economics,* vol. 114 (August 1999), pp. 739–67.

24. Zipf's law, named for George Zipf, is an example of a power law. Power laws are ubiquitous in nature and are also quite common in economics.

25. Our Brookings colleague Robert Axtell has presented the most persuasive case for Zipf's law as a natural economic phenomenon. See Robert L. Axtell and Richard Florida, "Emergent Cities: A Microeconomic Explanation of Zipf's Law" (Brookings, 2000). Also, Robert L. Axtell, "Zipf Distribution of U.S. Firm Sizes," *Science*, vol. 293 (7 September 2001), pp. 1818–20. Note that while the failure of a country's city-size distribution to conform to Zipf's law may imply that nonmarket forces were at work over time, the converse is not true. A Zipf distribution of city sizes does not imply the dominance of market forces. After all, central planners could have made (although it is fairly certain they did not do so in reality) a Zipf distribution the planning objective and used command-administrative methods to achieve it. Thus the market is a sufficient, but not necessary, condition for a Zipf city-size distribution.

26. Timothy R. Gulden and Ross A. Hammond, "An Agent-based Model of City-size Distribution," working paper, Center on Social and Economic Dynamics, Brookings (forthcoming, 2003).

Chapter 3

1. This was true, for instance, on 105 days out of 110 in the listings given in the *Washington Post* between October 12, 2002, and February 7, 2003.

2. The world's low temperature record, outside Antarctica, is -68° C. It was recorded three times: in Verkhoyansk on February 5 and February 7, 1892, and in Oymyakon on February 6, 1933. Both locations are in the Republic of Sakha (Yakutiya) in Siberia. "Siberian Cold Snap," *Weatherwise*, January/February 2002, www.weatherwise.org/qr/qry.siberiancold.html. Antarctica's cold record is -89° C. See www.ncdc.noaa.gov/oa/climate/globalextremes.html.

3. Nicholas Riasanovsky, *A History of Russia*, 3d ed. (Oxford University Press, 1977), p. 77.

4. Michael Wines, "Baltic Soil Yields Evidence of a Bitter End to Napoleon's Army," *New York Times*, 14 September 2002, p. A5. Wines cites sources from 1812 that describe how "the soldiers throw away their guns because they cannot hold them; both officers and soldiers think only of protecting themselves from the terrible cold," and talk of French forces dressing themselves in as many items as they can find, including women's clothing, but still perishing en masse from the cold.

5. Andrey P. Parshev, *Pochemu Rossiya ne Amerika: kniga dlya tekh, kto ostayetsya zdes'* [Why Russia is not America: A book for those who remain here](Moscow: Krymskiy Most-9D, 2000).

6. Ibid., p. 40.

7. L. V. Milov, *Velikorusskiy pakhar' i osobennosti rossiyskogo istoricheskogo protsessa* [The Great Russian ploughman and the specific features of the Russian historical process] (Moscow: Rossiyskaya politicheskaya entsiklopediya [ROSSPEN], 1998).

8. Ibid., p. 5.

9. Tatiana Mikhailova, "Where Russians Should Live: A Counterfactual Alternative to Soviet Location Policy," Pennsylvania State University, 2002.

10. Gunars Abele, "Effect of Cold Weather on Productivity," in *Technology Transfer Opportunities for the Construction Engineering Community*, Proceedings of Construction Seminar, February 1986 (U.S. Army Cold Regions Research and Engineering Laboratory).

11. The devastating effects of wind chill are familiar to people who spend time in the outdoors in Alaska and Canada. Alaskans often cite the "30-30-30" rule, which states that at -30° F, with winds of 30 miles per hour, human flesh will freeze solid in 30 seconds. An official Canadian occupational safety brochure warns that "exposed human flesh freezes within one minute at -29° C (-20° F) when wind speed is 8 km/h (5 mph)." *Cold Weather Workers Safety Guide*, prepared by the Canadian Centre for Occupational Health and Safety (no date), p. 13.

12. Deborah Herbert and Ian Burton, "Estimated Costs of Adaptation to Canada's Current Climate and Trends Under Climate Change," unpublished paper (Toronto, Atmospheric Environment Service, 1994).

13. Robert Anderson Jr. calculated the health costs of cooling: "The Health Costs of Changing Macro-Climates," in Anthony Broderick and Thomas M. Hard, eds., *Proceedings of the Third Conference on the Climatic Impact Assessment Program*, Conference Proceedings 1974, DOT-TSC-OST-74-15, 1974, pp. 582–92. Ralph D'Arge estimated other economic costs of cooling, including agriculture, forestry, and marine resources: "Economic Impact of Climate Change: Introduction and Overview," in Conference Proceedings, pp. 564–74. The work on the value of climate amenities drew on the work of Irving Hoch: "Variations in the Quality of Urban Life Among Cities and Regions," in Lowdon Wingo and Alan Evans, eds., *Public Economics and the Quality of Life* (Johns Hopkins University Press, 1977).

14. Moore himself did not use the DOT research to study the costs of the cold, but rather the benefits of warmer temperatures. See Thomas Gale Moore, *Climate of Fear. Why We Shouldn't Worry about Global Warming* (Cato Institute, 1998); and Thomas Gale Moore, "Health and Amenity Effects of Global Warming," *Economic Inquiry*, vol. 36 (July 1998), pp. 471–88.

15. Owing to that slower growth, the economy would be around 12–17 percent smaller at the end of the fifteen-year period than it would have been without the extra degree of cold. Note that saying that the economy would incur the extra cost each year for fifteen years assumes that no one adjusts during that period so as to reduce the cost. This is unlikely. For instance, some people and businesses would move to warmer areas. Others would shift to different kinds of activity that are better suited to (less penalized by) the cold.

16. Victor L. Mote, "Environmental Constraints to the Economic Development of Siberia," in Robert G. Jensen, T. Shabad, and A. Wright, eds., *Soviet Natural Resources in the World Economy* (University of Chicago Press, 1983), p. 22.

17. Ibid., p. 22.

18. Ibid., p. 21, citing Yu. M. Dogayev, "Ekonomicheskaya effektivnost' novoy tekhniki na Severe," *Nauka*, no. 36 (1969), pp. 38–40.

19. Tatiana Mikhailova, "Where Russians Should Live: A Counterfactual Alternative to Soviet Location Policy," Ph.D. diss., Pennsylvania State University, 2002.

20. Ibid.

21. Niall Ferguson's recent edited volume, *Virtual History: Alternatives and Counterfactuals* (Basic Books, 1999), is a good example of this popular approach. In that book, authors ask such questions as: "What if there had been no American War of Independence?" "What if Britain had stayed out of the First World War?" "What if Hitler had invaded Britain or had defeated the Soviet Union?"

22. Langdon White and George Primmer, "The Iron and Steel Industry of Duluth: A Study in Locational Maladjustment," *Geographical Review,* vol. 27, no. 1 (1937), pp. 82–91. Figures rounded to the nearest thousandth and based on the U.S. Census Metropolitan Statistical Area (MSA) of Duluth-Superior. Source: Demographic Brief, Metropolitan Area Population: 1900 to 1998, www.demographia.com.

23. White and Primmer, "Iron and Steel Industry of Duluth," pp. 89–90.

24. Ibid., p. 90.

25. Clifford G. Gaddy, *The Price of the Past* (Brookings, 1996), figure 9-1, "Defense Industry and City Growth: The Case of Perm."

Chapter 4

1. Richard Pipes, *Russia under the Old Regime* (Scribner's, 1974), p. 83.

2. Klyuchevskiy's most famous work is his comprehensive history of Russia: Vasiliy Klyuchevskiy, *Kurs russkoy istorii* (Moscow, 1937), 4 vols.

3. Dominic Lieven, *Empire: The Russian Empire and Its Rivals* (London: John Murray, 2000), p. 207.

4. Pipes, *Russia under the Old Regime*, pp. 6-12.

5. Pipes discusses how, until the mid-sixteenth century, the core of Russia's population was in a zone of mixed forests that lay between 50 and 60 degrees latitude, which approximates the latitude of modern Canada. Pipes observes, however, that in Canada the population is largely confined to 45–52 degrees latitude. North of 52 degrees latitude, in stark contrast to Russia, there is hardly any population or agriculture. Pipes describes how Russia's climate and poor soils meant that it was unable to produce agriculture yields sufficient to create the surplus necessary to sustain economic development. In the early modern period, this set Russia behind other European states, like Great Britain, which were able to generate agricultural surpluses and thus promote the development of internal markets and, ultimately, international trade.

6. Ibid., p. 13. There are no reliable population sources for this period, and the first official census in Russia was only in 1897. Pipes reached his prerevolutionary figures from a range of Soviet-era sources, including S. V. Voznesenskiy, *Ekonomika Rossii XIX-XX vv. v tsifrakh* (Leningrad, 1924); A. I. Kopanev, "Naseleniye russkogo gosudarstva v XVI v," *Istoricheskiye zapiski,* vol. 63 (1959), p. 254; V. M. Kabuzan, *Narodo-naseleniye Rossii v XVIII-pervoi polovine XIX v* (Moscow, 1963); and A. G. Rashin, *Naseleniye Rossii za 100 let (1811–1913 gg)* (Moscow, 1956).

7. Pipes, *Russia under the Old Regime*, p. 13. Pipes attributes as much as ten million of this growth to the incorporation of new territories into the Russian state, leaving natural increase to account for the rest.

8. Ibid., p. 169.

9. Cited in ibid., p. 14, referencing S. M. Dubrovskiy, *Stolypinskaya reforma* (Moscow, 1930).

10. Pipes, *Russia under the Old Regime*, p. 13. Unfortunately, tsarist statistical records often cover different periods, making it difficult to obtain a neat snapshot of key developments over time.

11. Ibid., p. 167.

12. Thomas Malthus, *An Essay on the Principle of Population, as It Affects the Future Improvement of Society with Remarks on the Speculations of Mr. Godwin, M. Condorcet, and Other Writers* (London: J. Johnson, 1798). Accessed online at www.ac.wwu.edu/~stephan/malthus/malthus.0.html.

13. Richard Pipes, *The Russian Revolution* (Knopf, 1990), p. 103.

14. The term "embarrassment of space" is from Roy Mellor, *The Soviet Union and Its Geographic Problems* (London: Macmillan, 1982), p. xi.

15. Pipes, *The Russian Revolution*, pp. 103–04. Here Pipes is referring to Vasiliy Klyuchevskiy's statement that "the history of Russia is the history of a country which colonizes itself."

16. Malthus, *Essay on the Principle of Population*, chap. 6.

17. Pipes, *Russia under the Old Regime*, pp. 11–12, referencing nineteenth-century German and other European agricultural experts.

18. In 1992 an Aborigine, Eddie Mabo, successfully sued Australia's State of Queensland in the High Courts. The so-called Mabo Judgement resulting from the case said that Australian territories were already inhabited by Aborigines in the eighteenth century, and that British and European settlers had no legal basis for invoking *terra nullius* in establishing land claims. See C. L. Ogleby, "Terra Nullius, the High Court, and Surveyors," *Australian Surveyor,* vol. 38, no. 3 (September 1993), pp. 171–89; and also Stan Pelczynski, "The Australian High Court Recognition of Native Title—The Mabo Judgement and Its Implications," 27 July 1993, www.innu.ca/mabo.html.

19. In the age of empires, the European Great Powers used the first definition of *terra nullius* in their efforts to colonize the rest of the (non-European) world, and they thus "[supplied] sovereignty where none existed." Henry Reynolds, *The Law of the Land* (Ringwood, Victoria: Penguin Books, 1987), p. 12. The British legal scholar T. J. Lawrence, in his 1910 treatise *The Principle of International Law*, maintained that all territory "not in the possession of states who are members of the family of nations" (e.g., the European Great Powers) should be viewed "as technically [*terra nullius*] and therefore open to occupation." See T. J. Lawrence, *The Principle of International Law* (London: Macmillan, 1910), p. 151, cited in Reynolds, *The Law of the Land,* p. 12.

20. Prussian legal scholar Friedrich Carl Von Savigny, in his seminal *Treatise on Possession* of 1848, was one of the first to suggest that possession had to have two

clear components: actual physical presence on the land and a "desire" to possess the land. Gaining a presence allowed the occupant to use the land in any way he saw fit, but if the land was not actually "used" (lived on in permanent settlements, farmed, or mined, etc.), or it was "physically abandoned and a determination exists to give it up," then possession could be forfeited and lost. See Reynolds, *The Law of the Land,* pp. 14–15. As early as the 1820s, in diplomatic correspondence with Russia, Great Britain managed to secure an agreement that "use and occupation" would "constitute the best titles by which a state [could] lay claim to rights of sovereignty over any part of the continent," in reference to their respective interests in Asia. See James Simsarian, "The Acquisition of Legal Title to Terra Nullius," *Political Science Quarterly*, vol. 53, no. 1 (March 1938), p. 124.

21. This sense of obligation is encapsulated in a famous 1895 quotation by German chancellor Bernhard von Bülow, who declared that "the question is not whether we [Germany] want to colonize or not, but that we must colonize, whether we want it or not." Cited in William Langer, *The Diplomacy of Imperialism 1890–1902* (Knopf, 1956), p. 85.

22. Cited in Wolfgang Mommsen, *Theories of Imperialism* (Random House, 1980), p. 5.

23. The appellation "Great" [*velikiy*] is endowed with considerable political and cultural symbolism and used sparingly in Russian political discourse, always in conjunction with ideas of giant size or magnitude, magnificence and splendor, nobility, grandness, excellence, majesty and glory. In Russian history, very few rulers, wars, and events have been designated as "Great": Peter the *Great*, Catherine the *Great*, the *Great* Northern War, the *Great* Reforms of Alexander II, the *Great* October Revolution, and the *Great* Patriotic or Fatherland War. In each case the designation marks a crucially important period or juncture for the Russian state in its relationship to the outside world, respectively: the expansionist and modernizing reigns of Peter and Catherine, which were seen as the apogee of the Russian Empire; the war that marked Russia's emergence as a European Great Power after the defeat of Sweden at the Battle of Poltava in 1709; the reforms of the nineteenth century that brought an end to the perceived shame of serfdom; the Bolshevik revolution, which transformed old tsarist Russia into a modern industrial (and purportedly the world's first communist) state; and World War II—Russia's punishing victory over Germany—which saw Russia's rise as a superpower rival to the United States and its dominance of Eastern Europe and half the globe. For a more detailed discussion of this issue see Fiona Hill, "In Search of Great Russia: Elites, Ideas, Power, the State, and the Pre-Revolutionary Past in the New Russia 1991–1996," Ph.D. diss., Harvard University Department of History, March 1998.

24. The indigenous population of Siberia comprises a mixture of Asiatic nomadic peoples (Altaic, Aleutian, Samoyedic, Tungus-Manchu, Turkic, Ugric, and others), with some related to the Mongols to the south and others to the native peoples of North America across the Bering Strait. For a good study of the history and culture of the native peoples of Siberia see Marjorie Mandelstam Balzer, *The*

Tenacity of Ethnicity: A Siberian Saga in Global Perspective (Princeton University Press, 1999).

25. John Cole, "Changes in the Population of Larger Cities of the USSR, 1979–1989," *Soviet Geography,* vol. 31, no. 3 (March 1990), p. 160. Cole notes: "The process of Soviet urban growth has to a large extent been the result of centrally planned decisions about the location of investment and the creation of jobs in different sectors of the economy, rather than the result of market forces only partially affected by government decisions."

26. See Roger Thiede, "Industry and Urbanization in New Russia from 1860 to 1910," in Michael F. Hamm, ed., *The City in Russian History* (University of Kentucky Press, 1976).

27. Pipes, *Russia under the Old Regime,* p. 9.

28. Pipes, *The Russian Revolution,* p. 296.

29. William Blackwell, "Modernization and Urbanization in Russia: A Comparative View," in Hamm, *The City in Russian History,* p. 303.

30. See M. E. Falkus, *The Industrialization of Russia, 1700–1914* (London: Macmillan, 1972), p. 11. If Poland and Finland were excluded from the Russian Empire, the urban population of Russia was smaller—just over 15 percent (18.6 million) of the population in 1913 (p. 34). This compares relatively well with urban populations in other countries in this period. For example, in 1913, 34.6 percent of Britain's population was urban, 23.1 percent in the United States, 21 percent in Germany, and 14.8 percent in France. See Paul Kennedy, *The Rise and Fall of the Great Powers* (Random House, 1987), p. 200.

31. Pipes, *The Russian Revolution,* p. 237.

32. Ibid., p. 724.

33. *Narodnoye khozyaystvo SSSR v 1990 g* (Moscow, 1991), p. 68.

34. *Naseleniye Rossii za 100 let (1897–1997): Statisticheskiy sbornik* (Moscow: Goskomstat Rossii, 1998), pp. 32–33.

35. Chauncy Harris, *Cities of the Soviet Union* (Chicago: Rand McNally, 1970), pp. 269–70 (internal footnotes omitted).

36. Ibid, pp. 270–71.

37. Ibid., p. 271. Odessa's population fell from approximately 500,000 in 1915 to about 420,000 in 1926.

38. Blackwell, "Modernization and Urbanization in Russia: A Comparative View," p. 320.

39. Ibid., p. 295.

40. Ibid., p. 320.

Chapter 5

1. Mark Bassin, "Inventing Siberia: Visions of the Russian Far East in the Early 19th Century," *American Historical Review,* vol. 96, no. 3 (June 1991).

2. Alexander Solzhenitsyn, "Repentance and Self-Limitation in the Life of Nations," in A. Solzhenitsyn, ed., *From under the Rubble*, trans. A. M. Brock and others (Bantam Books, 1976), p. 141.

3. The Council on Foreign and Defense Policy is a Moscow-based group led by Russian political analyst Sergey Karaganov that brings together leading figures from politics, the analytical community, and the press; it was established to produce reports on critical security issues for the Russian government. See "Sovet po vneshney i oboronnoy politike," *Sibir' i dal'niy vostok v sotsial'no-ekonomicheskom i politicheskom prostranstve Rossii,* www.svop.ru/yuka/856.shtml (accessed 11 July 2002).

4. Bassin, "Inventing Siberia," p. 767.

5. John Harrison estimates that the fur-trade share of Russia's revenues was almost 25 percent. See *The Founding of the Russian Empire in Asia and America* (University of Miami Press, 1971), p. 71, cited in Gary Hausladen, "Russian Siberia: An Integrative Approach," *Soviet Geography*, vol. 30, no. 3 (1989), p. 240. Benson Bobrick provides a lower estimate of 10 percent in *East of the Sun: The Epic Conquest and Tragic History of Siberia* (Poseidon Press, 1992), p. 72. In any case, it is clear that the fur trade was lucrative. Anna Reid in her book on Siberia points out that in the 1620s, two pelts of black fox fur could be sold for a sum that would purchase fifty acres of land, a cabin, five horses, ten head of cattle, twenty sheep, and much more besides. See Anna Reid, *The Shaman's Coat: A Native History of Siberia* (New York: Walker, 2002), p. 26.

6. Gary Hausladen, "Russian Siberia: An Integrative Approach," *Soviet Geography*, vol. 30, no. 3 (1989), p. 237.

7. Marc Raeff, *Siberia and the Reforms of 1822* (University of Washington Press, 1956), p. 13.

8. A. P. Sukhodolov, *Sibir' v nachale XX veka: territoriya, granitsy, goroda, transportniye magistrali, sel'skoye khozyaystvo* (Irkutsk: Irkutskaya ekonomicheskaya akademiya, 1996), pp. 26–27.

9. Martin Gilbert, *Russian History Atlas* (MacMillan, 1972), p. 54.

10. Excerpts from Mikhail Speranskiy's survey of Siberia (1821), cited in Raeff, *Siberia and the Reforms of 1822*, pp. 7–8.

11. N. M. Yadrintsev, *Sibir' kak koloniya* (1892; reprint, Tyumen': Yu. Mandriki, 2000), p. 167.

12. Bassin, "Inventing Siberia," p. 777.

13. Ibid., p. 790. In the mid-nineteenth century, the romanticism of the frontier life in Siberia became so strong that the tsarist government had to head off a nascent Siberian autonomy movement—spurred on by the sense of distance from European Russia and intermarriage with native peoples. See Dominic Lieven, *Empire: The Russian Empire and Its Rivals* (London: John Murray, 2000), p. 229.

14. In the 1880s, an estimated 72 percent of migration into Siberia was illegal. See J. William Leasure and Robert A. Lewis, "Internal Migration in Russia in the Late Nineteenth Century," *Slavic Review*, vol. 27, no. 3 (September 1968), p. 382.

240 NOTES TO PAGES 77–83

15. S. I. Bruk and V. M. Kabuzan, "The Dynamics and Ethnic Composition of the Population of Russia in the Era of Imperialism (From the End of the 19th Century to 1917)," *Istoriya SSSR*, no. 3 (1980), pp. 74–93, reprinted in translation in *Soviet Geography*, vol. 30, no. 2 (1989), pp. 130–54, table 3 ("Number and Direction of Internal Migrants, Emigrants, and Immigrants in Russia, 1871–1916"), p. 140.

16. V. M. Kabuzan, "The Settlement of Siberia and the Far East from the Late 18th to the Early 20th Century (1795–1917)," *Istoriya SSSR*, no. 3 (1979), trans. James R. Gibson in *Soviet Geography*, vol. 32, no. 9 (1991), pp. 617, 625.

17. Ibid., pp. 619–21. Kabuzan notes that high rates of natural increase accounted for three-quarters of the aggregate population growth in Siberia in this period. He also points out that in periods when penal settlement was high, the rate of natural increase declined, as there were usually few women among exiles to Siberia.

18. Gilbert, *Russian History Atlas*, p. 62.

19. Kabuzan, "The Settlement of Siberia and the Far East," p. 625.

20. Kathleen Barnes, "Eastward Migration within the Soviet Union," *Pacific Affairs*, vol. 7, no. 4 (December 1934), p. 397. Also Anatoly Khodorkovsky and others, "Russia's Peculiar Path," *The Moscow Times*, 15 January 2001.

21. Kabuzan, "The Settlement of Siberia and the Far East," p. 629. Gilbert provides a figure of nine million people in *Russian History Atlas*, p. 62.

22. Kabuzan, "The Settlement of Siberia and the Far East," p. 622.

23. See Donald Treadgold, *The Great Siberian Migration: Government and Peasant in Resettlement from Emancipation to the First World War* (Princeton University Press, 1957), p. 78.

24. See, for example, Victor Mote, *Siberia: Worlds Apart* (Boulder, Colo.: Westview Press, 1998), pp. 45–51.

25. A. P. Sukhodolov, *Sibir' v nachale XX veka : territoriya, granitsy, goroda, transportniye magistrali, sel'skoye khozyaystvo* (Irkutsk: Irkutskaya ekonomicheskaya akademiya, 1996), p. 28.

26. Gilbert, *Russian History Atlas*, p. 60.

27. Treadgold, *The Great Siberian Migration*, p. 70.

28. Kabuzan, "The Settlement of Siberia and the Far East," p. 625.

29. Gilbert, *Russian History Atlas*, p. 60. See also Kabuzan, "The Settlement of Siberia and the Far East," pp. 618–19.

30. Kabuzan, "The Settlement of Siberia and the Far East," pp. 628–29.

31. For a good general discussion of the tsarist financial constraints, see Paul Kennedy, *The Rise and Fall of the Great Powers: Economic Change and Military Conflict from 1500–2000* (Random House, 1987), pp. 234–36.

32. Kathleen Barnes, "Eastward Migration within the Soviet Union," pp. 399–400.

33. James R. Harris, "The Growth of the Gulag: Forced Labor in the Urals Region, 1929–31," *Russian Review*, vol. 56 (April 1997), pp. 269–70.

34. Ibid., p. 270.

35. M. B. Smirnov, S. P. Sigachev, and D. V. Shkapov, "Sistema mest zaklyucheniya v SSSR. 1929–1960," in M. B. Smirnov, ed., *Sistema ispravitel'no-trudovykh lagerey v SSSR, 1923–1960: spravochnik* (Moscow: Zven'ya, 1998), pp. 25–74. Anne Applebaum notes that the idea of using prisoners to develop specific underdeveloped regions was first formulated as early as November 1925 in a letter to Feliks Dzerzhinzkiy, the head of the Bolshevik secret police, although no action was taken at that juncture. Applebaum, *Gulag: A History* (Doubleday, 2003), p. 30.

36. Applebaum, *Gulag*, pp. 31-40.

37. David Dallin and Boris Nikolaevsky, *Forced Labor in Soviet Russia* (Yale University Press, 1947), pp. 197–98.

38. Applebaum, *Gulag*, p. 87; see also Robert Conquest, *The Great Terror: Stalin's Purges of the Thirties* (Macmillan, 1968), p. 351.

39. Ibid., pp. 352, 355.

40. Dallin and Nikolaevsky, *Forced Labor in Soviet Russia*, p. 146.

41. Smirnov, Sigachev, and Shkapov, "Sistema mest zaklyucheniya." In 1947 the Soviet government had issued a decree prescribing a minimum of five years imprisonment in the GULAG for "misappropriation of state property."

42. According to G. M. Ivanova, *GULAG v sisteme totalitarnogo gosudarstva* (Moscow, 1997), p. 136, cited in Smirnov, Sigachev, and Shkapov, "Sistema mest zaklyucheniya, p. 73, fn. 212, production under the control of the Soviet internal affairs ministry, the MVD, accounted for 10 percent of the total industrial output of the USSR in 1949. Russia's industrial output share was around two-thirds of the USSR total.

43. Galina Ivanova, "The 'Camp Economy' of the Postwar Period," in *Novaya perspektiva: voprosy istorii ekonomicheskikh i politicheskikh otnosheniy v Rossii* (XXV), vol. 2.

44. Dallin and Nikolaevsky, *Forced Labor in Soviet Russia*, pp. 50–51.

45. Ibid., p. 51. Between the Soviet censuses of 1926 and 1939, the Soviet Union's urban population leaped from 26 million to nearly 56 million.

46. Ibid., p. 31.

47. See "10. Amurskiy zheleznodorozhniy ITL (Amurlag)," pp. 143–44; "47. Bureyskiy ITL (Burlag, Bureylag)," pp. 177–78; "84. Dal'nevostochnyy ITL (Dal'lag)," pp. 208–09; "465. Shosdorlag," pp. 515–16, all in M. B. Smirnov, ed., *Sistema ispravitel'no-trudovykh lagerey v SSSR: spravochnik* (Moscow: Zven'ya, 1998).

48. See also "284. Primorskiy ITL (Primorskoye LO, Primorlag)," pp. 362–63; "335. Stroitel'stvo 201 i ITL (Nikolaevskiy ITL)," pp. 413–14; and "444. Khabarovskiy ITL (Khabarlag)," pp. 501–02, in ibid.

49. *Rossiyskiy statisticheskiy yezhegodnik 2001* (Moscow: Goskomstat), p. 99.

50. Mote, *Siberia: Worlds Apart*, p. 92.

51. Cited in David MacKenzie and Michael Curran, *A History of Russia and the Soviet Union*, rev. ed. (Homewood, Ill.: Dorsey Press, 1982), p. 594. The bulk of the ethnic Russian and Ukrainian settlers relocated in northern Kazakhstan. Today they straddle Kazakhstan's border with the Russian Federation and account for more than 30 percent of Kazakhstan's total population.

52. Robert N. Taaffe, "The Conceptual, Analytical, and Planning Framework of Siberian Development," in George Demko and Roland Fuchs, eds., *Geographical Studies on the Soviet Union: Essays in Honor of Chauncy D. Harris,* Research Paper 211 (University of Chicago Department of Geography, 1984), p. 169.

53. Leslie Dienes, "The Development of Siberia: Regional Priorities and Economic Strategy," in Demko and Fuchs, eds., *Geographical Studies on the Soviet Union,* p. 194.

54. Friedrich Engels, *Herr Eugen Dühring's Revolution in Science [Anti-Dühring],* trans. Emile Burns, ed. C. P. Dutt (New York: International Publishers, 1939), pp. 322–24.

55. For more on Lagovskiy, see Clifford Gaddy, *The Price of the Past,* chap. 3, "The Logic of a Hypermilitarized Economy" (Brookings, 1996).

56. Dienes, "The Development of Siberia," pp. 199–200.

57. Taaffe, "The Conceptual, Analytical, and Planning Framework of Siberian Development," p. 170.

58. See Gaddy, *Price of the Past,* pp. 39–40.

59. Taaffe, "The Conceptual, Analytical, and Planning Framework of Siberian Development," p. 166.

60. Ibid., pp. 178, 180–81.

61. Ibid., p. 158.

62. Dienes, "The Development of Siberia," pp. 189–92.

63. Yu. Sobolev, "Narodnokhozyaystvennaya programma osvoyeniya zony BAM," in *Planovoye khozyaystvo* 7 (1978), cited in Taaffe, "The Conceptual, Analytical, and Planning Framework of Siberian Development," p. 159.

64. Ibid., p. 166.

65. G. Mil'ner, "Problems of Ensuring the Supply of Labour Resources for Siberia and the Far Eastern Regions," *Problems of Economics,* vol. 22, no. 4 (1979), p. 88, cited in Taaffe, "The Conceptual, Analytical, and Planning Framework of Siberian Development," p. 161.

66. Taaffe, "The Conceptual, Analytical, and Planning Framework of Siberian Development," pp. 167, 165.

67. Dienes, "The Development of Siberia," pp. 200, 204–05.

68. Taaffe, "The Conceptual, Analytical, and Planning Framework of Siberian Development," pp. 163, 168.

69. Dienes, "The Development of Siberia," p. 212.

70. Ibid., p. 213.

71. Abel Aganbegyan, *Inside Perestroika: The Future of the Soviet Economy,* trans. Helen Szamuely (Harper & Row, 1989), p. 192; Andrei Kokoshin, "Defense Industry Conversion in the Russian Federation," in Teresa Pelton Johnson and Steven Miller, eds., *Russian Security after the Cold War: Seven Views from Moscow* (Washington: Brassey's, 1994), p. 52; cited in Gaddy, *Price of the Past,* p. 40.

72. Taaffe, "The Conceptual, Analytical, and Planning Framework of Siberian Development," pp. 168–69, 173, 177.

73. Ibid., p. 181. Other sources discuss development projects extending as far as 2010.

74. S. G. Prociuk, "The Manpower Problem in Siberia," *Soviet Studies,* vol. 19, no. 2 (1967), pp. 190–210.

75. Prociuk, "The Manpower Problem in Siberia," p. 196.

76. Ibid., p. 198.

77. Ibid., p. 205.

78. Ibid., p. 206.

79. Cited in William Wohlforth, "The Perception of Power: Russia in the Pre-1914 Balance," *World Politics,* vol. 39, no. 3 (April 1987), p. 362.

80. Especially to the Don and Kuban regions. Soviet economist M. Ya. Sorin, cited in Prociuk, "The Manpower Problem in Siberia," p. 199.

81. Taaffe, "The Conceptual, Analytical, and Planning Framework of Siberian Development," p. 160.

82. Constantine Krypton, "The Economy of Northern Siberia, 1959–1965," *Russian Review,* vol. 19, no. 1 (1960), p. 51.

Chapter 6

1. See Alexis de Tocqueville, *Democracy in America,* trans. George Lawrence, ed. J. P. Mayer (New York: Perennial Classics, 2000); Robert Putnam, *Making Democracy Work: Civic Traditions in Modern Italy* (Princeton University Press, 1993); and Robert Putnam, *Bowling Alone* (Simon & Schuster, 2000).

2. Cf. the medieval Central European slogan: "*Stadtluft macht frei*" ["City air brings freedom"].

3. Russia scholar S. Frederick Starr emphasizes "the strange modernity of serfdom and slavery" as one of the unique features of Russia. He notes that given that land is an almost free good in Russia, it has created an inordinate emphasis on controlling the scarce commodity (labor). Slavery elsewhere is ancient. In Russia it is more modern because of the land. This is what is different about Russia when comparing it with other European states. Personal exchange with the authors on the first draft of *The Siberian Curse,* 10 March 2003.

4. According to Pipes, in 1861 a little under half of Russian peasants and just under 38 percent of the total population of Russia were serfs or peasants personally bonded to a landlord. See Richard Pipes, *Russia under the Old Regime* (Scribner's, 1974), p. 144. Serfs were not technically owned in their person by the landlord, as slaves in the Americas were in this same period. The landlord owned the actual land itself, or at least the right to dispose of the rents from the land that the serfs lived on. Serfs were thus obligated to perform labor services for the landlord. However, once that service was fulfilled, the agricultural product of the serfs' labor was then their own—to be used for personal or family subsistence or sold if they so chose. In addition, almost half of Russia's serfs were more like tenant farmers in the sense that they paid dues (taxes) to the landlord rather than performed labor. As

long as they paid the required remittance, they were free to move away from the land and seek other employment. Only 12–15 percent of the Russian Empire's total population fell into the category of labor-performing serfs, who were tied to the land and the landlord and entirely at the mercy of the latter. After the emancipation of the serfs, landlords were generally not compensated for the loss of serfs and their labor or remittances. Ibid., pp. 150–51.

5. Ibid., pp. 17, 158–59; and Edward Keenan, "Muscovite Political Folkways," *Russian Review,* vol. 45 (1986), pp. 122–25.

6. Pipes, *Russia under the Old Regime,* p. 141.

7. William Blackwell, "Modernization and Urbanization in Russia: A Comparative View," in Michael F. Hamm, ed., *The City in Russian History* (University of Kentucky Press, 1976), pp. 297–300.

8. Pipes, *Russia under the Old Regime,* p. 200.

9. Marc Raeff, "Imperial Policies of Catherine II," in James Cracraft, ed., *Major Problems in the History of Imperial Russia* (Lexington, Mass.: D.C. Heath, 1994), p. 239.

10. Roger Thiede, "Industry and Urbanization in New Russia from 1860 to 1910," in Hamm, ed., *The City in Russian History,* pp. 125–38, 126.

11. These were Moscow, Kiev, Smolensk, Azov, Kazan', Arkhangel'sk, Ingermanland (St. Petersburg), Siberia, Nizhegorod, and Astrakhan', created between 1707 and 1714. See Lindsey Hughes, *Russia in the Age of Peter the Great* (Yale University Press, 1998), p. 115; and Evgeniy Anisimov, *The Reforms of Peter the Great: Progress through Coercion in Russia,* trans. John T. Alexander (Armonk, N.Y.: M. E. Sharpe, 1993) p. 89.

12. See Paul Dukes, trans. "The institution of the administration of the provinces of the Russian Empire (7 November 1775)," *Russia under Catherine the Great: Select Documents on Government and Society, vol. 1* (Newtonville, Mass.: Oriental Research Partners, 1978), pp. 140–57; and Irina Isakova, *Regionalization of Security in Russia,* Whitehall Paper Series 53 (London: Royal United Services Institute for Defence Studies, 2001), p. 2.

13. Isakova, *Regionalization of Security in Russia,* p. 2.

14. See Nicholas Riazonovsky, *A History of Russia,* 3d ed. (New York: Oxford University Press, 1977), pp. 415–16.

15. On Russia's defense industry cities, see Clifford G. Gaddy, *The Price of the Past: Russia's Struggle with the Legacy of a Militarized Economy* (Brookings, 1996), esp. chaps. 8, 9.

16. The Russian Federation comprises twenty-one republics, one autonomous oblast (the Jewish AO), ten autonomous okrugs, six krays, forty-nine oblasts, and two cities with special status (Moscow and St. Petersburg). For a detailed discussion of the administrative system of the USSR, see D. L. Zlatopol'skiy, *Gosudarstvennoye ustroystvo SSSR* (Moscow: Izd. Yuridicheskoy literatury, 1960).

17. A good discussion of this period and these issues can be found in Daniel Triesman, *After the Deluge: Regional Crises and Political Consolidation in Russia* (University of Michigan Press, 2000).

18. The 1992 federal treaty consisted of three separate documents, signed between the federal government and the republics; between the federal government and the krays, oblasts and cities; and between the federal government and the autonomous okrugs and the Jewish autonomous oblast (Birobidzhan).

19. See James Hughes, "Moscow's Bilateral Treaties Add to Confusion," *Transition* (20 September 1996), pp. 39–43.

20. Jeff Kahn, "The Parade of Sovereignties," *Post-Soviet Affairs,* vol. 16, no. 1 (2000), p. 83. See also Kathryn Stoner-Weiss, "Central Weakness and Provincial Autonomy: Observations on the Devolution Process in Russia," *Post-Soviet Affairs,* vol. 15, no. 1 (1999), pp. 87–106.

21. Author interview with Sergey Kiriyenko, former Russian prime minister and presidential representative for the Volga region, Washington, D.C., 29 January 2002.

22. For more on this story, see Nonna Chernyakova, "Far East Residents Fight for Warmth," *The Moscow Times,* 18 January 2001, p. 1; and Otto Latsis, "Who Defeated Nazdratenko?" *Russia Journal,* 10 February 2001.

23. Grigory Ioffe and others, "Russia's Fragmented Space," in Blair Ruble, Jodi Koehn, and Nancy Popson, eds., *Fragmented Space in the Russian Federation* (Johns Hopkins University Press, 2001), p. 31.

24. Nicholas Lynn and Alexei Novikov, "Refederalizing Russia: Debates on the Idea of Federalism in Russia," *Publius,* vol. 27, no. 2 (Spring 1997), pp.187–203.

25. Isakova, *Regionalization of Security in Russia,* pp. 3, 6.

26. See Putin's references to increasing the polpreds' responsibilities in his April 2002 State of the Nation address to the Russian parliament. English language source: BBC Monitoring Service, 18 April 2002, Johnson's Russia List #6195 at www.cdi.org/russia/johnson/6195.txt. Russian language source at: www.kremlin.ru/appears/2002/04/18.shtml. See also Isakova, *Regionalization of Security in Russia,* p. 13.

27. Matthew Hyde, "Putin's Federal Reforms and Their Implications for Presidential Power in Russia," *Europe Asia Studies,* vol. 53, no. 5 (July 2001), pp. 719–43.

28. The ratio of the largest region (oblasts, krays, and republics) to the smallest is over 400:1 by territory and around 30:1 by population. For the okrugs, the corresponding ratios are approximately 11:1 (territory) and 5:1 (population).

29. "Kremlin Hints at Redrawing City and Village Boundaries," *RFE/RL Newsline—Russia,* vol. 6, no. 129, part 1 (12 July 2002).

30. Isakova, *Regionalization of Security in Russia,* p. 11.

31. Pipes, *Russia under the Old Regime,* pp. 121–22. In 1705 Peter the Great introduced conscription, an institution that persisted through the Soviet period and is still in place today. Whereas military service is currently obligatory for every male, in its original form only one male was drafted from every twenty Russian households. See also Lindsey Hughes, *Russia in the Age of Peter the Great* (Yale University Press, 1998), pp. 114, 120.

32. There are two major exceptions to the overlap between Russia's eight Soviet-era military districts and Putin's new federal districts. The first is that the head-

quarters of the Volga Military District was in Samara (formerly named Kuyby-shev), while the capital of the Volga Federal District is Nizhniy Novgorod. The sec-ond is that the regions that were included in the Transbaykal Military District (headquarters: Chita) and the Far East Military District (headquarters: Khabarovsk) have been merged into the Far Eastern Federal District, with the capital in Khabarovsk.

33. See Hyde, "Putin's Federal Reforms," p. 724. The polpreds with a military and security service background were Viktor Cherkessov of the Northwestern Federal District, a veteran of the Soviet KGB; Konstantin Pulikovskiy of the Far Eastern Fed-eral District, a former military officer; Petr Latyshev of the Ural Federal District, a former colonel-general in the Russian interior ministry (federal police) forces; Georgiy Poltavchenko of the Central Federal District, a former lieutenant-general in the tax police; and Viktor Kazantsev of the Southern Federal District, a former army general.

34. See Darrell Slider, "Russia's Governors and Party Formation," in Archie Brown, ed., *Contemporary Russian Politics* (Oxford University Press, 2001), p. 226; and Steven Solnick, "Gubernatorial Elections in Russia, 1996–1997," *Post-Soviet Affairs,* vol. 14, no. 1 (1998), pp. 49–50.

35. Indeed, in November 2002, the Russian Duma, still dissatisfied with the functioning of the Russian Federation's territorial-administrative structure, held hearings to discuss the possibility of further divisions of the federation, with one proposal put forward by Vladimir Zhirinovskiy (leader of the Liberal Democratic Party of Russia and deputy speaker of the Duma) to divide Russia into fifteen ter-ritories with at least ten million people living in each (to manufacture a more even distribution of population). See Maxim Glikin, "Russia May Be Left with 15 Regions," *Nezavisimaya gazeta,* 15 November 2002, p. 2.

36. This is not to deny the massive presence of unfree labor in and around Moscow in the Soviet period. As Timothy Colton describes in his book on Moscow, there were GULAG camps around Moscow, and GULAG labor was used to build some of Moscow's major structures, including road, water and drainage networks, the Volga-Moscow canal, one of the largest and most imposing housing complexes along the Moscow River (the *Kotel'nicheskaya naberezhnaya* apartment tower), and the Ministry of Foreign Affairs building. German and Japanese prisoners of war were also used to construct the new Moscow State University (MGU) building in the 1940s. For the Volga-Moscow canal, an army of 200,000 GULAG workers was deployed, and the project gave rise to the "*zek*" moniker for prisoners assigned to the canal construction [*zaklyuchennyye kanalstroya*], which was later used for prison camp laborers in general. Russian author Alexander Solzhenitsyn, one of the most famous *zeks,* spent a year after World War II in a small labor camp erected at Moscow's Kaluga Gates (later *Ploschad' Gagarina,* close to the city center) con-structing an apartment block for Interior Ministry (MVD) officers. He described the camp in his writings as "a tiny islet of the savage Archipelago, more closely tied to Noril'sk and the Kolyma [icy MVD colonies in the far north and east] than to

Moscow." Quoted in Timothy Colton, *Moscow: Governing the Socialist Metropolis* (London: The Belknap Press of Harvard University Press, 1995), pp. 258, 335. See also figure 5-1, showing the large GULAG population around Moscow.

37. For a discussion of some of Moscow's advantages over other cities, see Valentina Moiseyenko, Viktor Perevedentsev, and Natal'ya Voronina, *Moskovskiy region: migratsiya i migratsionnaya politika*, Working Paper 3 (Moscow: Carnegie Moscow Center, 1999).

38. The old Soviet national anthem was restored in December 2000, after an interim period of a new, but wordless, "patriotic song'" by nineteenth-century Russian composer Mikhail Glinka. The revived anthem—written during World War II to rally the Red Army against the invading Germans—was given a different text to reflect the demise of the Communist party and Vladimir Lenin as central features in Russian political life. See "Duma Approves Soviet Anthem," *BBC News* Europe, 8 December 2000, http://news.bbc.co.uk/2/hi/europe/1060975.stm. In conjunction with the restoration of the red star, Russian defense minister Sergey Ivanov noted: "The star is a sacred concept. Our grandfathers and fathers fought for this star, and we already have it on our epaulets." See "[Putin] Backs Defense Ministry's Request to Restore the Red Star," *RFE/RL Security and Terrorism Watch*, vol. 3, no. 43 (3 December 2002). See also Nikolay Poroskov, "Vozvrashcheniye krasnoy zvezdy. Vladimir Putin vernul armii 'simvol ottsov i dedov'," *Vremya novostey*, 27 November 2002. The public reception of these efforts was mixed. Some Russian commentators, like military analyst Pavel Felgenhauer, noted, "Returning the star could boost morale. It may look like a trifle, but it gives an important signal to both the top brass and the civilian bureaucracy that the Soviet military machine will remain;" others expressed concern. Russian human rights activist Lyudmila Alexeyeva, head of the Moscow Helsinki Group, observed that "[although] no one is left out: Communists get their anthem, the conservatives have a double-headed eagle and democrats their tricolor flag. . . . It makes one wonder what kind of national ideology such a state has." Both cited in NUPI Center for Russian Studies, "Putin restores red star as the symbol of Russian armed forces," 26 November 2002, www.nupi.no/cgi-win/Russland/krono.exe?5182.

39. Caroline Wyatt, "A tomato too far for Putin," *BBC News*, 6 August 2002, http://news.bbc.co.uk/1/hi/world/europe/2177306.stm; Douglas Birch, "Putin's popularity reaches high note. Pop song celebrates Russian president's sobriety, responsibility; 'I Want Someone Like Putin'," *Baltimore Sun*, 3 September 2002, p. 1A; and Mark Mackinnon, "A 'Personality Cult' Bedevils Wary Putin: Fearing Comparison with Stalin or Lenin, Kremlin Frowns on Wave of Adoring Art," *Globe and Mail*, 27 September 2002, p. A14.

Chapter 7

1. Michael Bradshaw, "The Geographic Factor in Russia's Modernization," presentation at Center for Strategic and International Studies, Washington,

7 November 2002. See also Allen C. Lynch, "Russia's Illiberal Geography," *Europe-Asia Studies,* vol. 54, no. 1 (January 2002).

2. Note that the definition of the North and Far North varies in Russian and other sources, as we discuss in appendix C.

3. "Exodus Continues from Russian Far North," *ITAR-TASS Weekly News,* 20 November 2001. The ministry noted that the largest exodus—almost 250,000 people—from the North occurred immediately after the dissolution of the Soviet Union in 1992, with the bulk of these migrants leaving Chukotka, Kamchatka, Magadan, Murmansk, and the island of Sakhalin. Since then, the level of migration has tapered off—although population numbers have continued to fall as a result of the fact that most migrants tended to be young people and those with families.

4. Robert Kaiser, "Siberian Diary: Carrying Chevys to Krasnoyarsk," *Washington Post,* 3 September 2001, p. C1.

5. Goskomstat, the Russian state statistics agency, listed Moscow's resident population as of January 1, 2002, as 8,539,200. *Chislennost' naseleniya Rossiyskoy Federatsii po gorodam, poselkam gorodskogo tipa i rayonam na 1 yanvarya 2002 g.* (Moscow: Goskomstat, 2002), p. 14.

6. "Census Turns Up 2 Million More Russians Than Expected," *RFE/RL Newsline—Russia,* vol. 6, no. 216 (18 November 2002).

7. "Russian Population Becoming Increasingly Mobile," *RFE/RL Newsline—Russia,* vol. 6, no. 230 (10 December 2002).

8. Note, for instance, that 43.4 million Americans moved in the period March 1998–March 1999. That is, relative to the total population, more Americans moved in a single year than did Russians in over a decade. www.census.gov/prod/2001pubs/p23-205.pdf.

9. Timothy Heleniak, "Migration Dilemmas Haunt Post-Soviet Russia," *Migration Information Source,* October 2002, www.migrationinformation.org/feature/display.cfm?ID=62 (11 April 2003).

10. For information on the North Caucasus, see Fiona Hill, *Russia's Tinderbox: Conflict in the North Caucasus and Its Implications for the Future of the Russian Federation* (Cambridge, Mass.: Strengthening Democratic Institutions Project, September 1995).

11. In 1989, 43 percent of the North Caucasus population lived in rural areas, in contrast with 23 percent for the population of the Russian Federation as a whole. Ibid., p. 2.

12. See Leslie Dienes, "Reflections on a Geographical Dichotomy: Archipelago Russia," *Eurasian Geography and Economics,* vol. 43, no. 6 (2002), p. 449.

13. Before 1991, 50–70 percent of the budget revenues of the autonomous republics of the North Caucasus came directly from federal government subsidies, with Chechnya, Ingushetiya, and Dagestan the most heavily subsidized. Hill, *Russia's Tinderbox,* p. 3.

14. Timothy Heleniak, personal communication.

15. Figures from Goskomstat RF 1998, cited in I. G. Kosikov and L. S. Kosikova, *Severnyy Kavkaz: sotsial'no-ekonomicheskiy spravochnik* (Moscow, 1999), p. 9.

16. Ibid., p. 13. Dagestan and Ingushetiya both had a rate of 12 births per 1,000 people in this period. In 1998 Krasnodar kray received the largest number of migrants in the North Caucasus (20 for every 1,000 people), followed by Stavropol kray (14.5 for every 1,000), and then Rostov oblast (7.4 per 1,000).

17. Ibid., p. 12.

18. Ibid., pp. 23–41.

19. See appendix C for the World Bank's definition of the Russian North. 1989 population data from *Naseleniye Rossii za 100 let (1897–1997)* (Moscow: Goskomstat Rossii, 1998).

20. The North today is variously described as holding half of the world's palladium, significant deposits of platinum, and the bulk of Russia's oil, gas, gold, diamonds, and timber—all estimated at as much as $27 trillion by the European Bank for Reconstruction and Development (EBRD). As a result of its mineral wealth, in the 1990s, the North was reported to provide Russia with 20 percent of national income, 25 percent of tax revenues, and 35 percent of GDP. Figures cited in Alla Startseva, "Pulling Far North out of the Cold," *The Moscow Times,* 10 July 2001, p. 1 Also cited in Vladimir Kitov," EBRD Sets Sights on Russia's Northern Expanses," *Russia Journal,* vol. 4, no. 25 (29 June–5 July 2001), p. 118.

21. Figures cited in Startseva, "Pulling Far North out of the Cold."

22. Sarah Karush, "Harnessing the North," *The Moscow Times,* 28 November 2000, p. 1.

23. Ibid.

24. Ibid.

25. Leonid Vinogradov, "Houses Encapsulated in Ice in Magadan," *ITAR-TASS Weekly News,* 29 March 2001.

26. Alek Akhundov and Grigoriy Punanov, "Obratnyy bilet: Severyan gotovyat k pereseleniyu," *Izvestiya,* 9 June 2001, p. 2.

27. "Duma Deputy Says Northern Delivery Severely Underfunded," *RFE/RL Newsline—Russia* (10 July 2001). Russian analyst Mikhail Delyagin, director of the Institute for the Problems of Globalization, has suggested that the actual cost of fuel and food deliveries to the North is always at least three times larger than the amount allotted in the federal budget. Cited in Karush, "Harnessing the North."

28. Karush, "Harnessing the North."

29. "Siberian City to Swap Shares for Fuel," *RFE/RL Russian Political Weekly,* vol. 2, no. 30 (19 September 2002).

30. "Economic and Social Issues of Migration from Russian North," World Bank staff memorandum, November 1998.

31. "Statistics Committee Gives Details of Food Costs across Russia," *ITAR-TASS Weekly News,* 4 September 2002.

32. A basket of four food items (ground beef, potatoes, lettuce, bread) in Anchorage, for example, cost $8.82 in 2001, while in New York the same basket cost $12.27. It cost, in comparison, $6.83 in Los Angeles. Four Alaskan cities made the rankings in the American Chamber of Commerce Researchers Association's 20

highest cost urban areas in the United States in 2001: Juneau (ninth), Kodiak (thirteenth), Anchorage (fourteenth), and Fairbanks (twentieth). Data as of December 2001. Source: "Average Price for Select Goods and Services in Select U.S. Cities," American Chamber of Commerce Researchers Association (ACCRA) *Urban Area Index Data* (fourth quarter 2001) as cited in *Alaska Economic Trends* (June 2002), pp. 14–15.

33. Startseva, "Pulling Far North out of the Cold."

34. Figures cited in ibid.

35. Nicholas George, "Westernising the Far North: Low Costs May Not Be Enough to Keep the Barents Region Alive," *Financial Times*, 22 July 2002, p. 10. Murmansk and the surrounding region have been included in the Barents Euro-Arctic Council (BEAC) created by the Nordic countries and the European Commission to promote economic development and stimulate trade and investment in the northernmost regions of Finland, Norway, Sweden, and Russia. In the 1990s, Swedish entrepreneurs, themselves used to conducting business in cold climates, moved into the Murmansk region to take advantage of its large labor pool, the comparatively low production and assembly costs, and its relatively developed transportation networks. Most of these investments and new businesses have yet to show significant results. See also Startseva, "Pulling Far North out of the Cold"; and Kitov, "EBRD Sets Sights on Russia's Northern Expanses."

36. See chapter 10, note 6, for later developments regarding this program.

37. All information on the project is from "Russian Federation: World Bank Supports Restructuring of Country's Northern Economy," *World Bank Group Press Release*, Press Release No. 2001/369/ECA, Washington, 7 June 2001, www.worldbank.org.ru/eng/projects/portfolio/north_rest_01.htm. For press coverage of the program and the regions it encompasses see, for example, Giles Whittell, "Hope for the Abandoned: The World Bank Is to Spend Millions of Dollars Resettling the Victims of Stalin's Labor Camps. But Many Former Detainees Have Not Seen the Outside World for Decades," *The Times*, 1 June 2001.

38. Andrew Jack, "Pioneering Migration Scheme Offers Hope to Inheritors of Stalin's Arctic Penal Colonies," *Financial Times*, 17 July 2002, p. 20.

39. "Unemployment Soars in Pockets of Siberia and Far East," *RFE/RL Newsline—Russia*, vol. 6, no. 143 (1 August 2002). Unemployment rates in 2002 rose by almost 50 percent for Chita and 73 percent for Tuva compared with 2001. Unemployment figures in Russia are also traditionally underreported by the government.

40. "Children Born in 1991–2000 to Live No More than 70 Years," *Interfax*, 31 July 2002.

41. Siberia Airlines website: http://english.s7.ru/company/10.shtml.

42. "Trans-Siberian Railroad Now Electrified," Associated Press, 25 December 2002. Plans are also being made to connect the Trans-Siberian to a railroad running through North and South Korea and adding connections to China, Japan, Iran, and other countries. The Trans-Siberian still has great potential as a shipping route.

From 1998 to 2001, the number of shipping containers transported along the line trebled from 15,000 to 45,000, and yet the current volume is less than one-third of the railroad's full capacity. See Sergei Ivanov, "Business, Transport and Logistics: Bridging the Gap between Europe and Asia," *Russia Journal,* 22 March 2002.

43. "Feel Like Going for a Drive?" *RFE/RL Newsline—Russia,* vol. 6, no. 177 (19 September 2002).

44. "Russia-Housing-Results," *ITAR-TASS Weekly News,* 27 January 1999.

45. Alla Startseva, "Audit Chamber Takes Over 3rd Ring Road," *The Moscow Times,* 5 September 2001, p. 5.

46. "EBRD Allots USD 100 Million for St. Petersburg Ring Road Construction," www.rosbalt.ru, 22 May 2003.

47. Akhtyam Akhtyrov, "Underground metro is experiencing a decline: Moscow will soon have the new surface metro," *Pravda.ru,* 28 September 2002, http://english.pravda.ru/society/2002/09/28/37431.html.

48. Y. E. Krouk, "Metro Development in Russia," *Tribune (Newsletter of the International Tunneling Association),* vol. 7 (July 1998), www.ita-aites.org/tribune7/FOR4.html.

49. Grigory Ioffe and others, "Russia's Fragmented Space," in Blair Ruble, Jodi Koehn, and Nancy Popson, eds., *Fragmented Space in the Russian Federation* (Johns Hopkins University Press, 2001), p. 32.

50. Ibid., p. 31.

51. Ibid., p. 34.

52. Ibid., p. 34.

53. Ibid., p. 77.

54. According to international telecommunications survey data for the year 2000, Russia had only twenty-two telephone lines per one hundred inhabitants in comparison with sixty-one in Germany and seventy in the United States—although this was more than the eleven lines in China and twelve in Mexico, and also slightly ahead of the eighteen lines per one hundred inhabitants in Brazil. All figures from International Telecommunication Union, January 2002, www.itu.int/ITU-D/ict/statistics/, as cited in Jeremy Azrael and D. J. Peterson, *Russia and the Information Revolution,* RAND Issue Paper (IP-229-CRE), 2002.

55. See Azrael and Peterson, *Russia and the Information Revolution.* The figure of 25 percent computer use comes from a Russian survey conducted by the ROMIR independent research center in January 2001, cited in "Most Russians Do Not Use Computers—Poll," *ITAR-TASS Weekly News,* 28 January 2001. According to the ROMIR poll, almost 75 percent of Russians in January 2001 had never used a computer at all. This figure put Russia slightly behind both Mexico and Brazil in this indicator, but still ahead of China. Of the 25 percent of Russians in the January 2001 ROMIR poll who stated that they were regular computer users, fewer than 16 percent actually had their own computer at home. Most (34 percent) used a computer at work, 27 percent at school or university; 14 percent used a relative or friend's computer; and around 5 percent used public libraries and Internet or cyber cafes.

56. "Number of Internet Users Grows by 40 Percent," *Moscow Tribune*, 5 February 2002. The Russian Communications and Information Technology Ministry projected an increase to around eight million regular users by the end of 2002.

57. Azrael and Peterson, *Russia and the Information Revolution*, p. 2. Not every Russian with access to a computer actually has access to the Internet. In a survey conducted in the summer of 2001 by the European research agencies MASMI Research and Pro Active International, only 2.3 percent of Russians were reported to have Internet access at home, and only 6.3 percent had access at work. Cited in Brian Arengi, "Study Reveals RuNet Demographics," *The Moscow Times*, 31 July 2001, p. 8. In January 2002, as part of an effort to address this deficiency, the Russian government officially launched the "E-Russia" program to promote efforts to upgrade Russia's telecommunications infrastructure, increase the use of information technology in government and business, and expand public Internet access.

58. "Russian Ministry Promises Better Public Access to Internet by Year End," *Prime-TASS*, 23 October 2002. Regular users of the Internet in Russian surveys were defined in Russian sources as those who were online for more than an hour a week. In this regard, in August 2000, a Russian Internet survey firm, Monitoring.ru, reported that while some 9.2 million Russians were accessing the Internet, only about 20 percent of those were regular users. See Sam Gerrans, "Slowly, Shakily, Democratic Russia Goes Online," *TechWeb News*, 27 November 2000, www.techweb.com/wire/story/TWB20001127S0017. The ROMIR January 2001 poll, cited earlier, also indicated that only 7.7 percent of Internet users in Russia actually used the network every day.

59. All these facilities, however, provided limited access to the Internet. For example, only one out of fifty Russian schools offered Internet access to its pupils in 2001. Azrael and Peterson, *Russia and the Information Revolution*, p. 3.

60. See, for example, some of the strategies outlined under the U.S. government–sponsored "Nuclear Cities Initiative," www.nn.doe.gov/nci/about_strategy.shtml; and the creation in 2000–01 of the Siberian Information Technology Center in Akademgorodok, Novosibirsk's so-called city of science. The Technology Center and the city have an impressive website at www.sibitc.com/news/index.html with full information about the initiative.

61. Timothy Egan, "Bill Gates Views What He's Sown in Libraries," *New York Times*, 6 November 2002, p. 18A. Consultants advising the Bill Gates project also noted that 22 percent of new computer users in libraries used them to find new jobs, with some indication that the new jobs were often in other regions.

62. Increased access to the Internet is also likely to act as a spur to more out-migration in remote areas of Russia by facilitating information about potential destinations. Lack of information is one of the greatest barriers to migration in most countries, not just in Russia.

63. Kaiser, "Siberian Diary: Carrying Chevys to Krasnoyarsk."

64. Edward L. Glaeser, "Demand for Density? The Functions of the City in the 21st Century," *Brookings Review*, vol. 18, no. 3 (Summer 2000), pp. 10–13. Glaeser's

findings are presented in greater detail in Edward L. Glaeser, Jed Kolko, and Albert Saiz, "Consumer City," Working Paper 7790 (Cambridge, Mass.: National Bureau of Economic Research, July 2000).

65. Vladimir Kaganskiy, *Kul'turnyy landshaft i sovetskoye obitayemoye pros-transtvo* (Moscow: Novoye literaturnoye obozreniye, 2001), pp. 388–89.

66. Ibid., p. 393.

67. Ivan Ivanov, "Situation Controlled Despite Severe Frosts—Kasianov," *ITAR-TASS Weekly News*, 9 January 2001; Robert Serebrennikov, "Duma Invites Premier to Attend Session on Energy Issue," *ITAR-TASS Weekly News*, 17 January 2001; Ian Traynor, "For Siberia, a Return to Wasteland: Population Drains Away as Brutal Project to Colonize Frozen Wilderness Is Reversed," *Guardian*, 12 June 2002, p. 3.

68. Leonid Drachevskiy, polpred of the Siberian federal district, cited in Traynor, "For Siberia, a Return to Wasteland."

69. Applebaum, "The Great Error," *Spectator*, 28 July 2001.

Chapter 8

1. Runaway serfs and Cossacks were the most frequent groups to head for the Russian expanses and avoid the reach of the state. But those whom the state sought to exile could also effectively disappear for good to their own advantage. For example, in the tsarist era, after church reforms in the mid-seventeenth century, those who clung to the old practices and liturgy—the Old Believers, or *starovery*—were expelled from European Russia and forced to move to Siberia. Thanks to the region's vastness and their own consequent remoteness from the center of power, various Old Believer sects and groups flourished even in the Soviet era, maintaining their customs and communities and defying predictions of their demise after the collapse of the USSR. See Steve Nettleton, "Old Believers End Isolation in Siberian Border-lands," *CNN.com*, March 2000, www.cnn.com/SPECIALS/2000/russia/story/train/old.believers; and "Census Takers Discover Remaining Members of Low-Profile Religious Sect," *RFE/RL Russian Political Weekly*, vol. 2, no. 32 (2 October 2002). Likewise, Russian census takers in 2002 turned up quite a few other surprises, including a previously unknown ethnic group—the Chalymtsy—about 130 strong and living out in the most inaccessible reaches of the Taymyr autonomous okrug (home of Noril'sk Nickel). See "New Ethnic Group Discovered," *RFE/RL Newsline—Russia*, 2 October 2002.

2. Susan Brazier, "Propiska," www.nelegal.net/articles/propiska.htm. The Nelegal.net website is managed by Russian residents who lack *propiski* and others concerned about the *propiska* regime.

3. Cynthia Buckley, "The Myth of Managed Migration: Migration Control and Market in the Soviet Period," *Slavic Review*, vol. 54, no. 4 (Winter 1995), p. 906.

4. Ira Gang and Robert Stuart, "Mobility Where Mobility Is Illegal: Internal Migration and City Growth in the Soviet Union," *Journal of Population Economics*, vol. 12 (1999), p. 118.

5. *Raionnaya planirovka economicheskikh, administrativnykh rayonov, promysh-lennykh rayonov i uzlov* (Moscow, 1962), p. 62. Cited in Valentina Moiseyenko, Vik-tor Perevedentsev, and Natal'ya Voronina, "Moscow Region: Migration and Migration Politics," Working Paper 3 (Moscow: Carnegie Moscow Center, 1999), pp. 32–33. Part of this decision was actually attributed to cost. Soviet planners estimated that government expenditures were 9 percent higher per resident in a city with a population of 800,000 than per resident in a city of 50,000. At the same time, how-ever, labor productivity in the industries of cities with a population of over one mil-lion was also seen (in 1961) as 38 percent higher than in cities of 100,000–250,000 residents. See V. G. Davidovich, "O razvitii seti gorodov za 40 let," *Voprosy geografii,* vol. 45 (1959), p. 67; and V. G. Davidovich, *Planirovka gorodov i rayonov* (Moscow) 1964, p. 30, cited in Moiseyenko, Perevedentsev, and Voronina, "Moscow Region," p. 33.

6. Gang and Stuart, "Mobility Where Mobility Is Illegal," p. 119.

7. Ibid., pp. 131–32.

8. Including Resolution No. 713 of the Administration of the Russian Federa-tion of July 17, 1995, which was deemed unconstitutional by the Constitutional Court of the Russian Federation on 2 February 1998 (Moiseyenko, Perevedentsev, and Voronina, "Moscow Region," p. 47). See also Brazier, "Propiska"; and "Justice Ministry Might File Suit to Block 'Propiska' System [in Moscow]," www.nelegal.net/articles.htm.

9. Cited in Andrew Jack, "Pioneering Migration Scheme Offers Hope to Inher-itors of Stalin's Arctic Penal Colonies," *Financial Times,* 17 July 2002, p. 20.

10. Nancy Ries, "Food and Hunger: The Living Memory of War in Russia," paper presented at War and Memory Workshop, History Department, Pennsylvania State University, 16 March 2002, p. 1.

11. Ibid., p. 5.

12. Ibid., p. 8.

13. In their discussions of Russia's "virtual economy," Clifford G. Gaddy and Barry W. Ickes describe this phenomenon as "householdization" or "personaliza-tion" of social safety nets. They argue that it is a major cause of a general status quo bias in today's Russia that militates against all forms of radical economic reform (including migration). See Gaddy and Ickes, *Russia's Virtual Economy* (Brookings, 2002), pp. 169–70, 210–12.

14. Ries, "Food and Hunger," p. 9.

15. Anton Ushkov, "Russia to Draft Children of the North Special Program," *ITAR-TASS Weekly News,* 26 November 2002.

16. Andrew Jack, "Pioneering Migration Scheme Offers Hope."

17. The official statistics on enterprise profitability leave much to be desired, but the picture they give of regional differences, especially the difference between Moscow and St. Petersburg, on the one hand, and the rest of the country on the other, seems to accord with much anecdotal evidence. Officially, in 2002, no fewer than 46.7 percent of all enterprises in Russia were loss-making. Only the cities of

Moscow (27 percent) and St. Petersburg (28 percent) had fewer than 30 percent loss-makers. In thirty-nine of Russia's eighty-nine regions, more than half of the enterprises were loss-makers. Authors' calculations from *Interfax Weekly Reports*.

18. The relatively high rates of foreign direct investment (FDI) in Sakhalin, Krasnodar, and Tyumen' (ranks 2, 3, and 5 in table 8-1) deserve comment. They can all be explained by their importance to Russia's energy industry and related trade. Sakhalin is one of Russia's new target areas for energy development for Northeast Asian markets (see chapter 10). Krasnodar is dominated by the Russian port and oil terminal of Novorossiysk, which is being heavily developed to support the transit of Caspian energy resources as well as the bulk of Russian Black Sea freight. Tyumen' is the center of Russia's Siberian oil industry.

19. Moiseyenko, Perevedentsev, and Voronina, "Moscow Region," p. 43.

20. Timothy Colton, *Moscow: Governing the Socialist Metropolis* (London: The Belknap Press of Harvard University Press, 1995), p. 462.

21. Ibid., pp. 463–65.

22. Ibid., pp. 456–65.

23. For example, Colton states that "although manufacturing employment grew by only 2,000 during [the 1970s], 250,000 *limitchiki* entered Moscow through the industrial revolving door." Ibid., p. 467.

24. Ibid., p. 577.

25. Ibid., p. 720.

26. Ibid., p. 723.

27. *Demograficheskiy yezhegodnik Rossii 2000* (Moscow: Goskomstat, 2000), p. 366.

28. "Census Turns Up 2 Million More Russians than Expected," *RFE/RL Newsline—Russia*, vol. 6, no. 216 (18 November 2002).

29. For a general overview of recent court challenges, see Public Interest Law Initiative, "Russian NGOs challenge national propiska system in district courts," *Pursuing the Public Interest: A Handbook for Legal Professionals and Activists* (New York, 2001), pp. 90–91, www.pili.org/library/discrimination/propiska.htm.

30. Michael Gordon, "Moscow Blast 3rd in 2 Weeks, Kills at Least 95," *New York Times*, 14 September 1999, p. 1A.

31. Maria Arzumanova, "Cleansing Moscow," *Moscow News*, 29 September 1999.

32. Anna Nochuikina, "Unbidden Guests," *Moscow News*, 23 February 2000.

33. Rusudan Nikuradze, "Moscow Gets Tough on Caucasian Migrants," *IWPR Caucasus Reporting Service*, No. 155, 14 November 2002, www.iwpr.net/index.pl/archive/cau/cau_200211_155_1_eng.txt.

34. Ibid.

35. "Moscow Mayor Again Calls for 'Propiska' System," *RFE/RL Newsline—Russia*, vol. 6, no. 223 (27 November 2002).

36. See, for example, Witold Rybczynski, "Downsizing Cities: To Make Cities Work Better, Make Them Smaller," *Atlantic Monthly*, vol. 276, no. 4 (October 1995), pp. 36–47. Also, Robert Putnam, "Mobility and Sprawl," in *Bowling Alone* (Simon & Schuster, 2000).

37. Deidre A. Gaquin and Katherine A. DeBrandt, *County and City Extra: Special Decennial Edition* (Lanham, Md.: Bernan, 2002).

38. This policy was terminated, however, in the late 1970s, after people either failed to find new jobs in new locations or refused to move out of their homes because of local and family ties. It was replaced by regional and local government policies to promote community development and regeneration.

39. Paul Zielbauer, "As Eastern Germany Rusts, Young Workers Leave," *New York Times*, 25 December 2002, p. A3.

40. ABC News Transcripts, "In Search of America: 1-Room Schools," *ABC World News Tonight with Peter Jennings*, 13 November 2002 (06:30 PM ET), based on U.S. census data, accessed on Lexis-Nexis.

41. Richard Rowland, "Russia's Disappearing Towns: New Evidence of Urban Decline, 1979–1994," *Post-Soviet Geography and Economics*, vol. 37, no. 2 (February 1996), pp. 63–87. The towns that "vanished" were usually very small settlements that, after shedding population, were often reclassified as "villages."

42. Ibid., pp. 84–85.

43. Donald R. Davis and David E. Weinstein. "Bones, Bombs and Break Points: The Geography of Economic Activity," Working Paper 8517 (Cambridge, Mass.: National Bureau of Economic Research, October 2001), p. 5.

44. Rowland, "Russia's Disappearing Towns," p. 76. From 1989 to 1994, Magadan's population dropped from 151,700 to 135,200. The populations of both Moscow and St. Petersburg also contracted initially in the late 1980s and early 1990s before bouncing back again through in-migration.

45. Many power plants in Russia were combined heat and power plants, although the bulk of municipal heat (75 percent) was produced by more inefficient heat-only boilers, also operated by the power generators. See International Energy Agency, "District Heating," in *Energy Policies in the Russian Federation* (Moscow: IEA, September 1995), pp. 249–56.

46. Personal communication from Boris Brevnov, former head of Unified Energy Systems (Russia's power utility monopoly), 14 June 2001. Power plants in Russia are notoriously inefficient, most still operating on 1950s–1960s standards (from the time period they were built). Nothing can be out-sourced, and all maintenance is performed by on-site teams.

47. Ibid.

48. Oleg Nekhayev, "Sealed-Off Cities. Unlike the U.S., Russia Has Not Opened Its 'Nuclear Cities' after the End of the Cold War. In the Meantime, the Cities Are Dying, Since the State's Support Does Not Let Them Develop," *Rossiyskaya gazeta*, 20 July 2002, p. 1.

49. Housing utilities (for water, electricity, heating, maintenance, sewage, and so on) are variously estimated by the Russian government and the World Bank to account for between 30 and 40 percent of municipal budgets and sometimes in excess, with a total annual expenditure of $4.1 billion. Of that amount, 102.5 million is accounted for by discounts on household bills. See Valeria Korchagina, "Putin Orders $20 Billion Housing Reform," *The Moscow Times*, 30 May 2001, p. 1.

50. Carolyn Gochenour, *District Energy Trends, Issues, and Opportunities: The Role of the World Bank*, World Bank Technical Paper no. 493 (March 2001), p. 15.

51. International Energy Agency, *Energy Policies in the Russian Federation.* Russian Duma members have also estimated that large Russian cities lose up to 50 percent of their heat before it reaches its destinations thanks to antiquated and poorly maintained public utilities and infrastructure; see ". . . As Leading Communist Criticizes Housing Reforms," *RFE/RL Newsline—Russia*, vol. 6, no. 237 (19 December 2002).

52. See the Moscow Center for Energy Efficiency's website at www.cenef.ru/about/cenef.htm. The World Bank has several projects since the mid-1990s to renovate Russia's direct heating system: The "Russian Energy Efficiency Project" (1996), "Russia Enterprise Housing Divestiture Project" (1996), "Russia Severstal Heat and Power Project" (1998), and the "Russia Municipal Heating Project" (2001), which is designed to help alleviate the financial burden associated with the supply of district heating on municipal governments (www.worldbank.org). Information on the Institute for Urban Economics programs is available at www.urbaneconomics.ru.

53. The goal of housing utility reform is to raise housing and utility costs to a level sufficient to cover all expenses and to subsidize utilities for those with the lowest incomes. See Otto Latsis, "Special Report: Uneasy Balance for a Rickety Economy. With Little Chance of Further Growth, Hope Lies in Market Reform. But a Key Question Remains: How Will Reform Be Carried Out," *Russia Journal*, 11–17 May 2001. By 2010 the Russian government hopes that Russian households will cover 90 percent of their utility and other communal services costs; see "Coming Soon: Shock Therapy, Part II?" *Jamestown Monitor*, vol. 7, no. 121 (25 June 2001).

54. Fred Weir, "Capitalism Hits Home in Russia: Next Month the Kremlin Unveils a Plan to Wean the Country away from Housing and Other Subsidies," *Christian Science Monitor*, 20 June 2001, p. 6.

55. Nick Paton Walsh, "Power—But Not to the People: Russians Pray That Their Neighbors Pay Their Electricity Bills: Thanks to Soviet Wiring, if One Gets Cut, They All Get Cut. And Privatization Threatens to Make Things Even Worse," *Statesman* (UK), 15 July 2002, p. 24.

56. International Energy Agency, *Energy Policies in the Russian Federation*, p. 254.

57. Boris Rumer, *Investment and Reindustrialization in the Soviet Economy* (Boulder, Colo.: Westview Press, 1984), pp. 118–19, 132.

58. Robin Munro, "10,000 Canadian Homes Set to Invade Russia," *The Moscow Times*, 6 November 2001, p. 9.

59. Anatoliy Chubays, translated from full version of presentation available in "Stenogramma soveshchaniya po problemam sotsial'no-ekonomicheskogo razvitiya Dal'nevostochnogo federal'nogo okruga" [Vladivostok], 23 August 2002, www.president.kremlin.ru/text/appears/2002/08/18503.shtml.

60. Alla Startseva, "A Blackout Looms in Kamchatka," *The Moscow Times*, 11 July 2002, p. 5.

61. Gas-fired power stations are confined mostly to European Russia. The breakdown of the power generation system in European Russia is about 70 percent gas, 15 percent nuclear power, 10 percent hydroelectric power (mostly in the Volga region), with fuel oil accounting for the rest. In contrast, in Siberia, 40–50 percent of power is generated by coal-fired thermal plants, with the rest accounted for by hydroelectric power. Siberian power plants, however, can rely on hydroelectric power only in the spring and summer. In winter, with the rivers frozen, they are heavily dependent on coal. The coal-fired power plants in the Russian Far East (which account for 55 percent of power generation there, with fuel oil covering the remainder) are the largest in the Russian Federation, designed to serve extremely large areas. They are dependent on heavily subsidized coal supplies and are not self-sustainable (self-financing) given the relatively small size of the population and low profitability of the industrial base in the region. (Authors' interview with Boris Brevnov, 14 June 2001.) For more information on Russian power generation, see the UES website at www.rao-ees.ru/ru.

62. Arthur Andersen Consulting, *Russian Electricity Reform*, Report, April 2001, p. 5.

63. Boris Brevnov with Cameron Half, *From Monopoly to Market Maker? Reforming Russia's Power Sector* (Cambridge, Mass.: Strengthening Democratic Institutions Project, April 2000), p. 17.

64. Brevnov, personal communication.

Chapter 9

1. "Eurasianism" was first espoused as a theory positing Russia's distinctive fusion of European (Slavic) and Asian (Turkic) elements in the 1920s and 1930s by a group of Russian émigré writers, including religious philosopher Ivan Ilyin (1866–1949) and linguist Nikolay Trubetskoy (1890–1938). It was later elaborated by historian Lev Gumilev (1912–93), son of the celebrated Russian poets Nikolay Gumilev and Anna Akhmatova. Eurasianism was seen as an ideological alternative to communism and a basis for the reorganization of a restored Russian Empire in the same geographic space it had occupied before the Revolution. As a philosophy, it bridged the gap between an exclusive ethnic-Russian concept of Russia and the reality of the state's multiethnicity. It allowed a Slavic, Orthodox Russia to coexist with an embrace of the non-Russian Asian peoples of the steppe and restored the idea of a multiethnic, multiracial, multinational, and multireligious "*Rossiya*" (Russia in a neutral rather than ethnic Russian, *russkaya*, form). For a detailed discussion of the history of Eurasianism, see Rafael Khakimov, ed., *Panorama-Forum: Yevraziystvo: za i protiv* (Kazan'), vol. 8, no. 1 (1997). In 1995 Russian scholar Aleksandr Panarin revived the basic ideas of Eurasianism from the geopolitical perspective in a series of articles and books—arguing that Russia could only find its true political identity and destiny in the geographic and historic space stretching between "Western Europe and the Pacific" and between "the Arctic Ocean and the

Great Steppe." See, for example, Aleksandr Panarin, *Rossiya v tsivilizatsionnom protsesse: mezdhu atlantizmom i yevraziystvom* (Moskva: RAN, 1995).

2. See the group's website, www.arctogaia.com, which also refers to Russia as "Arctogaia" or the land/goddess of the North, making a play on the Arctic and "Gaia," the Greek goddess of the Earth or "Mother Earth."

3. Aleksandr Dugin, *Osnovy geopolitiki: geopoliticheskoye budushcheye Rossii* (Moscow: Arktogeia-Tsentr, 2000). "Eurasianism" presents itself as a "lowest common denominator" for Russia, a movement that seeks to include ethnic Russians as well as the many religious and ethnic minorities with whom Russians have cohabited for centuries in the Volga region, the Urals, and across Siberia; see Dmitriy Chernov, "Vremya politiki. 'Evraziya' prevyshe vsego," *Vremya MN*, 25 April 2001, p. 3. See also Igor' Mal'tsev, "Obshchestvo. Evraziya über alles," *Kommersant-Daily*, 20 April 2001, p. 9; "Program of the Socio-Political Movement EURASIA," http://arctogaia.com/public/eng/Program.htm; and "Eurasia above All: Manifest of the Eurasist Movement," http://arctogaia.com/public/eng/Manifesto.htm.

4. Oleg Rashidov, "Partstroitel'stvo," *Komsomol'skaya pravda*, 24 April 2001, p. 6; and Aleksandr Maksimov and Orkhan Karabaagi, "Oni v svoikh koridorakh. Yevraziytsev prizvali na gosudarevu sluzhbu," *Obshchaya gazeta*, 31 May 2001, p. 7.

5. For a detailed discussion of the political influence of the Eurasianists at the end of the 1990s, see Charles Clover, "Dreams of the Eurasian Heartland: The Reemergence of Geopolitics," *Foreign Affairs*, vol. 78, no. 2 (March/April 1999), pp. 9–13. Putin referred to Russia as a "Euro-Asiatic country" at an Asia Pacific Economic Cooperation (APEC) meeting in November 2000; the reference was seen in the Russian press as an explicit nod to the Eurasianists. See Dmitriy Radyshevskiy, "Politika. Soblazn yevraziystva," *Moskovskye novosti*, 8 May 2001, p. 14.

6. Sergei Golubchikov, "Great Spaces a Burden? A Vast Territory—Is It a Blessing or a Curse? We Have Yet to Learn to Benefit from It even though Northern Riches Have Been Faithfully Supplementing the State Treasury," *Moscow News*, 23 October 2002, Home section.

7. James Billington, "Okay, They've Met. Now Let's Get Engaged," *Washington Post*, 17 June 2001, p. B2.

8. Richard Solomon and Masataka Kosaka, eds., *The Soviet Far East Build-Up: Nuclear Dilemmas and Asian Security* (Dover, Mass.: Auburn House Publishers, 1986); and Harold Gelman, "The Soviet Far East Military Build-Up and Soviet Risk-Taking against China," RAND, doc. no. R-2943AF, 1982. Soviet military strategy was also directed toward the containment of Japan and toward U.S. Pacific bases during the cold war, which led to the heavy military build-up of the Kamchatka Peninsula and the region around the Sea of Okhotsk, including Sakhalin Island and the Kuriles. Discussion with Mark Kramer, director of Harvard University's Cold War Project, 7 September 2001.

9. Gilbert Rozman, "A New Sino-Russian-America Triangle?" *Orbis*, vol. 44, no. 4 (Fall 2000), pp. 541–56; Tim Whewell, "Russians Fear Takeover by Chinese in East," *Independent on Sunday* (UK), 10 December 2000, p. 26; "Moscow Urged Not

to Cut Troops in Far East," *RFE/RL Security Watch*, vol. 2, no. 4 (29 January 2001); Alexander Lukin, "Russia and China," presentation at the Brookings Institution, 17 April 2001; "A Chinatown the Size of Siberia," *Obshchaya gazeta*, 5 July 2001; Oleg Zhunusov, "Konstantin Pulikovskiy, polpred prezidenta: Na Dal'nem Vostoke sushchestvuyu vse ugrozy," *Izvestiya*, 23 July 2001, www.izvestia.ru/politic/article21470; Andrei Piontkowski, "You Can't Beat the Chinese: In Ten Years Russia Could Lose Its Far East Possessions," *Nezavisimaya gazeta*, 14 August 2001; Vladimir Meshcheryakov, "Russia's Cross: Russia Is Dying as a Great Power—and Its People Are Dying Too," *Tribuna*, 15 August 2001; Andrei Vaganov, "Russians Are Asians: By 2010 Chinese Will Become the Second Largest Ethnic Group in Russia," *Nezavisimaya gazeta*, 6 August 2002.

10. See, for example, Vitaliy Denisov, "Solntse vskhodit za Uralom," *Krasnaya zvezda*, 5 July 2002, p. 2. In a rebuttal to an article critical about Siberia that had appeared in *Literaturnaya gazeta* in April 2001, two distinguished Russian geographers went so far as to produce a series of World Bank statistics suggesting that if the wealth of nations were calculated according to the value of the country's natural resources rather than human production, then Russia would be the richest country in the world: "It turns out that the USA, the most developed country in the world, has [natural resources valued at] about $400,000 per person, while Canada, which is significantly less developed [sic] but which possesses vast natural resources, has a much higher figure, over $700,000 per capita. We estimate that for Russia the figure would be $1 [million]–1.2 million per person. Consequently, we are three times richer than Americans." Vladimir Kotlyakov and Grigoriy Agranat, "Otvet rebrom. Shiroka strana moya! I mnogo!" *Literaturnaya gazeta*, 5 September 2001, p. 11. The original article to which they were replying was Aleksey Tsvetkov, "Kto, chto, pochemu? Shiroka? Strana moya? Mnogo l' v ney?" *Literaturnaya gazeta*, 18 April 2001, p. 8.

11. "Prime Minister Calls for Arctic Economic Development," *RFE/RL Newsline—Russia*, vol. 6, no. 223, part 1 (November 2002), p. 27; Bruce Stanley, "U.S. Looks to Russia as Vital Oil Supplier: Burgeoning Arctic Outpost Symbolizes New Push to Tap its Rich Reserves," Associated Press, 1 December 2002. Some of Russia's richest energy deposits are in some of the remotest and harshest regions of the North. Russian oil-sector ambitions to increase exports to the U.S. market in 2002 put a new emphasis on increasing production in older fields in western Siberia as well as opening up new oil reserves within the Arctic Circle, especially in the oil-bearing regions of the Barents Sea with access to international sea transportation routes.

12. Krasnoyarsk is Russia's second largest administrative unit. It is the third richest in natural resources, producing 75 percent of Russia's cobalt and 70 percent of its copper, along with 24 percent of lead, 15 percent of coal, and 10 percent of Russia's gold. It is also home to Noril'sk Nickel and the Krasnoyarsk Aluminum Smelter, which accounts for 27 percent of all Russian aluminum production. See Azim Mamanov, "Regional Corner: Krasnoyarsk Krai, Russia," *Business Information Service for the Newly Independent States (BISNIS)*, November 1998, www.bisnis.doc.gov/bisnis/bulletin/9811corn.htm.

13. Roman Abramovich declared Chukotka effectively bankrupt in June 2001 (see "Chukotka Goes Bankrupt," *RIA Novosti*, 15 June 2001), leading the Russian government to propose "liquidating" many of the region's most inaccessible and nonviable settlements to cut back on budgetary outlays for fuel and supplies (see Tatyana Kuzmina, "Chukotka: Authorities Discuss Liquidation of Remote Villages," *ITAR-TASS Weekly News*, 20 September 2001). Between September and November 2001, Abramovich assisted in relocating 339 families (881 people) from four of the remotest villages in Chukotka to European Russia (including the Leningrad, Tula, Tver', Kursk, Novgorod, Belgorod, Rostov, and Voronezh regions and the cities of Omsk, Taganrog, Astrakhan', Kursk, and Voronezh). See Tatyana Kuzmina, "Chukotka Resettlement: Over 300 families Move to Central Russia from Chukotka," *ITAR-TASS Weekly News*, 27 November 2001.

14. Abramovich has paid wage arrears with his own money and helped elderly and disabled citizens of Chukotka relocate permanently to European Russia. He has arranged and paid for summer vacations for the region's children and has helped to rebuild municipal and other critical infrastructure. For more information on Abramovich's activities in Chukotka see Elena Dikun, "Abramovich's Golden Hills in Chukotka," *Jamestown Foundation Prism*, vol. 7, no. 9 (30 September 2001), http://russia.jamestown.org/pubs/view/pri_007_009_005.htm; Wayne Allensworth, "Russia-USA: The Chukotka-Alaska Connection," *JRL Research And Analytical Supplement*, no. 11 (JRL #6401, 14 August 2002), www.cdi.org/russia/johnson/6401-6.cfm; and Yuri Zarakhovich, "Meet the Richest Man in Russia: Who Is Roman Abramovich? And What's He up to in Chukotka, a Desolate Province in Russia's Far North," *Time Europe*, 2 December 2002, p. 76.

15. For other basic information on Chukotka, see *Regiony Rossii 2000, vol. I*, (Moscow: Goskomstat), pp. 549–53.

16. See, for example, V. Yu. Malov and B. V. Melent'ev, "Otsenka posledstviy otkaza ot federal'noy podderzhki ekonomiki Sibiri" [An Assessment of the Consequences of Refusing to Give Federal Support to the Siberian Economy], *Eko*, no. 8 (2002), pp. 89–99.

17. Sergei Blagov, "Russian Water on Troubled Soils," *Asia Times*, 18 December 2002, www.atimes.com/atimes/Central_Asia/DL18Ag01.html.

18. A similar declaratory strategy for the Russian Arctic (the North) ("On the Draft Foundations of Russian Federation State Policy in the Arctic") was adopted in June 2001. This is available on the website of the Russian Ministry of Foreign Affairs, www.mid.ru.

19. Cited in Denisov, "Solntse vskhodit za Uralom," *Krasnaya zvezda*.

20. Cited in Yevgeniya Kvitko, "Russian North Will Live On," *Moscow News*, 24 April 2002, p. 3. The *Moscow News* concluded this article with an editorial comment that once again reviewed and posited Siberia's natural resource base as the ultimate justification for its development: "Seventy-seven percent of Russia's petroleum reserves, 85 percent of its natural gas, 80 percent of its coal, 99 percent of its platinum, 70 percent of its nickel, and 41 percent of its gold. Overall some 80 percent of Russia's total mineral deposits are located in Siberia."

21. For another variation on this line of thinking, see Sergei Golubchikov, "Great Spaces a Burden?" *Moscow News*, 23 October 2002, p. 3.

22. A complete transcript of this meeting, chaired by President Putin, is available on the Russian presidential website, www.kremlin.ru, and what follows has been taken directly from this transcript: "Stenogramma soveshchaniya po problemam sotsial'no-ekonomicheskogo razvitiya Dal'nevostochnogo federal'nogo okruga," 23 August 2002, www.president.kremlin.ru/text/appears/2002/08/18503.shtml.

23. Ibid.

24. Ibid.

25. Vladimir Putin, "Speech to the Meeting on Questions of Natural Monopolies' Rates Policies in Siberia and the Far East," on the Trans-Siberian Railway, 16 February 2001, www.kremlin.ru/text/appears/2001/02/10296.shtml.

26. Vladimir Sluzhakov, "Delovoy zavtrak. Yevgeniy Primakov: My na poroge demograficheskoy katastrofy," *Rossiyskyia gazeta*, 9 July 2002 (RGA, no. 123), p. 1.

27. "Stenogramma soveshchaniya."

28. Ibid.

29. Timothy Heleniak, "Migration Dilemmas Haunt Post-Soviet Russia," *Migration Information Source*, Migration Policy Institute (October 2002), www.migrationinformation.org.

30. See Clifford G. Gaddy and Barry W. Ickes, *Russia's Virtual Economy* (Brookings, 2002).

31. Aleksandr Kisel'nikov, the chairman of the regional committee for government statistics in Novosibirsk, asserted in an interview in a Siberian newspaper in December 2000 that Siberia ought to be more attractive for Russian migrants given that half of European Russia was still suffering from the aftereffects of the 1988 Chernobyl nuclear accident, that the traditional Soviet "south" was now "foreign territories" (the South Caucasus and Central Asia), that the Ural Mountains were "mostly poisoned and devastated" (by heavy industry), and that the (North) Caucasus is at war. Kisel'nikov declared: "We do not have any national conflicts, earthquakes, floods. The soil is good . . . and the climate is not as bad as they keep saying." V. Zhuravlev, "A v Rossii teper' luchsheye mesto—Sibir'" [The best place in Russia now is Siberia], *Sovetskaya Sibir'*, 29 December 2000.

32. See Heleniak, "Migration Dilemmas Haunt Post-Soviet Russia," for a detailed analysis of this issue.

33. Ibid. In 1994, 915,000 immigrants from the former non-Russian republics of the USSR moved to Russia, with only 124,000 moving in 2001.

34. Ibid.

35. Ibid.

36. Ye. S. Krasinets, "Vneshnyaya trudovaya migratsiya v Rossiyu," in *Migratsiya naseleniya*, supplement to the journal *Trudovaya migratsiya v Rossii*, no. 2 (2001), pp. 79–107. The exact number cited is 213,300 (p. 84).

37. Ibid., p. 99. Heleniak notes that there are plausible estimates of as many as six million illegal immigrants in Russia, with many originating in East Asian coun-

tries and Africa. The lower figures would be similar to the figures for illegal immigrants in the United States. Heleniak, "Migration Dilemmas."

38. Krasinets, "Vneshnyaya trudovaya migratsiya," p. 84.

39. The Central Asian states were the poorest and least developed in the USSR and had to begin almost from scratch in their development in the 1990s. In losing Moscow as the center of gravity, the states lost crucial subsidies for budgets, enterprises, and households; inputs for regional industries; markets for their products; transportation routes; and communications with the outside world—much of which was filtered through the Soviet capital. The World Bank estimates that as a result of these losses, between 1990 and 1996, the Central Asian states saw their economies decline by 20–60 percent of GDP. Thanks to extensive borrowing from international financial institutions, reforms in the 1990s also saddled regional states with high and unsustainable debt burdens. Landlocked, resource-poor Tajikistan and Kyrgyzstan have fared particularly badly. A staggering 70–80 percent of their populations have now fallen beneath the poverty line, which puts them among the poorest of the developing countries. Soviet-era attainments in health, education, infrastructure, and industrial development have gradually eroded. See Fiona Hill, "Areas for Future Cooperation or Conflict in Central Asia and the Caucasus," presentation at conference on "The Silk Road in the 21st Century," Yale University, 19 September 2002, www.brookings.edu/views/speeches/hillf/20020919.htm. The Kyrgyz and Tajik governments have begun to keep detailed figures on their migrant workers because worker remittances and trade with Russia play an increasingly important role in the economies of both Kyrgyzstan and Tajikistan. Some sources suggest that there may be as many as one million Tajiks working temporarily or permanently in Russia. Migrant workers from Uzbekistan are also reported to be seeking work in Russia in large numbers, but there are no reliable figures.

40. Tyntchtykbek Tchoroev, "Government Delegation Meets with the Kyrgyz Labor Migrants in Russia," RFE/RL Kyrgyz News, 22 December 2002.

41. Personal communication from Central Asian sociologist Anara Tabyshaliyeva, executive director of the Institute for Regional Studies, Bishkek, Kyrgyzstan, Washington, 12 December 2002.

42. Council on Foreign and Defense Policy, "Siberia and the Far East in Russia in the 21st Century: New Assessments, New Priorities, and New Decisions" (Moscow, June 2001), cited in Andrei Piontkovsky, "Does Russia Want to Keep Its Far East," Russia Journal, 24–30 August 2001.

43. See, for example, Whewell, "Russians Fear Takeover by Chinese in East." Whewell points out that there are fewer than ten million Russians in the Far East and at least 250 million Chinese in China's three northern provinces close to the Russian border—sufficient evidence in his mind, and in those of regional leaders, of Chinese designs on Russia's newly "empty lands." Similarly, Zhanna Zayonchkovskaya, head of the Russian Academy of Science's Institute of Economic Forecasting, claimed in 2001 that by the middle of the twenty-first century, Chinese would inevitably become the second largest ethnic group in Russia after Rus-

sians. See "Chinese Immigration Important for Russian Economic Revival," *BBC Monitoring*, 23 June 2001.

44. Galina Vitkovskaya and Sergey Panarin, eds., *Migratsiya i bezopasnost' v Rossii* (Moscow: Interdialekt, 2000), p. 188.

45. Mikhail Alexseev, comment on "Borderguards and the 'Yellow Peril,'" *PONARS-list*, Thursday, 30 November 2000. For a detailed discussion of this issue, see Mikhail Alexseev, "Socioeconomic and Security Implications of Chinese Migration in the Russian Far East," *Post-Soviet Geography and Economics*, vol. 42, no. 2 (2001), pp. 95–114.

46. See Mikhail Alexseev, *The Chinese Are Coming: Public Opinion and Threat Perception in the Russian Far East*, PONARS Policy Memo #184, January 2001, www.csis.org/ruseura/ponars/policymemos/pm_0184.pdf. Alexseev notes that all official data and his own research indicate that the number of Chinese migrants in the Primor'ye region of Russia, around Khabarovsk and Vladivostok, cannot be significantly higher than 1–1.5 percent of the region's Russian population on any given day. He found "no evidence of Chinese presence that would be even remotely similar to the Chinese presence in New York, San Francisco, or even Moscow." Heleniak estimates the Chinese population in the Far East to be between 100,000 and 300,000 (both legal and illegal), with most arriving under official labor contracts. See Heleniak, "Migration Dilemmas," p. 7.

47. Heleniak, "Migration Dilemmas," p. 7.

48. Ibid., p. 8. Lidiya Grafova, "Russia Does Not Need People," *Novaya gazeta*, 29 July 2002.

49. "Russian Rights Activists Attack 'Repressive' Draft Migration Policy Paper," *BBC Monitoring*, 10 December 2002; Natalia Yefimova, "Migrants Come, Refugees Leave," *The Moscow Times*, 10 December 2002, and "Duma and Nationalities Ministry Hash Out Migration Policy," *RFE/RL Russian Political Weekly*, vol. 2, no. 42 (11 December 2002).

50. Malik Mansur, "Uzbekistan: Migrants Suffer Russian Humiliation," *IWPR Reporting Central Asia*, no. 121 (24 May 2002); Abdukholik Rakhmatullaev, "Migrant Tajiks Face Racist Violence," *IWPR Reporting Central Asia*, no. 136 (9 August 2002); and Vladimir Davlatov, "Russia: Tajiks Fear Deportation," *IWPR Reporting Central Asia*, no. 162 (19 November 2002).

51. The classically trained economist will likely object to this point on the basis of Pareto efficiency and the idea that everyone gains something from this transaction. In this instance, however, the gains come only from heavy subsidization of declining industries and the presence and availability of cheap labor from Central Asia (and other immigrant labor). This provides a means of keeping otherwise loss-making enterprises in operation.

52. See Gillian Sandford, "Concerns Mount at Racial Unrest in Northern England: Burnley Hit by Two Nights of Riots, Is the Fourth Town to Erupt in Recent Months," *Christian Science Monitor*, 26 June 2001, p. 7.

53. Claudia Rosett, "The Promised Land," *Wall Street Journal Opinion Journal*, 9 August 2001, www.opinionjournal.com.

54. Ibid.

55. Alla Startseva and Valeria Korchagina, "Pyongyang Pays Russia with Free Labor," *The Moscow Times*, 6 August 2001, p. 1.

56. Ibid.

57. Cited in Ian Traynor, "For Siberia, a Return to Wasteland: Population Drains Away as Brutal Project to Colonize Frozen Wilderness Is Reversed," *Guardian*, 12 June 2002, p. 3.

58. See Sergei Golubchikov, "Great Spaces a Burden?" and the discussion of Soviet Space [*Sovetskoye prostranstvo*] by Vladimir Kaganskiy in *Kul'turnyy landshaft i sovetskoe obitayemoe prostranstvo* (Moscow, 2001), pp. 135–246.

59. Cited in Lidia Grafova, "Russia Does Not Need People," *Novaya gazeta*, 29 July 2002.

60. See, for example, Julie DaVanzo and Clifford Grammich, *Dire Demographics: Population Trends in the Russian Federation* (Santa Monica: RAND, 2001); Stephen Massey, "Russia's Maternal and Child Health Crisis: Socio-Economic Implications and the Path Forward," *EastWest Institute Policy Brief*, vol. 1, no. 9 (December 2002); David F. Gordon, "The Next Wave of HIV/AIDS: Nigeria, Ethiopia, Russia, India, and China," *NIC Intelligence Community Assessment*, September 2002 (ICA 2002-04 D).

61. Interfax Statistical Report, no. 18 (2003).

62. U.S. Census Bureau, International Data Base, www.census.gov/ipc/www/idbnew.html. Goskomstat has three scenarios: 138 million (best-case), 134 million (mid), and 128 (worst-case). See Tat'yana Smol'yakova, "Demografiya. Tri tsenariya zhizni i smerti" [Demography. Three scenarios of life and death], *Rossiyskaya gazeta*, 6 March 2002, p. 6. Looking further into the future, the scenarios become even gloomier. As a high-range estimate, demographer Murray Feshbach predicts that by 2050, Russia's population will drop to about 100 million, while Goskomstat's medium prediction is 102 million. See Murray Feshbach, *Russia's Health and Demographic Crises: Policy Implications and Consequences* (Washington: Chemical and Biological Arms Institute, 2003), pp. 5–7.

63. See, for example, Igor Chubays, *Ot russkoy idey k idei Novoi Rossii: kak nam preodolet' ideinyy krizis* (Moscow: Izdatel'stvo "GITIS," 1996). The classic discussion of the U.S. ideologization of its expansion across the North American continent from the Atlantic seaboard to the Pacific is in Frederick Merk, *Manifest Destiny and Mission in American History: A Reinterpretation* (Knopf, 1963).

64. Andrey Myaken'kiy, "Soyuz nerushimyy. Alyaska, ser!" *Moskovskaya pravda*, 2 December 2000, p. 2; Denis Babichenko, "Pis'mo bashkirskomu sultanu. Vladimir Putin repetiruyet rol' sobiratelya zemli russkoi," *Segodnya*, 12 May 2000; Ivan Trefilov, "Sobiratel' postsovetskikh zemel'. Integratsiya ot Vladimira Putina: snachala politika, potom ekonomika," *Segodnya*, 11 October 2000, p. 3; and "... As Analyst Explains Putin's Tactics," *RFE/RL Newsline—Russia*, vol. 6, no. 153, part 1 (15 August 2002).

65. Maura Reynolds, "It's Colder than Siberia—Even in Siberia," *Los Angeles Times*, 20 January 2001, p. 1A.

66. Ibid.

67. Nick Paton Walsh, "Situation Normal: Russia Is Frozen Solid," *Guardian*, 10 January 2003, p. 18.

68. Municipal governments keep a grim annual account of the number of street deaths from the cold. For example, on December 6, 2002, the Moscow city government reported that 133 people had succumbed to hypothermia on city streets so far that winter. See Gregory Feifer, "Russia: Country Digs in for Another Long Winter," *RFE/RL*, 6 December 2002.

69. "... As Putin Again Calls for Someone to Be Held Accountable," *RFE/RL Russian Federation Report*, vol. 3, no. 4 (24 January 2001).

70. Vladimir Putin, "Vystupleniye na soveshchanii, po voprosy o khode vosstanovitel'nykh rabot v Yuzhnom federal'nom okruge," 5 November 2002, www.president.kremlin.ru/text/appears/202/11/21248.shtml. Although in this specific instance Putin was speaking after serious, devastating floods in southern Russia in the late summer of 2002, he was referring also to the response to other instances of flooding in the previous year, including Lensk in 2001.

71. David Stern and Andrew Jack, "Muscovites Freeze as Temperature Hits −32° C," *Financial Times*, 10 January 2003, p. 6; Sergei Borisov, "Russia: A Cold Snap and Snapping Tempers," Transitions Online, 13 January 2003, www.tol.cz.

72. Reynolds, "It's Colder than Siberia."

73. Ibid.

74. "... And Country Braces for Another Winter," *RFE/RL Newsline*, vol. 6, no. 200, part 1 (23 October 2002).

75. Alexander Tsipko, "Privatization Is No Longer Popular in Russia," *Jamestown Foundation Prism*, vol. 7, no. 2 (February 2001), part 1.

76. For a detailed discussion of these and other examples of environmental pollution, see D. J. Peterson, *Troubled Lands: The Legacy of Soviet Environmental Destruction*, RAND Research Study (Boulder, Colo.: Westview, 1993).

77. Sergei Blagov, "Environmental Protection Agency to Be Axed," *Asia Times*, 31 May 2000.

Chapter 10

1. Leslie Dienes, "Reflections on a Geographic Dichotomy: Archipelago Russia," *Eurasian Geography and Economics*, vol. 43, no. 6 (September 2002), p. 455. Russian scholar Boris Rodoman has designated at least ten million square kilometers (about two-thirds) of Russian territory as part of the *glubinka*, claiming that these territories are in the process of a reverse modernization. Boris Rodoman, "Novaya polyarizatsiya rossiyskogo prostranstva," in Yu. G. Lipets, ed., *Polyusa i tsentry rosta v regional'nom razvitii* (Moscow: IGRAN, 1998), p. 35, as cited in Grigory Ioffe and others, "Russia's Fragmented Space," in Blair Ruble, Jodi Koehn, and Nancy Popson, eds., *Fragmented Space in the Russian Federation* (Johns Hopkins University Press, 2001), p. 77.

2. Dienes makes the point that Siberia's oil, gas, and metal-producing centers are connected to and integrated into the national and global economies, while at the same time implying that the bulk of the region's population is not, and also does not benefit appreciably from the "multiplier effect of successful resource exports." Ibid., pp. 450–51.

3. Victor Mote notes that "until the twentieth century, Greater Siberia was not commonly regarded as an organic part of Russia." See Mote, *Siberia: Worlds Apart* (Boulder, Colo.: Westview Press, 1998), p. 57. Siberia's role as part of Russia's heartland is very much a modern construction and a fiction.

4. However, at the same time, targeted, limited residence restrictions, in a small number of places east of the Urals, like Noril'sk, might in fact prove helpful. In this instance, Siberian one-enterprise cities should clearly be downsizing, and migrants tend to be attracted to Noril'sk by enterprise and local government subsidies or, in the case of illegal immigrants, by extremely low-paying temporary jobs, rather than by the prospect of new, stable employment.

5. In Tulare County and other regions of California with high unemployment rates, local governments have paid welfare recipients to leave the area in search of jobs in other states. In 2001, under the More Opportunity for Viable Employment (MOVE) program, for example, 750 people were paid an average of $1,600 to relocate to the Midwest and other areas with relative labor shortages. See Evelyn Nieves, "A Fertile Farm Region Pays Its Jobless to Quit California," *New York Times*, 18 June 2001; and M. Mindy Moretti, "Counties Pay Residents on Welfare to Move. Program Gets High Marks from Participants and County Financial Officers," Online County News, National Association of Counties, 33, 13 (2 July 2001) www.naco.org/pubs/cnews/01-7-2/counties.htm.

6. In 2002 the Russian government passed a new law on resettlement assistance for northern regions. In the summer of 2003, it announced the allocation of 900 million rubles ($30 million) to finance its implementation. Russian government and other sources indicate that as many as 780,000 people or households (the specification is unclear) are registered on local waiting lists for assistance in resettling from the North. The World Bank–financed resettlement project in Moscow is currently testing new, more effective and efficient schemes for public assistance for out-migration from the North that would provide migrants with certificates for finished housing in a destination of *their choice*. The new Russian resettlement law also stipulates the federal funding of housing certificates and free choice of destination. World Bank officials in Moscow note that the "old thinking" about the government's needing to specify migrants' final destinations is gradually eroding as government experts realize that "administrative definition of the destination places would increase significantly the risks of return migration and reduce effectiveness of migration assistance." The overall World Bank allocation for migration assistance from the Russian North in 2003 was $70 million for a three-year period. As of May 2003, the first 1,800 households had applied for participation in the World Bank–financed project, and the actual out-migration process had begun. Personal

email communication with Andrei Markov, senior human development specialist, World Bank, Moscow office, 19 June 2003.

7. See, for example, Richard Burger and Charles Undeland, *Center-Region Relations in the Russian Federation: A Case Study of Nizhny Novgorod Oblast*, Occasional Paper (Strengthening Democratic Institutions Project, Harvard University, August 1993); Andrei Makarychev, *The Region and the World: The Case of Nizhnii Novgorod*, Working Paper 6 (Zürich: Center for Security Studies and Conflict Research, May 2001); and the city's website, www.unn.runnet.ru/nn/.

8. Dienes lists the cities with the highest rates of consumption as Moscow, St. Petersburg, Novosibirsk, Nizhniy Novgorod, Yekaterinburg, Samara, Omsk, Kazan', Ufa, Chelyabinsk, and Rostov-na-Donu. He notes that these cities, all with populations of over one million, account for three-quarters of the Russian "middle class," or those earning from $150 to $2,500 per month. He also points out that the Russian "mean monthly income . . . seems to decrease rapidly outside the capital, and diminish fairly regularly with city size." "Reflections on a Geographic Dichotomy," p. 448.

9. Michael Bradshaw, "The Geographic Factor in Russia's Modernization," presentation at Center for Strategic and International Studies, Washington (7 November 2002); Mote, *Siberia: Worlds Apart*, p. 2.

10. Robert N. Taaffe, "The Conceptual, Analytical and Planning Framework of Siberian Development," in George Demko and Roland Fuchs, eds., *Geographical Studies on the Soviet Union: Essays in Honor of Chauncy D. Harris,* Research Paper 211 (University of Chicago Department of Geography, 1984), p. 166; Leslie Dienes, "The Development of Siberia: Regional Priorities and Economic Strategy," in Demko and Fuchs, eds., *Geographical Studies on the Soviet Union,* pp. 204–05.

11. Dienes, "The Development of Siberia," pp. 204–05.

12. German journalist Michael Thumann described how abandoned gold mines in Siberia had reopened using imported seasonal labor brigades with no support services during his summer 2000 journey through Siberia ("Dossier: Abschied vom Ende der Welt" [Dossier: A Farewell from the End of the World], *Die Zeit*, 31 December 2000); as did British journalist Andrew Jack when visiting similar regions in the summer of 2002 (Jack, "Pioneering Migration Scheme Offers Hope to Inheritors of Stalin's Arctic Penal Colonies," *Financial Times*, 17 July 2002, p. 20).

13. Indeed, between 1996 and 2001, Canada's population concentrated even further in four broad urban regions—in southern Ontario, Montreal, mainland British Columbia and southern Vancouver Island, and Calgary-Edmonton—which now account for 51 percent of Canada's population. In contrast, the population in the northern territories declined by 5 percent in the same period, with high net outflows of migration to the rest of Canada. Taken from the 2002 census data from Statistics Canada, available at www.statcan.ca.

14. Statistics Canada, CANSIM II, table 051-0001, available at www.statcan.ca. One percent of Russia's population would be around 1.5 million, but the broader region of the Russian North currently contains about 12 million or about 8 percent of the Russian population. See Timothy Heleniak, *Migration from the Russian*

North during the Transition Period (Washington: The World Bank, September 1999), pp. 8–9.

15. In 1998 the GDP of the Northwest Territories was approximately $2.4 billion, about 15 percent of which was from mining. Yukon's GDP reached $947 million, 7 percent of which was from mining. In comparison, mining composed 3.6 percent of Canada's overall GDP that same year. Mining was second only to government services in northern Canada's top industries. "Canada Mining Facts," Mineral and Mining Statistics, http://mmsd1.mms.nrcan.gc.ca/mmsd/facts/canFact_e.asp?regionId=12.

16. Northern Indicators, 2000. Published under the authority of the Minister of Indian Affairs and Northern Development, Ottawa, 2000, www.ainc-inac.gc.ca/pr/sts/pu2000_e.pdf.

17. Elena Sabirova, "Sakhalin Island Oil and Gas Projects Potential," U.S Department of Commerce, International Trade Administration, Business Information Service for the Newly Independent States (BISNIS), presentation, 2002, www.bisnis.doc.gov/outreach02/sakhalin.ppt; Elena Sabirova and Michael Allen, "Summer 2000 Update on Sakhalin Oil and Gas Projects," BISNIS, www.bisnis.doc.gov/bisnis/ISA/010112sakhog.htm. See also Fiona Hill and Florence Fee, "Fueling the Future: The Prospects for Russian Oil and Gas," *Demokratizatsiya*, vol. 10, no. 4 (Fall 2002), pp. 462–87.

18. Michael Lelyveld, "Russia: Foreign Energy Investment Lagging in Ex-Soviet Region," *RFE/RL Features*, 27 November 2002.

19. Vladimir Kontorovich, "Can Russia Resettle the Far East?" *Postcommunist Economies*, vol. 12, no. 3 (2000), p. 374.

20. Ibid., p. 379.

21. Vladimir Kontorovich, "Economic Crisis in the Russian Far East: Overdevelopment or Colonial Exploitation," *Post-Soviet Geography and Economics*, vol. 42, no. 6 (2001), p. 395, citing Russian economist Yuriy Pivovarov.

22. Ibid., pp. 400–01.

23. Ibid., p. 404.

24. Kontorovich's proposals are similar to those of prominent Russian analysts who have been critical of the Russian government's approach to the region. See, for example, Mikhail Delyagin, director of the Moscow Institute for Globalization Problems, and his recommendations for the Russian North in Sarah Karush, "Harnessing the North," *The Moscow Times*, 28 November 2000.

25. Mikhail Alexseev, "Socioeconomic and Security Implications of Chinese Migration in the Russian Far East," *Post-Soviet Geography and Economics*, vol. 42, no. 2 (2001), pp. 95–111.

26. Several distinct regions of Russia have already been designated as UNESCO World Heritage sites: the Virgin Komi Forests in the Urals in 1995, Lake Baykal in 1996, the volcanoes of Kamchatka in 1996, the Golden Mountains of Altai (southwest of Novosibirsk) in 1998, other locations on the Kamchatka Peninsula in 2001, and Central Sikhote-Alin in the Primorsk kray also in 2001. See UNESCO's website www.unesco.org/whc/ for more information.

27. It is important to distinguish the kind of special fund we suggest here from some special resource funds established in other countries. The State of Alaska, for example, has established the Alaska Permanent Fund Corporation (for more information see the Corporation's website, www.apfc.org) for the purpose of redistributing natural resource revenues to the inhabitants of that state. Dividends from the fund have put more than $10 billion into the regional economy and account for as much as 10 percent of the annual income of some Alaskans in rural areas. Our proposed Siberian resource fund would be used to move people *away from* the region, *not* encourage them to stay, as the Alaska Permanent Fund does. This would not be a fund for the development and maintenance of Siberia and its inhabitants.

Appendix B

1. Thomas C. Peterson and Russell S. Vose, "An Overview of the Global Historical Climatology Network Temperature Database," p. 5, www.ncdc.gov/ol/climate/research/ghcn/ghcnoverview.html.

2. Russian HydroMetCenter City Climactic Data, http://meteo.infospace.ru/climate/html/index.ssi.

3. John F. Griffiths, "Some Problems of Regionality in Applications of Climate Change," in *Proceedings of the Fourteenth International Congress of Biometeorology*, 1–8 September 1996, Ljubljana, Slovenia, pp. 384–90.

Appendix C

1. S. V. Slavin, *The Soviet North: Present Development and Future Prospects* (Moscow: Progress Publishers, 1972), pp. 38–39.

2. See, for instance, Michael Bradshaw, "The Russian North in Transition: General Introduction," *Post-Soviet Geography*, vol. 36, no. 4 (1995), p. 196.

3. Timothy Heleniak, "Out-Migration and Depopulation of the Russian North during the 1990s," *Post-Soviet Geography and Economics*, vol. 40, no. 3 (1999), p. 157, fn 5.

Appendix D

1. Tatiana Mikhailova, "Where Russians Should Live: A Counterfactual Alternative to Soviet Location Policy," Ph.D. diss., Pennsylvania State University, 2002.

2. See, for instance, Philip E. Graves, "Migration and Climate," *Journal of Regional Science*, vol. 20, no. 2 (1980), pp. 227–37; M. I. Cropper, "The Value of Urban Amenities," *Journal of Regional Science.*, vol. 21, no. 3 (1981), pp. 359–74; and Jennifer Roback, "Wages, Rents, and the Quality of Life," *Journal of Political Economy*, vol. 90, no. 6 (1982), pp. 1257–79.

Bibliography

Abele, Gunars. "Effect of Cold Weather on Productivity, in Technology Transfer Opportunities for the Construction Engineering Community." Proceedings of Construction Seminar, February 1986. U.S. Army Cold Regions Research and Engineering Laboratory.

Aganbegyan, Abel. *Inside Perestroika: The Future of the Soviet Economy.* Translated by Helen Szamuely. Harper and Row, 1989.

Alexseev, Mikhail. *The Chinese Are Coming: Public Opinion and Threat Perception in the Russian Far East.* PONARS Policy Memo no. 184 (January 2001).

———. "Socioeconomic and Security Implications of Chinese Migration in the Russian Far East." *Post-Soviet Geography and Economics* 42, no. 2 (2001): 95–111.

Anderson, Benedict. *Imagined Communities: Reflections on the Origin and Spread of Nationalism.* London: Verso and NLB, 1983.

Anderson, Jeffrey J. *The Territorial Imperative: Pluralism, Corporatism, and Economic Crisis.* Cambridge University Press, 1992.

Anderson, Robert, Jr. "The Health Costs of Changing Macro-Climates." In *Proceedings of the Third Conference on the Climatic Impact Assessment Program*, edited by Anthony Broderick and Thomas M. Hard. Department of Transportation Conference Proceedings, DOT-TSC-OST-74-15 (1974).

Andreev, Vasily. "Nationalism in Russia: Past, Present, and Prospects for the Future." *Prism* 2, no. 7, part 4 (5 April 1996).

Anisimov, Evgeniy. *The Reforms of Peter the Great: Progress through Coercion in Russia.* Translated by John T. Alexander. Armonk, N.Y.: M. E. Sharpe, 1993.

Applebaum, Anne. *Gulag: A History.* New York: Doubleday, 2003.

Arbatov, Alexei. "Voyennaya reforma: doktrina, voiska, finansy." *Mirovaya ekonomika i mezhdunarodnyye otnosheniya* 17 (July 1997).

Arbatov, Alexei, and others, eds. *Managing Conflict in the Former Soviet Union: Russian and American Perspectives.* MIT Press, 1997.

Arthur Andersen Consulting. *Russian Electricity Reform: Recommendation Report.* Moscow: April 2001.

Åslund, Anders. *How Russia Became a Market Economy.* Brookings, 1995.

Axtell, Robert L. "Zipf Distribution of U.S. Firm Sizes." *Science* 293 (7 September 2001): 1818–20.

Axtell, Robert L., and Richard Florida. "Emergent Cities: A Microeconomic Explanation of Zipf's Law." Mimeo. Brookings, 2000.

Azrael, Jeremy, and D. J. Peterson. "Russia and the Information Revolution." RAND Issue Paper (IP-229-CRE), 2002.

Ball, Deborah Yarsike, "The Political Views of the Russian Officer Corps: A Survey of 600 Field-Grade Officers." Presentation at Harvard University's Davis Center for Russian Studies, 19 September 1996.

Ball, Deborah Yarsike, and Theodore Gerber. "The Political Views of Russian Field Grade Officers." *Post-Soviet Affairs* 12, no. 2 (1996):155–80.

Baluev, D. G. "O natsional'nykh interesakh Rossii i ee meste v mezhdunarodnykh otnosheniyakh." *Vestnik.* Moscow: Fonda Rossiyskiy Obshchestvenno-politicheskiy Tsentr, December 1996.

Balzer, Marjorie Mandelstam. *The Tenacity of Ethnicity: A Siberian Saga in Global Perspective.* Princeton University Press, 1999.

Bandera, V. N. *The Soviet Economy in Regional Perspective.* Praeger, 1973.

Barber, John, and Mark Harrison. *The Soviet Defence Industry Complex from Stalin to Khrushchev.* New York: Macmillan, 2000.

———. *The Soviet Home Front 1941–1945: A Social and Economic History.* New York: Longman, 1991.

Barnes, Kathleen. "Eastward Migration within the Soviet Union." *Pacific Affairs* 7, no. 4 (1934): 395–405.

Bartlett, Robert, and Janet Hartley. *Russia in the Age of Enlightenment: Essays for Isabel de Madariaga.* Houndmills, Basingstoke, Hampshire: Macmillan and SSEES, University of London, 1990.

Bassin, Mark. "Inventing Siberia: Visions of the Russian Far East in the Early 19th Century." *American Historical Review* 96, no. 3 (June 1991): 763–94.

Berdyaev, Nikolay. *Russkaya ideya: osnovnyye problemy russkoy mysli XIX veka i nachala XX veka.* Paris: YMCA Press, 1946.

Berlin, Isaiah. *Russian Thinkers.* Harmondsworth, Middlesex: Penguin Books, 1978.

Besançon, Alain, "Les Frontières Orientales de l'Europe: Le Cas Russe." *Commentaire* 18, no. 71 (Autumn 1995): 493–500.

Best, Geoffrey. *War and Society in Revolutionary Europe, 1770–1870.* Leicester University Press, 1982.

Bestuzhev, Igor. *Bor'ba v Rossii po voprosam vneshney politiki 1906–1910.* Moscow: Akademiya Nauk SSSR, 1961.

Billington, James. *The Icon and the Axe: An Interpretative History of Russian Culture.* Vintage Books, 1970.

Blackwill, Robert, and Sergei Karaganov, eds. *Damage Limitation or Crisis: Russia and the Outside World.* CSIA Studies in International Security no. 5, 1994.

Blasi, Joseph, Maya Kroumova, and Douglas Kruse. *Kremlin Capitalism: Privatizing the Russian Economy.* Cornell University Press, 1997.

Bobrick, Benson. *East of the Sun: The Epic Conquest and Tragic History of Siberia.* New York: Poseidon Press, 1992.

Bonnell, Victoria E. *Russia in the New Century: Stability or Disorder.* Boulder, Colo.: Westview Press, 2001.

Boycko, Maxim, Andrei Shleifer, and Robert Vishny. *Privatizing Russia.* MIT Press, 1995.

Bradshaw, Michael J. "Economic Relations of the Russian Far East with the Asian-Pacific States." *Post-Soviet Geography* 35, no. 4 (April 1994): 234–46.

———. "The Energy Crisis in the Russian Far East." *Europe-Asia Studies* 50, no. 6 (September 1998): 1043–63.

———. "The Russian North in Transition." *Post-Soviet Geography* 36, no. 4 (April 1995): 195–203.

———. "Russia's Illiberal Geography." Paper presented at the Center for Strategic and International Studies, Washington, 7 November 2002.

Bradshaw, Michael, and Philip Hanson, eds. *Regional Economic Change in Russia.* Northampton, Mass.: E. Elgar, 2000.

Brevnov, Boris, and Cameron Half. *From Monopoly to Market Maker? Reforming Russia's Power Sector.* Cambridge, Massachusetts: Strengthening Democratic Institutions Project, April 2000.

Broderick, Anthony, and Thomas M. Hard, eds. *Proceedings of the Third Conference on the Climatic Impact Assessment Program.* Department of Transportation Conference Proceedings, DOT-TSC-OST-74-15, 1974.

Brovkin, Vladimir. "The Emperor's New Clothes: Continuity of Soviet Political Culture in Contemporary Russia." *Problems of Post-Communism* 43, no. 2 (March/April 1996): 21–28.

Brown, Archie, ed. *Contemporary Russian Politics.* Oxford University Press, 2001.

———. *The Gorbachev Factor.* Oxford University Press, 1996.

Brown, Archie, and Lilia Shevtsova. *Gorbachev, Yeltsin, and Putin: Political Leadership in Russia's Transition.* Washington: Carnegie Endowment for International Peace, 2001.

Bruk, S. I., and V. M. Kabuzan. "The Dynamics and Ethnic Composition of the Population of Russia in the Era of Imperialism (From the End of the 19th Century to 1917)." *Soviet Geography* 30, no. 2 (1989): 130–54.

Buckley, Cynthia. "The Myth of Managed Migration: Migration Control and Market in the Soviet Period." *Slavic Review* 54, no. 4 (1995): 896–916.

Burbulis, Gennady. *Stanovleniye novoy rossiyskoy gosudarstvennosti: real'nost' i perspetivy.* Moscow: "Strategy" Center, 1996.

Burger, Richard, and Charles Undeland. *Center-Region Relations in the Russian Federation: A Case Study of Nizhny Novgorod Oblast.* Cambridge, Mass.: Strengthening Democratic Institutions Project, August 1993.

Campbell, R. W. *Soviet and Post-Soviet Telecommunications: An Industry under Reform.* Boulder, Colo.: Westview Press, 1995.

Chandler, Tertius, and Gerald Fox. *3000 Years of Urban Growth.* New York: Academic Press, 1974.

Charques, Richard. *The Twilight of Imperial Russia.* Oxford University Press, 1958.

Chenery, H., and T. N. Srinivasan, eds. *Handbook of Development Economics,* volume 2. Elsevier Science, 1988.

Chepelkin, M. A., and N. M. Dyakova. *Istoricheskiy ocherk formirovaniya gosudarstvennykh granits rossiyskoy imperii (2-aya polovina XVII-nachalo XX v.v.).* Moscow: Rossiyskiy nauchnyy fond, 1992.

Chinyaeva, Elena. "The Search for the Russian Idea." *Transition,* June 1997.

Chislennost' naseleniya Rossiyskoy Federatsii po gorodam, poselkam gorodskogo tipa i rayonam na 1 yanvarya 2002 g. Moscow: Goskomstat, 2002.

Chubais, Igor'. *Ot russkoy idey k idei Novoi Rossii: kak nam preodolet' ideinyy krizis.* Moscow: Izdatel'stvo "GITIS," 1996.

Chubais, Igor', and Vladimir Vedrashko, eds. *Novye vekhi: obshchestvennyy al'manakh demokraticheskoy nauchno-publitsistechskoy mysli o rossiiskoy probleme,* no. 1. Moscow: Izdatel'stvo Prava Cheloveka, 1996.

Ciccone, Antonio, and Robert E. Hall. "Productivity and the Density of Economic Activity." *American Economic Review* 86, no. 1 (March 1996): 54–70.

Clayton, Anthony. *End of Empire.* Sandhurst, England: Conflict Studies Research Center, 1995.

Clem, Ralph. *Research Guide to the Russian and Soviet Censuses.* Cornell University Press, 1986.

Clover, Charles. "Dreams of the Eurasian Heartland: The Reemergence of Geopolitics." *Foreign Affairs* 78, no. 2 (March/April 1999): 9–13.

Cole, John P. "Change in the Population of the Larger Cities of the USSR." *Soviet Geography* 31, no. 3 (March 1990): 160–72.

Colton, Timothy. *Moscow: Governing the Socialist Metropolis.* The Belknap Press of Harvard University Press, 1995.

Conger, Dean. "Siberia: Russia's Frozen Frontier." *National Geographic* 131, no. 3 (March 1967).

Conolly, Violet. *Beyond the Urals: Economic Development in Soviet Asia.* Oxford University Press, 1967.

———. *Siberia Today and Tomorrow: Study of Economic Resources, Problems, and Achievements.* New York: Taplinger, 1976.

Conquest, Robert. *The Great Terror: Stalin's Purges of the Thirties.* Macmillan, 1968.

Council on Foreign and Defense Policy, "Will the Union Be Revived? The Future of the Post-Soviet Space." Cambridge, Mass.: Strengthening Democratic Institutions Project, June 1997.

Cracraft, James, ed. *Major Problems in the History of Imperial Russia.* Lexington, Mass.: D. C. Heath, 1994.

Custine, Adolphe, marquis de. *Empire of the Czar: A Journey through Eternal Russia.* Doubleday, Anchor Books, 1989.

Dallin, David, and Boris Nikolaevsky. *Forced Labor in Soviet Russia.* Yale University Press, 1947.

Danilevskiy, Nikolay. *Rossiya i Yevropa.* St. Petersburg, 1869.

D'Arge, Ralph. "Economic Impact of Climate Change: Introduction and Overview." In *Proceedings of the Third Conference on the Climatic Impact Assessment Program,* edited by Anthony Broderick and Thomas M. Hard. Department of Transportation Conference Proceedings, DOT-TSC-OST-74-15 (1974).

DaVanzo, Julie, and Clifford Grammich. *Dire Demographics: Population Trends in the Russian Federation.* RAND, 2001.

Davidovich, V. G. "O razvitii seti gorodov za 40 let." *Voprosy geografii* 45 (1959).

———. *Planirovka gorodov i rayonov.* Moscow, 1964.

Davis, Donald R., and David. E. Weinstein. "Bones, Bombs and Break Points: The Geography of Economic Activity." Working Paper 8517. Cambridge, Mass.: National Bureau of Economic Research, October 2001.

De Madariaga, Isabel. *Russia in the Age of Catherine the Great.* Yale University Press, 1981.

Demko, George, and Roland Fuchs. *Geographic Studies on the Soviet Union: Essays in Honor of Chauncy D. Harris.* University of Chicago Press, 1984.

Demograficheskiy yezhegodnik Rossii 2000. Moscow: Goskomstat, 2000.

De Nevers, Renee. *Russia's Strategic Renovation.* Adelphi Paper 289. London: IISS/Brassey's, July 1994.

Derluguian, Georgi M., and Scott Greer. *Questioning Geopolitics: Political Projects in a Changing World System.* Westport, Conn.: Greenwood Press, 2000.

De Villepin, Xavier. "Face aux Incertitudes Russes." *Commentaire* 18, no. 71 (Autumn, 1995): 511–14.

Diamond, Jared. *Guns, Germs and Steel: The Fates of Human Societies.* W. W. Norton, 1999.

Dienes, Leslie. "Economic and strategic position of the Soviet Far-East." *Soviet Economy* 1, no. 2 (April 1985): 146–76.

———. "Reflections on a Geographic Dichotomy: Archipelago Russia." *Eurasian Geography and Economics* 43, no. 6 (September 2002): 443–58.

————. "Regional Planning and the Development of Soviet Asia." *Soviet Geography* 28, no. 5 (May 1987): 189–213.

————. *Soviet Asia: Economic Development and National Policy Choices.* Boulder, Colo.: Westview Press, 1987.

Diment, Galya, and Yuri Slezkine. *Between Heaven and Hell: The Myth of Siberia in Russian Culture.* New York: St. Martin's Press, 1993.

Dobson, Richard. *Is Russia Turning the Corner? Changing Russian Public Opinion 1991–1996.* Washington: United States Information Agency, September 1996.

Dogayev, Yu. M. "Ekonomicheskaya effektivnost' novoy tekhniki na Severe." *Nauka* 36 (1969): 38–40.

Domenach, Jean-Marie. "Leninist Propaganda." *Public Opinion Quarterly* 15, no. 2 (Summer 1951): 265–73.

Doyle, Michael W. *Empires.* Cornell University Press, 1986.

Drage, Geoffrey. *Russian Affairs.* London: John Murray, 1904.

Drobizheva, L. M., and others. *Demokratizatsiya i obrazy natsionalizma v Rossiyskoy Federatsii 90-kh godov.* Moscow: Mysl', 1996.

Drobizheva, Leokadia. *Govorit elita respublik Rossiyskoy Federatsii.* Moscow, 1996.

Duff, J. D., ed. *Russian Realities and Problems.* Cambridge University Press, 1917.

Dugin, Aleksandr. *Osnovy geopolitiki: geopoliticheskoye budushcheye Rossii.* Moscow: Arktogeia-Tsentr, 2000.

Dukes, Paul, ed. *Russia and Europe.* London: Collins & Brown, 1991.

————. trans. *Russia under Catherine the Great: Select Documents on Government and Society,* vol. 1. Newtonville, Mass.: Oriental Research Partners, 1978.

Duncan, Peter J. S. *Russian Messianism: Third Rome, Holy Revolution, Communism and After.* New York: Routledge, 2000.

Dunlop, John. "Alexander Lebed and Russian Foreign Policy." *SAIS Review,* Winter-Spring 1997: 47–72.

————. *The New Russian Nationalism.* The Washington Papers. Praeger, 1985.

————. *The Rise of Russia and the Fall of the Soviet Empire.* Princeton University Press, 1993.

Energy Policies in the Russian Federation: 1995 Survey. Paris: OECD/IEA, 1995.

Engels, Friedrich. *Herr Eugen Dühring's Revolution in Science (Anti-Dühring).* Translation. New York: International Publishers, 1939.

EPIcenter. *Social Policies in Russia,* no. 1 (25), January–February 1997; and no. 2 (26), March–May 1997.

Eranti, Esa, and George Lee. *Cold Region Structural Engineering.* McGraw-Hill, 1986.

Falkus, M. E., *The Industrialization of Russia, 1700–1914.* Studies in Economic and Social History. London: Macmillan, 1972.

Federov, Yuri. "L'institution militaire, le pouvoir et la société civile en Russie." *Politique Étrangère* (Paris) (December 1996): 777–89.

Ferguson, Niall. *Virtual History: Alternatives and Counterfactuals.* Basic Books, 1999.

Ferris, Wayne. *The Power Capabilities of Nation-States: International Conflict and War.* Lexington, Mass.: Lexington Books, 1973.

Feshbach, Murray. *Russia's Health and Demographic Crises: Policy Implications and Consequences.* Washington: Chemical and Biological Arms Control Institute, 2003.

Fieldhouse, D. K., *Economics and Empire 1830–1914.* Cornell University Press, 1973.

Figes, Orlando. *A People's Tragedy: The Russian Revolution, 1891–1924.* Penguin Books, 1996.

Florida, Richard. "Bohemia and Economic Geography." *Journal of Economic Geography* 2, no. 1 (January 2002): 55–71.

———. *The Rise of the Creative Class.* Basic Books, 2002.

French, Hugh M., and Olav Slaymaker, eds. *Canada's Cold Environments.* McGill-Queen's University Press, 1993.

French, R. Antony. *Plans, Pragmatism and People: The Legacy of Soviet Planning for Today's Cities.* Pitt Series in Russian and East European Studies, no. 26. University of Pittsburgh Press, 1995.

Fuller, William C., Jr. *Civil-Military Conflict in Imperial Russia, 1881–1914.* Princeton University Press, 1985.

———. *Strategy and Power in Russia: 1600–1914.* Free Press, 1992.

Gabaix, Xavier. "Zipf's Law for Cities: An Explanation." *Quarterly Journal of Economics* 114 (August 1999): 739–67.

Gaddy, Clifford G. *The Price of the Past: Russia's Struggle with the Legacy of a Militarized Economy.* Brookings, 1996.

Gaddy, Clifford G., and Barry W. Ickes. "The Cost of the Cold." Unpublished working paper, Pennsylvania State University (May 2001).

———. *Russia's Virtual Economy.* Brookings, 2002.

Gang, Ira, and Robert Stuart. "Mobility Where Mobility Is Illegal: Internal Migration and City Growth in the Soviet Union." *Journal of Population Economics* 12 (1999): 117–34.

Ganz, Hugo. *The Land of Riddles: Russia Today.* New York and London: Harper & Brothers, 1904.

Gaquin, Deidre A., and Katherine A. DeBrandt, *County and City Extra: Special Decennial Edition.* Lanham, Md.: Bernan, 2002.

Gare, Frédéric, ed. *La Russie dans Tous Ses États.* Brussels and Paris: Collection Axes Savoir, 1996.

Garnett, Sherman. "The Impact of the New Borderlands on the Russian Military." Occasional Paper 9 (August 1995). Cambridge, Mass.: American Academy of Arts and Sciences, 1995.

———. "Russian Power in the New Eurasia." *Comparative Strategy* 15 (1996): 31–40.

———. "Russia's Illusory Ambitions." *Foreign Affairs* 76, no. 2 (March/April, 1997): 61–77.

Gellner, Ernest. *Nations and Nationalism.* Cornell University Press, 1983.

Gelman, Harold. "The Soviet Far East Military Build-Up and Soviet Risk-Taking against China." R-2943AF. Santa Monica, Calif.: RAND, 1982.

Gerschaft, Mikhail. "The Economic Grounds for Russian Nationalism." *Prism* 1, no. 22, part 4 (20 October 1995).

———. "The Sour Grapes Syndrome." *Prism* 2, no. 11, part 2 (31 May 1996).

Geyer, Dietrich. *Russian Imperialism: The Interaction of Domestic and Foreign Policy 1860–1914.* Yale University Press, 1987.

Gilbert, Martin. *Russian History Atlas.* Macmillan, 1972.

Glaeser, Edward L. "Demand for Density? The Functions of the City in the 21st Century." *Brookings Review* 18 (Summer 2000): 10–13.

Glaeser, Edward L., Jed Kolko, and Albert Saiz. "Consumer City." Working Paper 7790. Cambridge, Mass.: National Bureau of Economic Research, 2000.

Gochenour, Carolyn. *District Energy Trends, Issues and Opportunities: The Role of the World Bank.* World Bank Technical Paper 493. Washington: World Bank, 2001.

Gold, L. W., and T. H. W. Baker. *Research and Development for Engineering in Cold Regions.* Ottawa: National Research Council of Canada, 1979.

Goldman, Marshall. *Lost Opportunity: Why Economic Reforms in Russia Have Not Worked.* W. W. Norton, 1994.

Goldstein, Judith, and Robert Keohane, eds. *Ideas and Foreign Policy: Beliefs, Institutions and Political Change.* Cornell University Press, 1993.

Gordon, David F. "The Next Wave of HIV/AIDS: Nigeria, Ethiopia, Russia, India, and China." *NIC Intelligence Community Assessment,* ICA 2002-04 D, September 2002.

Gorin, N. "Strana po imeni provintsiya," *Ekspertnyi institut: diskussionnyi material,* no. 14, December 1995.

Gorodetskii, A., and Iu. Pavlenko. "The Reform of Natural Monopolies." *Problems of Economic Transition* 43, no. 12 (April 2001): 50–62.

Graham, Stephen. *Changing Russia.* London: John Lane, 1912.

Grandstaff, Peter. *Interregional Migration in the USSR: Economic Aspects, 1959–1970.* Duke University Press, 1980.

Greenfeld, Liah. *Nationalism: Five Roads to Modernity.* Harvard University Press, 1992.

Griffiths, John F. "Some Problems of Regionality in Applications of Climate Change." In *Proceedings of the Fourteenth International Congress of Biometeorology,* 384–90. Ljubljana, Slovenia, September 1996.

Gulyga, Arseny, ed. *Russkaya ideya i ee tvortsy.* Moscow: Soratnik, 1995.

Gumilev, Lev. *Etnogenez i biosfera Zemli.* Leningrad: Izdatel'stvo Leningradskogo gosudarstvenogo universiteta, 1989.

———. *Geografiya etnosa v istoricheskii period.* Leningrad: Nauka, 1990.

Hajda, Lubomyr, and Mark Beissinger, eds. *The Nationalities Factor in Soviet Politics and Society.* Boulder, San Francisco, and Oxford: Westview Press, 1990.

Hamm, Michael F., ed. *The City in Russian History.* University of Kentucky Press, 1976.

Harcave, Sidney, ed. *The Memoirs of Count Witte.* Armonk, N.Y.: M. E. Sharpe, 1990.

Harris, Chauncy. *Cities of the Soviet Union: Studies in Their Function, Size, Density, and Growth.* Chicago: Rand McNally, 1970.

Harris, James R. "The Growth of the Gulag: Forced Labor in the Urals Region, 1929–31." *Russian Review* 56 (April 1997): 265–80.

Harrison, John. *The Founding of the Russian Empire in Asia and America.* University of Miami Press, 1971.

Hausladen, Gary. "Recent Trends in Siberian Urban Growth." *Soviet Geography* 28, no. 2 (February 1987): 71–89.

———. "Russian Siberia: An Integrative Approach." *Soviet Geography* 30, no. 3 (March 1989): 231–46.

Heleniak, Timothy. "Economic Transition and Demographic Change in Russia, 1989–1995." *Post-Soviet Geography and Economics* 36, no. 7 (September 1995): 446–58.

———. "Internal migration in Russia during the Economic Transition." *Post-Soviet Geography and Economics* 38, no. 2 (February 1997): 81–104.

———. "Migration and Restructuring in Post-Soviet Russia." *Demokratizatsiya* 9, no. 4 (Fall 2001): 531–49.

———. *Migration from the Russian North during the Transition Period.* Social Protection Discussion Paper 9925. Washington: World Bank, 1999.

———. "Out-Migration and Depopulation of the Russian North during the 1990s." *Post-Soviet Geography and Economics* 40, no. 3 (April 1999): 155–205.

Herbert, Deborah, and Ian Burton. "Estimated Costs of Adaptation to Canada's Current Climate and Trends under Climate Change." Unpublished paper. Toronto: Atmospheric Environment Service, 1994.

Hietala, Thomas. *Manifest Destiny: Anxious Aggrandizement in Late Jacksonian America.* Cornell University Press, 1985.

Hill, Fiona. "In Search of Great Russia: Elites, Ideas, Power, the State, and the Pre-Revolutionary Past in the New Russia 1991–1996." Ph.D. dissertation. Harvard University, 1998.

———. *Russia's Tinderbox: Conflict in the North Caucasus and Its Implications for the Future of the Russian Federation.* Cambridge, Mass.: Strengthening Democratic Institutions Project, September 1995.

Hill, Fiona, and Florence Fee. "Fueling the Future: The Prospects for Russian Oil and Gas." *Demokratizatsiya* 10, no. 4 (Fall 2002): 462–87.

Historical Statistics of the United States: Colonial Times to 1970: Part 1. U.S. Census Bureau, 1975.

Hobsbawm, E. J. *Nations and Nationalism since 1780: Program, Myth, Reality.* Cambridge University Press & Canto, 1991.

Hoch, Irving. "Variations in the Quality of Urban Life among Cities and Regions." In *Public Economics and the Quality of Life,* edited by Lowdon Wingo and Alan Evans. Johns Hopkins University Press, 1977.

Hosking, Geoffrey. *Russia: People and Empire, 1552–1917.* Harvard University Press, 1997.

Hughes, James. "Moscow's Bilateral Treaties Add to Confusion." *Transition* (20 September 1996): 39–43.

Hughes, Lindsey. *Russia in the Age of Peter the Great.* Yale University Press, 1998.

Hyde, Matthew. "Putin's Federal Reforms and Their Implications for Presidential Power in Russia." *Europe Asia Studies* 53, no. 5 (July 2001): 719–43.

International Energy Agency. *Energy Policies of the Russian Federation.* Paris: OECD, 1995.

———. *Russia's Energy Efficient Future: A Regional Approach.* OECD Washington Center, 1996.

Ioffe, Gregory. "History and Geography of Forced Migrations in the USSR." *Post-Soviet Geography and Economics* 42, no. 6 (September 2001): 464–68.

Ioffe, Grigory, and Tatyana Nefedova. "Areas of Crisis in Russian Agriculture: A Geographic Perspective." *Post-Soviet Geography and Economics* 41, no. 4 (June 2000): 288–305.

Isakova, Irina. *Regionalization of Security in Russia.* Whitehall Paper Series 53. London: Royal United Services Institute for Defence Studies, 2001.

Isham, Heyward, ed. *Remaking Russia: Voices from Within.* Armonk, N.Y.: M. E. Sharpe, 1995.

Ivanova, Galina. "The 'Camp Economy' of the Postwar Period." *Novaya perspektiva: voprosy istorii ekonomicheskikh i politicheskikh otnosheniy v Rossii* (25), vol. 2.

Ivanova, Galina M. *Labor Camp Socialism: The Gulag in the Soviet Totalitarian System.* Armonk, N.Y.: M. E. Sharpe, 2000.

Jelavich, Barbara. *A Century of Russian Foreign Policy, 1814–1914.* Philadelphia: Lippincott, 1964.

———. *St. Petersburg and Moscow: Tsarist and Soviet Foreign Policy, 1814–1974.* Indiana University Press, 1974.

Jensen, Robert G., T. Shabad, and A. Wright, eds. *Soviet Natural Resources in the World Economy.* University of Chicago Press, 1983.

Jervis, Robert. *Perception and Misperception in International Politics.* Princeton University Press, 1976.

Johnson, Teresa Pelton, and Steven Miller, eds. *Russian Security after the Cold War: Seven Views from Moscow.* CSIA Studies in International Security no. 3. Washington: Brassey's, 1994.

Joll, James. *The Origins of the First World War.* 2d ed. New York: Longman, 1992.

Kabuzan, V. M. "The Settlement of Siberia and the Far East from the Late 18th to the Early 20th Century (1795–1917)." Translated by James R. Gibson in *Soviet Geography* 32, no. 9 (1991): 616–32.

Kahn, Jeff. "The Parade of Sovereignties." *Post-Soviet Affairs* 16, no. 1 (January 2000): 58–89.

Karaganov, Sergei. "The Idea of Russia." *International Affairs* (Moscow), December 1992.

———. *Where Is Russia Going? Foreign and Defense Policies in a New Era.* Peace Research Institute Frankfurt Report no. 34. April 1994.

Karamzin, Nikolai. *Letters of a Russian Traveler, 1789–1790: An Account of a Young Russian Gentleman's Tour through Germany, Switzerland, France, and England.* Columbia University Press, 1957.

Keenan, Edward. "Muscovite Political Folkways." *Russian Review* 45 (1986): 122–25.

Kennan, George. *Siberia and the Exile System.* London: James R. Osgood, McIlvaine & Co., 1891; New York: Praeger, 1970.

Kennan, George F., *The Decline of Bismarck's European Order.* Princeton University Press, 1979.

———. *The Fateful Alliance: France, Russia, and the Coming of the First World War.* Pantheon, 1984.

Kennaway, Alexander. *The Mental and Psychological Inheritance of Contemporary Russia.* Sandhurst, England: Conflict Studies Research Center, 1996.

Kennedy, Paul. *The Rise and Fall of the Great Powers: Economic Change and Military Conflict from 1500 to 2000.* Random House, 1987.

Khakimov, Rafael, ed. "Yevraziystvo: za i protiv." *Panorama-Forum* 8, no. 1 (1997).

Kirkow, Peter. *Russia's Provinces: Authoritarian Transformation versus Local Autonomy.* St. Martin's Press in association with the Centre for Russian and East European Studies, University of Birmingham, 1998.

Kissinger, Henry. *Diplomacy.* Touchstone, 1994.

Klyamkin, Igor. *Narod i politika.* Moscow: Fond Obshchestvennoe Mnenie, 1992.

Klyuchevskiy, Vasiliy. *Kurs russkoy istorii.* Moscow, 1937.

Knorr, Klaus. *Power and Wealth: The Political Economy of International Power.* Basic Books, 1973.

Kobrinskaya, Irina. *Vnutripoliticheskaya situatsiya i prioritety vneshnei politiki Rossii.* Moscow: Rossiiskii Nauchnyi Fond, 1992.

Kochan, Lionel, and Richard Abraham. *The Making of Modern Russia.* 2d ed. Harmondsworth, Middlesex: Penguin Books, 1983.

Koebner, Richard, and Helmut Dan Schmidt. *Imperialism: The Story and Significance of a Political Word, 1840–1960.* Cambridge University Press, 1964.

Kohn, Hans. *Nationalism: Its Meaning and History.* Princeton, N.J.: Van Nostrand, 1965.

Kokoshin, Andrei. *Reflections on Russia's Past, Present, and Future.* Cambridge, Mass.: Strengthening Democratic Institutions Project, June 1997.

Komachi, Kyoji. *Concept-Building in Russian Diplomacy: The Struggle for Identity from "Economization" to "Eurasianization."* Cambridge, Mass.: Center for International Affairs, May 1994.

Kontorovich, Vladimir. "Can Russia Resettle the Far East?" *Postcommunist Economies* 12, no. 3 (2000): 365–84.

———. "Economic Crisis in the Russian Far East: Overdevelopment or Colonial Exploitation?" *Post-Soviet Geography and Economics* 42, no. 6 (2001): 391–415.

Kortunov, Andrei, and Andrei Volodin. *Contemporary Russia: National Interests and Emerging Foreign Policy Perceptions.* Cologne: Bundesinstitut für ostwissenschaftliche und internationale Studien, 1996.

Kortunov, Vadim. *Istina v iskusstve: russkiy mistitsizm v sisteme mirovozzrenii Vostoka i Zapada.* Moscow: Rossiyskiy nauchnyy fond, 1992.

Kosikov, I. G., and L. S. Kosikova. *Severnyy Kavkaz: sotsial'no-ekonomicheskiy spravochnik.* Moscow, 1999.

Kosolapov, Nikolai A. "Rossiya: v chem vse-taki sut' istoricheskogo vybora." *Mirovaya ekonomika i mezhdunarodnaya otnosheniya* 10 (1994).

Kozyrev, Andrei. "Russia: Chance for Survival." *Foreign Affairs,* Spring 1992.

Kramer, Mark "The Early Post-Stalin Succession Struggle and Upheavals in East-Central Europe: Internal-External Linkages in Soviet Policy (Part 1)." *Journal of Cold War Studies* 1, no. 1 (Winter 1999).

———. "The Early Post-Stalin Succession Struggle and Upheavals in East-Central Europe: Internal-External Linkages in Soviet Policy (Part 2)." *Journal of Cold War Studies* 1, no. 2 (Spring 1999).

———. "The Early Post-Stalin Succession Struggle and Upheavals in East-Central Europe: Internal-External Linkages in Soviet Policy (Part 3)." *Journal of Cold War Studies* 1, no. 3 (Fall 1999).

Krasinets, Ye. S. "Vneshnyaya trudovaya migratsiya v Rossiyu." *Migratsiya naseleniya* (supplement to the journal *Trudovaya migratsiya v Rossii*) no. 2 (2001): 79–107.

Krivokhizha, Vasily, ed. *Problemy vneshnei i oboronnoi politiki Rossii: sbornik statei,* no. 3. Moscow: Russian Institute of Strategic Studies, 1995.

———. "Rossiya v novoy strukture mezhdunarodnykh otnosheniy." *Polis,* no. 3 (1995).

Krypton, Constantine. "The Economy of Northern Siberia, 1959–1965." *Russian Review* 19, no. 1 (1960): 47–55.

Kuchins, Andrew, ed. *Russia after the Fall.* Washington: Carnegie Endowment for International Peace, 2002.

Kudryavtsev, Aleksey Osipovich. *Ratsional'noye ispol'zovaniye territorii pri planirovke i zastroike gorodov SSSR.* Moscow: Izdatel'stvo Literatury po Stroitel'stvu, 1971.

Lacis, M. *Agrarnoye perenaselenie i perspektivy bor'by s nim (v svete 5-letnego perspektivnogo plana khozyaystvennogo stroitel'stva).* Moscow: Gosudarstvennoye izdatel'stvo, 1929.

Landes, David. *The Wealth and Poverty of Nations: Why Some Are So Rich and Some So Poor.* W. W. Norton, 1998.

Langer, William. *The Diplomacy of Imperialism, 1890–1902.* Alfred A. Knopf, 1956.

Langlais, Richard. *Reformulating Security: A Case Study from Artic Canada.* Göteborg University, 1995.

Lappo, G. M., ed. *Goroda Rossii: entsiklopediya.* Moscow: Bol'shaya Rossiyskaya Entsiklopediya, 1994.

Laqueur, Walter. *Black Hundred: The Rise of the Extreme Right in Russia.* HarperCollins, 1993.

Leasure, J. William, and Robert A. Lewis. "Internal Migration in Russia in the Late Nineteenth Century." *Slavic Review* 27, no. 3 (September 1968): 375–94.

Lebed, Alexander. *Za derzhavu obidno.* Moscow: Moskovskaya Pravda, 1995.

Lederer, Ivo. *Russian Foreign Policy: Essays in Historical Perspective.* Yale University Press, 1962.

LeDonne, John P. *The Russian Empire and the World.* Oxford University Press, 1997.

Lee, Lisa. *Housing Maintenance and Management in Russia during the Reforms.* Washington: Urban Institute, 1996.

Lewis, Robert, Richard Rowland, and Ralph Clem. *Nationality and Population Change in Russia and USSR: An Evaluation of Census Data, 1897–1970.* Praeger, 1976.

Lieven, Dominic. *The Aristocracy in Europe, 1815–1914.* Columbia University Press, 1992.

———. *Empire: The Russian Empire and Its Rivals.* London: John Murray, 2000.

———. *Nicholas II: Twilight of the Empire.* St. Martin's Press, 1993.

———. *Russia and the Origins of the First World War.* St. Martin's Press, 1983.

———. *Russia's Rulers under the Old Regime.* Yale University Press, 1989.

Linz, Susan J. *The Impact of World War II on the Soviet Union.* Totowa, N.J.: Rowman & Allanheld, 1985.

Lipets, Yu. G., ed. *Poliusa i tsentry rosta v regionalnom razvitii.* Moscow: IGRAN, 1998.

Lockwood, David. *The Destruction of the Soviet Union: A Study in Globalization.* St. Martin's Press, 2000.

Lomborg, Bjorn. *The Skeptical Environmentalist: Measuring the Real State of the World.* Cambridge University Press, 2001.

Lukin, Alexander. "Russia's Image of China and Russian-Chinese Relations." Brookings Center for Northeast Asian Policy Studies, 2001.

Lydolph, Paul E. *Climates of the Soviet Union.* New York: Elsevier Scientific, 1977.

Lynch, Allen C. "Roots of Russia's Economic Dilemmas: Liberal Economics and Illiberal Geography." *Europe-Asia Studies* 54, no. 1 (2002): 31–49.

Lynn, Nicholas, and Alexei Novikov. "Refederalizing Russia: Debates on the Idea of Federalism in Russia." *Publius* 27, no. 2 (Spring 1997): 187–203.

MacKenzie, David, and Michael Curran. *A History of Russia and the Soviet Union.* Revised ed. Homewood, Ill.: Dorsey Press, 1982.

Mackinder, Halford J. "The Geographical Pivot of History." *Geographical Journal* 23, no. 4 (April 1904): 421–44.

Makarychev, Andrei. *The Region and the World: The Case of Nizhnii Novgorod.* Working Paper 6. Zurich: Center for Security Studies and Conflict Research, May 2001.

Malov, V. Yu., and B. V. Melent'ev. "Otsenka posledstviy otkaza ot federal'noy podderzhki ekonomiki Sibiri." *Eko* 8, no. 338 (2002): 89–99.

Malthus, Thomas. *An Essay on the Principle of Population, as It Affects the Future Improvement of Society with Remarks on the Speculations of Mr. Godwin,*

M. Condorcet, and Other Writers, June 7, 1798. London: Printed for J. Johnson, in St. Paul's Church Yard, 1798.

Manilov, Valery. *The National Security of Russia.* Cambridge, Mass.: Strengthening Democratic Institutions Project, June 1997.

Martov, L., ed. *Obshchestvennoye dvizheniye v Rossii v nachale XXogo veka,* I-IV. St. Petersburg, 1912.

Maslin, M. A. *Russkaya ideya.* Moscow: Respublika, 1992.

Massey, Stephen. "Russia's Maternal and Child Health Crisis: Socio-Economic Implications and the Path Forward." *EastWest Institute Policy Brief* 1, no. 9 (December 2002).

Matthews, Melvyn. *The Passport Society: Controlling Movement in Russia and the USSR.* Boulder, Colo.: Westview Press, 1993.

May, Ernest. *American Imperialism: A Speculative Essay.* New York: Atheneum, 1968.

McDaniel, Tim. *The Agony of the Russian Idea.* Princeton University Press, 1996.

McDonald, David. *United Government and Foreign Policy in Russia, 1900–1914.* Harvard University Press, 1992.

McNeil, Robert, ed. *Russia in Transition 1905–1914: Evolution or Revolution?* Huntington, N.Y.: Robert E. Krieger Publishing Company, 1976.

McNeill, William. *The Pursuit of Power: Technology, Armed Force, and Society since AD 1000.* Oxford: Basil Blackwell, 1983.

Medvedev, S., and P. Podlesnyy, eds. *Geopoliticheskiye peremeny v Yevrope, politika zapada i al'ternativy dlya Rossii.* Moscow: Institute of Europe Reports no. 19. Moscow, 1995.

Mellor, Roy. *The Soviet Union and Its Geographic Problems.* London: Macmillan, 1982.

Mendras, Marie, "La Russie dans les têtes," *Commentaire* 18, no. 71 (Autumn 1995): 501–10.

Merk, Frederick. *Manifest Destiny and Mission in American History: A Reinterpretation.* Knopf, 1963.

Mikhailova, Tatiana. "Where Russians Should Live: A Counterfactual Alternative to Soviet Location Policy." Unpublished paper. Pennsylvania State University (3 December 2002).

Miller, Steven. ed. *Military Strategy and the Origins of the First World War: An International Security Reader.* Princeton University Press, 1985.

Mil'ner, G. "Problems of Ensuring the Supply of Labour Resources for Siberia and the Far Eastern Regions." *Problems of Economics* 22, no. 4 (1979).

Milov, L. V. *Agrarnye tekhnologii v Rossii IX-XX vv.: materialy XXV sessii Simpoziuma po agrarnoy istorii Vostochnoy Yevropy.* Arzamas: Arzamasskiy gosudarstvennyy pedagogicheskiy institut, 1999.

———. *Mentalitet i agrarnoye razvitiye Rossii: materialy mezhdunarodnoy konferentsii, Moskva, 14-15 iyunya 1994 g.* Moscow: Rosspen, 1996.

———. *Osobennosti rossiyskogo zemledeliya i problemy rasseleniya IX-XX vv. XXVI sessiya Simpoziuma po agrarnoy istorii Vostochnoy Yevropy: tezisy dokladov i soob-*

shcheniy, Tambov, 15–18 sentyabrya 1998 g. Moscow: Rossiyskaya akademiya nauk, 1998.

———. *Velikorusskiy pakhar' i osobennosti rossiyskogo istoricheskogo protsessa.* Moscow: Rossiyskaya politicheskaya entsiklopediya (ROSSPEN), 1998.

———. *Zazhitochnoye krest'yanstvo Rossii v istoricheskoy retrospective: zemlevladeniye, zemlepol'zovaniye, proizvodstvo, mentalitet: XXVII sessiya Simpoziuma po agrarnoy istorii Vostochnoy Yevropy: tezisy dokladov i soobshcheniy Vologda, 12–16 sentyabrya 2000 g.* Moscow: Institut rossiyskoy istorii RAN, 2000.

Milov, L. V., and V. A. Kuchkin. *Rossiya v sredniye veka i novoye vremya: sbornik statey k 70-letiyu chl.-korr. RAN L. V. Milova.* Moscow: Rosspen, 1999.

Milov, L. V. "Prirodno-klimaticheskiy faktor osobennosti rossiyskogo istoricheskogo protsessa." *Voprosy istorii* no. 4/5 (1992): 37–56.

———. "Yesli govorit ser'yezno o chastnoy sobstvennosti na zemlyu . . . Rossiya. Klimat. Zemel'nyye otnosheniya i natsional'nyy kharakter." *Svobodnaya mysl',* no. 2 (1993): 77–88.

Milyukov, Pavel. *Political Memoirs* 1905–1917. University of Michigan Press, 1967.

———. *Russia and Its Crisis.* New York: Collier, 1962.

———. *Russia Today and Tomorrow.* New York: Macmillan, 1922.

Mitchneck, Beth. "Geographical and Economic Determinants of Interregional Migration." *Soviet Geography* 32, no. 3 (March 1991): 168–89.

Mitrofanov, Alexei. *Novaya ideya rossiiskoi geopolitiki: taktika i strategiya na sovremmenom etape.* Moscow, 1997.

Moiseyenko, Valentina, Viktor Perevedentsev, and Natal'ya Voronina. *Moskovskiy region: migratsiya i migratsionnaya politika.* Working Paper 3. Moscow: Carnegie Moscow Center, 1999.

Mommsen, Wolfgang. *Theories of Imperialism.* Random House, 1980.

Moore, Thomas Gale. *Climate of Fear: Why We Shouldn't Worry about Global Warming.* Washington: Cato Institute, 1998.

———. "Health and Amenity Effects of Global Warming." *Economic Inquiry* 36 (July 1998): 471–88.

Morehouse, Thomas. *Alaskan Resources Development.* Boulder, Colo.: Westview Press, 1984.

Moskoff, William. *The Bread of Affliction: The Food Sully in the USSR during WWII.* Cambridge University Press, 1990.

Mote, Victor L. *Siberia: Worlds Apart.* Boulder, Colo.: Westview Press, 1998.

Moul, William. "Measuring the 'Balances of Power': A Look at Some Numbers." *Review of International Studies* 15, no. 2 (April 1989): 101–21.

Narodnoye khozyaystvo SSSR, 1922–1982. Moscow: Goskomstat, 1982.

Neumann, Iver. *Russia and the Idea of Europe: A Study in Identity and International Relations.* The New International Relations Series. New York: Routledge, 1996.

Novikova, L. I., and I. N. Sizemskaya, eds. *Rossiya mezhdu Yevropoy i Aziyey: yevraziyskiy soblazn'*. Moscow: Nauka, 1993.

Odom, William, and Robert Dujarric. *Commonwealth or Empire? Russia, Central Asia, and the Transcaucasus*. Indianapolis: Hudson Institute, 1995.

Ogleby, C. L. "Terra Nullius, the High Court, and Surveyors." *Australian Surveyor* 38, no. 3 (September 1993): 171–89.

OMRI. "Post-Communism: A Search for Metaphor," *Transition* (Prague) 2, no. 6 (22 March 1996).

Orr, Michael. *The Current State of the Russian Armed Forces*. Sandhurst, England: Conflict Studies Research Center, November 1996.

Orttung, Robert, Danielle Lussier, and Anna Paretskaya. *Republics and Regions of the Russian Federation: A Guide to Politics, Policies, and Leaders*. Armonk, N.Y.: M. E. Sharpe, 2000.

Panarin, Aleksandr. *Rossiya v tsivilizatsionnom protsesse: mezdhu atlantizmom i yevraziystvom*. Moscow: RAN, 1995.

———. "Geopoliticheskiy pessimizm protiv tsivilizovannogo optimizma." *Znamya*, no. 6, 1994.

Parshev, Andrey P. *Pochemu Rossiya ne Amerika: kniga dlya tekh, kto ostayetsya zdes'*. Moscow: Krymskiy Most-9D, 2000.

Parrott, Bruce, ed. *State Building and Military Power in Russia and the New States of Eurasia*. Vol. 5, *The International Politics of Eurasia*. New York and London: M. E. Sharpe, 1995.

Parshev, Andrey P. *Pochemu Rossiya ne Amerika: kniga dlya tekh, kto ostayetsya zdes'*. Moscow: Krymskiy Most-9D, Forum, 2000.

Peterson, D. J. *Troubled Lands: The Legacy of Soviet Environmental Destruction*. Boulder, Colo.: Westview Press, 1993.

Peterson, D. J., and Eric K. Bielke. "Russia's Industrial Infrastructure: A Risk Assessment." *Post-Soviet Geography and Economics* 43, no. 1 (January–February 2002): 13–25.

Petro, Nikolai. *The Rebirth of Russian Democracy: An Interpretation of Political Culture*. Harvard University Press, 1995.

Petrov, N. V. "Settlement in Large Cities of the USSR." *Soviet Geography* 28, no. 3 (March 1987): 135–57.

Pinsky, Donne. *Industrial Development of Siberia and the Soviet Far East*. Santa Monica, Calif : RAND, 1984.

Pipes, Richard. *The Formation of the Soviet Union: Communism and Nationalism, 1917–1923*. Revised ed. Harvard University Press, 1997.

———, ed. *P. B Struve Collected Works in Fifteen Volumes*. Ann Arbor, Mich.: University Microfilms, 1970.

———. *Russia under the Bolshevik Regime*. Alfred A. Knopf, 1993.

———. *Struve: Liberal on the Left, 1870–1905*. Harvard University Press, 1970.

———. *Struve: Liberal on the Right, 1905–1944*. Harvard University Press, 1980.

———. *Russia under the Old Regime.* Charles Scribner's Sons, 1974.

———. *The Russian Revolution.* Alfred Knopf, 1990.

Pleshakov, Konstantin. *The Tsar's Last Armada: The Epic Journey to the Battle of Tsushima.* Basic Books, 2002.

Porter, Michael E., "The Competitive Advantage of Nations." *Harvard Business Review* (March-April 1990): 73–93.

Posen, Barry. "Nationalism, the Mass Army, and Military Power." *International Security* 18, no. 2 (1992).

Pressman, Norman, and Xenia Zepic. *Planning in Cold Climates: A Critical Overview of Canadian Settlement Patterns and Policies.* Winnipeg, Canada: Institute of Urban Studies, 1986.

Prociuk, S. G. "The Manpower Problem in Siberia." *Soviet Studies* 19, no. 2 (1967): 190–210.

Putnam, Robert. *Bowling Alone.* Simon & Schuster, 2000.

———. *Making Democracy Work: Civic Traditions in Modern Italy.* Princeton University Press, 1993.

Ra'anan, Uri, and Kate Martin, eds. *Russia: A Return to Empire?* St. Martin's Press, 1995.

Raeff, Marc, ed. *Catherine the Great: A Profile.* Hill and Wang, 1972.

———. *The Decembrist Movement.* Englewood Cliffs, N.J.: Prentice-Hall, 1966.

———. *Siberia and the Reforms of 1822.* University of Washington Press, 1956.

Ragsdale, Hugh. *Imperial Russian Foreign Policy.* Cambridge University Press, 1993.

Rashin, G. *Naseleniye Rossii za 100 Let (1811–1913 gg.). Statisticheskiye ocherki.* Moscow: Gosstatizdat, 1956.

RAU Corporation. "Kontseptsiya natsional'noi bezopasnosti Rossiiskoi Federatsii v 1996–2000 godakh," *Obozrevatel'* (Moscow), 1995.

Raviot, Jean-Robert. "Fédéralisme et Gouvernement Régional en Russie," *Politique Étrangère* (Paris) (December 1996): 803–12.

Redmond-Howard, L. G., ed. *The Nations of the War: Russia and the Russian People.* London: Simpkin, Marshall, Hamilton, Kent & Co., 1914.

Regulations and Standards for the Planning and Development of Towns. Boston Spa, Yorks.: National Lending Library for Science and Technology, 1962.

Reid, Anna. *The Shaman's Coat: A Native History of Siberia.* New York: Walker, 2002.

Remnick, David. *Resurrection: The Struggle for a New Russia.* Random House, 1997.

Reynolds, Henry. *The Law of the Land.* Ringwood, Victoria: Penguin Books, 1987.

Riasanovsky, Nicholas. *A History of Russia.* 3d ed. Oxford University Press 1977.

———. *Nicholas I and Official Nationality.* University of California Press, 1959.

Robinson, Georid Tanquary. *Rural Russia under the Old Regime: A History of the Landlord-Peasant World and a Prologue to the Peasant Revolution of 1917.* Macmillan, 1949.

Rosen, Roman. *Evropeyskaya politika Rossii: doveritel'nyy memorandum sostavlennyy letom 1912 goda.* Petrograd: A. Benke, 1917.

———. *Forty Years of Diplomacy*, vol. 2. Alfred A. Knopf, 1922.

Rossiyskaya diplomatiya v portretakh. Moscow: Mezhdunarodnye otnosheniya, 1992.

Rossiyskiy statisticheskiy yezhegodnik 2001. Moscow: Goskomstat, 2001.

Rothgeb, John M., Jr. *Defining Power: Influence and Force in the Contemporary International System.* St. Martin's Press, 1993.

Rousselet, Kathy. "Les Modes d'Adaptation de la Société Russe." *Politique Étrangère* (Paris) (December 1996): 823–33.

Rowland, Richard. *Regional Population Trends in the Former USSR, 1939–51, and the Impact of World War II.* University of Pittsburgh Press, 1997.

———. "Russia's Disappearing Towns: New Evidence of Urban Decline, 1979–1994." *Post-Soviet Geography and Economics* 37, no. 2 (1996): 63–87.

Rozman, Gilbert. "A New Sino-Russian-America Triangle?" *Orbis* 44, no. 4 (Fall 2000): 541–56.

Ruble, Blair, Jodi Koehn, and Nancy Popson, eds. *Fragmented Space in the Russian Federation.* Johns Hopkins University Press, 2001.

Rumer, Boris. *Current Problems in the Industrialization of Siberia.* Russian Research Council at Harvard University, 1982.

———. *Investment and Reindustrialization in the Soviet Economy.* Boulder, Colo.: Westview Press, 1984.

Rusk, David. *Cities without Suburbs.* Washington: Woodrow Wilson Center Press, 1993.

Russian Independent Institute of Social and Nationalities Problems. *Mass Consciousness of the Russians during the Period of Social Transformation: Reality versus Myths.* Moscow, January 1996.

Russian Socio-Political Center. "Natsional'naya doktrina Rossii: doklad kruglogo stola." Moscow, 1995.

Rutskoi, Alexander. *Obreteniye very.* Moscow, 1995.

Ryabushinsky, V. P., ed. *Velikaya Rossiya: sbornik statey po voennym i obshchestvennym voprosam*, vol. 1, 2. Moscow, 1910, 1911.

Rybczynski, Witold. "Downsizing Cities: To Make Cities Work Better, Make Them Smaller." *Atlantic Monthly* 276, no. 4 (October 1995): 36–47.

Sarolea, Charles. *Great Russia: Her Achievement and Promise.* Alfred Knopf, 1916.

Sazonov, Sergei. *Fateful Years, 1909–1916.* New York: Frederick A. Stokes, 1928.

Schmidt, Jeremy. "Russia's Frozen Inferno." *National Geographic* 200, no. 2 (August 2001): 56–73.

Sestanovich, Stephen. "Geotherapy: Russia's Neuroses, and Ours." *National Interest* 45 (Fall 1996): 3–13.

Sherr, James. *Russian Great Power Ideology: Sources and Implications.* Sandhurst, England: Conflict Studies Research Center, July 1996.

Shlapentokh, Vladimir. *How Russians See Themselves Now: In the Aftermath of the Defeat in Chechnya.* Special Adviser for Central and Eastern European Affairs Briefs. Brussels: NATO HQ, 4 December 1996.

————. *Russia—Privatization and Illegalization of Social and Political Life.* Sandhurst, England: Conflict Studies Research Center, August 1995.

Shoshin, A. A. "Geographical Aspects of Public Health." *Soviet Geography,* 1964.

Simmons, Ernest J., ed. *Continuity and Change in Russian and Soviet Thought.* Harvard University Press, 1955.

Simsarian, James. "The Acquisition of Legal Title to Terra Nullius." *Political Science Quarterly* 53, no. 1 (March 1938): 111–28.

Skrine, Francis Henry. *The Expansion of Russia.* Cambridge University Press, 1915.

Slezkine, Yuri. *Arctic Mirrors: Russia and the Small Peoples of the North.* Cornell University Press, 1994.

Smirnov, M. B., ed. *Sistema ispravitel'no-trudovykh lagerey v SSSR: spravochnik.* Moscow: Zveniya, 1998.

Smith, M. A. *Russia's State Tradition.* Sandhurst, England: Conflict Studies Research Center, June 1995.

Snyder, Jack. *Myths of Empire: Domestic Politics and International Ambition.* Cornell University Press, 1991.

Sobolev, Yu. "Narodnokhozyaystvennaya programma osvoyeniya zony BAM." *Planovoye khozyaystvo* 7 (1978): 77–84.

Solnick, Steven. "Gubernatorial Elections in Russia, 1996–1997." *Post-Soviet Affairs* 14, no. 1 (1998): 48–80.

Solomon, Richard, and Masataka Kosaka, eds. *The Soviet Far East Build-Up: Nuclear Dilemmas and Asian Security.* Dover, Mass.: Auburn House Publishers, 1986.

Soloviev, Vladimir. *Sochineniya v dvukh tomakh.* Moscow: Izdatel'stvo Mysl', 1988.

Solzhenitsyn, Alexander. "Repentance and Self-Limitation." In *From under the Rubble.* Translated by A. M. Brock and others. Bantam Books, 1976.

Sorokin, Konstantin. *Geopolitika sovremennosti i geostrategiya Rossii.* Moscow: Rosspen, 1996.

Stalin, I. V., "Marksizm i natsional'nyy vopros." In I. V. Stalin, *Sochineniya.* Vol. 2, *1907–1913,* 290–367. Moscow: Izdatel'stvo politicheskoy literatury, 1953.

Starr, Frederick, ed. *The Legacy of History in Russia and the New States of Eurasia.* Vol. 1 of *The International Politics of Eurasia.* Armonk, N.Y.: M. E. Sharpe, 1994.

Statistical Abstract of the United States: 2002. U. S. Census Bureau, 2001.

Stoll, Richard J., and Michael D. Ward, eds. *Power in World Politics.* Boulder, Colo.: Lynne Rienner, 1989.

Stolypin, Petr. "Rech' Predsedatelya Soveta Ministrov P. A. Stolypina, proisnesennaya v Gos. Dume 16 noyabrya." *Okrainy Rossii,* no. 47 (24 November 1907).

Stoner-Weiss, Kathryn. "Central Weakness and Provincial Autonomy: Observations on the Devolution Process in Russia." *Post-Soviet Affairs* 15, no. 1 (1999): 87–106.

Storper, Michael, and Richard Walker. *Capitalist Imperative: Territory, Technology and Industrial Growth.* New York: Basil Blackwell, 1989.

Sukhodolov, A. P. *Sibir' v nachale XX veka: territoriya, granitsy, goroda, transportniye magistrali, sel'skoe khozyaystvo.* Irkutsk: Irkutskaya ekonomicheskaya akademiya, 1996.

Sumner, B. H., *Peter the Great and the Emergence of Russia*. New York: Collier Books, 1962.

Swearingen, Roger. *Siberia and Soviet Far East: Strategic Dimensions in Multinational Perspective*. Hoover Institution Press, Stanford University, 1987.

Szporluk, Roman. *Communism and Nationalism: Karl Marx versus Friedrich List.* Oxford University Press, 1988.

———. "Dilemmas of Russian Nationalism." *Problems of Communism* (July–August 1989): 15–35.

———, ed. *National Identity and Ethnicity in Russia and the New States of Eurasia.* Vol. 2 of *The International Politics of Eurasia*. Armonk, N.Y.: M. E. Sharpe, 1994.

Thomas, Clive S. *Alaska Public Policy Issues: Background and Perspectives*. Juneau: Denali Press, 1999.

Thornton, Judith. "Institutional and Structural Change in Pacific Russia." *Comparative Economic Studies* 34, no. 4 (Winter 2001): 1–8.

Tishkov, Valery. *Ethnicity, Nationalism and Conflict in and after the Soviet Union: The Mind Aflame*. London, Thousand Oaks, and New Delhi: International Peace Research Institute, Oslo, and United Nations Research Institute for Social Development, 1997.

———. *Kontseptual'naya evolyutsiya natsional'noy politiki v Rossii*. Moscow: RAN Institut Etnologii i Antropologii, 1996.

———. *Nationalities and Conflicting Ethnicity in Post-Communist Russia*. Ethnic Conflict Management in the Former Soviet Union Working Paper Series. Cambridge, Mass.: Conflict Management Group, April 1993.

———. "Natsiya i natsionalizm." *Svobodnaya mysl'*, no. 3 (1996).

———. "What Is Russia? Prospects for Nation-Building." *Security Dialogue* 26, no. 1 (March 1995).

Tocqueville, Alexis de. *Democracy in America*. Translated by George Lawrence and edited by J. P. Mayer. New York: Perennial Classics, 2000.

Treadgold, Donald. *The Great Siberian Migration: Government and Peasant in Resettlement from Emancipation to the First World War*. Princeton University Press, 1957.

Triesman, Daniel. *After the Deluge: Regional Crises and Political Consolidation in Russia*. University of Michigan Press, 2000.

Troitskiy, Yevgeniy, ed. *Russkaya ideya i sovremennost'*. Moscow, 1992.

———. *Russkaya natsiya i obnovlenie obshchestva*. Moscow, 1990.

———. *Vozrozhdenie russkoy idei: sotsial'no-filosofskiye ocherki*. Moscow, 1991.

Trubetskoy, Grigoriy. "Nekotoryye itogi russkoy vneshney politiki." In *Velikaya Rossiya: sbornik statey po voennym i obshchestvennym voprosam*. Vol. 2, edited by V. P. Ryabushinskiy. Moscow, 1911.

———. "Rossiya kak velikaya derzhava." In *Velikaya Rossiya: sbornik statey po voennym i obshchestvennym voprosam*. Vol. 1, edited by V. P. Ryabushinskiy. Moscow, 1910.

Tsipko, Alexander. "A New Russian Identity or Old Russia's Reintegration?" *Security Dialogue* 25, no.4 (December 1994): 443–55.

Tyutchev, Fedor. *Pol'noye sobraniye stikotvoreniy.* Leningrad: Sovetskiy pisatel', 1987.

United States Department of Defense. *Soviet Military Power: Prospects for Change, 1989.* 1989.

Ure, John. *The Cossacks.* London: Constable, 1999.

Vance, James E., Jr. *The Merchant's World. The Geography of Wholesaling.* Prentice-Hall, 1970.

Venturi, Franco. *Roots of Revolution: A History of the Populist and Socialist Movements in Nineteenth Century Russia.* New York: Grosset & Dunlap, The Universal Library, 1966.

Vitkovskaya, Galina, and Sergey Panarin, eds. *Migratsiya i bezopasnost' v Rossii.* Moscow: Interdialekt, 2000.

von Schierbrand, Wolf. *Russia: Her Strength and Weakness: A Study of the Present Conditions of the Russian Empire, with an Analysis of its Resources and a Forecast of its Future.* New York and London: G. P. Putnam's Sons, The Knickerbocker Press, 1904.

Walicki, Andrzej. *A History of Russian Thought from the Enlightenment to Marxism.* Stanford University Press, 1979.

———. *The Slavophile Controversy: History of a Conservative Utopia in Nineteenth Century Russian Thought.* Oxford University Press, 1975.

Wegren, Stephen, and A. Cooper Drury. "Patterns of Internal Migration during the Russian Transition." *Journal of Communist Studies and Transition Politics* 17, no. 4 (December 2001): 15–42.

Weinberg, Robert. *Stalin's Forgotten Zion. Birobidzhan and the Making of a Jewish Homeland: An Illustrated History, 1928–1996.* University of California Press, 1998.

White, Langdon, and George Primmer. "The Iron and Steel Industry of Duluth: A Study in Locational Maladjustment." *Geographical Review* 27, no. 1 (1937): 82–91.

White, Stephen, Richard Rose, and Ian McAllister. *How Russia Votes.* Chatham, N.J.: Chatham House Publishers, 1997.

Whiting, Allen. *Siberian Development and East Asia: Threat or Promise?* Stanford University Press, 1981.

Wieczynski, Joseph L., ed. *The Modern Encyclopedia of Russian and Soviet History.* Academic International Press, 1977.

Wingo, Lowdon, and Alan Evans, eds. *Public Economics and the Quality of Life.* Johns Hopkins University Press, 1977.

Wohlforth, William. "The Perception of Power: Russia in the Pre-1914 Balance." *World Politics* (April 1987): 353–81.

Wood, Junius B. "Far Eastern Republic of Siberia." *National Geographic* 41, no. 6 (June 1922): 565–92.

Woodruff, William. *The Struggle for World Power, 1500–1980.* St. Martin's Press, 1981.

World Bank. *World Development Report 1996.* Oxford University Press, 1996.

Wyckoff, William, and Gary Hausladen. "Settling the Russian Frontier: With Comparisons to North America." *Soviet Geography* 30, no. 3 (1989): 179–246.

Yadrintsev, N. M., *Sibir' kak koloniya*. 1892. Reprint, Tyumen': Yu. Mandriki, 2000.

Yavlinsky, Grigory. *Reforms from Below: Russia's Future*. Moscow: EPIcenter, Nika Print, 1994.

Yeltsin, Boris. *Against the Grain*. Summit Books, 1990.

———. *The Struggle for Russia*. Random House, Times Books, 1994.

Yuzhakov, S. N. "Politika: dvukhsotletiye rossiyskoy velikoderzhavnosti." *Russkoye bogatstvo*, no. 6, June 1909.

Zamaleyev, A. F., ed. *Rossiya glazami russkogo: Chaadayev, Leont'yev, Solov'yov*. Sankt-Peterburg: Nauka, 1991.

Zaslavskaya, T. I., and L. A. Arutyunyan, eds. *Kuda idet Rossiya? Al'ternativy obshchestvennogo razvitiya*. Moscow: Interpraks, 1994; Moscow: Aspekt Press, 1995.

Zlatopol'skiy, D. L. *Gosudarstvennoye ustroystvo SSSR*. Moscow: Izd. Yuridicheskoy literatury, 1960.

Zufelt, John. *Cold Regions Engineering: Putting Research into Practice*. Reston, Va.: American Society of Civil Engineers, 1999.

Zyuganov, Gennady. *Derzhava*. Moscow: Informpechat, 1994.

———. *Report to Congress of the Communist Party of the Russian Federation*, Official Transcript, 22 April 1997.

Index

Abele, Gunars, 41–44
Abramovich, Roman, 172, 261n14
Adygeya, 121
Aganbegyan, Abel, 94
Agriculture: in the North Caucasus region, 121, 122; population growth and, 62; serfs and, 243n4; in the Soviet Union, 87; in tsarist Russia, 61–62, 63–64, 67, 104–05, 235n5. *See also* Serfs
Alaska, 27; cold, 227, 234n11; cost of living, 126, 249n32; population and labor, 206; sold by Russia to the U.S., 60n
Alaska Permanent Fund Corporation, 270n27
Alexander I, 76
Alexseev, Mikhail, 210
ALROSA (diamond monopoly), 190
Amu-Darya River, 173
Amur oblast, 167, 209
Amur River, 58, 79, 80, 81, 87, 171, 207
Anadyr, 126
Anchorage, 126, 229, 249n32
Applebaum, Anne, 84, 130b–31b, 139
Arkhangel'sk, 105
Armenia, 59, 122, 153

Australia: application of *terra nullius*, 64–65, 76, 236n18; population and population distribution, 5, 14–15, 16
Austria-Hungary, 8, 63
Axtell, Robert, 233n25
Azerbaijan, 59, 122, 153

Baku, 68
Baltic Sea, 59
Baltic states, 60
BAM. *See* Baykal-Amur railroad
Bamlag. *See* Baykal-Amur Corrective Labor Camp
Barents Euro-Arctic Council (BEAC), 250n35
Bashkortostan, 111, 112
Bassin, Mark, 72–73
Baykal-Amur Corrective Labor Camp (Bamlag), 92
Baykal-Amur railroad (BAM), 84, 92, 170
BEAC. *See* Barents Euro-Arctic Council
Belgium, 63, 64
Billington, James, 171
Birobidzhan (Jewish Autonomous Oblast), 81, 82, 87, 99
Bishkek, 179–80
Black Sea, 59, 69, 122

293

35, 40; in U.S., 227, 229. *See also* Temperature

Coal and coal mining, 96, 131b, 167, 195, 258n61

Cold Regions Research and Engineering Laboratory, 41

Colton, Timothy, 151–52

Communist Party of the Soviet Union (CPSU), 107–08, 110, 116, 151

Conquest, Robert, 84

Cossacks, 58–59, 73, 75, 253n1

Cost of the Cold Project, 35, 217, 225

Council on Foreign and Defense Policy (CFDP), 73–74, 180, 239n3

CPSU. *See* Communist Party of the Soviet Union

Creative class, 13

Crimean War, 9

CSED. *See* Center on Social and Economic Dynamics

Dagestan, 121, 122

Dal'stroy project, 84, 86, 130b

Dallin, David, 86

Davis, Donald, 158

Decembrists and Decembrist Rebellion, 76–77

Democracy and democratization, 102, 107, 111, 115, 116

Department of Transportation, 46–47

Detroit, 17, 54, 138, 162

Diamond, Jared, 15

Dienes, Leslie, 197–98

Dnepr River, 67

Dnepropetrovsk (Yekaterinslav), 68

Donbass coalfields, 96

Don River, 67

Dotsenko, Konstantin, 124

Drachevskiy, Leonid, 173–74, 185, 201

Dugin, Alexander, 170

Duluth, 53–55, 227

EBRD. *See* European Bank for Reconstruction and Development

Economic issues: capitalism and socialism, 90b; cities and metropolitan areas, 22–24, 154–55, 157; climate and cold, 35–36, 234n15; competition, 116; connectedness, 23–24; cost-of-life calculations, 47; disamenities of agglomeration, 15–16; economic efficiency, 3; economic size, 4–5, 10–11, 154–55; Engels dictum, 88–89; global economy, 205; history of economic development, 11; institutions of, 24; labor issues, 102, 130, 143, 145, 177, 187; locational maladjustment, 54; market economy, 24, 35, 212; natural resources, 212–13, 232n14; population size and distribution, 14–17, 19, 102; positive externalities of agglomeration, 15; productivity and production, 5, 15, 16, 41, 41–44, 54, 63n; technology, 11, 15; territorial size, 10–12, 15; trade, 11, 24, 28n; value creation, 5; wages, 45. *See also* Cold; Industrialization

Economic issues, Russia: cities and metropolitan areas, 23, 154–57, 164, 198, 268n8; communication and technology, 136–37; competition, 31; connectedness, 5, 117, 140, 202; costs of food and fuel, 125–26; development of and transition to market economy, 24, 25, 102, 111, 119, 138–39, 147, 194, 196–98, 201–02, 208, 211; employment and jobs, 102, 145, 255n23; energy and power generation, 167–68, 207–08, 256n49; Engels dictum, 88–91, 100, 173, 175, 211; enterprise profitability, 254n17; infrastructure, 132–34; interregional economic associations, 114; investment in Russia, 30–31, 147, 151t, 204, 208, 255n18; labor and labor costs, 30, 175–82, 185, 201; local governments, 111; maintenance of the army, 9; mobility and migration, 143–46, 154, 176–82, 200–01; natural resources, 172; North Caucasus region, 123; population size and distribution, 16–17, 53, 101–02, 113, 121, 140, 154, 187, 197, 199–200; productivity and

302INDEX

ture, 33, 34t, 37, 46–47, 53; colonization and, 76–77; communication and technology, 136b, 137; cost
of food, 126; economic issues,
12–13, 16, 23, 154–55; in global
affairs, 8; health care and medical
issues, 47; history and background,
12, 102; immigration to, 122;
mobility and migration, 248n8;
national integration, 12–14; natural
resources, 260n10; population size
and distribution, 5, 15, 16, 137–38,
156–57, 158b–159b; relocation programs, 202; subsidies, 136b, 201–02
Urals and Ural Mountains: cities and
urbanization, 154, 161, 163; climate
and cold, 129; development of, 198,
206; economic issues, 164; history
and background, 75, 78; labor issues,
83; mobility and migration, 74, 77;
USSR and, 87, 108
Urals Metallurgical Trust, 83
Ussuri River, 207
Ust'-Kut, 99, 192b
Ust'-Nera, 144
Uzbekistan, 150, 173, 182b

Vancouver, 207
Virgin Lands campaign, 87–88
Vladivostok: blackout of *2001*, 193;
Chinese immigrants, 181; settle-
ment of, 58; transportation to, 77,
80–81, 133
Von Bethmann-Hollweg, Theobald, 97
Vorkuta, 127–28, 130b, 131b
Voronezh, 62, 68, 105
Voyenno-promyshlennyy kompleks (VPK),
108–09

Warsaw, 59
Washington, 17
Weinstein, David, 158
White, Langdon, 54
White Sea–Onega Canal, 173
Winn, Marjory, 218
Winnipeg, 227
World Bank: definition of Russian North,
123–24, 221–23; public assistance
for out-migration, 267n6; Russian
energy efficiency, 164; Russian
spending to support the North, 125;
resettling labor camp victims,
250n37. *See also* Northern Restructuring Project
World War I, 10, 68, 157, 232n12
World War II: bombing of Japanese cities,
157–61; city shrinkage due to, 157;
effects of, 52, 60, 70, 97; German
invasion of USSR, 27–28; Soviet
GULAG, 86; Soviet relocation of
industry, 87

Yadrintsev, Nikolay, 76
Yakutsk, 75, 129
Yaroslavl', 67
Yavlinskiy, Grigoriy, 186, 204
Yekaterinburg, 21, 40, 112, 129, 154, 179
Yeltsin, Boris, 112, 114, 116, 152, 153
Yenisey River, 81, 92
Yerakhtin, Aleksandr, 182b
Yezhov, Nikolay, 86
Yukon, 206

Zayonchkovskaya, Zhanna, 185
Zheleznogorsk, 163–64
Zipf's Law, 19–20, 21, 22, 40, 232n23,
232n24, 233n25